COURT
ARTS
OF
INDONESIA

HELEN IBBITSON JESSUP

THE ASIA SOCIETY GALLERIES, NEW YORK
in association with
HARRY N. ABRAMS, INC., NEW YORK

Published on the occasion of
Court Arts of Indonesia
an exhibition organized by
The Asia Society Galleries, New York
in association with the Arthur M. Sackler Gallery,
  Smithsonian Institution, Washington, D.C.

The Asia Society Galleries, New York
September 19–December 16, 1990

Dallas Museum of Art
February 10–April 7, 1991

Arthur M. Sackler Gallery, Washington, D.C.
May 19–September 2, 1991

Natural History Museum of Los Angeles County
October 19, 1991–January 5, 1992

KunstHAL Rotterdam, The Netherlands
November 1, 1992–January 17, 1993

AUTHOR'S NOTE: unless otherwise specified, dates
in this book refer to the Christian Era; dates
after rulers' names refer to the reign, not the
lifespan. Spelling of Indonesian words in almost
all cases conforms to Bahasa Indonesia. The
order of dimension information is height, width,
depth.

Published by The Asia Society Galleries, New York
Osa Brown, Acting Director, Publisher

Publications Coordinator: Becky Mikalson
Publications Assistant: Merantine Hens
Editor: Ellen Cochran Hirzy
Design: Dana Levy, Perpetua Press
Maps: Joseph Asherl
Printed and bound by South China Printing Co., Hong Kong

LIBRARY OF CONGRESS CATALOGUE CARD NUMBER 90-81136

This book is published in association with Harry N. Abrams, Inc.,
New York. A Times Mirror Company.

ISBN: 0-87848-072-2 (softcover, TASG)

0-8109-3165-6 (hardcover, Abrams)

0-8109-2514-1 (softcover, Abrams)

Second Printing

Cover: *Kris* (NO. 71)

Back cover: *Ukur* (NO. 154)

Page 1: *Wayang kulit* performance, *Kraton* Kasepuhan, Cirebon, 1989.
Photograph by John Gollings.

Pages 4–5: Complete *wayang kulit kotak* set up for performance by the
dalangs in the *Kraton* Ngayogyakarta Hadiningrat, Yogyakarta, 1989.
Photograph by John Gollings.

TABLE OF CONTENTS

FUNDING ACKNOWLEDGMENTS

The Asia Society Galleries gratefully acknowledges the generous support of the following funders for the *Court Arts of Indonesia* exhibition and catalogue.

MAJOR FUNDING

National Endowment for the Humanities
The Luce Foundation
UNOCAL
P.T. International Nickel Indonesia

ADDITIONAL SUPPORT

National Endowment for the Arts
Yayasan Nusantara Jaya
Garuda Indonesia
KLM Royal Dutch Airlines
A consortium of Bank Negara Indonesia 1946, Bank Bumi Daya, Bank Dagang Negara, Bank Ekspor Impor Indonesia, Bank Niaga, Bank Central Asia
J.P. Morgan & Co. Incorporated
Revlon, Inc.
The Chase Manhattan Corporation
Asian Cultural Council
Friends of The Asia Society Galleries
The Starr Foundation
The Andrew W. Mellon Foundation

LENDERS TO THE EXHIBITION

Dr. Mr. Ide Anak Agung Gde Agung, Puri Agung, Gianyar
University of Amsterdam, on loan to the Royal Tropical Institute, Tropenmuseum, Amsterdam
Australian Museum, Sydney
Australian National Gallery, Canberra
Raja of Baun
The British Library, Oriental Collections, London
The British Library, India Office Library and Records, London
Samuel Eilenberg
Samuel Eilenberg-Jonathan Rosen Collection
James J. Fox
Wieneke de Groot
Haryono Guritno
K. R. T. Hardjonagoro
Robert J. Holmgren and Anita E. Spertus
Istana Mangkunagaran, Surakarta
Istana Pakualaman, Yogyakarta
Kabupaten Bima, for the Sultan of Bima
Kabupaten Watampone
Family of Sultan Muhamad Kaharuddin III
Kraton Kasepuhan, Cirebon
Kraton Ngayogyakarta Hadiningrat, Yogyakarta
Kraton Surakarta Hadiningrat, Surakarta
Museum *Istana* Siak Sri Indrapura, Riau Lingga
Museum *Istana* Ternate, Maluku
Museum Nasional, Jakarta
Museum Negeri, Aceh
Museum Negeri Bali, Denpasar
Museum Negeri Nusa Tenggara Barat, Mataram
Museum Negeri Sonobudoyo, Yogyakarta
Museum Prabu Geusan Ulun, Sumedang
Museum Radya Pustaka, Surakarta
Museum Wayang, Jakarta
National Gallery of Victoria, Melbourne
Volkenkundig Museum Nusantara, Delft
Mr. and Mrs. Oorthuys, on loan to the Rijksmuseum, Amsterdam
The House of Orange-Nassau Historic Collections Trust, The Hague
Ibu Siti Maryam Rachmat, S. H.
Rijksmuseum voor Volkenkunde, Leiden
Royal Asiatic Society, London
Royal Tropical Institute, Tropenmuseum, Amsterdam
Tengku Luckman Sinar, Deli Sultanate
Society of the Friends of Asiatic Art on loan to the Rijksmuseum, Amsterdam
Suaka Peninggalan Sejarah dan Purbakala, Ujung Pandang
Iwan Tirta
Peter Worsley

FOREWORD

ALTHOUGH INDONESIA IS A HUGE, culturally diverse entity, its overall historical experience has been uniform. From its diversity was created a unity, which is expressed by our national motto: *Bhinneka Tunggal Ika*, or Diverse Yet One.

Court Arts of Indonesia is an exhibition that brings together aspects of Indonesian culture that, if seen in isolation, might not give a full understanding of the common basis of the civilization that developed as a result of the ability of Indonesian culture to absorb foreign influences and use them to create a new form. This new entity is never felt as something foreign because it has undergone a process of intense acculturation. The exhibition provides a profound view of this process and its results.

Although courts no longer exist in the real political sense in Indonesia, they are still regarded as centers of traditional art and culture. As such they continue to be held in high esteem.

Court Arts of Indonesia displays aspects of Indonesian culture that are little-known and rarely seen outside—or even within—Indonesia. These traditional artistic elements are still an important influence on the development of modern Indonesian art, however, and thus are an important source of insight for anyone interested in Indonesian art of any period.

I would like to express my deep gratitude to Dr. Andrew Pekarik of The Asia Society for conceiving and laying the groundwork for this exhibition and to Dr. Helen Jessup and Ms. Osa Brown and her associates for their dedication in realizing the project. I fully believe that this exhibition will contribute positively to a better understanding of the ancient arts of Indonesia and give a better insight into the culture of Indonesia in general.

DRS. BAMBANG SUMADIO
Head, Directorate of Museums

PREFACE

INDONESIA IS THE FIFTH MOST POPULATED COUNTRY IN THE WORLD WITH AN ANCIENT and rich culture, yet it remains remarkably little known in the West. The Asia Society, dedicated to introducing American audiences to the arts of Asia, has been unique in its commitment to exhibit Indonesian art. Nearly twenty years ago, it organized *Ancient Indonesian Art,* which was the first exhibition of Indonesian classical art ever to be held in the United States. *Splendid Symbols,* comprising textiles from throughout the archipelago, was presented in 1979, and in 1985 the Society and the Smithsonian Institution Traveling Exhibition Service co-organized *Power and Gold,* an exhibition that included a large selection of Indonesian jewelry. *Court Arts of Indonesia* is the most complex exhibition with the broadest scope ever organized by The Asia Society and, as no published research exists that exclusively examines the topic, this exhibition and catalogue have created a new field of study.

Court Arts of Indonesia has been organized over the course of five years, and has involved the dedication and collaboration of many people across four continents. Andrew Pekarik, former Director of The Asia Society Galleries, first went to Indonesia in 1985 to set the exhibition in motion. It was Dr. Pekarik who first conceived of the idea of the exhibition, and through his efforts the idea took shape.

The early commitment of Indonesian government officials helped turn Dr. Pekarik's vision into a reality, and we are profoundly thankful to them for their encouragement. They are Minister of Foreign Affairs Ali Alatas S.H., Minister for Coordination of People's Welfare Soepardjo Roestam, former Minister of Foreign Affairs Dr. Mochtar Kusuma Atmadja, Minister of Education and Culture Prof. Dr. Fuad Hassan, Director-General of Culture G.B.P.H. Puger and his predecessor Prof. Dr. Haryati Soebadio, and Director-General of Tourism Mr. Joop Ave.

Court Arts of Indonesia is part of the Festival of Indonesia, a nationwide celebration of the performing and fine arts of Indonesia held in 1990–1991 that has three major exhibitions at its core. The other two are *The Sculpture of Indonesia,* organized by the National Gallery of Art, and *Beyond the Java Sea,* organized by the National Museum of Natural History, Smithsonian Institution. The Asia Society joined the festival through Dr. Mochtar Kusuma Atmadja, initiator of the festival and the founder of the Yayasan Nusantara Jaya, a private Indonesian cultural foundation. Dr. Kusuma Atmadja's foresight and leadership was the force by which the festival was propelled so successfully forward, and we are grateful to him for his enthusiastic support. We would also like to thank Ted M.G. Tanen, who coordinated the festival in the United States.

Helen Jessup traveled continuously over a five-year period throughout Indonesia, Europe, Australia, and the United States to research and construct the exhibition. She did extensive field work in Indonesia, interviewing royal families, discovering royal treasures, and identifying themes to link together the vastly diverse cultures comprising Indonesia's courts. The success of the exhibition and catalogue is a tribute to her scholarship, diplomacy, and tireless and uncompromising dedication to developing a cultural dialogue between Indonesia and the United States.

We are also indebted to Drs. Bambang Sumadio, Head of the Directorate of Museums, Jakarta, who was co-curator and led the team of Indonesian scholars assembled to work on this project. I would like to express my deep gratitude for his gracious guidance through the often intricate and delicate negotiations necessitated by so complex an exhibition.

As part of *Court Arts of Indonesia*, The Asia Society collaborated with the Museum Nasional, Jakarta, to present a landmark exhibition there in July 1990, featuring the works of art borrowed from public and private Indonesian collections. It was the first time that objects were assembled from so many different regions throughout the archipelago, particularly from hitherto unseen court collections. We are thankful to Dra. Suwati Kartiwa, M. Sc., Director of the Museum Nasional, for making the Jakarta exhibition a success.

Court Arts will travel to three museums after its presentation in New York. We would like to thank Milo Beach, Director of the Arthur M. Sackler Gallery in Washington, D.C., who played a major role in planning the exhibition from its developmental stages. Dr. Beach, with his staff, worked in close association with The Asia Society to bring the project to fruition. We are also thankful to Dr. Peter Keller, Associate Director for Public Programs, Natural History Museum of Los Angeles County and to Emily Sano, Deputy Director of the Dallas Museum of Art, for their commitment to the exhibition.

The organization of the vastly complex details of *Court Arts of Indonesia* was implemented by a very small and devoted staff at The Asia Society. Becky Mikalson, Production Assistant, was particularly skillful and diligent in coordinating many aspects of the exhibition and catalogue production. Merantine Hens, Publications Assistant, organized and prepared the catalogue's manuscript and myriad photographs with great competence and good humor. Dana Stein Dince, Registrar, oversaw the innumerable logistical details involved in assembling, packing, displaying and transporting the works of art. Nancy Blume was responsible for the docent program. The installation was designed by Cleo Nichols, who gave form to the intricate concepts presented in the exhibition, and David Harvey was the graphic designer.

We are indebted to the lenders to this exhibition, both private individuals and public institutions from Indonesia, Europe, Australia, and the United States, who permitted us to borrow objects of such extraordinary beauty and cultural significance. Without their generosity this exhibition would not have been possible.

It is with deepest gratitude that we thank the sponsors of *Court Arts of Indonesia* for their financial and enthusiastic support. We received major funding from the National Endowment for the Humanities, The Luce Foundation, UNOCAL, and P.T. International Nickel Indonesia. Additional support was provided by the National Endowment for the Arts; the Yayasan Nusantara Jaya; Garuda Indonesia; KLM Royal Dutch Airlines; a consortium of banks comprising Bank Negara Indonesia 1946, Bank Bumi Daya, Bank Dagang Negara, Bank Ekspor Impor Indonesia, Bank Niaga and Bank Central Asia; J.P. Morgan & Co. Incorporated; Revlon, Inc.; The Chase Manhattan Corporation; the Asian Cultural Council; Friends of The Asia Society Galleries; The Starr Foundation; and The Andrew W. Mellon Foundation.

OSA BROWN
Acting Director
The Asia Society Galleries

ACKNOWLEDGMENTS

The genesis of this exhibition would not have been possible without the long-term cooperation and encouragement of hundreds of people in many countries. It is difficult to know where to begin acknowledging the help received over the past almost five years, and it is all too likely that some names will inadvertently be left out, for which I apologize in advance.

First of all, I would like to thank Andrew Pekarik for entrusting me with the task of preparing an exhibition in a previously unexplored field and for giving his warm support to the project throughout his tenure as Director of The Asia Society Galleries. Others in the Galleries have been helpful as well, notably Osa Brown, who took over the project direction for most of the final two years, published the catalogue and, as Acting Director, sustained the constructive role of The Asia Society Galleries in the evolution of the exhibition. Dana Stein-Dince's talents as Registrar ensured the success of the exhibition's detailed planning process and the safety of the objects. Becky Mikalson and Merantine Hens were dedicated, meticulous and cheerful throughout the demanding production of the catalogue, while Pam Sapienza, Pauline Sugino, Kathy Lee, and Iris von Braun generously offered their unflagging support. The Arthur M. Sackler Gallery staff has also been supportive from the beginning; in particular, I would like to thank Milo Beach and Jane Norman.

No words can fully express my gratitude to the Indonesian counterpart team; the Indonesian officials who smoothed my way throughout Indonesia; and the Yayasan Nusantara Jaya under the dynamic leadership of Dr. Mochtar Kusuma Atmadja. In particular I would like to mention Minister for Coordination of People's Welfare Soepardjo Roestam (formerly Minister for Home Affairs); Foreign Minister Ali Alatas S.H. (formerly Ambassador to the United Nations); and Drs. Bambang Sumadio, Head of the Directorate of Museums. Pak Bambang, Co-curator of all three core exhibitions of the Festival of Indonesia, worked tirelessly and devotedly to implement our complex plans. In this task he was helped by Pak Basrul Akram, B.A., of his own staff, as well as by members of the counterpart team, Teguh Asmar, M.A., and Dra. Sri Soejatmi Satari. Additional assistance was provided by the staff of the Yayasan Nusantara Jaya, Pak Rahmad Adenan, Pak Supono Hadisudjatmo, Ibu Raya Sumardi, Pak Djoko Soejono, M.A., Pak Erman Soehardjo, S.H., Dra. Nani Woerjani, Ibu Anggrek May Koetin, S.H., and Ibu Judi Achjadi, and special advisers Bapak H. Boediardjo and Bapak Haryono Guritno, whose encyclopedic knowledge of *wayang* was a constant guide. I would also like to express my gratitude for the support of Minister of Education and Culture Professor Dr. Fuad Hassan, Director-General of Culture G.B.P.H. Puger, Director-General of Tourism Mr. Joop Ave and former Director-General of Culture Dr. Haryati Soebadio.

Special mention should be made of the unwavering support of my husband, Philip Caryl Jessup, whose presence, patience, and advice concerning both large and small details were indispensable.

Particular thanks are due to the scholars who read and made valuable suggestions about the catalogue. These were Clifford Geertz, Philip Jessup, George Michell, Hugh O'Neill, Anthony Reid, the late Soedjatmoko, Jill Stowell and John Stowell. I would especially like to acknowledge the help of my editor, Ellen Cochran Hirzy, whose care and patience were unflagging. Dana Levy's design has greatly enhanced the material, while the photography of John Gollings, Paul Hickman, and also Dirk Bakker, has provided a dazzling permanent record of an outstanding group of objects.

Special mention is due to two people whose unstinted help was vital in planning and continuity and who, sadly, are not with us to share in the fulfillment of our ideas: my dear friends the late Paramita Abdurachman and the late Molly Bondan. They opened many doors, smoothed many paths and offered comradeship and wise counsel in our extensive travels together.

In addition to receiving help with the overall organization of the exhibition from those already mentioned, I was guided throughout by the advice and support of many other friends and scholars. One of the most inspiring of these is also no longer with us, namely, the late Soedjatmoko. To have known him will always remain one of life's blessings, and I know that his philosophy will have a continuing influence well beyond the personal sphere in matters of global understanding and in the world of the underprivileged for whose rights he so tirelessly worked.

Two other people were especially supportive in the development of ideas and scholarship and in our efforts to arrange loans. They are both major lenders as well, and their generosity has enriched the exhibition immeasurably. I refer to Dr. Mr. Ide Anak Agung Gde Agung and K.R.T. Hardjonagoro. In addition, special thanks are due to Iwan Tirta, Sabam Siagian, Wieneke de Groot, and Tom and Hoedel van Leeuwen whose liaison work and assistance, advice and hospitality buoyed me constantly.

Other scholars and museum curators who generously shared their ideas include Taufik Abdullah, Hasan Ambary, I Made Bandem, Sudarmaji Damais, Achadiati Ichram, H. Karkono Kamajaya PK, Umar Kayam, Adrien Lapian, La Ode Manarfa, But Muchtar, Soewito Santoso, Edi Sedyawati, R.M. Soedarsono, Panuti Sudjiman and Sumartini, as well as many others, who will be mentioned in a region-by-region acknowledgment. Non-Indonesian scholars who gave valuable advice include Encik Wan Alias, Mariann Binti An, Benedict Anderson, Monique Barbier-Mueller, Tim Behrend, James Boon, P.T. Boskma, Koos van Brakel, Michael Brand, Peter B. Carey, Henri Chambert-Loir, John Darling, Anthony Day, Christine Dobbin, Jane Drakard, Brian Durrans, David van Duuven, Samuel Eilenberg, Owen Eilbracht, Alan Feinstein, Hartmut Ortwin Feistel, Nancy Florida, Anthony Forge, James Fox, Annabel Gallop, Clifford Geertz, Godfrey Goodwin, Sarah Goodwin, Henk-Jan Gortzak, Walter Gronert, Willem van Gulik, John Guy, Hedi Hinzler, Michael Hitchcock, Robert J. Holmgren and Anita E. Spertus, Gerd Höpfner, Itie van Hout, Fiona Jack-Hinton, Rebecca Jewell, Schuyler Jones, Wilhelmina Kal, Mohammad Kassim Bin Haji Ali, Dr. Kreisel, Ann Kumar, Dr. Kurio, M. Laman, Stephan Lansing, John Legge, Willy Lim, Martin Loonstra, Jerry Losty, Pauline Lunsing-Scheurleer, Margot Lyon, Jamie Mackie, Campbell Macknight, Pierre-Yves Manguin, Virginia Matheson-Hooker, Robyn Maxwell, George Michell, John Miksic, George Miller, Anthony Milner, Willem van der Molen, James Mollison, M-L. Nabholz-Kartaschoff, Stanley O'Connor, William O'Malley, Hugh O'Neill, Mae Anna Pang, Christian Pelras, Jaap Polak, Sarah Posey, Urs Ramseyer, Anthony Reid, P. Richardus, Merle Ricklefs, Henk van Rinsum, Adrian Roberts, Stuart Robson, Monika Rohrbach-Benton, Reimar Schefold, Tan Sri Dato' Mubin Sheppard, James Siegel, Garrett Solyom, E.G. Spruyt, Jill Stowell, John Stowell, David Stuart-Fox, Heather Sutherland, Paul Michael Taylor, Pieter ter Keurs, H. Thode Arora, Allen Thomas, Alit Veldhuizen-Djajasoebrata, Adrian Vickers, Zoe Wakelin-King, Rita Wassing-Visser, Michael Watson, Kees van der Wilk, Margaret Wiener, B. Woelderink, Peter Worsley, Inger Wulff, Father Zoetmulder and Dr. Zwernemann.

The cooperation of our biggest lender, the Museum Nasional, was vital to the success of the exhibition in both Jakarta and the United States. I greatly appreciate the support of its Director, Dra. Suwati Kartiwa, and her staff members Arifin, Ariyo, Intan, Noeriya, Paulina, Razak, Suhardini and Sutrisno, as well as the design contributions for the installation of the Jakarta exhibition from Gagi Soebagiono.

Without lenders there would be no show, and I wish to thank all who so generously allowed us to view, photograph and borrow objects that in many cases have never been seen by the public before. The names of these people have already been formally listed in the front of the book, as have those of our financial supporters.

I feel special gratitude and affection for those who were my traveling companions on field trips. In addition to Paramita Abdurachman and Molly Bondan, these include Sonya Joesoef,

Sri Soejatmi Satari, Victor Tanja and Rini Waworuntoe. I would also like to thank Frank Morgan, who generously offered to provide us with a *bale* from Bali, and Peter Bost, who helped us with ticketing costs for travel to New York. Thanks also to all my friends in Jakarta who offered support in many forms: Roekmini and Zainal Abidin, Mara and Kim Adhyatman, Pia Alisjabana, Joni Adiputra, Anak Agung Gde Agung, Lynn L. Cassel, Donna E. Culpepper, Herawati Diah, Teguh S. Djamal, G.P.H. General Djatikusumo, Anak Agung Oka Djelantik, Australian Ambassador Philip Flood, Anthony Granucci, Jozeph Groenewoud, Bambang Gunardjo, Jenne and Hendra Hadiprana, Daisy Hadmoko, Tina Hamzah, General Andi Jusuf, Jennifer Lindsay, William Lowrey, U.S. Ambassador John Monjo and Sirkka Monjo, former Australian Ambassador Bill Morrison and Marta Morrison, Kartini Muljadi SH, Julia Musfian, Anak Agung Muter, Lukman Nurhakim, Caecil and Alex Papadimitriou, Titi and Jusuf Ronodipuro, Mini Salim, Jo Seda, Peter Sie, Dien and Hitler Singawinata, Ellis Gene Smith, Min and Darpo Soedarpo Sastrosatomo, Dewi Savitri Soedibio, Ratmini Soedjatmoko, Happy Soeryadjaya, Judith Soerydjaya, G.W. de Vos van Steenwijk, F. Sugiri, H. Sutardjo, Jean and Julius Tahija, Soffie and Beni Wahyu, Jusuf Wanandi, former U.S. Ambassador Paul Wolfowitz and Claire Wolfowitz and Mike Yaki.

In the course of the preparations for the exhibition I traveled to twenty-two of Indonesia's twenty-seven provinces. I found people everywhere who were similarly enthusiastic and helpful and I would like to mention those not already listed. In Central Java, these include, in Surakarta, His Royal Highness Pakubuwono XII, Susuhunan of Surakarta, G.P.H. Puger, G.R.Ay. Himbo Kusumo, G.R.Ay. Koes Moertiya and G.R.Ay. Soepiyah from the Kraton Surakarta Hadiningrat; K.G.P.A. Djiwo Kusumo, Mangkunagoro, and G.R.Ay. Satuti Yamin, G.R.Ay. Rosati Kadarisman, R.Ay. Hilmiyah Darmawan Pontjowolo, R.T.M. Husodo Pringgokusumo, Pak Woerjanto Darmosarkoro and Sri Sadoyo Ipong at the Istana Mangkunagaran; Pak Sanjata, Drs. Slamet and others from the Department of Education and Culture; and Mas Warno and Marlene Heins. In Yogyakarta I am indebted to His Highness Sultan Hamengkubuwono X, to his father, the late Sultan Hamengkubuwono IX, and to the late G.P.B.H. Poeroeboyo, G.P.B.H. Joyokusumo, G.P.B.H Hadidjoyo, G.B.P.H. Hadisuryo and G.B.P.H. Hadiwinoto at the Kraton Ngayogyakarta Hadiningrat; G.P.H.A.A. Pakualam VIII, K.P.H. Ambarkusumo, K.P.H. Anglingkusumo, Drs. Soetamdaru Tjokrowerdojo and Drs. Soemidjian at the Pakualaman; and Dr. Boechari, Pak Kasman, Drs. Bambang Prasetyo, Drs. Roedjito, Pak Fatjah Siddik, Drs. Pak Soedarso S.P., Pak Soekarto Kusumaatmadja, Drs. Djoko Soekiman, Pak Soenarto and Pak Warno Waskito.

In East Java I would like to acknowledge the Governor and Pak Gunarto as well as Drs. Sunardjo at Trawulan; in Madura, the Bupatis of Sumenep and Bangkalen and also Drs. Abdullah Muin and Pak Edhisetiawan. In West Java I was helped in Cirebon by P.R.A. Maulana Pakuningrat SH, Sultan Sepuh, Kraton Kasepuhan, the late Haji Mohammad Noeroes, Sultan Anom, Kraton Kanoman, P.M.M. Amir Natadiningrat, Sultan Kecirebonan, Kraton Kecirebonan, Pak Djana, Pak R.J. Djayakelana, Pak Sjafei Soeryagoenawan and R.M. E. Yusuf; Pak Abdullah Hamid and R.M. Abdullah Kartadibrata in Sumedang; Drs A.D. Pirous and Pak Gagi Subagiono Soepeno in Bandung; and Drs. Halwany Michrob in Banten.

In East Kalimantan, besides the Governor and his staff, I wish to mention Pak Usman Achmad, Drs. Aziz, Pak Abdullah Djabar, Drs. Chaidir Hafiedz, Pak Imdaad Hamid, Drs. H.M. Mazkoer Hasran, Sdri. Meiliana Sabirin, Pak Aji Sastra Wijaya, Pak Sanusi Saudek and Drs. Ali Syamsudin. In West Kalimantan I thank the Governor and Pak Hartadi, Pak A. Kahar, Pak Agus Achmad Kamaruddin, Drs. Koestarto and Ibu Koestarto, Drs. Anton S. Ruatu, Pak Soepardal, Pak Soeparno, Ibu Wartini and Pak Yatimin in Pontianak. In Mempawah I acknowledge Drs. Muchalli Taufik; in Singkawan, Drs. Muazie Harun; and in Sambas, the Bupati. In South Kalimantan thanks are due to the Governor, Drs. H. Gusti Hasan Aman, Pak Abdul Hamid, Pak M. Machli, Pak B. Mariso, Drs. Mussani Noor, Pak Rahimsyah, Drs. M. Idwar Saleh, Drs. Syarifuddin and Pak Umar Mahlan.

Thanks are due to many people in South Sulawesi as well. These include Governor Amiruddin, the Bupatis of Gowa and Watampone, Andi Mackulau Opu Daeng Parebba, Andi Babu Tayang Karaeng Bontolangkasa Makmun, Andi Mappasissi, Andi Rifai, Andi Sapada Nurhani, Andi Sulthani Opu Daeng Mangngerang, Pak Djufri Tenribali, Andi Wati Sulthani,

Pak Abdullah Husein, Ibu Ita, Pak Sam Habibie, Ibu Endang Indiardjo, Pak Harun Kadir, Pak Kenchana Sebayang, Pak Fritz Limbunan, Pak H.A. Muddarijah, Drs. Abdul Muttalib, Drs. Saharuna Amiruddin and Pak Soeroto Brodjo.

In Bali I am grateful to the former Governor, Dr. Ida Bagus Mantra and to Drs. Putu Budiastra, to the Bupati of Klungkung and also to Mr. Pino Confessa, Dr. Made Djelantik, Kol. Pol. Purn. Anak Agung Gde Karang, Anak Agung Ngurah Anom Mayun, Ms. Kristina Melcher, Pak Sutedja Neka, I Gusti Gde Raka, Dr. Ida Bagus Rata, Made Rusta, I.G.N. Ketut Sangka, Pak Wayan Suanda, Tjokorda Putra Sukawati, Wayan Widiantara, Pak Wija Wawo Runtu and Ibu Tati Wawo Runtu and Pak Made Wijaya.

In Nusa Tenggara Barat I thank Governor H. Gatot Suherman, Ibu Suri Kaharuddin, Pak Daeng Kaharuddin, Pak Massir Q. Abdullah, Ibu Aisah, Ibu S. Maryam Rachmat and Ibu Saleha, also Pak Robby G. Anthonysz, Pak Umar Berlian, Ibu Siti Hadidjah, Drs. Abdul Manaf M. Said Husny, La Sangi, Drs. H. Abdul Kadir, the Bupati of Raba, Drs. H. Madilaoe, Pak Abdul Madjid, Pak M. Natsir, Pak H. Oemarkaroen, Pak H. Parwoto, Drs. Lalu Ratmadji, Drs. H.L. Srigede, Drs. I I.L. Wacana and Dra. Alit Widiastuti. Thanks also in Nusa Tenggara Timur to former Governor Dr. Ben Mboi and Dr. Nafsiah Mboi, to Vice-Governor G. Boeky and Ibu Boeky, to Drs. J.J. Djeki, Raja Baun Pak Victor Korah and Ibu Korah, Dr. Franz and Ibu Cory Rajahaba and Pak Jes Therik.

In Maluku, I am indebted to the Governor, to the staff of the Department of Education and Culture, the Director of the museum in Ambon, Drs. Nizam Gani and Drs. Frans Rijoly in Ambon; in Ternate I thank Pak L. Rajilun, Pak Mohammad Samsuddin and Drs. Supanji, the Bupati; and in Tidore, Pak Tukan, the Bupati, and Pak Togubu.

I was similarly helped in many provinces of Sumatra. In Lampung I would like to mention the Governor as well as Pak Yaman Aziz, Pak Syamsuhara Hadi, Pak Hamzah, Drs. Subekti Elyas Harun, Drs. Man Hasan, Pak Barlian Jayadilampung, the Kepala Desa of Cahaya Negeri, Pak Mansyur, Pak Sutan Raja Medan, Ibu Ifu Ratu Mupun, Pak Raja Sutan, Drs. Amir Syarifuddin and Pak Dulhai Tabahhassa. In Padang I am grateful to Governor Hasan Basri Durin and Pak Abu Jazid. In Riau Lingga I thank the Governor and Ir. Djati Sussetya and the Caltex company, as well as Pak Tenas Effendi, Drs. Wan Galib, Dr. H. Tabrani Rab and Drs. M. Bosman Saleh in Pekanbaru. In Siak Sri Indrapura, thanks to Drs. Chairi Thalib and Pak Terigan and to other local officials. In South Sumatra I am indebted to the Governor and members of the Department of Education and Culture and also to Ibu Roosmala Emmy, Pak M. Iskandar, Ibu Irsen Luki Radjamin and Pak H. M. Katrawi Rahim. The Governor of Aceh was also helpful, as were Drs. Afifudin Jamal, Drs. Zaccharia Rachman, Pak Nasruddin Sulaiman and Tengku M. Yunan. In North Sumatra I am grateful to Tengku Luckman Sinar and Tengku Dra. Sitta Syaritsa.

Outside Indonesia there were many who provided assistance, including Ted Tanen, Maggie Weintraub and staff in the New York Festival of Indonesia Office. We enjoyed working with our colleagues at the National Gallery of Art in Washington D.C. who were concerned with *The Sculpture of Indonesia* exhibition, particularly Anne Robertson, Frances Smyth and Joe Krakora, and those at the National Museum of Natural History working on *Beyond the Java Sea*, especially Paul Taylor, Lorraine Aragon, Anna Rice and Margery Stoller. We also appreciate the help of the Embassy of Indonesia in Washington under Ambassador Abdul Rachman Ramly. In addition I am grateful to Sir Anthony Acland, Chief Emeka and Mrs. Bunmi Anyaoku, Colonel George Benson, Robertson Collins, Brikkenaar van Dijck, Edward Elson, David and Pamela Evans, Gudrun Feller, the late Donald Friend, Dominique Gardan, Bryce Harland and Anne Blackburn, Barbara Harvey, Cavan and Mira Hogue, Kohar Rony, Daisy Leong, George and Angie Loudon, Jonkheer R. Loudon, Des and Felicity Moore, Andrew Paneyko, Ted and Megan Pocock, Ambar Pramono, John Randall, Brian and Pam Read, the late Hans Rhodius, Richard W. Teare, Sir Ralph Verney, Charles Warner, Ingeborg Weber and Elizabeth Wilson.

As a result of the support of all the people on this long list the world has become a smaller and friendlier place, and, I hope, a little more Indonesian.

HELEN IBBITSON JESSUP

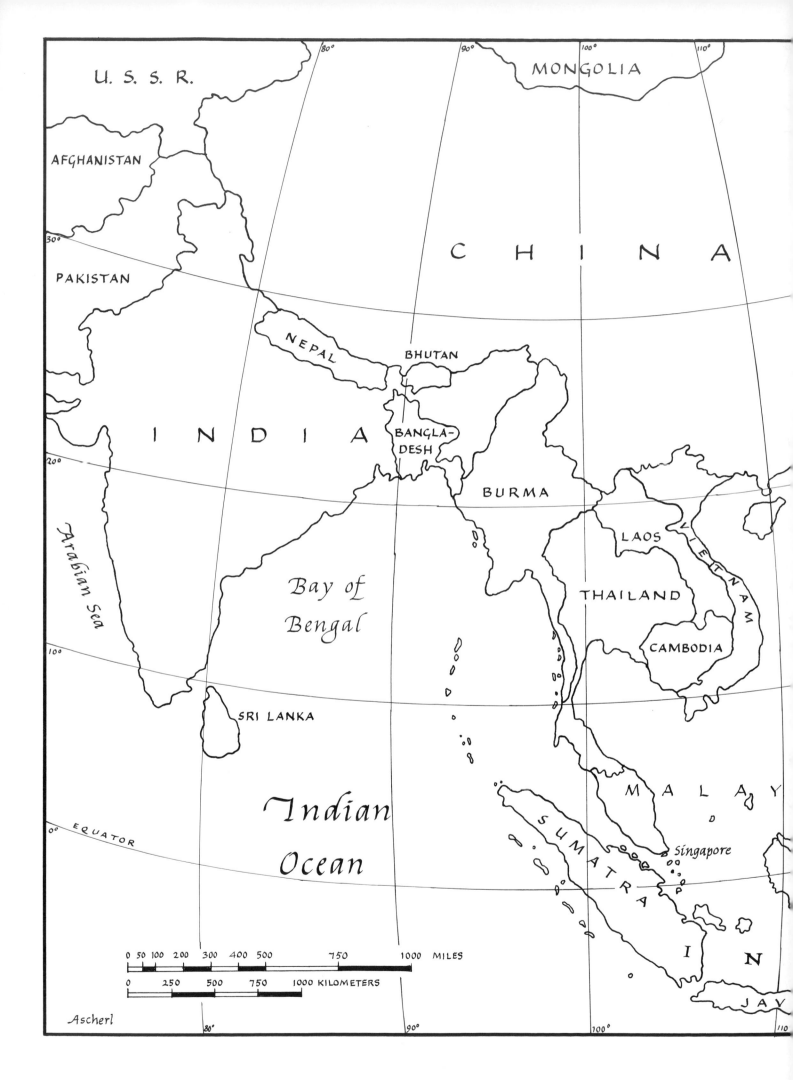

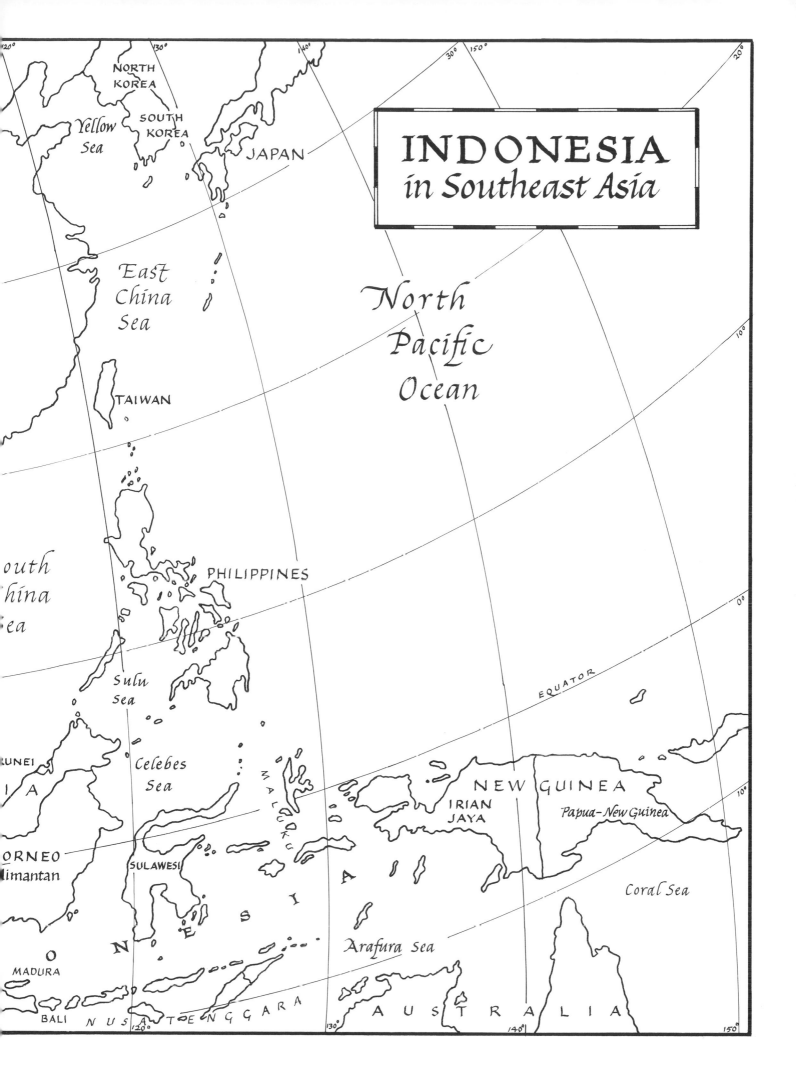

INDONESIA
in Southeast Asia

North
Korea

South
Korea

JAPAN

Yellow
Sea

East
China
Sea

North
Pacific
Ocean

TAIWAN

outh
hina
ea

PHILIPPINES

Sulu
Sea

RUNEI

Celebes
Sea

EQUATOR

NEW GUINEA

IRIAN
JAYA

Papua-New Guinea

ORNEO
limantan

SULAWESI

Coral Sea

O
N
E
S
I
A

MADURA

Arafura Sea

A U S T R A L I A

BALI   N U S A   T E N G G A R A

South
China
Sea

THAILAND

BURMA

LAOS

CAMBODIA

VIETNAM

[CHAMPA]

[FUNAN]

Andaman
Sea

ISTHMUS
OF
KRA

Gulf of
Siam

•6

•1

MEKONG R.

•46

12°

8°

•3

•53

ACEH

•38

DELI

•37 •42

L. Toba
Asahan R.

SIMEULUE

NIAS

EQUATOR

STRAITS OF MELAKA

PERAK

MALAY

PENINSULA

M A L A Y

•35

•43

•29

Singapore

12
•

Siak R.

•55 •63

RIAU

SA

•60

B O

•44

•56

4°

SUMATRA

17
•

•48 Inderagiri R.

•47

MT. MERAPI

SIBERUT

•45

MENTAWAI ISLANDS

•27

LINGGA

BUKIT-SI-GUNTANG

Musi R.

•49

BANGKA STRAIT

BANGKA

BELITUNG

(K A L I

KARIMATA STRAIT

0°

4°

•13

•54

Tulungbawang R.

LAMPUNG

•73

KRAKATAU

SUNDA STRAIT

•30

•9

•26

I N D O N

Java Sea

MAD

•28

•20 •59

Solo R. •25

•32 Brantas

75
•

•18

•64

MT. AGUNG

•34

•24 •22 •31

•72

•21

BALI

•15

•65

•67 •19

•4

•58 •11

J A V A

•62

•41 •71

•77

MT. MERAPI

MT. LAWU

8°

Indian Ocean

0 20 40 60 80 100   150   200 M.

0   50 100 150 200 K.

Ascherl

98°

102°

106°

110°

INDONESIA

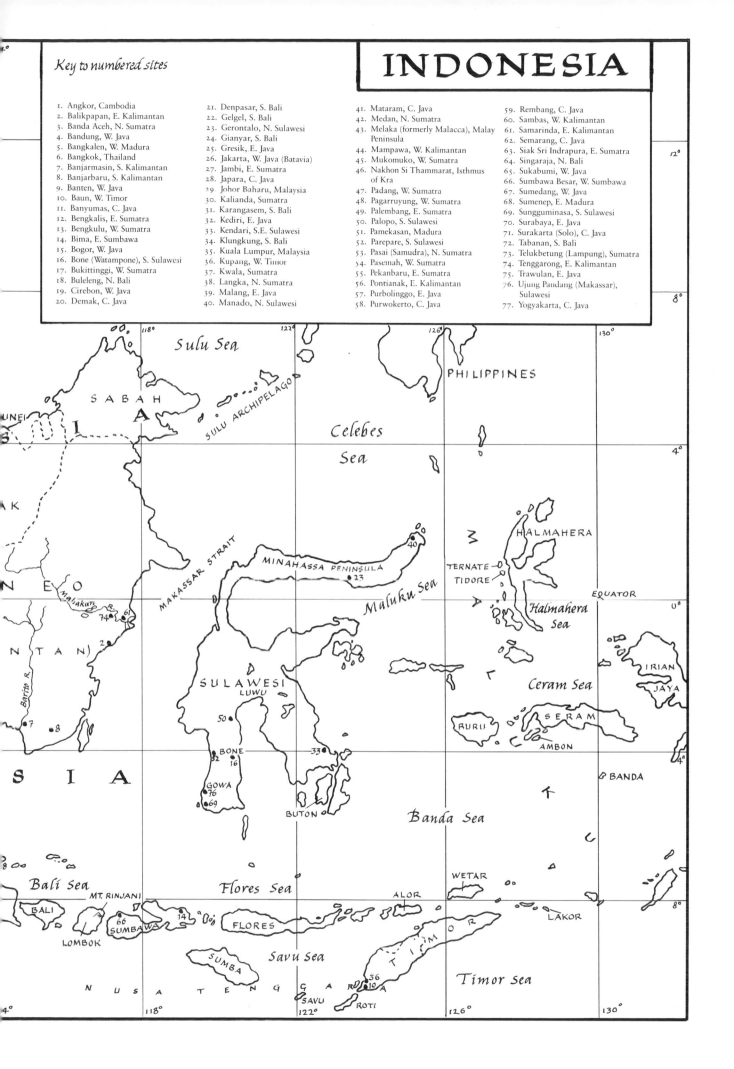

INTRODUCTION

*A person who can speak Malay can
be understood from Persia to the
Philippines.*

François Valentijn, ca. 1725.[1]

How remarkable it is that a cleric and historian from a small country on the North Sea, in a world where the ocean voyage from Europe to Southeast Asia took nine months, should have appreciated the importance of the language of the Indonesian archipelago and its speakers.[2] We in the West, who can send and receive long telefaxed documents from the antipodes in a few minutes, scarcely know where Indonesia is. The distance mentioned by Valentijn, who spent more than fifteen years in what was then the Netherlands East Indies, is roughly equal to that between Dublin and Ulan Bator. Such a distribution represents an impressive linguistic hegemony even by the standards of twentieth-century English.

Astonishment at the prospect of a united Europe, where twelve countries will merge their economic and cultural fate in 1993, may be tempered by the thought that Indonesia is a country where nearly three hundred languages and myriad cultures have been united by a lingua franca and a common purpose for more than forty years, since the proclamation of the independent nation in 1945. Even before that, during the three hundred fifty years of Dutch presence, and earlier under the empires of Srivijaya, Mataram, Majapahit and the second Mataram, communications and trade contacts flourished in a domain that stretches about as far as from Scotland to Athens or from New York to Los Angeles. There is no country of equal importance in today's world about which so little is known in the West, except by the Dutch. It is the world's fifth most populous country, approaching one hundred eighty million people. With more than thirteen thousand islands stretching along the equator from the Indian Ocean in the west to Papua New Guinea in the east, bordered to the north by Singapore and mainland Southeast Asia and to the south by Australia, Indonesia has a recorded history reaching two thousand years into the past and a future promising a role as the major state of Southeast Asia when its economic growth meets its population and development challenges.

Bas relief at *candi* Borobudur, Central Java, ca. 800 C.E., showing musicians.

The physical beauty of this tropical archipelago—"Insulinde," as the more romantically inclined Dutch called it—has long been recognized. As Thomas Stamford Raffles rhetorically asked, about a century after Valentijn:

> [W]here was there a country that could more invite the retreat of holy men, than the evergreen islands which rise in endless clusters on the smooth seas of the Malayan Archipelago, where the elevation and tranquillity of devotion are fostered by all that is majestic and lovely in nature?[3]

The cultures of Indonesia were noted by Chinese travelers like Ma Huan in the fifteenth century, by Europeans like Marco Polo in the thirteenth century and Tomé Pires in the sixteenth century and investigated by Dutch scholars from the seventeenth century. Between the writings of British historians like William Marsden, Raffles and John Crawfurd at the end of the eighteenth and beginning of the nineteenth century—accounts that were, like the Netherlands reports, predominantly Eurocentric—and the work of twentieth-century writers like Margaret Mead, Gregory Bateson, Walter Spies, Colin McPhee and Miguel Covarrubias, Indonesia received scant attention from the world at large. Furthermore, Bali, not Indonesia as a whole, gripped the foreign imagination earlier in this century. Since then, stimulated by the fascination of these amazing islands, the tide of scholarship has surged. Linguists, epigraphers, archaeologists, anthropologists, sociologists, geographers, geologists, biologists, ecologists, economists, political scientists, musicologists and historians of religion, art, architecture and the dance have penetrated the remotest regions and the most specialized areas of Indonesian culture.

Given the breadth of these studies, and the appearance over the last twenty years of a few notable exhibitions of sculpture, textiles and jewelry,[4] it seems extraordinary that so little awareness of this cultural cornucopaeia has been roused in the general Western public. Perhaps the very diversity of fields, the need for prolonged focus to gain accurate and deep insight into any single topic, and the daunting multilingual scholarship required for thorough comparative analysis all combine to bewilder a prospective student.

When visualizing Indonesia's location in relation to other countries, it should be remembered that although the archipelago occupies a portion of the globe roughly equal to the size of the mainland United States, extending more than three thousand miles east to west and about fifteen hundred miles north to south, much of this area is water. As a result, Indonesia in many respects is a maritime nation, with all that this implies in terms of connections in trade and politics and disjunctions in culture and language. Lying as it does across the equator, it is affected by both northern and southern monsoon systems. The heavy seasonal rains brought by these winds to most of the region foster forest growth and wet rice cultivation adequate throughout history for exportable surpluses as well as for support of a dense population. Indigenous plants yielding cloves, nutmeg and mace, pepper, sandalwood, benzoin and other aromatics provided the foundation for internal trade and early commercial links with China and India. The same products were the magnet drawing European colonizers from early in the sixteenth century—Portuguese, Spanish, French, Dutch and English—to eastern routes in search of the prized spices of "the Indies."

The very forces of sun, rain and wind that promote Indonesia's tropical abundance can also be destructive. With frequent earthquakes and volcanic eruptions, the climatic elements threaten the survival of cultural artifacts and historical evidence in general. Though prehistoric remains indicate early human settlement in the Indonesian region, we are dependent on Chinese dynastic records of the third century of the Christian era[5] (reported in fifth-century accounts) for the earliest dateable information identifying civilizations in Sumatra and Java that were involved early in the first millennium in trade with China. Indian evidence is available from about two hundred years later, while local epigraphic indications of early polities (the social and political structures of the groups were not developed enough to be designated as states) begin in the fifth century in Kalimantan and Java.

Although more than thirteen thousand islands make up modern Indonesia's twenty-seven provinces, those most important in its history are Java; Sumatra; Kalimantan (the Indonesian part of Borneo); Sulawesi (formerly known as Celebes); Bali; the smaller islands to the east comprising Nusa Tenggara (formerly known as the Lesser Sundas), which include Sumbawa, Sumba, Flores and Timor; and Maluku (or the Moluccas), the Spice Islands, to the northeast.

For most of its history the region has comprised many independent polities, even within the limits of relatively small islands like Java and Bali. From time to time larger powers emerged with wider regional hegemony. One of the earliest was Srivijaya. By the sixth century this seafaring state in Sumatra had achieved some regional power, and by the seventh century it was a noted center for Buddhist studies, with economic dominance over most of the states bordering the Straits of Melaka (formerly Malacca). From that time it vied with Javanese polities for control of regional trade and shipping until an attack in 1025 by the South Indian Chola state reduced its international importance.[6]

In the eighth and ninth centuries powerful dynasties emerged in Central Java. In the period known as the first Mataram era the Buddhist Sailendra line, which created the temple of Borobudur and other religious monuments, coexisted with but was eventually dominated by the Hinduistic Sanjaya line. In the tenth century there was a still-unexplained shift of government to East Java, where the kingdoms of Kediri and Singasari emerged in the twelfth and thirteenth centuries. The end of the latter saw the rise of the Majapahit empire, which by the second half of the fourteenth century claimed a tributary area extending over much of Sumatra, Kalimantan, Maluku and even parts of mainland Southeast Asia.

After the decline of Majapahit during the fifteenth century, Java's first Islamic state became powerful at Demak on the north coast, while the last years of the sixteenth century saw a shift of power back to Central Java with the emergence of the second Mataram kingdom. Though divided eventually into four branches, this dynasty was the origin of today's courtly families of Central Java. Like Srivijaya and probably Majapahit, all these polities were in reality loosely related trading and tributary networks rather than centrally administered empires. Even the most extensive hegemony of all before the 1945 proclamation of an independent Indonesia, that of the Netherlands as colonial overlord, was only truly a politically focused entity after 1817 and was not in control of the entire region until early in the twentieth century.[7]

The diversity inherent in such a geographic and historical spread is further complicated by major external cultural waves that washed over the original Austronesian societies of Indonesia with their animist and pantheistic mythologies. The first of these, beginning early in the Christian era, was Indic, and brought with it Hinduism and Buddhism. Later, from the fourteenth century in Java and earlier in Sumatra, Islam with its religious, cultural and moral modifications exerted a major influence. The European colonial period, beginning from early in the sixteenth century, introduced yet another strand. The effects of Chinese contacts, particularly on coastal areas, though never as pervasive or sharply focused as the others, were evident throughout Indonesian history in places such as North Java, East Sumatra and Bali.

Any effort to give an overview of Indonesian culture is complicated by the very diversity and richness that make it worthwhile. It is necessary to impose some shape on the geographical, historical and cultural variety in order not to lose the wood in the multiplicity of trees. Since the highest achievements of art have often been associated with the power and status of rulers and the prestige and patronage they provide, the courts of Indonesia offer a suitable framework for the endeavor.

The courts, while drawing on the raw material of indigenous art, had the power and the economic means to raise it to new levels and to preserve it; their world encompasses the foundations and the pinnacle, the seeds and the fruit, of Indonesian culture.

Even when the framework is established, challenges still abound. What is a court? In Indonesia the answer can include the fifth-century state of King Mulavarman in Kalimantan as well as the small princedoms in Roti, East Nusa Tenggara, where courts were in effect defined by the Dutch only in the nineteenth century. It can cover courts like Srivijaya, for which there is still only fragmentary evidence, as well as the second Mataram, where a wealth of literary and material records span more than four hundred years of a court culture that still exists. The answer must also take into account the challenge of great diversity: the nobility of the classical sculpture of Java and Sumatra between the seventh and fifteenth centuries is neither more nor less Indonesian than the funeral masks of the North Sumatran Batak people, the beaded baby-carriers of the Kalimantan Dayaks or the ruby-studded gold ritual offering bowls of the Balinese. One component in the definition of a court concerns the level of sophistication. Some polities could more accurately be described as courts in embryo, like the ruling centers in Timor and other eastern islands and the many fiefdoms within provinces like Lampung in Sumatra. Some were well defined centrally, with considerable local power, but were on a small scale, like the courts of Ternate and Tidore in Maluku and Gelgel in Bali; others, like the so-called empires of Java and Sumatra, achieved broadly based power over large areas and had well-developed hierarchies within their political structures.

Since the courts with current or traceable traditions number in the hundreds, a selection has been made to encompass a representative historical, geographical and cultural spread. This book addresses the ancient kingdoms of Srivijaya and Pasai, as well as later Aceh, Minangkabau, Lampung, Palembang, Deli, Siak and Riau Lingga courts in Sumatra. In Kalimantan, apart from the mention of Mulavarman's realm and the old kingdom of Sukadana, there is reference to Kadriah-Pontianak, Sambas and Mampawa in the west, Kutei in the east and Banjarmasin in the south. The most powerful of the Sulawesi courts, Gowa, Bone and Luwu, are represented, as are Gianyar, Karangasem, Klungkung, Tabanan and Singaraja in Bali. Ternate and Tidore in Maluku, Lombok, the Sumbawa courts at Sumbawa Besar and Bima, Baun in Timor, and Roti and Savu are all small island courts that have been included to represent the eastern region of Indonesia. In Java, always the most densely populated major island, the early kingdoms already mentioned are joined by Banten, two of the four courts of Cirebon and all four of Central Java: the Susuhunanan and the Mangkunagaran in Surakarta and the Sultanate and the Pakualaman in Yogyakarta.

Beyond the general geographical and historical representation offered by the framework of the courts, several underlying themes bind all the disparities and particularities together and keep the courts within the perspective of Indonesian culture in general. Court culture was by no means isolated from the mainstream; in most cases it was rather the zenith of a creativity that had its roots in the deepest autochthonous sources. A theme of great importance, dealt with in the first two chapters of this book, is the basic concept of kingship and the attendant questions of legitimacy and power. Legitimacy depends on spiritual conviction, possible only when rulers are believed to be connected to myths of origin and identity and seem to have divine sanction. Throughout Indonesia such links are implied by images that relate to this underlying mythology; prominent among these are mountains, rice, snakes, ships, and Trees of Life. The catalogue includes many objects that embody these symbols, including the *gunungan* or mountain-form puppet (FIG. I/NO. 107) that is central to the shadow play, daggers decorated with gold snakes

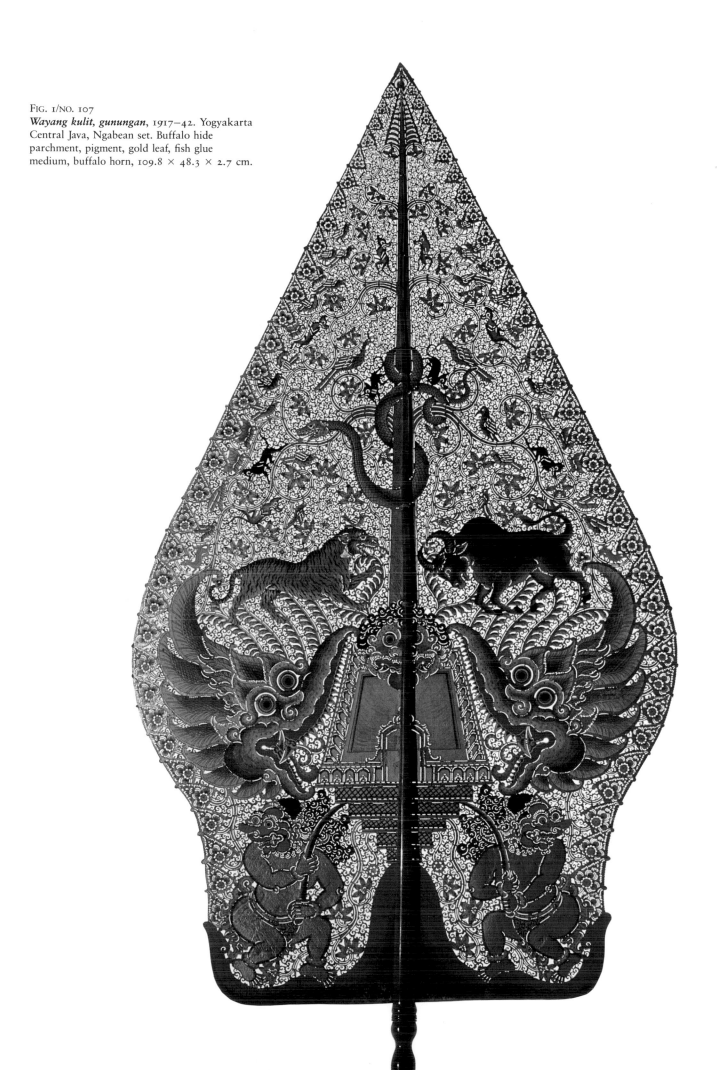

FIG. 1/NO. 107
Wayang kulit, gunungan, 1917–42. Yogyakarta
Central Java, Ngabean set. Buffalo hide
parchment, pigment, gold leaf, fish glue
medium, buffalo horn, 109.8 × 48.3 × 2.7 cm.

(FIG. 2/NO. 69), carved figures of Dewi Sri, the rice goddess and symbol of fertility (FIG. 3/NO. 146), a Dongson-era bronze ship (FIG. 44), textiles depicting ancestor ships and Trees of Life.

This book also deals with the material and spiritual sources and manifestations of kingly power, political, military and economic. The functions of the court for which the ruler was responsible include judicial processes, internal administration, revenue development, foreign diplomacy (FIG. 4/NO. 7) and military organization (FIGS. 5, 6/NOS. 20, 27), all of which entail material culture for fulfillment. The second chapter treats these topics, presenting the ruler in the world at large through weaponry (FIGS. 7, 8/NOS. 11, 12; 13, 14), ceremonial processional objects like litters, carriages (FIG. 9/NO. 31) and umbrellas of rank, and other symbols of office.

The ruler in his court is discussed in the third and fourth chapters. Chapter 3 concentrates on the connections between royal and vernacular architecture and the cosmic symbolism inherent in palace structures. The ruler as host and patron can be seen in chapter 4, which presents the artifacts connected with social receptions, the betel (or *sirih*) ceremony equipment (FIGS. 10, 11/NOS. 40, 44; NOS. 39, 46), courtly dress (FIGS. 12, 13/NOS. 78, 82) and jewelry (FIGS. 14, 15/NOS. 54, 58; NOS. 51, 59). In addition, chapter 4 describes the masks (FIG. 16; FIG. 17/NO. 131), textiles (FIG. 18/NO. 77), instruments (FIG. 19) and puppets (FIG. 20/NO. 114; FIGS. 21, 22; FIG. 23/NO. 124) made for the performing arts and the sculpture, manuscripts (FIGS. 24, 25/NOS. 99, 102) and painting (FIG. 26/NO. 103) that flourished within the courts. Also described in chapter 4 are the ruler's place in kingly and life-cycle rituals and the regalia and symbols (FIG. 27/NO. 139; FIG. 28)[8] for these ceremonies.

An understanding of Indonesian culture is an exciting goal. In the belief that an overview of it, with some insights into its main themes, may be useful in trying to reach such a goal, this book, enhanced by the illustrations of many splendid objects, offers an introduction to the remarkable civilization shared and nurtured by the people and rulers of Indonesia.

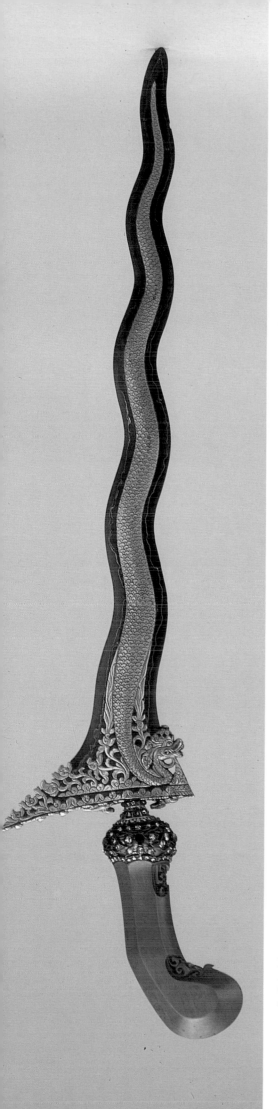

Fig. 3/no. 146
Loro blonyo, early 19th century. Yogyakarta,
Central Java. Wood, pigment, gold leaf, fish
glue medium, copper gilt, silk, cotton; male
figure 58 cm, female figure 54 cm.

Fig. 2/no. 69
Kris Nagasasra, early 19th century. Surakarta,
Central Java. Iron, nickel *pamor*, gold, silver,
diamonds, wood, 48 cm.

FIG. 4/NO. 7
Letter in *lontar* form, 1768. Badung or
Mengwi, Bali. Gold-copper alloy, 24 × 5.5 cm.

FIG. 5/NO. 137
State *kris*, 19th century or earlier. Gowa, South
Sulawesi. Iron, nickel *pamor*, gold, diamonds,
rubies, wood (sheath lining), 40 × 25 cm.

Opposite:
FIG. 6/NO. 27
Tali banang (**swordbelt**), 19th century. Bugis
people, South Sulawesi. Cotton, tablet woven,
natural dye, 380 × 12 cm.

FIG. 7/NOS. 11, 12
NO. 11 (left): *Tombak* (lance), 17th century.
Yogyakarta, Central Java. Head: gold, iron,
nickel *pamor*, silver or zinc; shaft: *timaha*
wood; 277.6 × 5.7 (shaft 3.3) cm.
NO. 12 (right): *Tombak*, 1872. Bone, South
Sulawesi. Head: gold, silver, iron, nickel *pamor*;
shaft: wood; 244.4 × 3.1 (shaft 2.4) cm.

FIG. 8/NOS. 13, 14
NO. 13 (below left): *Tombak*, 17th century.
Central Java. Head: gold, silver, iron, nickel
pamor; shaft: wood; 226 cm.
NO. 14 (below right): *Tombak*, 17th century.
Central Java. Head: gold, diamond, iron, nickel
pamor; shaft: wood; 230 cm.

FIG. 9/NO. 31
Wayang kulit, carriage, 19th century.
Surakarta, Central Java. Buffalo hide
parchment, buffalo horn, pigment, fish glue
medium, gold leaf, 63.7 × 76.7 × 1.7 cm.

FIG. 10/NO. 40
Wadah (containers) for tobacco and *sirih*
leaves, 19th century. Bangkalen, Madura. Gold,
11.4 × 9.7 × 4.8 and 11.3 × 10 × 5 cm.

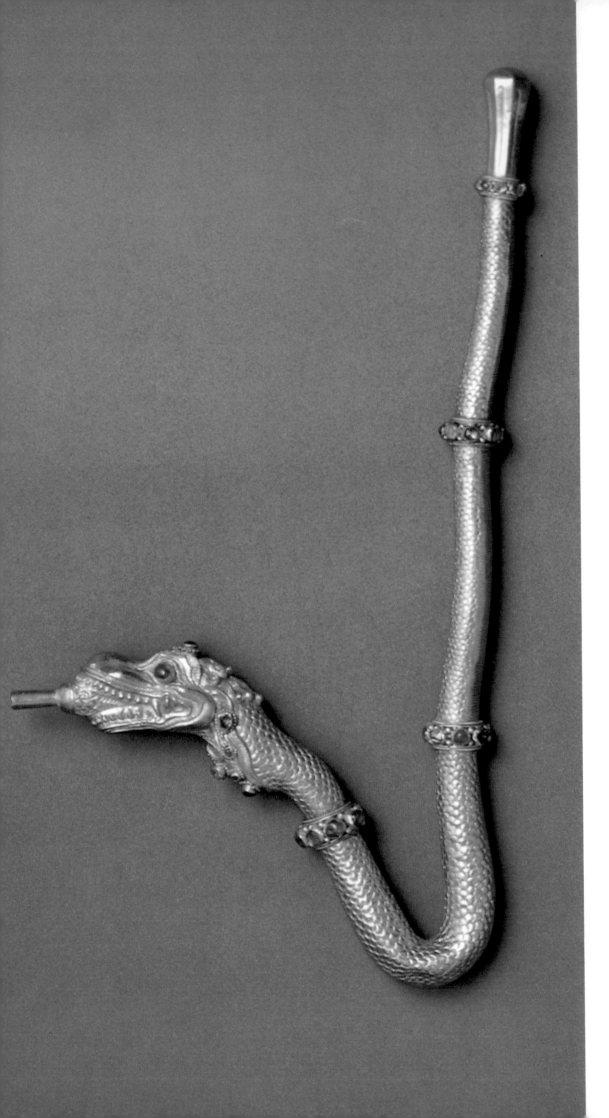

FIG. 11/NO. 44
Pipe, 19th century. Lombok.
Gold, rubies, diamonds,
23 × 12.1 × 2.2 cm.

FIG. 12/NO. 78
Kain songket, early 20th century(?). Semawa,
West Sumbawa (Sumbawa Besar). Silk, cotton,
silver thread, 117 × 164 cm.

FIG. 14/NO. 54
Glang (bracelets), 19th century. Kutei, East
Kalimantan. Gold, 10.5 × 7 and 10.1 × 7.2 cm.

FIG. 15/NO. 58
Ear pendants in quasi-bird form, 14th–15th
century. East Java. Gold, 7.5 × 3.4 cm.

FIG. 13/NO. 82
Kain songket, late 19th or early 20th century.
Pandai Sikek, Minangkabau, West Sumatra.
Silk, gold thread, 46 × 175 cm.

FIG. 16
Topeng (mask) **Raden Astra Miruda**, before
1815. Central Java. Wood, pigment, gold leaf,
fish glue medium, 18 cm.

FIG. 17/NO. 131
Telek (**mask**), 20th century(?). Bali. *Pole* wood,
fish glue patination, 15.6 × 12.5 × 6 cm.

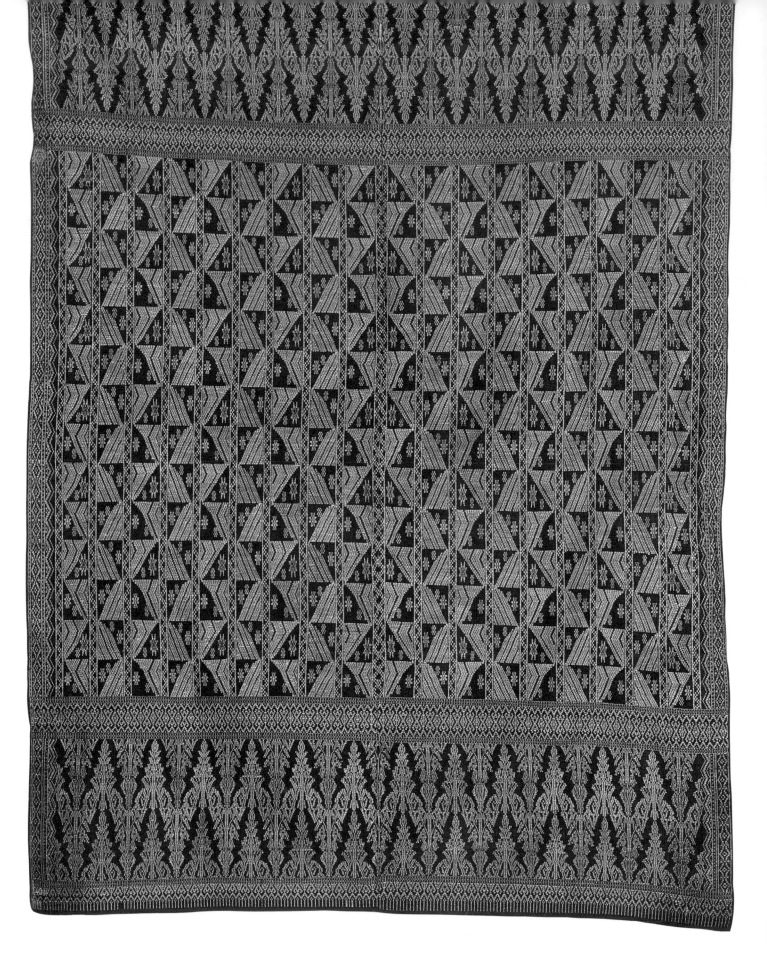

FIG. 18/NO. 77
Kain songket, late 19th century. Klungkung(?),
Bali. Silk, gold and silver thread, chemical dyes,
110 × 150 cm.

FIG. 19
Slentem (**metallophone**), before 1815. Java or
Madura. Bronze, wood, pigment, gold leaf,
tempera and fish glue medium, 54.5 × 142 cm.

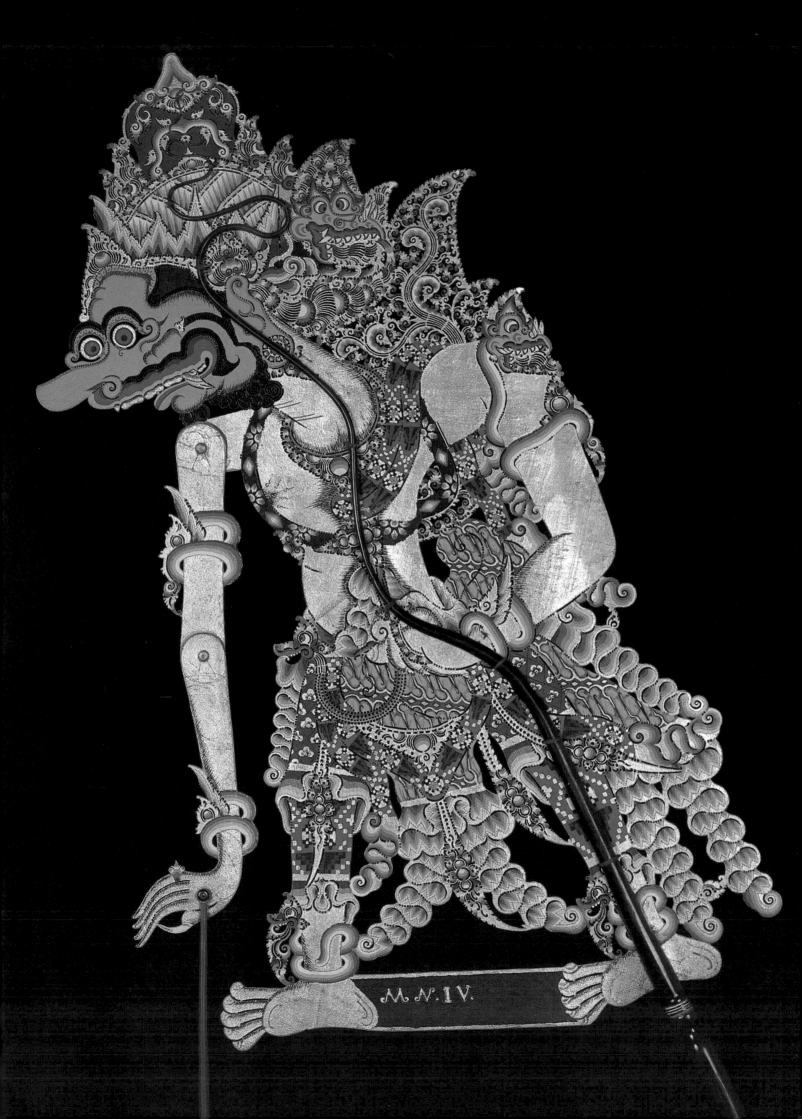

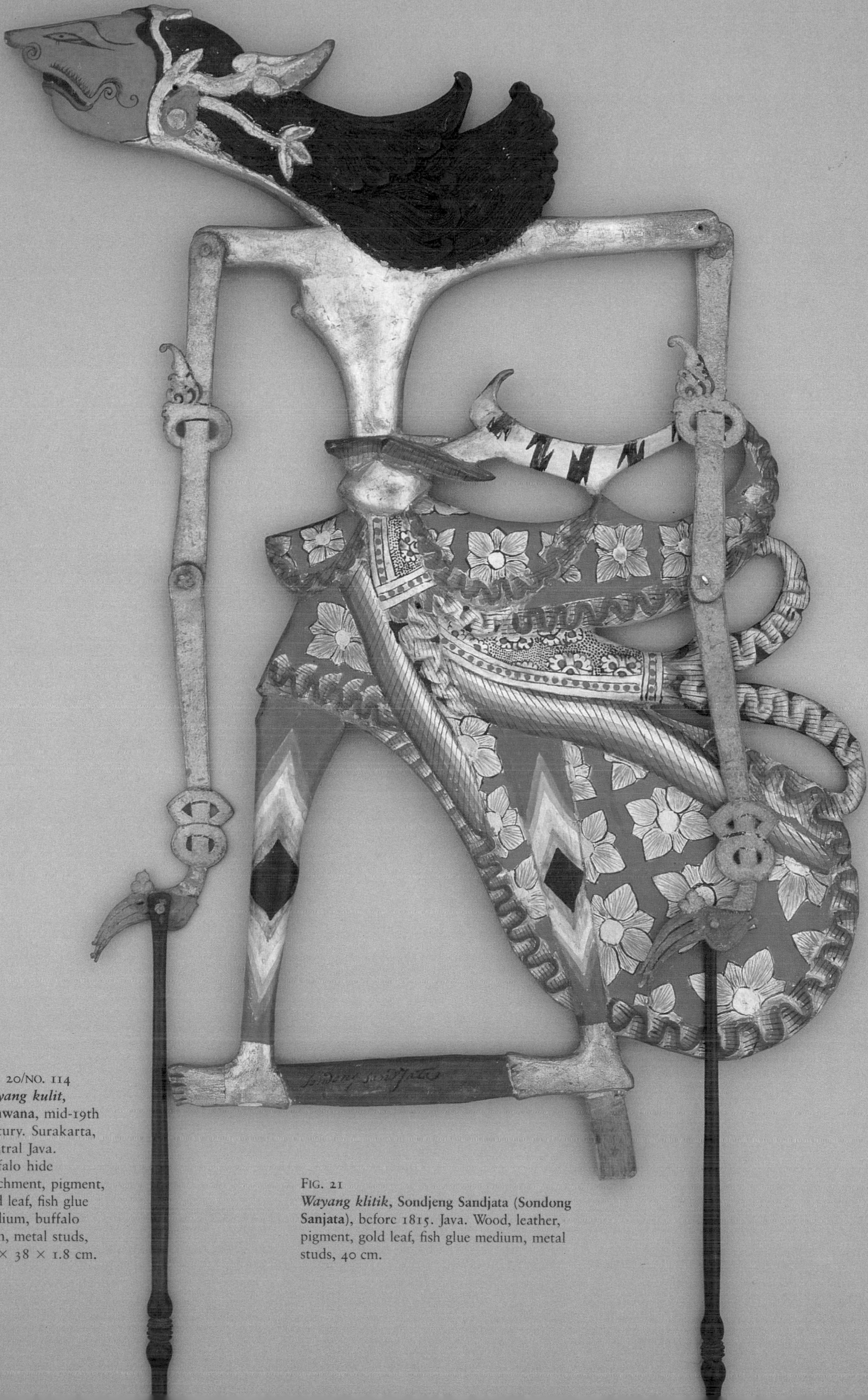

FIG. 20/NO. 114
Wayang kulit,
Rahwana, mid-19th
century. Surakarta,
Central Java.
Buffalo hide
parchment, pigment,
gold leaf, fish glue
medium, buffalo
horn, metal studs,
90 × 38 × 1.8 cm.

FIG. 21
Wayang klitik, Sondjeng Sandjata (Sondong
Sanjata), before 1815. Java. Wood, leather,
pigment, gold leaf, fish glue medium, metal
studs, 40 cm.

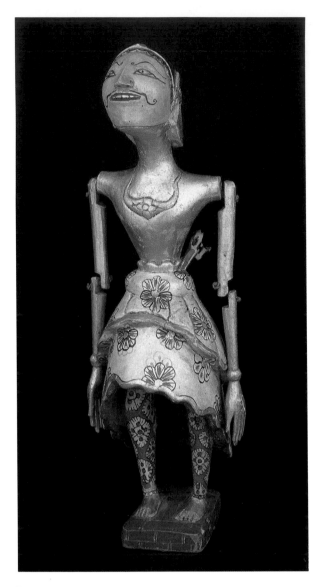

FIG. 22
Wayang gedog, **Ng Setro (Layang Seta)**, before
1815. Central Java. Wood, pigment, gold leaf,
fish glue medium, rattan fastenings, 38 cm.

FIG. 23/NO. 124
Wayang golek, **Kencana Wungu**, before 1881.
Cirebon, West Java. Wood, cotton and silk
cloth, pigment, gold leaf, fish glue medium,
metal fastenings, 47.1 cm.

Opposite above:
FIG. 24/NO. 99
Manuscript of *Serat Ambiya*, 1844.
Yogyakarta, Central Java. Ink on European
paper, polychrome watercolor and gold leaf,
leather binding, 38 × 28 × 15 cm.

Opposite below:
FIG. 25/NO. 102
Manuscript of *Rama Kawi*, late 18th century.
Yogyakarta, Central Java. Ink on Dutch paper,
polychrome watercolor and gold leaf, leather
binding, 31 × 19.5 cm.

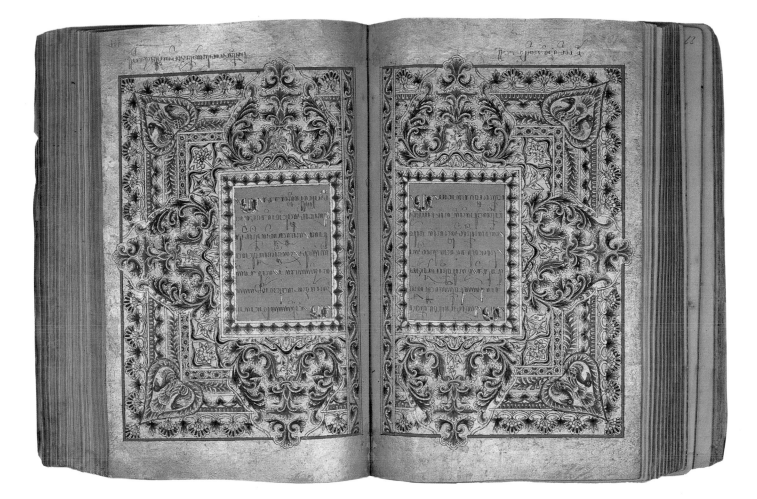

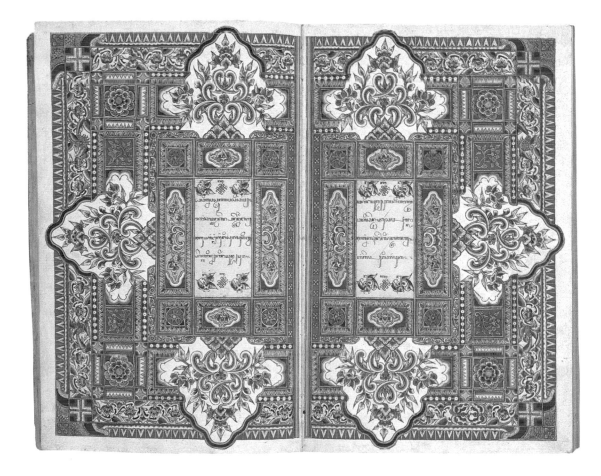

FIG. 26/NO. 103
Ramayana scene, 20th century. Klungkung
area, Bali. Pigment and gold leaf on cotton,
150 × 139 cm.

FIG. 27/NO. 139
Ceremonial *wadah* **(container)**, 19th century.
Banjarmasin, South Kalimantan. Silver, rock
crystal, gold, 40 × 64.2 × 14.7 cm.

FIG. 28
Sajen **(offering) bowl**, 18th century or earlier.
Gelgel, Bali. Silver, 12.5 × 17.1 cm.

I. FROM THE MOUNTAIN TO THE SEA

Myth, Legend and Literature in the Origin and Legitimacy of Princes

*[T]he tokens of His being
superhuman, wonderful, were: an
earthquake, the earth rumbled, rain of
ashes, thunder, flashes of lightning
turning about in the sky, the
mountain Kampud collapsed.*[1]

SUCH CONCATENATIONS OF NATURAL CATACLYSMS suggest divine intervention, but this passage from the *Nagarakertagama* is extolling the power of a king, not a deity. Even allowing for the hyperbole inherent in a court poet's celebration of his monarch, this excerpt from the 1365 poem by the Javanese poet Prapanca indicates the association with natural forces and the inference of divine status that were central to the conceptions of kingship in Indonesia's realms. The identification of the ruler with a deity is familiar to students of Egyptian, Japanese, Mayan and, in terms of sanctions at least, European imperial history, among others. More relevant to the Indonesian case is the Hindu *devaraja*, or divine king concept, found in many countries of Southeast Asia.[2]

Indic cultural influences that have left their overt signs in the dance, drama, music and Sanskrit vocabulary of Thailand, Burma and Cambodia, as well as in the ancient kingdoms of Funan and Campa, also helped form the courts of the Indonesian archipelago. How and at what period these influences took effect in Indonesia is a matter of some dispute, early theories emphasizing a direct Indian presence in a quasicolonizing sense, later interpretations stressing the effects of Indian traders. More recent assessments surmise that the high-caste nature of the Hindu cultural elements of Java and Sumatra indicates a sacral-scholarly shaping of the upper stratum of society.[3] Brahman priests and scholars, their mysterious and exotic lore lending the aura of the supernatural to the ceremonies they conducted, enhanced the king's status. The divine sanction and superhuman power thus invoked through ritual were crucial in the ruler's claim to legitimacy, particularly in times of changing and expanding political and economic development.

Such invocation of Hindu-Buddhistic authority seems to have occurred about a century after the earliest dated contacts with Indonesia by traders and Buddhist pilgrims from India and China. Fifth-century Chinese imperial histories quoting lost third-century sources indicate that trade with the Indonesian archipelago had begun early in the first millennium, but the first dateable Indian reference to Indonesia is in the records of a Buddhist pilgrim, the Kashmiri prince Gunavarman, who sailed from India to China via Java early in the fifth century. Within Indonesia the first evidence of Indian links with Indonesian rulers is epigraphic: Sanskrit inscriptions on three sacrificial posts of the first half of the fifth century in East Kalimantan compare the victories of the local king, Mulavarman, with the achievements of Yudhisthira (Yudistira in Bahasa Indonesia), one of the semidivine heroes of the classic Sanskrit epic, the Mahabharata, and mention the monarch's link with Brahmans from outside his realm.

A more direct parallel between the power of a god and the king is drawn in three inscriptions of the mid- to late fifth century in West Java, near Bogor, celebrating the victories of King Purnavarman of the kingdom of Tarumanagara. They relate to nearby carved footprints, representing three paces by Visnu that won earth, waters and sky for the side of the good, and identify Purnavarman with Visnu, one of the gods of the Hindu pantheon.[4]

Architectural evidence of the Hindu-Buddhist conception of the capital city as the center of empire, a microcosm of Mount Meru as the center of the Hinduistic universe, can be found in the eighth- and ninth-century monuments of Central Java. The Buddhist mandala-mountain of Borobudur (FIG. 29) and the Hindu temple complex of Loro Jonggrang at Prambanan are among the early structures expressing Indic cosmic ideas, which include the figure of the king as axis of the world, a position comparable to Indra's role in the cosmos. A gold plaque of this period from Banyumas, Central Java, invokes the image of divine power in the suggestion of the Buddha implicit in a lotus umbrella (FIG. 30/NO. 5).

By the time the center of power in Java had shifted from the Kedu plain of Central Java to the Brantas river basin of East Java in the tenth century, the identification of the ruler with a god was more specific. Airlangga (1019–49)[5] rides Garuda as an incarnation of Visnu in a sculpture from *candi* (temple) Belahan in East Java, while Prapanca's poem refers to Kertanagara (1268–92), king of Kediri, as both the Hindu god Siva and the Buddha Akshobhya. The fourteenth-century prose chronicle of kings, the *Pararaton*, identifies King Kertajaya of Kediri (1216–22) with Siva and Ken Angrok, the founder of the Singasari dynasty in 1222, with the gods Visnu and Brahma. Ken Angrok's stepson, Anusapati (1227–48), is depicted as Siva in his funerary statue of about 1260 (FIG. 31/NO. 6), while a similar sculpture of the early fourteenth century shows Vijaya, who became the first king of Majapahit as Kertarajasa Jayavardhana (1293–1309), as Visnu (FIG. 32).

THE DIVINE RULER AS LORD OF THE MOUNTAIN

The divine identity of Rajasanagara, the ruler celebrated by Prapanca in the *Nagarakertagama*, leads to a different consideration of the Indic component in Indonesian ideas of kingship. As the incarnation of Bhatara Girinatha (or Batara Guru, FIG. 33/NO. 108), Siva as Lord of the Mountain, he is related as well to an indigenous system of beliefs that is older than the Hindu influences in Java, Kalimantan and Sumatra and that also encompasses conceptions of kingly power in other parts of Indonesia. In Sumatra, the Srivijayan kings of the seventh and eighth centuries are connected with images of the Buddha[6] and also with the local beliefs in mountain spirits.

With the invocation of the mountain, the interpretation of kingship in Indonesia assumes a much broader and deeper aspect. The mountain pervades Indonesian ideas of the sacred, the spiritual and the royal, and it is no accident that the royal tombs of Java at *candi* Ijo and Imogiri and those of Madura at Asta Tinggi and Aros Baya, to cite only a few, are situated on the tops of mountains. The prominence of the mountain theme throughout the archipelago is a result of the central role the mountain plays in myths of origin, little wonder, considering the powerful volcanoes that dominate many parts of Indonesia. Maya Danawa, for example, the redeemed and reincarnated wicked king of the Danawa demons and the progenitor with the reincarnated Snake-Princess Malini of the kings of Bali, came from the mountain Tolangkir, the former top of the mountain Kelasa placed by the gods on Bali.[6] While this Balinese legend partly draws on Indic traditions, the East Indonesian myth from Timor of the origin of the clans of Makassae is more primordial. A bird removes the water covering the earth and reveals the mountain Mate Bian. From it emerges a hermaphrodite who splits twice, yielding brother and sister pairs who produce the race. Shepard Forman, who reports this myth, claims that common myths shape rituals that link otherwise independent princedoms in this eastern region of Indonesia.[8]

To the extreme west, Sumatran myths of origin are rich in mountain imagery. Palembang in the south, Perak on the Malay Peninsula and some parts of Minangkabau in the west refer to the mountain Bukit Si-Guntang (Bukit Seguntang) as the source of their rulers. A glow on its slopes one night is revealed by morning to be three men; one is mounted on a white buffalo (or in one version of the legend a white elephant) and claims to be descended from Alexander the Great. In the Palembang version he becomes Sri Turi Buwana (in other versions Tribuana, or Sang Sipurba), the first ruler of Palembang (or of other places like Pagarruyung in Minangkabau and Banjarmasin in Kalimantan). A variant of Minangkabau origins has the founders descending from Mount Merapi after a time of flood.[9] Bataks in Northwest Sumatra go to mountaintops to communicate with their ancestors, while further south in Pasemah a mountain-shaped shield called a *perubatan* is kept with a child until it is five years old to protect it from ill fortune; should the shield be lost or broken it must be replaced or harm will befall the child.[10]

To the northeast of the archipelago, some of the Bugis of South Sulawesi believe that the line of their rulers begins with Tomanurung (literally, he or she who descends), who descended from the Upperworld.[11] In Mambai, Timor, the ruling class is said to have come from a lonely house on a mountain, and in Lakor, South Maluku, an ancestor symbol takes the form of a mountain, or *gunungan*. These examples show the wide distribution of the mountain motif. Its application is equally broad, as can be gauged from its occurrence in such diverse objects as a *mamuli* earring from Sumba (FIG. 34/NO. 3), a head adornment from Central Java (FIG. 35/NO. 65), the back of a ceremonial seat (*pepadon*) from Lampung, South Sumatra (FIG. 178/NO. 132), a xylophone-type instrument from a court gamelan orchestra in Cirebon in West Java (FIG. 36/NO. 91) and the central piece in the *wayang kulit*, or shadow puppet drama, the *gunungan* (FIG. 37/NO. 2). This nineteenth-century example from the *Kraton* Kasepuhan with its dual implications of cosmic mountain and Tree of Life is typical of *gunungans* in all *wayang* sets.[12]

Perceiving the penetration of the mountain symbol into so many aspects of life in Indonesia, from the life-cycle essence of the animist *perubatan* child-protecting talisman through the sophistication of the court *wayang* and gamelan to the spiritual power of ancestors and gods, enables us to understand more clearly the vitality of Indonesian court culture. The power and legitimacy of the ruler and the strength of the culture he fosters derive not from the external trappings of Indic religious authority, important and impressive though these may be, but from the deep well of symbols that tap the indigenous mythology of existence itself. The images of kingship have meaning not just for the courts, but for society as a whole. Even in regions where Indic influences dominated princely culture for centuries, the Hindu-Buddhist cosmology fused so well with autochthonous mythology that the visual signs of this belief system belong to an archipelago-wide tradition. The syncretism for which Indonesia is renowned similarly wove Islamic, Chinese and European influences into the warp of indigenous civilization.

That the viability of the ruler springs from his links with myths of origin and pantheistic forces partly accounts for the respect, even reverence, for members of the old ruling family still apparent in many former kingdoms of Indonesia where loyalty to the Republic is now the paramount political commitment. This is clearest in those former realms where the physical structure of the courts has been better preserved—notably those of Surakarta, Yogyakarta and Cirebon in Java and of Karangasem, Gianyar and Tabanan in Bali—but is perhaps more remarkable in places where the material trappings of the court have been absorbed for the most part into the administrative or cultural government infrastructure. Notable among these are the South Sulawesi former kingdoms of Luwu, Bone and Gowa[13] and those on the island of Sumbawa at Bima and Sumbawa Besar.[14]

RICE, FERTILITY AND DEWI SRI

Mythical symbols are seldom isolated. At the deepest levels of culture they often relate to one another. The strength of the mountain image as a multilayered symbol of kingly power, its elemental significance expanded by Indic cosmic references, is further enhanced by its links with fertility concepts, which were important in establishing the ruler as a source of vitality and prosperity. The embodiment of the cosmic mountain in a terraced monument, as at Borobudur with its nine levels, possibly linked the ancestor worship associated with mountainous places having such terraces to fertility themes.[15] The stepped form of this monumental structure, where the bas-reliefs lining the galleries that surround each level

FIG. 29
Plan of Borobudur, ca. 800. Central Java. This Buddhist monument embodies the cosmic mountain in mandala plan. Square terraces with bas-reliefs and circular ones with stupa-covered Buddha statues lead to a central stupa. The pilgrim climbs from the sphere of desire (*kamadhatu*), through the sphere of form (*rupadhatu*) and finally reaches the sphere of formlessness (*arupadhatu*).

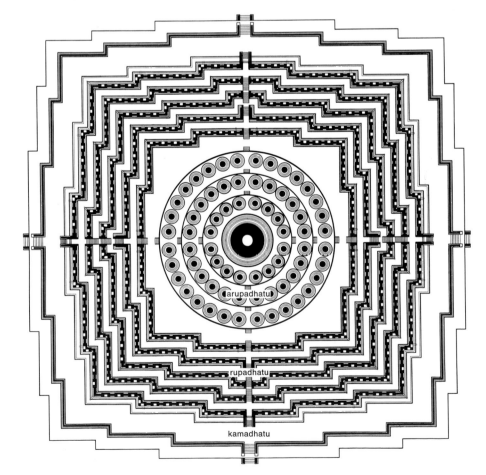

Fig. 31/no. 6
Anusapati, second king of Singasari, as Siva, ca. 1260. East Java. Andesite, 123 cm.

Fig. 30/no. 5
Plaque, 9th century. Banyumas, Central Java. 18-carat gold; frame: silver or zinc and copper alloy, 20 × 12.4 × 2 cm.

FIG. 32
Kertarajasa, first king of Majapahit, as Visnu,
ca. 1300. East Java. Stone, 200 cm.

FIG. 33/NO. 108
Wayang kulit, **Batara Guru**, 1870. Magelang,
Central Java. Buffalo hide parchment, pigment,
gold leaf, fish glue medium, buffalo horn,
semiprecious stones, 74.7 × 27 × 1.7 cm.

FIG. 34/NO. 3
Mamuli (**ear pendant**), 19th century. East
Sumba. Gold, 12 × 10 cm.

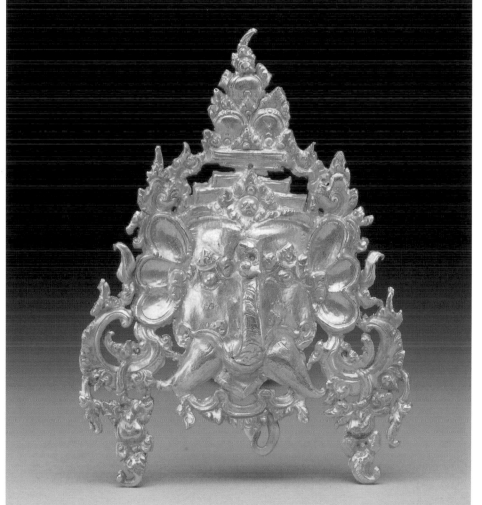

FIG. 35/NO. 65
Sumping (**head ornament**), 14th–15th
century(?). Java. Gold, 7.4 × 5.3 cm.

FIG. 36/NO. 91
Gambang (**xylophone**), 18th century. Cirebon,
West Java. Wood, bronze, rope, pigment,
29 × 65 × 23.3 cm.

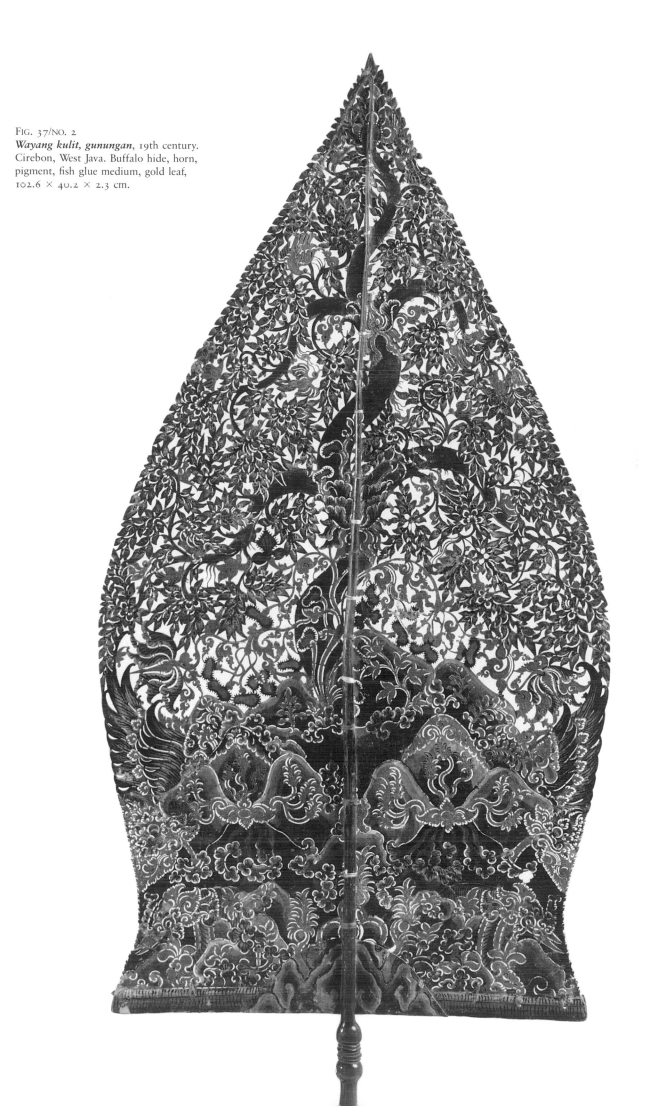

FIG. 37/NO. 2
Wayang kulit, gunungan, 19th century.
Cirebon, West Java. Buffalo hide, horn,
pigment, fish glue medium, gold leaf,
102.6 × 40.2 × 2.3 cm.

relate the story of the Buddha's life and that of his disciples, provides both physically and iconographically a paradigm of man's upward struggle to attain enlightenment. A precedent for monuments like Borobudur can be seen in a nine-stepped earthen pyramid at Lebak Sibedug in West Java, for which current archaeological research suggests a fourth-century date. This terraced structure may be an autochthonous mountain symbol, or it may be an early example of the architectural fusing of indigenous and Hindu symbols. The sometimes sacred terraces (*kahiangan*) on mountain slopes have a direct connection to rice growing and water control, activities indicating considerable social organization whose history is oldest in Java and Bali. Wet rice cultivation is known to have been practiced in Java since the eighth century or earlier and was widespread in Sumatra, Java and Bali by 1400.[16] Rice is considered to have a soul, and in some Indonesian languages the word for it is the same as that for the human soul (e.g., *tondi* in Batak).[17] As a support of life and a source of prosperity through exchange, rice is unsurprisingly prominent in Indonesian folk tales, its origin lying in heaven whence human ingenuity extracted it. There are several variants of the story of its coming to earth.

Indic overtones color one version, where the seed of life slips from heaven through seven levels of the lower world to the mouth of Nagaraja, king of snakes. When brought to heaven and slit open, Nagaraja yields not the seed but twins, a girl, Sri, and a boy, Sadana. Prohibited from marrying Sri, Sadana is cursed by Batara Guru and dies. The grieving Sri is in turn cursed by Batara Guru, and her body is taken to an earthly woman who has long prayed for the seed of life for earth's people. Seven days after Sri's interment, rice plants appear from her grave. It is significant that one of the most important of the annual ceremonies in the *kraton* (court or palace) of Surakarta in Central Java is the ritual cooking of rice by the Susuhunan, the king himself, as part of the annual ceremony of Garebeg, one of the religious celebrations where Islamic devotions are infused with indigenous beliefs. It is also noteworthy that at the time of the rice harvest, a *lakon* (play) from the shadow drama called *Sri Sadana* is performed that features Sadana (Sadono) and Dewi Sri in an episode linked to fertility rites.[18]

There are several variants of this theme, but the legend of Sri, who is deified and known as Dewi Sri, has passed into the general mythology of agriculture and fertility in Java and assumed a place in court customs. Like the mountain motif, the image of Dewi Sri pervades all layers of society. In the *wiwitan* ceremony in the harvest festival of Central Java, offerings are made to Dewi Sri; the first stalks of rice are cut and tied to make a bride or bridal couple (*mantenan*), which is identified as the goddess herself. This effigy is taken home and placed on a bed in the inner part of the house.[19] Similarly, simple effigies made of rice paste are formed as offerings to sacred *wayang kulit* (shadow play puppets) when these are removed from their storage chests in the *Kraton* Surakarta Hadiningrat (the court of the senior ruler of Java, the Susuhunan of Surakarta), while images of Dewi Sri are incised into the wood panels of small central rooms considered the heart of village houses in Java.[20] Her association with fertility has a more overt expression in the courtly *loro blonyo* figures (FIG. 38) placed in front of the *kobongan* (ritual marriage bed) in noble houses in Central Java and specifically named Dewi Sri and Dewa Sadana.

The placement of these figures in front of the *kobongan* signifies the importance accorded them. The *kobongan*, which is sometimes literally a bed, sometimes, especially in Sumatra and Sulawesi, a curtained alcove[21] and sometimes a screen (FIG. 39), is likely to be a completely enclosed shrine in the highest palaces of Java. In the *Kraton* Surakarta Hadiningrat, this shrine (FIG. 40) does not in fact have *loro blonyo* figures associated with it. Through its paired snakes cresting the roof and spitting real flames it suggests a complex mythology involving fire and *nagas* (the mythical snakes that are also central to Indonesian imagery), as well as the fertility symbolism implicit in the ritual marriage bed.

FIG. 39
Kobongan screen, 19th century. Kota Gede, Central Java. Wood, painted and gilded, 150 × 90 cm. Layered panels with patola motifs represent the *cindai*-covered cushions stacked in the ritual marriage bed.

Opposite:
FIG. 38
Loro blonyo, ca. 1875. By Wreksodiningrat. Surakarta, Central Java. Wood, pigment, fish glue medium, iron, gold, diamonds, semiprecious stones; male figure 55 cm, female figure 47 cm. Dewi Sri, goddess of rice, and her consort Sadono are placed before the ritual marriage bed.

FIG. 40
Kobongan, 20th century. The *dalem* of the
Kraton Surakarta Hadiningrat, Central Java. In
the ceremonial core of the palace is an exact
replica of the original ritual marriage bed
destroyed by fire in 1984. Flames spurt from
the mouths of the *nagas* on the roof.

Clearly the invocation in a courtly setting of elemental symbols of the cycles of nature identifies the ruler with the basic life force. Further associations with fertility are suggested in the use of the *naga* motif. Like the mountain, the mythical snake has both autochthonous and Indic sources, and its power can be for both good and evil. Like many symbols of primordial myths it has universal connotations, such as the Judaic association with the Garden of Eden and temptation or the Greek association with healing. One of the earliest examples of the *naga*'s enhancement of royal power can be seen in the Telaga Batu inscription near Palembang, South Sumatra, the probable site for the capital of the powerful maritime kingdom of Srivijaya, which dominated trade in the Melaka Straits area from the seventh to the eleventh century. This huge stone (now in the Museum Nasional in Jakarta), undated but from corroborating evidence thought to have been inscribed around the year 686,[22] is addressed to all the king's subjects. The inscription enunciates an oath of allegiance and describes the savage punishments that will befall any subject breaking the oath. The stone is in the form of a shield carved along the top curve with seven *naga* heads. The king, who is also associated with the spirit of water in contemporary inscriptions found near Palembang, invokes the locally held belief in the power of the snake, ruler of the waters, guardian of the life-force of water, source of fertility.[23] In an inscription of 775 dedicating a Buddhist monastery at Ligor in the north of the Malay Peninsula, the Srivijayan monarch is described as "patron of the *nagas*, their heads halved by the streaks of the luster of gems."[24] The fact that the Srivijayan kingdom was Buddhist adds importance to the *naga* symbol, since the snake is venerated as the protector, with seven coils and his hood, of the seven-day meditating Buddha.

Elsewhere in the archipelago the snake plays an important part in legend and symbol. The already quoted story of the snake-princess Malini indicates Balinese awareness of the *naga* as fertility source, while in Luwu there is a belief that the land was once occupied by snakes which on the eve of Friday (the Islamic holy day) were incarnated as humans. This introduces a syncretism binding autochthonous legend not with an Indic idea but with Islam. Among the Bataks the snake plays an important role in legends of the Karo people, who believe that they are descended from the daughter of a giant snake. In the court of the Batak spiritual leader, the Singamangaraja, snakes were tended and considered sacred. A Batak legend depicts Naga Padoha, the world serpent, causing the formation of mountains and earthquakes.[25] The daughter of the god Batara Guru, leaping from the upper world to the endless sea, is sent a handful of earth from her father via a swallow. Set on the sea, the soil grows and becomes the earth. This first earth, pushed off by Naga Padoha because it takes his light, is replaced by another; to ensure its survival the serpent is bound into a block. His struggles to move in this prison produce the mountain ridges and continuing earthquakes.

The association of snakes with princely regalia is apparent in Lampung, where the backs of *pepadons* (ceremonial seats) often depict serpents and where certain *pepadons* are said to have guardian snakes. At times the snake may subsume the *pepadon* into its own form to hide it from unauthorized viewers, or it may emerge to warn the owner of the presence of strangers.[26]

Perhaps the snake's most dramatic embodiment is in the carved figureheads of royal boats in Java, Sulawesi and Kalimantan (FIG. 41/NO. 9). It has been suggested that the amphibious nature of the snake emphasizes the duality of the king's power over land and water.[27] The magnificence of royal processions by water where the king's majesty was enhanced by the power of his serpent vessel is well expressed in the historical poem *Sja ir Perang Mengkasar*. It describes the

FIG. 42/NO. 8
Drawing of a river scene with *naga*-head boat,
1811–13. Java. Watercolor on paper,
50.8 × 30.5 cm.

FIG. 41/NO. 9
Boat head in *naga* form, 19th century(?).
Surakarta, Central Java. Teak wood, painted
and gilded, 78 × 30 × 71 cm.

King of Tallo, brother of the Sultan of Gowa in South Sulawesi, being carried to battle in a ship with a snake-monster figurehead that was

> carved in a pattern of clouds and curving lotus leaves. The King had his quarters in the Flowery Column. . . . The ship was . . . carved in fretted lines, stamped with sparkling gold leaf, so that it glittered and shone in dazzling fashion. . . . It looked as if it had come down from heaven. Encountering it at sea one would think it to be some monstrous animal. It took two hundred and sixty oarsmen to row the ship and the oars were gold-mounted. They shone like so many torches.[28]

Something of the power of such a snake-monster ship is expressed in the drawing (FIG. 42/NO. 8) made in Central Java during the British interregnum of 1811–16. Impressive also are the carved entwined snakes expressing *sangkala*, the encoded date formulas that characterize the Javanese expression of time, that are found in the *kratons* of Java over entrances and on gong stands, as well as in jewelry throughout the region. The gold bracelet pair called Ponto Janga-Jangaya (FIG. 43), in the *pusaka* (sacred heirloom) collection of the Gowa kingdom, is an outstanding example. The most dazzling of all manifestations of the *naga*, however, are probably those forged on the blades of many examples of the ceremonial *kris* (NO. 70), that acme of Indonesian weaponsmithing that reached its apogée under court patronage.

The history and philosophy of the *kris* deserves and has stimulated several dedicated studies.[29] No other object in Indonesia is more enshrined in mythology, stimulates more interest or is held in such esteem and awe (see chapter 4). Its implications of power, of sexuality, of harmony are complex, and each *kris* is thought to have a spirit of its own that must be compatible with the owner's lest

FIG. 43
Bracelets in *naga* form, 14th century. Makassar, South Sulawesi. 22-carat gold, sapphires, 8 cm. These bracelets, called Ponto Janga-Jangaya, are in the *pusaka* collection of the former Kingdom of Gowa.

misfortune follow. This spirit may have a positive aspect: the form of certain weapons may invoke protection (FIG. 49/NO. 4). Possession of certain *krises* is equated with royal power, and there are many *krises* among the *pusaka* of all courts (FIGS. 120, 172/NOS. 72, 136). Some of them have names and aristocratic titles (FIG. 173/NO. 138). Ceremonial exchange of gifts among rulers often involved *krises* (FIG. 52/NO. 67; NO. 70), and although the *kris* was traditionally associated with male symbolism, females also wore them (FIG. 121/NO. 73).

SHIPS AND THE RULERS OF THE SEA

In an archipelagic nation like Indonesia, the importance of ships in practical development and economic expansion is inevitable and confirmed by the historical record (see chapter 2). As with the images of rice and fertility, the prominence of ships and the sea in the symbols of all regions and all strata of society is another example of the visual signposts indicating the outlines of the overarching grid of Indonesian culture and reaching their fullest expression in the courts. The *naga* boat just described expressed the power of a Sulawesi ruler. We know from the *Nagarakertagama* that boats were also important in Majapahit ceremonies demonstrating the king's might. The *lancang kuning*, or yellow boats,[30] of Kalimantan and Sumatra played a similar role, and indeed even offered a metaphor for the state. A poem from the Malay region of Riau, East Sumatra, implies the common characteristics of a ruler and a ship's captain, or *nahkoda*:

> The Lancang Kuning sails at night
> Her bows towards high seas
> If her *nahkoda* is ignorant
> She is bound to be wrecked[31]

In Perak, across the Straits of Melaka from Riau, the terminology of shipping is used for government, the ruler being called "captain" and officials "mate."[32] Bali, Sunda and Java employ ship-shaped containers for the important ceremony of *sirih* (betel) preparation and presentation; an example in gold is one of the *pusaka* of the Surakarta court. Its form inspired the present from Pakubuwono X to Queen Wilhelmina of the Netherlands on the occasion of her 1901 marriage (FIG. 128/NO. 140). In Savu, East Nusa Tenggara, a large communal boat is drawn on the ground and villagers sit in appointed places named after boat positions to carry out important rituals.[33] In Sulawesi both houses and boats are correlatives for the body as metaphor for the world; shavings saved during ship construction are wrapped and hung on the mast in much the same way that the human umbilicus, considered the brother of the baby in many areas of Indonesia, is saved as an amulet.[34]

Recent research in Indonesian history and mythology has emphasized the importance of maritime contacts in the development of trade and international relations. Another clearly emerging aspect is the persistence of the Austronesian cultural factors that underlie all subsequent cultural and religious influences in the archipelago.[35] These indigenous factors include the importance in Austronesian societies of the sea, of women and of the links between them, compared to the patriarchal and land-oriented features that characterize Indo-Aryan and Chinese societies. Areas of Indonesia where Indic influences did not penetrate, as in the eastern islands and the interior regions of Sumatra, Kalimantan and Sulawesi, tend therefore to have societies where the female role is strong.

In this context, myths of origin and royal genealogies are concerned less with mountains and men than with princesses who emerge from the sea or are involved with ships of fortune. As with the pantheistic-Indic founding myths, which link timeless elements with known history, so these legends are a blend of real and mythological. The *Hikayat Banjar* and the *Salasilah Kutai* are nineteenth-

FIG. 44
Boat, Dongson period, ca. 3rd century B.C.–1st century C.E. Sikka, Flores. Bronze, 27 × 61 × 8 cm.

FIG. 46/NO. 1a
Tampan (**ritual weaving**), 19th century.
Lampung south coast, Sumatra. Cotton,
supplementary weft, 80 × 77.5 cm.

FIG. 45/NO. 156a
Palepai (**ceremonial hanging**), 19th century.
Kalianda, Southeast Lampung, Sumatra.
Cotton, supplementary weft, 63.5 × 266.7 cm.

century texts of earlier legends presenting what Ras calls "the Malay myth of origin."[36] The central personage in these legends is a princess who emerges from a mass of foam in the water and eventually marries a prince whose origin is the sky.[37] Together they found the Banjarmasin (or Kutei) royal dynasty. Ras posits them as the representatives of the water and the sky, with the earth being introduced in later episodes with the appearance of a princess who arises from a clump of bamboo. This myth is the most explicit expression of royal legitimacy based on elemental values.

Other important links between the ruling dynasty and the forces of the sea can be seen in the role played by Ratu Kidul, Queen of the Southern Ocean, in the courts of the Javanese second Mataram kingdom. Its earliest progenitor, *Panembahan* Senapati (1582–1601), was ritually married to Ratu Kidul, as was his grandson Sultan Agung (1613–45), to propitiate her and gain her support in times of trouble. Still today in the annual *labuh* ceremony the *Kraton* Ngayogyakarta Hadiningrat's Sultan renews the links between his dynasty and the goddess. In Srivijaya the king acknowledged the power of the sea in the practice of ritually throwing gold bricks into it as tribute, a custom attested to by the Arab geographer Ibn Khurdadhbih in 846.[38] In Riau the propitiation originally involved the sacrifice of a maiden; today in the Bengkalis district it is expressed in the ceremony of *Penyemahan Ikan Terebuk*, in which a girl is bathed with seawater; in Serasen decorations made of dried rice porridge are hung on coconut palms and a small boat filled with food offerings is sacrificed to the sea.[39]

A more pragmatic myth of origin, one with links to the ruler's need for economic viability as well as spiritual legitimacy, concerns the legend of the richly laden ship. Many versions of this tale exist, in essence describing how the capture

FIG. 47/NO. 61
Ring in phoenix form, 14th–15th century(?). Java. Gold, 2.28 cm.

of a merchant vessel, or its rescue, leads to the acquisition of leadership by an outstanding local personality.[40] Sometimes the hero Dampu Awang is involved, with admixtures of possible references to the Ming admiral Zheng He (Cheng Ho). Courts where the story occurs in the genealogy include Buleleng in Bali, Sumenep in Madura, Jepara on the north coast of Java, Cirebon in West Java, Palembang and Lampung in Sumatra and Banjarmasin in Kalimantan. A slightly different version in Buton, Sulawesi Tenggara, has a princess, the daughter of Kublai Khan, arriving by boat and becoming the mother of the Buton royal line.[41]

Among the most striking objects epitomizing the vital role that the sea and ships play in the rituals of Indonesia are various expressions of death symbols. Perhaps the oldest is a bronze boat of mysterious provenance (FIG. 44), which is the most treasured *pusaka* of a village in the eastern part of Flores, East Nusa Tenggara. Though there was a tradition of casting small ritual objects from brass in Flores, there is no evidence that this ship, which was largely cast in the lost wax technique, was locally made. It is probably contemporary with Dongson bronze drums made in the two or three centuries preceding and following the birth of Christ; the drums are named for the place in Vietnam where archaeologists first unearthed them in the 1930s.

Quite unlike the Indonesian bronzes of the Indo-Javanese period (eighth to fifteenth centuries) and differing also from ships depicted on the bas-reliefs of Borobudur, the ship relates to the iconography of indigenous ship mythology concerned with the arrival of founding ancestors, prosperity and the conveyance of the soul to the world of the dead. While the figures on the ship's superstructure and those seated along the hull seem to be manning the vessel, the interior figures seem to be involved in ritual. Three male figures braced against uprights are in dancing posture, while a female sits with splayed legs in a position resembling figures in Kalimantan Dayak beadwork and Sumba textiles. The scene is reminiscent of Lampung ship cloths and may be a similar microcosmic metaphor showing the great antiquity of the symbolism of ships in ancestor origins and soul destinations. Carved wooden boats of similar shape with similarly disposed human forms can be found in Central Kalimantan and in Batak illustrations, but this carefully guarded treasure seems to be unique.

The association of boats with death and the journey of the soul is borne out by coffins in boat form found in Nias, Batak lands, Lampung and Dayak villages in Kalimantan.[42] The most complex version of soul ships, however, undoubtedly occurs in the *palepai* and *tampan* ship textiles of Lampung (FIGS. 45, 46/NOS. 156a, 1a). These ceremonial cloths, with their complex imagery of ships bearing courtiers, pavilions, treasures, royal animals and Trees of Life, were made for aristocratic families of Lampung in the nineteenth century. They are not only extraordinary achievements of the weaver's art, but rich expressions of an entire culture. In recent years they have received much scholarly attention[43] and are a high point in the conjunction of courtly manifestations of primordial themes with uniquely indigenous skills of Indonesia.

THE TREE OF LIFE

Other images combine ancient symbols with courtly usage, among them those of birds. These include the *garuda*, the giant mythical bird that is Visnu's steed; the cock, which still plays an important role in the life of the Balinese; the phoenix (FIG. 47/NO. 61), which is particularly visible in areas affected by Chinese culture; and the peacock, a motif that probably dates from the Islamic era. Also important are images of the yoni-linga, the Indic male and female sexual symbols. The only remaining image that can be said to be pervasive, however, is that of the Tree of Life. Its ambiguous depiction with the mountain on the central figure in the *wayang kulit* drama, the *gunungan* or *kayon*, has already been mentioned. Fre-

Above:
FIG. 49/NO. 4
Kris, late 19th century. Surakarta, Central Java.
Iron, nickel alloy, gold; grip: sandalwood;
sheath: teak wood; 44 × 15 × 3.7 cm.

FIG. 48/NO. 16
Trisula (three-pronged) lance head, 17th
century. Central Java. Gold, iron, nickel *pamor*,
52.5 cm.

quently it is found with ships of the soul, as if to complete the duality of existence. Perhaps its form can even be fused with that of the terraced mountain and have a correlative in the shape of a many-tiered umbrella (compare the plant-become-umbrella in FIG. 30/NO. 5 with FIG. 165). It can be seen on the decks of the ships in *tampan* and *palepai*, on shrouds in Tanimbar, on woven mats in East Kalimantan and on lances (FIGS. 8, 48/NOS. 13, 14; 16) and *krises* (FIG. 49/NO. 4). The Batak think of the totality of the cosmos as a tree, its roots in the Underworld and its branches in the Upperworld, while the people of Baun in Timor have a myth of origin in which the ancestor of their rajas descended from a tree.[44]

Trees with their own symbolism—the *sawo* tree for prosperity, for example—are closely associated with palaces and sometimes also with carvings on the monuments of Central and East Java from the eighth century to the fifteenth century. The specific tree in the latter case is the *nagasari* tree, under which the king of Kutei was instructed in royal lore; the *nagasari* tree is also the symbol of Uma and Siva, lords of the universe. The importance of the *waringin* (banyan) tree in Hindu-Buddhist iconography is familiar to scholars of the Indic tradition, but it has a uniquely Indonesian connection with the courts of Java: a pair is always found on the *alun-alun*, the square in front of the palace. These trees have sacred status, and under their spreading branches subjects could sit for specified long periods to attract the attention of the king in matters of justice.

This account of the images and themes associated with the legitimacy and origin of rulers and peoples in Indonesia shows that the courts evolved from and gave expression to primordial forces having clear affinities with universal mythologies. The artifacts of courtly culture, such as the *kris*, jewelry and *wayang* puppets, embody imagery that can be seen as epistemological signs of the cycle of life. They can also be read as more direct evidence of royal power and economic success, which will be examined in subsequent chapters. It was this aspect of court life and kingly status that testified to the wealth of the state and imbued the Indonesian courts with their magnificence. Such brilliance convinced the people of the might of their ruler and the harmony and prosperity of their world and dazzled visiting foreigners from Marco Polo to the nineteenth-century British.

II. WARRIORS, TRADERS AND THE CELESTIALLY GRAND KING

Establishing and Maintaining Princely Power

The Emperor was famous for his love of justice. The empire grew prosperous. People in vast numbers thronged the city. At this time every kind of food was in great abundance. There was a ceaseless coming and going of people from the territories overseas which had submitted to the king, to say nothing of places inside Java itself.[1]

[M]ost revered Susunan, who is held on high by all the Company soldiers . . . who rules the people of Java, and has authority over lords in religion, the commander in battle, who is made glorious by God, who exercises supreme power, who enjoys all the good things of the earth, who rules all rulers, who is protected by the Supreme Soul.[2]

THESE TWO WRITERS were separated by four hundred years and more than twelve hundred miles. The first was describing the monarch of the East Java Majapahit empire; the second was addressing the king of Mataram in Surakarta, Central Java. Seemingly alike in their adulation of a ruler, who is seen as the "celestially grand king" in a phrase used often in the *wayang kulit* (shadow puppet) drama,[3] the meanings of the remarks are nevertheless as divergent as their subjects. The first reasonably can be reckoned a genuine and impartial account, written as it was by an inhabitant of Pasai after a devastating attack on that city by Majapahit forces. The more extravagantly phrased second passage conceals a company official's cynical use of traditional compliments to mask an internal assumption within the United East Indies Company (the VOC) that it had supremacy in Java.[4]

Throne dais, *Istana* Maimun, 1990. Medan, Sumatra.

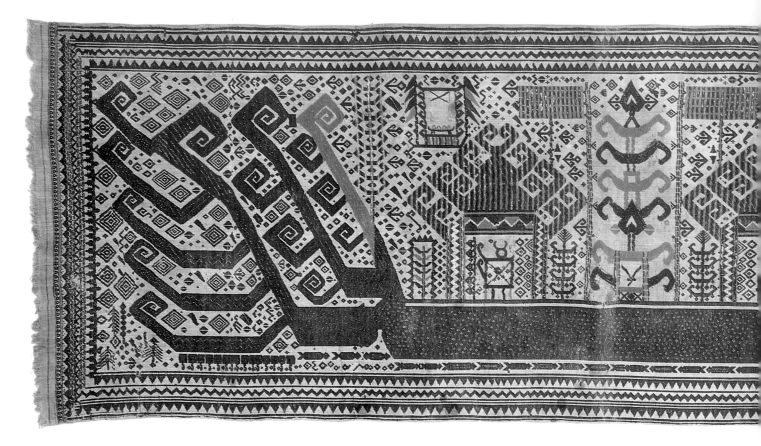

Fig. 50/no. 156b
Palepai (**ceremonial hanging**), 19th century.
South Lampung, Sumatra. Cotton,
supplementary weft, 67.7 × 245.1 cm.

FIG. 51/NO. 1b
Tampan (ritual weaving), 19th century.
Lampung south coast, Sumatra. Cotton,
supplementary weft, 85 × 70 cm.

FIG. 53/NO. 71
Kris, 19th century. Riau Lingga, East Sumatra.
Iron, nickel *pamor*, gold, rubies, diamonds,
wood, 37 × 11 cm.

Opposite:
FIG. 52/NO. 67
Kris, 19th century. Surakarta, Central Java.
Gold, iron, nickel *pamor*, diamonds, rubies,
wood, pigment, gold leaf, lacquer, copper,
52 × 17 × 4 cm.

Tombak (lance) head, 17th century. Central
Java. Gold, silver, iron, nickel *pamor*, 64.5 cm.

At the heart of this contrast in attitudes to the ruler of Java lies the question of power. By the fourteenth century the Majapahit empire was at its apogée, whereas by the late eighteenth century the influence of the second Mataram kingdom (founded around 1576 by *Panembahan* Senapati) had been steadily eroded by internal dissension and VOC control since its days of glory under Sultan Agung (1613–45).[5] Although in outward signs the eighteenth-century court was probably more splendid than Sultan Agung's, its revenues were severely curtailed by the steady VOC abrogation of rights over coastal trading centers, overseas trade and shipping, and tribute and produce from both West and East Java.

Sultan Agung's successor, Amangkurat I (1645–77), had neither the military nor the political ability of his father.[6] A series of succession struggles continued through the years following the end of VOC rule in 1798[7] until the eventual control of Indonesia by the Netherlands government in 1817. The struggles culminated in the bitter Java War of 1825–30, when the controversial Prince Dipanagara (1785–1855) led a revolt against the Yogyakarta court. After this civil war, which cut deeply into loyalties throughout Java, the control of the overt power of the courts by the Netherlands government was virtually complete.[8]

Beyond such simple manifestations of power as military strength or economic control lie many variants of a less quantifiable kind. These involve spiritual, political and genealogical manipulations that help explain the importance of Indonesia's courts even in the absence of political supremacy. The complexities of power can best be understood in the context of the equally complex form of the state in Indonesia.

FIG. 55/NO. 25
Golok **La Nggunti Rante**, 15th century(?). Bali or Sri Lanka(?). Blade: iron, silver alloy, copper; handle: horn or wood;
28.5 × 5.4 × 2.3 cm.

Early Chinese dynastic records note delegations from kingdoms in the Indonesian archipelago that scholars have identified with several areas in Sumatra and Java.[9] The earliest of these for which reliable records exist was the seventh- to eleventh-century Srivijayan empire with its capital where Palembang is situated now (and perhaps later in Jambi). Its fame was widespread, and it seems to have dominated much of the Malay Peninsula, Sumatra itself and the region of the Straits of Melaka. I Tsing, the Chinese Buddhist scholar who traveled to and from Srivijaya between 671 and 695, refers to a thousand monks in the city, by then an important center for Buddhist scholarship, but calls it a "fortified city."[10] Until today no definitive archaeological evidence has been established to pinpoint a settlement of the size that would indicate a large center of empire.[11]

Similar absence of urban construction, or indeed of secular architectural remains of any kind on a scale consistent with empire, makes it difficult to establish the location and nature of the Javanese kingdoms of the first Mataram era contemporary with Srivijaya. The most powerful of these were either connected with the Sailendra monarchs, Buddhist like the rulers of Srivijaya, or with the Saivite Sanjaya line. Even the Majapahit empire, for which documentation is more plentiful, has not yet been archaeologically fathomed to prove with material evidence what is known from epigraphic and literary evidence. Taken alone, its remains in the modern town of Trawulan, extensive though they are, so far offer insufficient proof to postulate an empire that held sway, according to the poem, the *Nagarakertagama*, over most of what is now Indonesia as well as parts of the Southeast Asian mainland from the late thirteenth century to the middle of the fifteenth century.

Many theories have been developed about the nature of Indonesian polities before the existence of written records, which are not extensive in indigenous or foreign sources before the fourteenth century. These theories apply even more to centers of power in Kalimantan, Sulawesi, Nusa Tenggara and Maluku than to Java, Bali and Sumatra. Earlier assumptions about the domination of indigenous societies by external Indic overlords have been rejected by scholars since World War II.

Unsatisfactory, too, are conceptions of exploitative monarchs dominating the uncoordinated and unhierarchical village substratum through control of water reticulation. Clear linear descent through succeeding dynastic eras has also been shown to be inaccurate, leaving out of account as it does the considerable historical overlapping of polities. The "empire" appears not to have been an organization controlling subject lands as much as a loose confederation of tributary states. These states' trading rights depended on sea-lane security and protection from piracy offered by the superior power, whether Srivijaya or Majapahit, and their credibility and prestige in international exchange were enhanced by their connections with that power. Similar relationships between early states and China offer precedents for such alliances.

The proposal that the *negara*, the capital as ritual center, can define the kingdom,[12] with the image of power like a cone of light radiating down from the ruler,[13] explains much of the theoretical power of the king and his centrality in the realm and is helpful in understanding many aspects of court evolution. The role of the king in solemn ceremony and glittering display is a legacy from Majapahit times, if not earlier, inherited by subsequent rulers of the more powerful states of Indonesia.

In practical terms, the most convincing theory of state development is that of an emerging focus of villages around a center of trade or a charismatic leader within traditional structures of agriculture and small-scale commerce. The linking of such trade centers around a dominant cluster, Wolters's *mandala* concept,[14] provided a nucleus that in the presence of productive agriculture and other favorable resource and trading factors could develop into a center of empire.[15] The leader of such a center, as we have seen, drew both on the power of autochthonous myth and on the supernaturally enhancing powers of exotic religions, not excluding priestly rituals and the talismanic nature of the language they were expressed in. The notion of the expanding polity based on long-established and quite sophisticated village organization and water and agricultural control, at least in Java and Bali, has been demonstrated more recently.[16]

Charters from the ninth to the fourteenth century inscribed on stone and copper plates in Bali and Java reveal well-developed systems of village officials and of hierarchies within local agriculture, trade and market organizations.[17] They also contain highly specific decrees (*sima* grants) offering exemption from royal taxation or state taxation obligations. Eighth-century inscriptions in Sumatra give considerable detail about the structure of the Srivijayan court and the duties and relative ranks of royal and nonroyal officials.[18]

Such evidence provides an enabling theory for court polity development without cutting it off too sharply from other Indonesian societies that offer many parallels in myth, symbol and ceremony yet lack a centralized monarchy. Among these is the world of the Minangkabau in Sumatra, whose social organization depended on three rulers, *Raja Nan Tiga Sila* (kings of the three seats).[19] These were the *Raja Alam* (king of the world), *Raja Ibadat* (king of religion) and *Raja Adat* (king of customary practices). This fragmentation of political power and the rise of democratic expression was magnified by the division of the matriarchal Minangkabau people into powerful clans led by chieftains with the title *penghulu*.

The *Raja Alam*, or *Tuanku*, was considered the head of the Minang world in his mountain palace in Pagarruyung, yet he had no physical might to substantiate a claim to kingship and received little more than token tribute. Although he was protected by a bodyguard, there was no standing army in Minangkabau. Access to its highlands from coastal regions was difficult, and its economic power rested on the possession and mining of gold. In 1783 William Marsden quoted local opinion that there were at least twelve hundred gold mines in Minangkabau.[20]

Leadership was not acquired by the usual hereditary or combat means in Minangkabau, and the authority of the *Raja Alam* rested on the tradition of his invincibility in moral strength and his adherence to the principles of the state ethos expressed in oral traditions, particularly the legend *Kaba Cindua Mato*. He was considered to have supernatural powers and insights into character that made him a good and just arbitrator. A lay of the laws of Muko-Muko, one of the many subsidiary polities in the external regions near the west coast that owed allegiance to the moral center of the Minangkabau world, describes the characteristics of the *Tuanku*, the extent of his lands, his duties and the obligations of his subjects. His sovereignty, expressed in terms as extravagant as any used for Javanese rulers, is described as being established first in Roum (which primarily means Turkey but also loosely includes Constantinople and Rome), second in China and third in Pulo Mas (golden isle), or Minangkabau. He is entitled to "the umbrella," a symbol of royal rank. Invoking an interesting parallel to the ship myths mentioned in chapter 1, he is also entitled to tribute because he made float again

> the ship overlaid with gold, which was lost ... on the shoals of the burning mountain, on arriving from the country of Roum, the crown of the world, and which was navigated by *Nakhoda kaya* [rich captain]; a ship which was inlaid with diamonds and rubies, equal in price to the price of a kingdom, and comparable in value to the crown of the son of Solomon.[21]

The religiously motivated Padri wars of the nineteenth century in Minangkabau led to the further fragmentation of centralized power, the abolition of the titular heads of society and the control of the Dutch. Regalia no longer exists, but

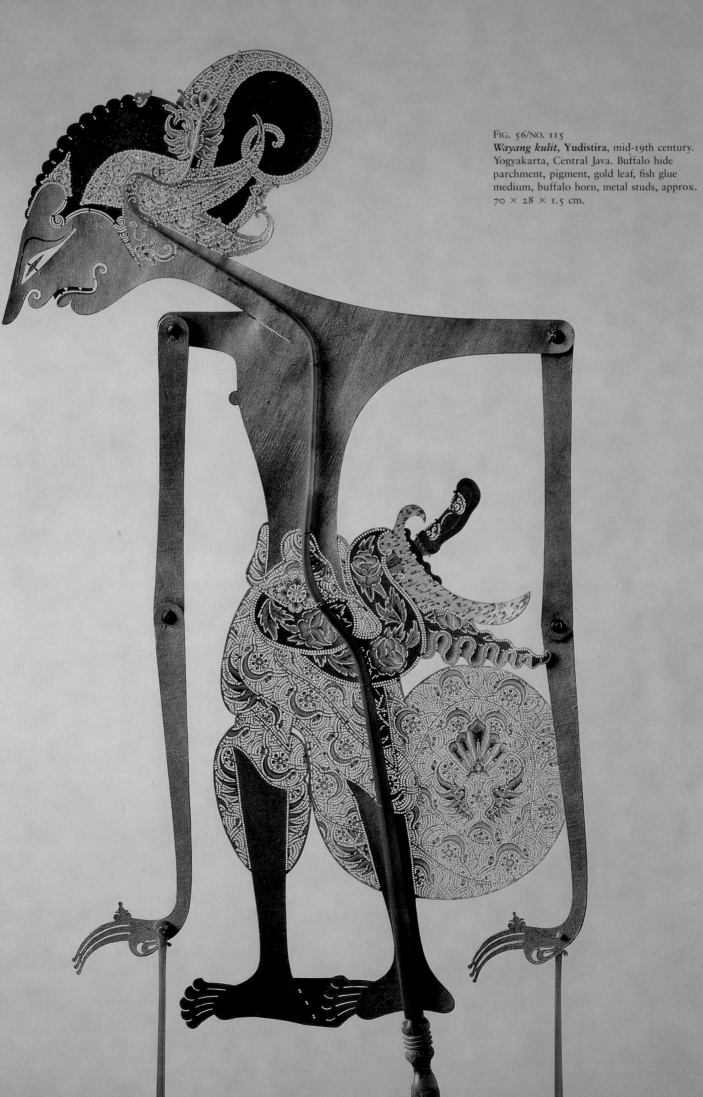

FIG. 56/NO. 115
Wayang kulit, Yudistira, mid-19th century.
Yogyakarta, Central Java. Buffalo hide
parchment, pigment, gold leaf, fish glue
medium, buffalo horn, metal studs, approx.
70 × 28 × 1.5 cm.

FIG. 57/NO. 109
Wayang kulit, Arjuna, 1917–42.
Yogyakarta, Central Java,
Ngabean set. Buffalo hide
parchment, pigment, gold leaf,
fish glue medium, buffalo horn,
bone studs, 69.5 × 28 × 1.5 cm.

surviving jewelry and the richness of textile traditions give some indication of the previous wealth of the state.

Other polities with myths of origin and power similar to those of princely states include the territories of the Batak. So lacking in central focus are the patriarchal clans of the Bataks, however, that they do not offer a court entity to compare with princely states. Like the inhabitants of Minangkabau, the Bataks think of themselves as a people, not a state. Their *Singamangaraja* (great lion-king), though imbued with supernatural powers including the ability to cause rain, is a spiritual leader, not a political figure, despite his potential to raise taxes and armies at times of crisis.[22] In Lampung there is a similar dispersal of authority into clans that precludes the development of true courts, though ceremonial trappings like the *pepadon* throne, the litter with hornbill frontal decoration and the rich *tampan* and *palepai* shipcloths (FIG. 50/NO. 156b) argue for princely grandeur. This is further suggested by the courtly imagery of the textiles (FIG. 51/NO. 1b).

There are many differences in political structure and social organization between the fully developed courts of Java, Madura, Sumatra, Kalimantan, Bali and Sulawesi, as well as the smaller realms of Ternate, Tidore, Lombok, Sumbawa and Bima, on the one hand, and the proto-courts in such places as Lampung, the princely clans of Minangkabau, Roti, Sawu and Sumba and the more straightforward chiefdoms of Nias, Tanimbar, Flores and Timor, on the other. However, the ceremonial traditions, myths of ancestors and sophisticated symbolism of the second group are evidence of their common heritage with the first.[23] The importance of supernatural power is one of the shared elements.

In extended analyses of the nature of power,[24] which pervades both the material and nonmaterial world in Indonesian belief, one aspect emerges clearly: power is paradoxical. The more it is exercised or needs to be demonstrated, the less effective it is; perceptibility diminishes its substance, knowledge of it implies control.[25] Anderson's much-quoted definition is so apt that it bears repetition:

> Power exists, independent of its possible users. It is not a theoretical postulate but an existential reality. Power is that intangible, mysterious and divine energy which animates the universe. . . . In Javanese traditional thinking there is no sharp division between organic and inorganic matter, for everything is sustained by the same invisible power. This conception of the entire cosmos being suffused by formless, constantly creative energy provides the basic link between the "animism" of the Javanese villages and the high metaphysical pantheism of the urban centers.[26]

Such a concept of power and energy is expressed by the Indonesian word *semangat*, meaning soul or spirit and also zest and courage; a variant is found in Sulawesi in the Bugis-Makassarese word *sumange'*.[27] A compromise between the absolute potency of absolute incomprehensibility and the ineffectiveness of complete perceptibility is found in the half-realized expressions of the nonmaterial world. Examples of these are whispers, smoke and fragrances, which are somewhat reminiscent of the Nias conception of the third component of man, *lumolumo*, the detached image of the soul—as in a reflection in water or a shadow—that leaves the body in dreams or illness. Similarly, emanations of *sumange'* such as shadows, bodily warmth, footprints and the voice, as well as such physical excrescences as sweat, tears, urine, and nail and hair clippings, diminish the reservoir of potency. Applied to a ruler this concept of power implies inertia: the power lies within the king's presence itself; the need to demonstrate effectiveness, to materialize the intangible, erodes potential. The truly powerful king is the still center of the kingdom, the nail of the world,[28] the navel of the universe. This is explicitly depicted in the insignia of the Susuhunan of Surakarta (FIG. 52/NO. 67).

An Islamic overtone is added to the primordial derivations of *kesakten* and *sumange'* in the Malay word *daulat* (royal power). In the *Sja'ir Perang Mengkasar* Enci' Amin writes: "As long as the Royal Power [*daulat*] of our great ruler is there/

Above:
FIG. 60/NO. 153
Wahana (miniature vehicle for a votive figure),
20th century. Bali. Wood, pigments, gold leaf,
fish glue medium, lacquer, 48.5 × 49 × 22 cm.

FIG. 59/NO. 149
Sangku (holy-water beaker) with lid, 19th
century or earlier. South Bali. Silver gilt, rubies,
11.2 × 6 cm.

no harm will come to Makassar."[29] The orthodox Islamic interpretation of this Arabic-derived word supposes the power in question to be the inspiration of God to achieve what is spiritually desirable. Any overtones of the personification of divine power in the person of the monarch, which older Indic beliefs might have added to the concept in Indonesia, would of course be contrary to the teachings of Islam. In many areas and at many times there have been efforts to force the nature of Moslem belief into lines less heterodox than has been typical of that faith in Indonesia. Some blurring of the edges between Islamic and *adat* (traditional) belief was expressed even in a state as committed to the teachings of the Prophet as Aceh, as will be seen in an analysis of palace architecture in chapter 3.

The invincibility of and unquestionable rights to absolute royal power, familiar to students of the theory of the divine right of kings in the West, achieve their ultimate fulfillment in *wahyu*. This sign of supernatural power was usually manifested by a glowing light and left the body on death. In some cases a princess with a "flaming womb" was perceived as the mother of kings; Ken Angrok, first king of Singasari (1222–27), was advised to marry Ken Dedes because her flaming womb guaranteed a line of monarchs. In a second case, tailored to legitimize the power of the Dutch, a princess with a flaming womb was sold to a Dutchman whose descendants thereby acquired legitimacy in Java. In a different version, the *wahyu* of Amangkurat II (1677–1703) was said at his death to have taken the form of a grain of light on his penis. Perceived and drawn in by his nephew Prince Puger, manifestation of the *wahyu* and its possession eventually confirmed Puger as Pakubuwono I (1705–19) over the direct claims of his cousin, Amangkurat III (1703–05).

Less mysterious forms of power than *kesakten* and *wahyu* serve to enhance the position of the ruler. Among these is the strength lent by ancestors. While this strength has links with the primordial role of ancestors still so dominant in Nias, for example, in the courtly setting it has a more practical expression in genealogical trees, or *silsilah* (literally, chain) as they were known after the arrival of Islam. Typically these trees not only trace the origin of the ruler and race in a mythical or divine figure, but also demonstrate his connections with important historical figures. The charter from the year 907 in Kedu, Central Java, lists the predecessors of King Balitung for eight generations, though it is not certain that they were in fact his direct ancestors.

A remarkable genealogy for the kings of Mataram provides a double line of ancestors, left and right.[30] The left begins with Adam and Seth and includes Hindu gods, indigenous kings and forebears of the heroes of the Mahabharata epic, as well as historical figures from other parts of Java. The right begins with Mohammed and lists characters from other countries in Asia, Sunan Ngampel—one of the nine *wali sanga*[31]—and the preceding kings of Mataram. The king's descent lines thus invoke authority and power from all possible sources in an impressive disregard for feasibility. The Islamic practice of incorporating names of ancestors into one's own indicates an attitude to genealogy similar to Indonesian autochthonous beliefs.

Another of the *walis*, Sunan Gunung Jati, also identified in some accounts as Tagaril, Falatehan, Fatahillah and Fadillah Khan,[32] but probably a different person, founded the sultanates of Cirebon and Banten in the early sixteenth century. To legitimize his right to rule, his genealogy claimed that the son and daughter of the last king of the earlier West Java kingdom of Pajajaran went to Arabia, where the daughter married a son of the monarch of Egypt. She bore a son, who returned to Java and became Sunan Gunung Jati.[33] In Sulawesi the long and complicated *silsilah* of the royal family of Gowa was a state *pusaka* (sacred heirloom), as was that of Luwu, La Galigo. In Roti genealogies were an oral tradition, in the care not of the leader of the family but of an official whose task it was to recite them in public.[34]

More pragmatic than the invocation of real or mythical forebears was the custom of consolidating political or trade relationships by marriage ties, a habit familiar to most royal histories and clearly visible in such European dynastic records as the Almanach of Gotha. In Java even a ruler as militarily secure as Sultan Agung allied himself with many other royal houses. He himself married daughters of the Sultan of Cirebon and a prince of Batang, on the north coast of Java, and gave sisters in marriage to Cakraningrat I of Madura and Prince Pekik of the powerful trading center of Surabaya.

Earlier, in a complementary process where smaller polities initiated alliances, princes from Kalimantan, Melaka (a powerful Malay Peninsula kingdom), Palembang, Bali, Surabaya, Minangkabau, Banten and Makassar had sought spouses among the children of the Majapahit ruler.[35] Until this century the tendency has continued.[36] These alliances show a wide spread of Bugis and Makassarese representatives, reflecting the reputation for journeying, daring and strength that these seafaring peoples of Sulawesi have earned. There is a saying that if the Dutch had not brought the archipelago under one flag, the Bugis would have done it. Certainly their maritime skills led to their prominence in external trade throughout the archipelago.

In fact, the Bugis role went beyond kinship links: they were actively involved in the government of Riau Lingga, having been called in by the Sultan early in the eighteenth century to help solve inheritance disputes and remaining as a stabilizing presence in perpetuity.[37] Their leader was given the title Yang Dipertuan Muda, and for such members of the nobility *krises* from Riau showing strong Bugis influence were made (FIG. 53/NO. 71). In other examples of far-reaching Bugis power, the forces of the noted warrior of Bone, Arung Palakka, were called on by the Dutch and English to fight their wars during seventeenth-century uprisings in Sumatra, Sulawesi and Java. In one such action against the Minangkabau, Arung Palakka is said to have taken the state umbrella with gold structural parts, and perhaps also the flag (NO. 32) as booty. Possibly the regalia was presented to him by residents of the area, who are reported to have been impressed by his valor.

In spite of such complex relationships, certain elements in concepts of nobility were unaffected by strategic alliances of blood or commerce. Perhaps the most interesting of these, particularly given the ubiquitous role of the Bugis in Indonesia, is the Sulawesi concept of white blood.[38] This quality of inherited spiritual superiority could not be acquired; one was born with it. Marriage patterns were based on the aim of increasing the proportion of white blood in the family. Avoiding its dilution underlay the immutability of one's place in the social hierarchy, and no matter how intimate a relationship between people of different levels might become, it did not negate the acceptance of permanent distinction. The integrity of white blood is in harmony with the Sulawesi notion of *siri'*, a blend of pride and shame that distinguishes man from beast and must be defended without material motives.[39]

Pusaka were mentioned in connection with the genealogical trees (*silsilah*) of Sulawesi. Such heirlooms are not merely the treasured tokens of a ruler's past, but potent signs of legitimacy. They rank as qualifications for leadership with spiritual and genealogical proofs; sometimes their mere possession was sufficient to establish a ruler. In 1677, for instance, the retention of some of the court *pusaka* by Amangkurat I (when he fled his court after the attack of the Maduran prince Trunajaya, losing his treasury and army) and their subsequent possession by his son, gave the latter a claim to become Amangkurat II even in the absence of any other signs of power. Similarly, when Raja Kecil of Minangkabau tried to usurp the throne of Riau Lingga in 1700, his temporary success was largely a result of his capture of the *pusaka* regalia; its recapture by Riau forces, bolstered by Bugis forces from Luwu, ensured their candidate's legitimacy in the eyes of the population.[40]

FIG. 61
Kerta Gosa, early 18th century. Klungkung, Bali. This judgment pavilion is lined with paintings depicting the consequences of immoral and sacrilegious behavior.

FIG. 62
Balai undangan, 18th century(?). Tabek, West Sumatra. This judgment pavilion in traditional Minangkabau style is an important meeting place for the Minangkabau people.

FIG. 63/NO. 18
Dwisula (two-pronged) lance head, 17th century. Central Java. Silver, iron, nickel *pamor*, 42.5 × 11.5 × 3.5 cm.

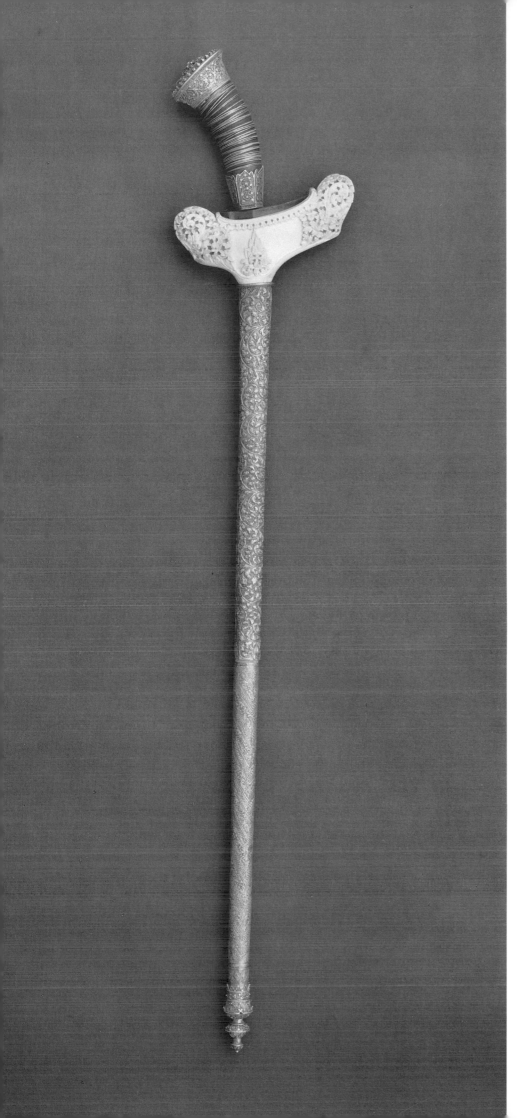

FIG. 64/NO. 22
Kris panjang, 19th century. Deli, Medan,
North Sumatra. Gold, iron, nickel *pamor*;
sheath and grip: wood, ivory; 72 × 13.2 × 3.8 cm.

FIG. 65/NO. 23
Kris pedang luwuk, 19th century or earlier.
Surakarta, Central Java. Gold, silver, diamonds,
iron, nickel *pamor*; sheath and grip: wood;
67.5 × 7.2 × 3.5 cm.

FIG. 66/NO. 26
Perisai (**shield**), 19th century. Banjarmasin, Kalimantan. Gold, iron, 46.5 diameter × 9.3 cm.

FIG. 67/NO. 24
Siwai (rencong), 18th century. Aceh, North Sumatra. Gold, enamel, diamonds, iron; sheath and grip: wood; 37.4 × 11.2 cm.

Some *pusaka* are guardians of the court's safety and prosperity. One of the most powerful is the jacket Kotang Antakusuma belonging to the Sultans of Yogyakarta. Its provenance is said to be from Sunan Kalijaga, one of the nine *walis*, who made it from a goatskin containing a relic of a garment of the Prophet, and while wearing it the king stands between earth and both Upper- and Under-worlds. It is worn only at times of great danger and offers protection to the realm.[41]

Episodes in the *wayang* epics often show heroes receiving magical weapons of invincibility from the gods, and weapons are important in *pusaka* collections. Typically these are lances (FIG. 54/NO. 17) and *krises*, but modern and even foreign ordnance are found. The sacred cannon Nyai Setomi of Surakarta is well known, but *pusaka* cannon are to be found throughout Indonesia. Among the most revered are seven miniature cannon in the Kalimantan court of Sambas that are tucked like so many slender fetishes into a bed covered with sheets in royal yellow, their heads laid on a royal yellow pillow, the whole in a protective glass case.[42]

The *golok* (fighting knife) La Nggunti Rante of Bima (FIG. 55/NO. 25) has been one of the most important symbols of the kingdom since the sixteenth century. At the beginning of a crucial battle it was said to have flown sponta-neously between the army of Bima and opposing forces from Flores. So impressed were Bima's enemies at this sign of supernatural power that they ceded the struggle without loss of blood. Perhaps the strongest *pusaka* power is found in Sulawesi, where it, not the ruler, is considered the earthly representative of the gods.[43]

THE KING AND THE WORLD

The state of kingship presented so far has been ideal, its power absolute. In practice, of course, rulers have to exist in the real world. Acknowledgment of this compromise is made in many ways, one of them being to fill in the template of the inimitable monarch with moral qualities. Some of these qualities derive from Indic models. The *Serat Rama*, an eighteenth-century translation by the court writer Jasadipura I of the Old Javanese version of the *Ramayana*, conveys the Hindu virtues of kings in the *Asta Brata*. Eight qualities are identified with the eight *Lopakalas*, the Indic guardians of the four cardinal and four intermediate points of the universe. These virtues include beneficence, the ability to restrain evil, kind-ness, wise behavior, insight into truth, generosity, intelligence in difficult situations and courage in opposing enemies. Together they contribute to the Javanese idea of the *Ratu Adil*, or just king, who, somewhat like King Arthur of the Britons, is expected to materialize to save the world in times of danger.

In Java a traditional vehicle for moral guidance is the *wayang* dramatic repertory. One character frequently invoked is the Indic character Yudistira (FIG. 56/NO. 115), one of the five princely Pandawa brothers, who is mentioned as a model leader, never lying or showing anger. A younger brother, the very popular Arjuna (FIG. 57/NO. 109) is valued for courage and his prowess with women. In Old Javanese *kidung* verse (in Javanese language and meter), Panji (NO. 117), the indigenous hero who is often compared with Arjuna, is also a model for princely conduct. Javanese rulers themselves produced literary works prescribing proper kingly behavior and implying the indissoluble mutual dependence of subject and king, the *kawula-gusti* relationship. One such is the *Serat Wulangreh* by Pakubuwono IV (1788–1820); another is the *Wedatama* of Mangkunagoro IV (1853–81).

In a more overtly Islamic context, Raja Ali Haji of Riau Lingga (ca. 1809–ca. 1870), the cousin of the Bugis ruler of that Malay kingdom, writes in his *Tuhfat al-Nafis* (The Precious Gift) that kings should ensure conditions for the proper following of Islamic laws. Prosperity naturally follows the harmony achieved in lands where religion dictates the conduct of affairs. The early Malay chronicle,

Hikayat Iskandar Dzu'l-Karnain, points out through a story about Alexander the Great that kings can subvert the ways of God by failing to control *hawa nafsu* (material desire). Only through *akal*, a quality of rationality and response to God that has something in common with the Bugis *siri'*, can man and, as implied through the parable of Alexander, kings, foster the ideal world.[44]

The idea of the ruler's responsibility for maintaining the correct environment for the fulfillment of divine will is common to most of the religions that shaped Indonesian society. Although glorification of the king was undeniably a motive, the construction of the great Buddhist and Hindu temples of Central and East Java (FIG. 58) demonstrates the defining role of religion in that island for more than eight hundred years. Iskandar Muda (1607–36) of Aceh, the greatest military conqueror of Sumatra who established Acehnese control over much of the island, was an absolutist monarch feared for his ruthless extermination of possible rivals. He was nevertheless noted for his building of mosques, though Islamic beliefs were more central during the reign of his successor, his son-in-law Iskandar Thani Alauddin Mughayat Syah (1636–41); orthodoxy was encouraged and religious writings flourished, as they continued to do under the queen Taj ul-Alam (1641–75), Iskandar Thani's widow, Iskandar Muda's daughter.[45]

The Indonesian society most completely pervaded by religion is certainly Hindu Bali, where offerings and attempts to interpret and express the will of the gods and to honor them affect all aspects of life. Rulers in Bali still gain their authority from their role as intermediaries for divine will, and the focus of artistic and economic forces is the glorification of the gods (FIG. 59, 60/NOS. 149, 153). Neglect of such obligations to the temple or failure to consult its priests would seriously undermine the cohesion of Balinese society, just as failure to set a spiritual example was considered to undermine cosmic harmony in both Javanese and Islamic contexts.

Another expectation in most Indonesian polities was that the ruler should take an active part in the processes of justice. Javanese kings received subjects in the *siti inggil* (high place) within the *kraton* (court) precincts. Rajas in Bali adjudicated disputes, the exquisite pavilion of Kerta Gosa in Klungkung (FIG. 61) having been built for such practices; the ruler of Gianyar is still involved in counseling his people in a more democratic version of the old custom. In Minangkabau the large *balai undangan* (law pavilion) in Tabek *desa* (village) (FIG. 62) continues to be used as a central judgment place for Minang clans. In Siak the Sultan adjudicated disputes in a special judgment hall reached by paired staircases to left and right. Those awaiting verdict could determine the decision by the ruler's choice of staircase to descend to ground level: use of the left staircase announced a negative decision, the right, a positive one. It is interesting that in most realms the place of judgment is set apart from the ruler's palace, though close by, a possible example of the separation of what we would designate the executive and judicial branches of government.

In practical terms the ruler's success and the criteria by which his people judged him depended on his ability to organize, sustain and protect his kingdom. Administration varied greatly from state to state, depending on whether the underlying indigenous system strongly retained its character and structure—as in Minangkabau and Savu, to take two different and widely separated examples—or whether the system of kingship pervaded society and dominated the existing system, as under Iskandar Muda in Aceh and in eighteenth-century Madura. In most places there was a compromise. In Majapahit Java, for example, the organization of agriculture, in particular wet rice cultivation, was carried out in the traditional village setting without outside organization. The independence of agriculture from royal dictates also holds true for Bali, where the *subak* (the organization that controls water) to this day exercises authority that does not defer to princes.[46]

FIG. 68
**Manuscript of *Serat
Bratayudha***, 1873–83.
Yogyakarta, Central
Java. Ink on European
paper, polychrome
watercolor, gold leaf,
leather binding, gold
embossing,
46 × 29 × 7 cm.

ᮊᮤᮒ ᮃᮓᮨᮌ ᮔ ᮃᮊᮨ ᮃᮊᮨ ᮃᮊᮨ ᮃᮊᮨ ᮃᮊᮨ ᮃᮊᮨ ᮃᮊᮨ
ᮃᮊᮨ ᮃᮊᮨ ᮃᮊᮨ ᮃᮊᮨ ᮃᮊᮨ ᮃᮊᮨ ᮃᮊᮨ ᮃᮊᮨ
ᮃᮊᮨ ᮃᮊᮨ ᮃᮊᮨ ᮃᮊᮨ ᮃᮊᮨ ᮃᮊᮨ ᮃᮊᮨ ᮃᮊᮨ
ᮃᮊᮨ ᮃᮊᮨ ᮃᮊᮨ ᮃᮊᮨ ᮃᮊᮨ ᮃᮊᮨ ᮃᮊᮨ ᮃᮊᮨ
ᮃᮊᮨ ᮃᮊᮨ ᮃᮊᮨ ᮃᮊᮨ ᮃᮊᮨ ᮃᮊᮨ ᮃᮊᮨ ᮃᮊᮨ

Rural market organization was also a local concern in Java, with market cycles in evidence in the ninth century closely resembling current systems.[47] Wider distribution and taxation were controlled from above. Members of the ruler's family, specially appointed court officials or powerful landholders were deputed to collect taxes on the king's behalf or to impose them on their own account—depending on the distance from the court—and subsequently to yield an agreed percentage of the total to the king.

In polities where external trade rather than interior agriculture was the moving force of society, such as coastal states like Jepara, Surabaya and Srivijaya itself, control of sea-lanes and harbors was more crucial than land organization. When the Portuguese overthrew the powerful straits kingdom of Melaka in 1511 there was no longer a stable power to police the waters of the straits, and trade and shipping were seriously disrupted by piracy.

Control of either hinterland or coast offered a basis for development, but as recent studies have shown, the inability of states to balance internal and external organization or to deal with the redistribution of profits to their people often underlay their loss of power.[48] The *Nagarakertagama* speaks of a royal ceremony where temples were supported by the king, and where "on the seven days without interruption money, clothes with food, unmeasured, were distributed."[49]

Notable examples of the failure of the redistribution process include Aceh in the late seventeenth century, where insufficient interior control led to an inadequacy of food supplies; this weakened the capital when booming trade expanded its population beyond the ability of the domestic market to sustain it. An example of the reverse situation, with an agriculturally based state deprived of trading possibilities because of loss of port control, occurred with Mataram in the same century, with the VOC gradually gaining ascendancy in external trade as their domination of the coasts increased. Such Dutch control of coastal shipping also prevented the spice-producing kingdoms of Maluku from reaping the profits of their production of cloves, cinnamon and nutmeg.

Administration of course requires expenditure as well as organization, so rulers needed resources. Income for monarchs often came from tribute as well as entrepôt profits and the sale of aromatics and medicines to China, as in the Srivijayan state. It came from fines imposed by the ruler as punishment, particularly in later Sumatran states. In Java, revenues were derived from the products of the land, as well as from land and production taxes, entrepôt profits and exports. In Sulawesi, the Makassarese nobility grew rice specifically for export to Maluku in return for spices as early as 1606.[50]

The prosperity of the realm depended, of course, on how well the ruler and his advisers could manage the economy, which was inevitably linked to both the internal and the external security of the state.[51] The appearance of prosperity, however, depended on how successfully the king could project an image of the beneficent and magnificent monarch. Ironically, the rulers appeared in greatest effulgence at a time when the military power of the Javanese courts was virtually gone and the hegemony of Netherlands forces had put an end to armed dynastic struggles. This important so-called "cult of glory"[52] was an important factor in the continuity of courtly power, and will be dealt with more extensively in chapter 4.

Before military domination by the Dutch turned Indonesia's courts into centers where culture rather than might played the leading role, the rulers were responsible for internal policing and external defense. At times there were large armies; the Kedukan Bukit inscription near Palembang from the year 682 records a journey of the king in search of *siddhayatra* (a quest for supernatural prowess), on which he took two thousand soldiers and was reported to be able to recruit up to twenty thousand more if necessary. These numbers must have been recruitable from the interior and underline the point that manpower resources were as important as other forms of wealth. Many raids from Aceh and other states were aimed at seizing slaves to bolster labor resources. The *Adat Aceh* records eight thousand troops in a ceremonial procession accompanying Sultan Iskandar Muda to a mosque on the feast of Id al-Adha, and in 1629 Iskandar Muda lost nineteen thousand troops and several hundred ships in an abortive raid against the Portuguese in Melaka. Even the relatively small coastal state of Jepara, under its King Yunus, could mount an attack against Melaka with an army of five thousand men in 1513.

Usually concerns about manpower resources led rulers to conserve forces. Sometimes this took the form of combat by a selected champion, possibly the relic of an ancient practice formalized on the installation of kings, as with the investiture of *Panembahan* Seda-ing-Krapyak (1601-13) after the death of Sultan Agung of Mataram. His younger brother challenged any who might oppose Krapyak's right to the throne to a testing duel. The value of a weapon such as La Nggunti Rante, the *pusaka* weapon of Bima (FIG. 55/NO. 25), gains new meaning in the context of manpower conservation; it is easy to understand how weapons acquired a cachet beyond their immediate technical potential and how their forging invoked some of the greatest skills of Indonesia's craftsmen. Lances (NO. 15), two- and three-pronged spears (FIG. 63/NO. 18), swords (NO. 21), *krises* (FIGS. 64, 65/NOS. 22, 23), knives and shields (FIG. 66/NO. 26) all raised weaponry from a functional to a formal status. Even cavalry trappings were elaborate and often made of precious metals (NO. 28). The Acehnese *rencong* and its variant the *siwai* (FIG. 67/NO. 24) were considered the embodiment of male strength, but symbolism reached its height in Indonesia in the *kris*, the essence of physical, spiritual and sexual potency.

Forming an elite corps that lent an aura of military superiority to the ruler and acted as a household guard was another way of acquiring visible warrior strength without being committed to the strains of maintaining a sizeable standing army. One of the earliest of these corps was the Tamtama, apparently formed around 1500 under Sultan Trenggana (1521–46) of Demak. To qualify for membership required superhuman physical powers and magical invulnerability. A later group for which better documentation is available is the women's corps (*prajurit estri*) formed in the household of Raden Mas Said, Mangkunagoro I (1757–95), in Surakarta.[53] The same palace maintained a legion that survived the atrophy of court troops after the Dutch had reduced most household corps to ceremonial status; the Dutch even called on this legion during the nineteenth century.

Given the framework of divinely sanctioned authority within which most Indonesian rulers exercised absolute power, it is interesting to try to identify possible means of redress available to their subjects. While the image of the ideal monarch was a widely distributed paradigm, even the few examples so far mentioned demonstrate that practice often fell far short of precept. Ronggawarsita, the great court poet of Surakarta, expresses his dismay at the spiritual vacuum at the heart of the late nineteenth-century kingdom in *Serat Kala Tida*:

> The lustre of the realm
> Is now vanished to the eye
> In ruins the teaching of good ways
> For there is no example left[54]

In fact, several mechanisms were available whereby subjects could express disapproval and sometimes even influence the behavior of their princes. The most effective of these methods were preventive rather than corrective. The norm of primogeniture, for example, could be bypassed if the Crown Prince was unsuitable in some way. In practice this happened more frequently without friction and succession wars outside Java than within. In the Sultanates of Buton and Ternate a council of elders approved the new ruler before he was confirmed. In Gianyar, Bali, consensus of family and councilors bypassed the direct heir in 1896, and for all Gianyar rulers there was a period of some years of trial before anointment. In Banjarmasin, Kalimantan, although outright rejection would probably have proved difficult, it was necessary for the people to sprinkle the Sultan-elect with consecrated water while he sat in the *alun-alun* (square in front of the palace) before coronation to signify their consent to his succession.[55]

One of the most effective means for the population to express their disapproval of the already consecrated ruler was simply to disappear into the hinterland. The *Nitisastra*, a Javanese text whose original version dated from Majapahit times, warns that a king with a cruel nature who does not pay attention to his subjects will be "left and evaded."[56] Given the knowledge that population was power for a ruler who needed to be able to count on reserves of labor to produce tradeable crops and man his armies, such tactics help to explain why the bond between ruler and subject, *kawula-gusti*, was strong indeed. A more direct means of access by a Javanese to his king was the custom known as *pepe*, which required sitting for three days under the *waringin* (banyan) trees on the *alun-alun*. After this demonstration of resolution the ruler was obliged to hear the petitioner's plea.

The most elegant and flexible means to express disapproval was certainly voiced by the *dalang*, the polymath master of the *wayang kulit* play. The art of the *dalang* is deeply respected and somewhat feared. He is considered to be capable of supernatural wisdom and therefore to have dangerous powers, particularly since he deals in the mystical realm of language: to name the thing is partly to control it. This attitude has resulted in elaborate word constructs to conceal specific identity in many parts of Indonesia—Sulawesi and Kalimantan, among others—and therefore the *dalang's* command of speech confers on him a status and power quite unconnnected to practical qualifications.[57]

The *wayang* stories contain behavior models based on royal characters within the Ramayana and, more particularly, the Bratayudha cycle (FIG. 68).[58] The scope for criticism is extended by the episodes involving the Panakawan, or clown figures, the most beloved of whom is Semar (FIG. 69/NO. 121), the clown-god. The *dalang* extemporizes the Panakawan dialogue, which sometimes concerns contemporary affairs. Instead of being delivered in classical Old Javanese, it is spoken in vernacular language and is thus more available to the audience. Through it the *dalang* may vocalize social anxieties or anger that have no other outlet and, given his special status, he can do it without fear of reprisal.

The separation of ruler and subject implied by the invocation of divine identity and absolute authority was based on power rather than difference of underlying beliefs. A shared cosmology provided a common body of symbols, so that the most important of thc plastic and performing arts, brought to their highest expression in the courts, as will be seen in chapter 4, sprang from roots that were meaningful for the peasant as well as for the prince.

FIG. 69/NO. 121
Wayang kulit, **Semar,** 19th century. Cirebon,
West Java. Buffalo hide parchment, pigment,
gold leaf, fish glue medium, buffalo horn, metal
studs, 66 × 39 × 3.5 cm.

III. PRINCELY PAVILIONS

Architecture as an Index to Court and Society

*Of the aspect of Moon and Sun, to
be sure, are the Royal compounds in
Tikta Shriphala there, peerless.*[1]

NO ART REVEALS AS MUCH about a civilization as architecture. From cathedrals and catacombs, from railway stations and rowhouses, from barracks, bathhouses and baseball stadiums, a visitor from outer space could reconstruct a great deal about the past of Western society. The level of technical skills, the mobility patterns, urban organization, recreation, religion, military power, personal habits and life rituals implicit in these random types of buildings would keep anthropologists and historians busy for decades. There is also meat for the art historian, the sociologist, the technician and the priest.

Studying the architecture of Indonesia is just as revealing of the history and art of its myriad societies as exploring this mythical scenario would be of Western society. It offers a mirror of civilization reflecting the same syncretism that characterizes Indonesian religious and political development. Nowhere is this clearer than in the architecture of the palaces of Indonesia's rulers.

THE *KRATON* AS PARADIGM OF THE UNIVERSE

Physical conditions in Indonesia are hostile to the built environment. Earthquakes, volcanic eruptions, tidal waves, hurricane-force winds, fierce sun, monsoon deluges and the destructive mold and insect foes that thrive in the tropical humidity all threaten the buildings that challenge untamed nature. Nothing but stone and sometimes brick can withstand the tropical elements for more than a few decades, and even structures made of these materials can be toppled by tremors, undermined by erosion and flooding exacerbated by forest-stripping, as at the great Buddhist monument Borobudur, or engulfed by resurgent jungle, as at Angkor Wat in Cambodia.

These facts explain why all the oldest architectural remains in Indonesia are made of stone. That they were all sacred buildings is probably a result of budget priorities: only structures of the highest importance justified the expense entailed by the relative scarcity and subsequent costliness of building-stone in most

Kerta Gosa (judgment pavilion), 1989.
Klungkung, Bali.

FIG. 71
Rice barns, 19th century. Mariya, East Lombok. These palm-thatched granaries on stilts are clustered on a hill overlooking a *Sasak* village. Protective spirits are said to make guards unnecessary.

FIG. 70
Bugis house, 20th century. Bone district, South Sulawesi. The stilt construction, peaked gable and fretwork carving are typical of Bugis vernacular architecture.

FIG. 72
Village houses and rice barn, 20th century. Pariangan, West Sumatra. The roof ridges of these typical Minangkabau structures exploit tensile strength.

FIG. 76
Siti inggil, early 17th century. *Kraton* Kasepuhan, Cirebon, West Java. The red brick gateways and the plinths of the *pendopos*, like their carved pillars and beams, show the stylistic heritage of Majapahit.

nections with other ninth-century sacred Indic structures; three inscriptions of about 856 and one of 863 found in the vicinity link the site with the erection of three linga sculptures and a Siva temple, respectively.[3]

The lingas celebrated the victory of a ruler and may well be connected with the supremacy of the Sanjaya Saivite line over the Buddhist Sailendra line, the dynasties apparently coexisting in Central Java from the early eighth century to the ninth century.[4] The Sanjaya line, connected to the Sailendra line by its king Rakryan Pikatan's marriage to the princess Pramodavardhani, daughter of King Samaratunga, achieved ascendancy over Java, for which the Ratu Boko plateau was an important focal point.[5]

The site of Ratu Boko, rising more than seven hundred feet above the plain, is clearly strategically important, dominating as it does much of the surrounding countryside. Not surprisingly, in light of the importance of mountains in Indonesian thought, it was also important spiritually. Whether or not its original architecture was exclusively sacred is not known, though a Buddhist Sailendra foundation preceded the Saivite Senjaya one. The fact that secular victories were recorded there suggests that at least by the ninth century a royal as well as a religious presence was identified with the place. At a time in Javanese history when the coincidence of divine and royal power was deliberately invoked, it is conceivable that what was originally sacred was later imbued with secular aspects. One theory suggests that Ratu Boko was a royal residence for only a short time: the carving on

Opposite:
FIG. 78
Candi **Brahu**, 14th century. Trawulan, East Java. The indented profile and red brick construction of this temple are characteristic of the architecture of the Majapahit empire.

FIG. 79
Gate, 18th century. Klungkung, Bali. The carved profile and red brickwork characteristic of Balinese architecture demonstrate the continuity of the Majapahit tradition in Bali.

the balustrades is unfinished, as is the staircase. Another theory infers from bones found on the site that at one time it was a cremation place.[6]

Whether or not a dual interpretation is possible, some of the structures, notably a *pendopo* with eight columns in eight rows that the archaeologists call a *kaputren* (female quarters), do seem distinctly secular.[7] Of greatest interest in the context of courtly architecture is the number of features at the site that are apparently precedents for later Javanese palaces.

First is the link with a mountain, the natural terrain here offering the foundation that in other monumental structures was partly built up, as at Borobudur and in the microcosmic mountain symbolized in the creation of the raised and walled *siti inggil* (high place) in the *Kraton* Surakarta Hadiningrat and the *Kraton* Ngayogyakarta Hadiningrat in the eighteenth century.[8] In the *siti inggil* the enthroned ruler appears to his subjects on ceremonial occasions.

One of the most beautiful *siti inggils* (FIG. 76), and indeed one of the finest architectural complexes in any court in Indonesia, is the early seventeenth-century example in the Kasepuhan *kraton* in Cirebon.[9] Symbolically and stylistically, it forms a link between the Hindu-Buddhist dynasties of Majapahit, which effectively came to an end in the mid-fifteenth century, and the Islamic era, which in Java had its first Moslem rulers around the turn of the sixteenth century. The oldest surviving building in the *kraton* in Cirebon is the exquisitely carved *pendopo* Langgar Alit of 1529 (FIG. 77). A little younger than the *Mesjid Agung* (Great Mosque) (which with the *Mesjid Agung* of Demak [FIG. 74] is one of the oldest and most venerated mosques in Indonesia), this small pavilion was origi-

Left:
FIG. 80
Site plan (detail). *Kraton* Surakarta Hadiningrat, Central Java. The plan shows important points on the ceremonial axis: A. *siti inggil*, B. *Srimanganti lor*, C. tower, D. *Pelataran* (large courtyard), E. *Sasanasewaka* (*pendopo agung*), F. *Sasanaparasedya* (*pringgitan*), G. *Prabasuyasa* (*dalem*), H. *kobongan*.

Right:
FIG. 82
Site plan, Majapahit, 14th century. Trawulan, East Java. This plan shows a similar sequence to FIG. 80: A. market, B. main gate and watch tower, C. *alun-alun*, D. former Buddhist temple, E. Saivite temple, F. *siti inggil*, G. throne pavilion, H. *dalem*, *pusaka* repository, I. king's residence, J. watch tower, K. Buddhist sanctuary L. Saivite sanctuary.

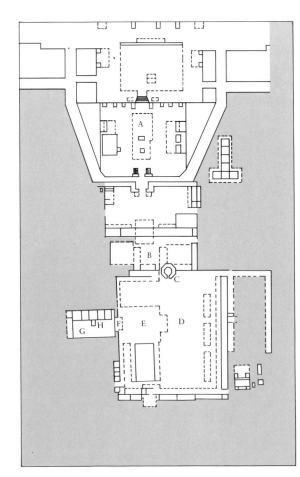

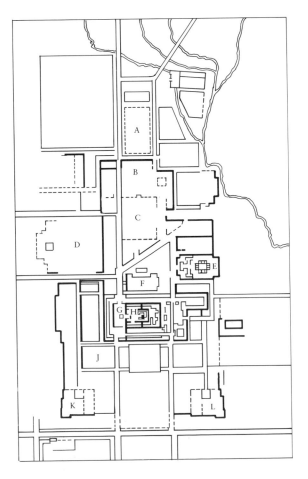

nally a private worshipping place for the Sultan's family. It formed part of the first palace, the *kraton* Pakungwati. The form of its rare central column with its four curved branches is echoed in one of the five *pendopos* in the *siti inggil*, the *Semar Tinandu* in its northeast corner. This *pendopo* has a pair of columns with three curved branches and represents the *kalimah sahadat*, or Moslem confession of faith, and is the place where the representatives of Islam sat during ceremonies.

The Islamic meaning of the *Semar Tinandu* fuses seamlessly with construction deriving directly from Majapahit techniques. The plinth is of soft red brick profiled like the walls of *candi* Brahu (FIG. 78), its refined surface possible because the Majapahit mortar of palm sugar sap and egg-white obviates the clumsy joints of modern mortars. The roof supports are the direct descendants of eighth-century prototypes, and the tiles are *sirap* shingles. The other four buildings in the walled compound, which is entered by Hindu-derived split gates reminiscent of the red brick gates found throughout Bali (FIG. 79),[10] illustrate four different ancient *pendopo* styles and also blend the Hindu-Javanese legacy with the Islamic. The smallest, the *Pandawa Lima* in the northwest corner of the *siti inggil*, has five columns that stand for the five tenets of adherence to Islam. Here sat the representative of the town government.

Directly to the south of the *Pandawa Lima* stands the *Tempat Sekaten*, a *pendopo* in square *joglo* form where the gamelan orchestra is played during religious festivals like Sekaten, or Mulud, the birthday of Mohammed. In the center of the compound stands another *joglo*, the *Palinggihan Sultan*, where the Sultan sat for religious ceremonies. To its north, overlooking the *alun-alun* in front

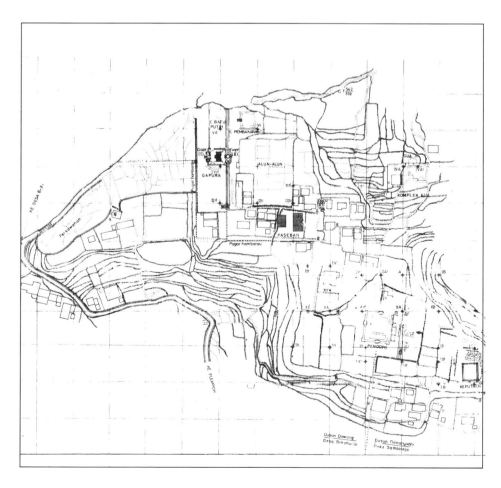

FIG. 81
Site plan, Ratu Boko, 9th century. Near Prambanan, Central Java. The plan shows early manifestations of features of Majapahit and later Mataram *kratons*: entrance portals, pools, *alun-alun*, *pringgitan* and *pendopos*.

FIG. 83
Pools, Ratu Boko, 9th century. Near Prambanan, Central Java. The pools offer early evidence of ritual bathing and pleasure gardens as part of palace complexes.

FIG. 84
Candi Tikus, 14th century, Trawulan, East Java. The profile relates to *Candi* Brahu (FIG. 78).
The pavilion set in a pool resembles bathing places for meditation and pleasure at Sunyaragi
(FIG. 86) and Taman Sari. (FIG. 85)

of the palace, is the rectangular *limasan pendopo* called the *Malang Semirang*, where the Sultan sat on a raised platform to receive subjects. Its twenty columns stand for various interpretations of Islamic principles, and with its raised platform, or *bale*, it demonstrates the direct inheritance that Cirebon, like Bali, received from Majapahit.

A second parallel between Ratu Boko and later Javanese courts is illustrated by a pair of buildings on raised plinths linked by staircases and surrounded by a moat and a wall. The larger of these has four rows of six columns, the smaller has two rows of six. Their spatial relationship is similar to the relationship in both Surakarta and Yogyakarta between the *Pendopo Agung*, the main *pendopo* for court ceremonies, and the *pringgitan*, a shallow hall in a similar form where dancing and *wayang kulit* performances sometimes take place.[11] This lies between and links the main *pendopo* and the *dalem* (inner sanctum) on the ceremonial axis,[12] which is central to the symbolism of the extant palaces in Surakarta and Yogyakarta and also in the Kasepuhan *kraton* in Cirebon. Archaeologists at the Ratu Boko site in fact refer to the columned platforms there as *pendopo* and *pringgitan*.

The main north-south axis of the eighteenth-century *kraton* in Surakarta leads the visitor from an *alun-alun*, the large square to the north of the palace, through a gateway into the first of the interior courts, the large *Pagelaran* containing several *pendopos* and other buildings. A privileged visitor might then proceed through another set of walls and gates to the *siti inggil* with its several *pendopos*, and possibly next to the main ceremonial court where the imposing main *pendopo* stands. The axis is not direct, but veers around baffle screens set behind gateways to prevent the entrance of evil spirits that cannot negotiate sharp turns, and turns to the right at the *Pendopo Agung* toward the *pringgitan* and the *dalem* (FIG. 80). The site plan of Ratu Boko (FIG. 81) shows a similar relationship between the main buildings, and from the reconstruction of the plan of the Majapahit capital at Trawulan (FIG. 82)[13] it is clear that the same directional principles determined the layout of its fourteenth-century *kraton*.[14]

A third link between Ratu Boko and later palaces, including Majapahit as well as present-day *kratons*, is the existence of clearly important pools that seem to have had both practical and ceremonial functions; these are sometimes set apart from the main palace buildings. Connected with the pools in some cases was a structure, either natural or artificial, representing a cave where meditation and recreation took place. The pools at Ratu Boko are numerous, from fifteen to twenty-five feet deep, rain-fed, and seem to follow natural formations. They appear to have been enclosed by walls and overlooked by buildings below the *pendopo-pringgitan* complex (FIG. 83). Another smaller pool is found to the north of the central group of principal structures and is considered by archaeologists to be part of a cave complex that could conceivably be a place of meditation and purification. The importance of caves as retreats for holy hermits and those seeking their spiritual guidance is clear in the *wayang* drama and exists today.

The pool at Majapahit, clearly manmade since it is strictly rectangular, was built on a much larger scale, 1200 feet long by 575 feet wide, and was enclosed by massive walls made of characteristic Majapahit red brick.[15] Called *Kolam Segaram* (sea pool), it was nearly ten feet deep, had a water gate leading to the river and a small inner pool for ingenious water control. It is one of three pools so far discovered of eight known to have existed in the Majapahit *kraton*. Another, known as *candi* Tikus (FIG. 84), lies a few miles away and seems more clearly to have been connected with ritual bathing. A small pavilion representing Mount Penanggungan (the East Javanese equivalent of Mount Meru, the center of the Indic cosmos) is set in the middle of a brick-walled pool that represents the sea. A gate known as *candi* Bajangratu leads to the pool.

The pools at Ratu Boko and Majapahit seem to be direct ancestors of many such complexes connected with later palaces. A Javanese poem of 1355 called *Sudamala* mentions a palace with a pavilion in a lake, while the *Babad Tanah Jawi* recounts that *Panembahan* Seda-ing-Krapyak (1601–13) of Mataram had a garden called Dana Raja that also had a lake. A Dutch prisoner in Sultan Agung's time reported that the river Opak had been dammed to form an artificial lake in front of the Mataram palace.

Other Dutch reporters include the eighteenth-century writer Stavorinus, who described the waterworks for the garden of Sultan Ageng Tirtayasa's Surosowan palace, near Banten, showing that water symbolism was important in West Java as well as in Central and East Java. Over a century earlier, De Houtman (commander of the Netherlands fleet that reached Banten in 1596) mentioned the artificial lake Tasik Ardi with a manmade island and two-storied pavilion at its center a few miles from the Banten kingdom's palace, a seventeenth-century replacement of the earliest palace which was destroyed by fire. This palace in turn was destroyed by the Dutch early in the nineteenth century.

Remains of terra-cotta pipes and holding ponds are visible in the ruins of this palace in Banten today, and the reconstructed pump-house shows how extensive the palace waterworks were. Originally under the control of the Hindu Sunda kingdom Pajajaran, Banten was conquered around 1525 by Fadillah Khan (Falatehan), born in Pasai, Sumatra, but coming from Demak. He became a son-in-law of the *wali* (saint) Sunan Gunung Jati, whose son Maulana Hasanuddin became the first crowned sultan in 1552.[16] Thriving on the pepper trade and as an important entrepôt in Sunda Strait commerce (especially after the Portuguese capture of Melaka in 1511 made the Melaka Straits less attractive to international

FIG. 85
Taman Sari, 18th century. (restored 20th century) Yogyakarta *kraton*, Central Java. This water palace with paired bathing pools is linked by underwater tunnel to a submerged meditation grotto.

shipping), Banten eventually conquered Pajajaran and controlled Lampung in South Sumatra. Until the late nineteenth century it maintained a considerable independence from the Dutch, whose chief center moved from Banten itself to the port of Sunda Kelapa, later named Batavia and now Jakarta.

Its role as a great international port (it was probably the largest city in Indonesia until the nineteenth century) and its location near the center of colonial trade and politics exposed Banten to European influences to a greater extent than was the case in more isolated Central Java courts. This is reflected in the ruins of the large palace for which a renegade Dutchman, Hendrik Lucasz Cardeel, was a builder and consultant. Links with the older Javanese *kraton* types are therefore more apparent in the parts of the palace that predate the seventeenth century, particularly the Tasik Ardi watergarden with its lake and mountain symbolism.

One of the best-known surviving palace pool-gardens in Java is the Taman Sari (pleasure garden) (FIG. 85), usually referred to as the Water Palace, at the Yogyakarta *kraton*.[17] Originally built by Sultan Hamengkubuwono I in 1758, in 1791 it was described by a Dutch major as having a colonnaded pavilion in the middle of an artificial lake and underwater corridors leading from women's bathing pools to a partly underwater mosque. Today water no longer links the garden's elements, and a restoration of the late 1960s did little to suggest its original purpose of meditation and pleasure.

Another extant palace complex combining water and cave elements is the elaborate *taman sari* Sunyaragi garden (FIG. 86)[18] a few miles beyond the Kasepuhan *kraton* in Cirebon to which it belongs.[19] Laid out in 1741, it was restored in the nineteenth century and is undergoing further restoration. It is a microcosm comprising three artificial mountains and numerous grottoes and caves linked by

Opposite above:
FIG. 86
Tamansari Sunyaragi, 18th century (restored 20th century). *Kraton* Kasepuhan, Cirebon, West Java. Artificial hills laced with connecting meditation grottoes flank a bathing pool with a central pavilion.

Opposite below:
FIG. 87/NO. 37
Carved panel, 16th century. Cirebon, West Java. Wood, 43.7 × 109 cm.

FIG. 88
Gunungan, 17th century. *Taman* Ghairah, Aceh, North Sumatra. The mountain structure's linked caves lead to the Sultan's meditation chamber. Lotus forms reveal earlier Indic influence on the Islamic palace.

hidden passages. The palace was once surrounded by water, and access was by boat across a large artificial pond. Before the whole complex lay an enormous artificial "sea" that the Sultan could contemplate when sitting in the highest pavilion.

The decoration encrusting the elaborate structure resembles the Chinese-derived *megamendung* and *wadasan* (clouds and rocks) pattern that is a pervasive motif in Cirebon and reflects the importance of Chinese influences in a coastal city where Chinese traders were active. Its incorporation into royal motifs is another striking example of the ability of Indonesian civilization to absorb foreign elements and fuse them with the original culture. The *megamendung* and *wadasan* can be seen in the distinctive Cirebon batiks, in carving (FIG. 87/NO. 37) in the architecture of the Kasepuhan *kraton* Jinem gate and in the rock creations in the garden, complete with small lake with central manmade island, behind the main *kraton*. At Sunyaragi the motif reinforces the mountain and water elements of what is clearly a microcosm created for the enactment of spiritual purification and physical entertainments. The garden features another primordial symbol, the tree. A gnarled *kapilaya* tree is associated with a *garuda* (giant mythical bird) sculpture, and a *sangkala* (cryptogram) indicates the date 1703; whether this applies to the tree's age or another event is not certain, but it is clearly an integral part of the grotto-palace complex.

The pervasiveness of the cosmology underlying the architecture of the palaces of Java—the incorporation of the mountain theme, the persistence of axis definition and its relationship to the importance of cardinal direction, and the recurrence of the motif of the sea-mountain-cave microcosm in a place of meditation—illustrates how radically the culture of the courts was bound to the main body of Indonesian culture. The continuity of structural principles between vernacular and monumental demonstrates this further. The power of such integrating forces can be judged from the remarkable fact that through sixteen hundred years they have survived many successive dynasties, the basic changes of belief entailed in the arrival of Buddhism, the Saivite form of Hinduism and Islam, continuous trade contacts with such dominant cultures as the Chinese and the European and the major intrusion of three and a half centuries of Dutch colonialism.

The wide distribution of these structural characteristics reinforces the theory that the determining source of Indonesian court culture lies in the mainstream of indigenous vernacular culture. Not only are they found throughout Java, but also in other islands. In Bali, for example, the importance of direction is paramount. The axis is calculated in reference to the mountain—the sacred Gunung Agung—and the sea. *Kaja*, toward the mountain, determines the placement of the ancestral shrine within the compound and is associated with the head, higher regions and the right side. *Kelod*, toward the sea, is the direction associated with the menial activities in a household, with the back and the lower parts of the body. The axis is therefore a basic determinant in Balinese architecture as it is in Javanese.

The *bale* Bengong in the *puri* (palace) at Gianyar, South Bali, a kingdom established in the nearby village of Beng in 1614 by a son of the ruling dynasty of Gelgel, is a small building raised high on a stone plinth. Built in 1710 when the court moved to its present site, it is clearly the equivalent of the *siti inggil*. Here the Raja sat to contemplate and to observe his subjects as they came to seek audience. Balinese palace compounds, like household compounds, devote a substantial space to temples, which are dedicated to deities and ancestors. The integration of daily life and religion in Bali is total. The differences between village and courtly art are narrower than elsewhere, perhaps because the inspiration for art—whether music or dance, the preparation of offerings, carving, painting or metalsmithing—is service to the gods, which subsumes other values and calls equally on all to contribute. Ideally, the ruler's glory exists to the extent that he manifests divine magnificence in his role as chief extoller and intermediary of the gods.

Just as the microcosmic theme of the high place and the relativizing determinant of the axis are found in Bali as in Java, so is the invocation of water and its purifying properties. The elaborate cremation ceremonies for which Bali is renowned are followed in due course by purification rituals, where an effigy of the dead is carried in solemn procession from the land to the seashore. The effigy is then burned and its ashes carried out to sea, thus completing the cycle of earth-fire-water to liberate the spirit and enable it to achieve a higher status in the cycle of life. Other evidence of reverence for the power of water is shown when the foundation stone of the sacred spring Tirta Mpul near Tampak Siring from the year 962 is bathed yearly under the full moon.[20] The ability of water to transmogrify a physical setting is invoked by the lake setting of the judgment *bale* Kerta Gosa at Klungkung; as in the other palace garden water pavilions, the material is sublimated to another dimension by isolation in another element, another world.

The Balinese dynasty of Karangasem dominated the island of Lombok in the nineteenth century, ruling as Hindus over the Moslem Sasak inhabitants until the Dutch conquest of 1894. The main *puri* was destroyed at that time, when the first of the *puputans* occurred. As in the *puputans* that were to take place in Bali later, all the members of the courts hurled themselves unarmed into advancing Dutch lines in what amounted to a ritual group sacrifice. What remains of the *puri* is two gardens with lakes in which stand *bales*: Taman Mayura, where the raja could meet with his people, and Taman Narmada, built by Anak Agung Gde Ngurah Karangasem (1870–94) to imitate the sacred mountain Rinjani. The Raja was too old to climb the mountain itself for sacred ceremonies, so he created a

FIG. 89
Balla Lampoa, 20th century. Gowa-Makassar, South Sulawesi. The five *tipe-tipe* (gable boards) of this vernacular-derived palace modeled on an older building indicate royal rank.

FIG. 90
Throne hall, 19th century. *Istana* Kadriah, Pontianak, West Kalimantan. Some Sumatran and
Kalimantan thrones are placed in structures like *pelaminans* (ritual marriage beds).

F<small>IG</small>. 91
Salakoa crown, 15th century(?). Gowa-Makassar, South Sulawesi. Gold, diamonds, approx.
20 × 30 cm. The stupa form of Salakoa resembles that of the Banten crown and may derive from
Buddhist headdresses with stylized Buddha curls.

symbolic mountain across the small valley, with its stream arising on Mount Rinjani, below the *bale* Kencana, where he retreated for relaxation and contemplation.

VERNACULAR PERSISTENCE AND THE ISLAMIC IMAGE

If in Bali and Lombok the symbolic features of palaces seem even closer to religious and elemental forces than in Java, in Aceh they are imbued with the principles of Islam. Whereas in Sumatra the Islamic palaces are usually stylistically further from indigenous architecture than any others in Indonesia, the strange building in Banda Aceh known as the Gunungan (FIG. 88) harks back to pre-Islamic themes, as the palace it was connected to also seems to have done.

Under Iskandar Muda (1607–36), Aceh was the greatest power in Sumatra, having inherited much of the international trading community displaced by the Portuguese dominance of Melaka a century earlier. The ships of Iskandar Muda's navy were capable of carrying seven hundred men, and his army had powerful horse, elephant, artillery and infantry brigades.[21] Islam was a more potent force in Sumatran polities than in Javanese, where pre-Islamic forces from earlier dynasties survived more successfully, and by the time of Iskandar Muda's successor, Iskandar Thani Alauddin Mughayat Syah (1636–41), Aceh was an important center of Islamic culture. Many chronicles survive from that time, including the *Bustan as-Salatin* (the Garden of Kings) by the Gujerati Nuruddin ar-Raniri. In one of its seven volumes this book describes the history of the kings of Aceh and of its court.

The palace was known as Dar ad-Dunya (abode of this world), a name implying a counterpart Dar al-Akhirah (heaven).[22] Set on the junction of two rivers, it was laid out on a north-south axis like Javanese *kratons*, with three successive courts and a *medan* (square) to the north that corresponded to the *alun-alun* in Java. Its garden, Taman Ghairah, was laid out by Iskandar Thani, and the *Bustan as-Salatin* indicates that the mountain-shaped structure at its center, the Gunungan, had connections with the *taman sari*, as microcosm of Indra's heaven, and the world-mountain Mahameru. Like the manmade mountains honeycombed with grottoes at Sunyaragi, the Gunungan is composed of corridors that climb the structure, weaving in and out of small caves and opening onto small ledges. The meditation of the king in the chamber at the top led to an Islamic version of insight into the divine through the dissolution of the self.[23] In a further parallel with microcosms of mountain, cave and water as places of meditation and enlightenment in other royal gardens of Indonesia, there is a diverted stream in the Taman Ghairah drawn from the river *Krueng* Daroy, or Dar ul-'isyq, which means river of love, and (as at Taman Sari in Yogyakarta) a mosque, which is called Isyqi Musyahadah, again invoking love in connection with a mystic insight into the divine.[24]

The palaces described so far have blended the pervasive *pendopo* form with Indic ideas of hierarchy and have expressed the autochthonous ordering of the universe fused with Hindu-Buddhist cosmogony and Islamic ideas of perfection. Often built partly in stone or brick, they have sometimes endured through several centuries. In other areas in Indonesia, palace types have remained closer to indigenous models and relied on a vertical ordering within one building to invoke the conception of a trinity of underworld, human world and the world above. They were seldom translated into more permanent materials, so although they may embody ancient principles, they are almost certainly recent copies of old structures.

One of the most striking of Indonesian building types is the Minangkabau house with its carved walls and upswept ridge-poles, the number of annex subsid-

Opposite above:
FIG. 92
Dalam Loka, 1885. Sumbawa Besar, West Sumbawa. The stilts, *tipe-tipe* (gable boards) and covered stairway of this vernacular-derived timber palace show Bugis influence (compare FIG. 89).

Opposite below:
FIG. 93
Palace, 19th century. Ternate, Maluku. The raised construction and double roof of the Sultan's palace have vernacular links while the bowed porch shows European influence.

iary ridges indicating the importance of the owner (FIG. 72). A tripartite division of the house designates the upper floors for the ruler and his women and the *pusaka* (heirlooms), the middle section for public events and the lower area for menial activities. Unfortunately, all the old palace buildings have disappeared, an inevitable result of the abolition of central leadership in the nineteenth century, which led to the disappearance of any impetus to conserve and renew vulnerable materials. The recent attempt to re-create the palace of the Raja Alam at Pagarruyung from old plans has ignored scale restraints and produced a structure so grandiose that the elegant proportions and flowing rhythms of buildings like the *balai undangan* (law pavilion) in Tabek (FIG. 62) have been lost. A more successful re-creation is the 1935 building for the Minangkabau Museum in Bukittinggi.

Some of the palaces of Sulawesi and Nusa Tenggara have fared better. Although the buildings of the sultanates of Luwu and Bone have been destroyed or dismantled, some carved components of the latter have been incorporated into the *Kabupaten* (regional government) office in Watampone. The Balla Lompoa palace of the Gowa-Makassar kingdom (FIG. 89) was built in 1936 by the thirty-third Sultan according to traditional form and has been maintained as a museum. Like Bugis vernacular houses (FIG. 70), the palace is raised on columns and made of wood. The region below the floor is the Underworld, the house itself represents the middle world of human beings, and the upper level under the roof is the Upperworld.

The palace has two sections, the roof-ridges parallel at right angles to the front facade and one, higher, set slightly back from the other. The rear, higher roof has five *tipe-tipe* (overlapping horizontal gable boards that signify status and are almost always in odd numbers) and the front one has three; the gable beams cross, a persistent Bugis characteristic. Access is by a roofed staircase to the front building. Inside, a large reception room is hung with banners and awnings in symbolic colors: red is uppermost, standing for heaven, gold symbolizing earth lies in the middle, and below is white, signifying the path that must be followed from earth to heaven. White for clothing is reserved for the ruler, a difference from most regions of Indonesia where the royal color is yellow.

Beyond the reception room, the equivalent of the main *pendopo* in Javanese palaces, lies a smaller room with a *lamming*. This curtained alcove with bed heaped with cushions is a ritual marriage bed like Java's *kobongan*. Variants of it are found throughout Indonesia—in Sumatra it is known as a *pelaminan*—and typically it is lined and framed with richly embroidered hangings, piled with cushions of silk and satin which are sometimes bejewelled or have appliqué gold plaques, and flanked with *pusaka* weapons and ceremonial umbrellas. In some courts, like the Kalimantan palaces in Mempawa, Sambas and Tenggarong, and the *Istana* (palace) Kadriah in Pontianak, and in the *Istana* Maimun of the Deli Sultanate in Medan, the *pelaminan* and throne platform have been combined (FIG. 90). In the *lamming* room in the Balla Lompoa palace are kept the *pusaka* of the Gowa kingdom, the crown (FIG. 91), *naga* bracelets, sacred weapons and chains of office of the Sultans.

Considering the widely distributed power and intermarriage patterns of Bugis-Makassarese nobility as revealed in the genealogical trees of royal houses throughout Indonesia, it is not surprising that Bugis architecture influenced that of many other regions. In Sumbawa the palaces of both Sumbawa Besar and Bima are patterned closely after the type of Gowa's Balla Lompoa in Sungguminasa outside Ujung Pandang (Makassar). In Bima the palace was built in 1927 to replace a 1911 building. Three *tipe-tipe*, crossing gable-ridges, roof-structure and surrounding galleries enclosed by carved wooden screens are all in the Bugis style, but the staircase has been modified into a covered veranda and the traditional stilts have not been used. The palace at Sumbawa Besar (FIG. 92) is similar to the one in

Bima, having been copied on a smaller scale by the last Sultan, Mohammad Kaharuddin (1938–65) as a gesture to his senior wife (*Permaisuri*), who was the daughter of the Sultan of Bima.

Not far from the new palace in Sumbawa Besar is the old one, the Dalam Loka of 1885. This is much closer to the structure of the Balla Lompoa, which it predates by fifty years, having two main buildings and an entrance section approached by a sloping covered ramp. There are unusually only two *tipe-tipe* on the gables. The roof ridges are decorated by carved snakes and their ends by birds. The palace is supported by ninety-nine pillars, signifying the ninety-nine names of God. Some of these penetrate the floor of the lower level, serving as supports for lamps, and some are painted or carved. Many of the beams and the threshold boards are carved also, in a variety of styles; craftsmen from all the provinces of West Sumbawa were invited to contribute to the building in whatever form they thought appropriate. Floorboards are wide and the sense of spaciousness is strong. The upper level of the palace was reserved for the princesses, who were not allowed to be viewed by outsiders; even the steep staircase they used to reach the top floor was screened from unauthorized eyes.

This palace, constructed entirely of wood, is grander than any others of the type, but like them retains a feeling of simplicity and human scale. Its links with the vernacular are clear, and the materials and forms, which are unchanged from village models except in size, show that the ruler was at one with his people. The same holds true for palaces in West Kalimantan and Maluku (FIG. 93), where wide verandas, wooden floors, wood-screened walls and nongrandiose proportions make them seem like comfortable, well-to-do family houses rather than grand palaces where the ruler was isolated from his subjects. In many places, such as

FIG. 96
Istana **Siak Sri Indrapura**, 1889. Riau Lingga, East Sumatra. Domes and Sassanian arches resembling the adapted Mughal forms of British colonial Malaya show Islamic inspiration for this palace.

Sambas, the palace mosque is considerably more distinguished architecturally than the palace.

Architecture may show close ties between the ruler and the ruled in West Kalimantan, South Sulawesi and Nusa Tenggara, but the same cannot be said about the Malay-culture states of Sumatra. Archival photographs in Netherlands collections show spectacular buildings in Langkat, Asahan, Medan and Siak that are closer to fantasy conceptions of what a palace should be than perhaps any others in Indonesia. While many of these structures are no longer standing, two notable examples remain: the *Istana* Maimun of the Deli Sultanate in Medan, North Sumatra (FIG. 94) and the *Istana* Siak Sri Indrapura in Riau.

The *Istana* Maimun, with its domed roofs and colonnaded arcades in Moorish style, has clearly looked to Mughal India (or perhaps European colonial conceptions of Mughal architecture) for inspiration for an Islamic palace. The arches and columns have no visual connections with the *pendopo* or any other indigenous form. Furthermore, the mass of the building relates to the encompassing totality of closed European models, and not to the series of free-standing structures in walled courts strung along an axis and separated by gates, each building designated to a specific function, characteristic of palace architecture in Java and Bali.

After climbing the double-tiered, roofed marble steps—yellow ceremonial umbrellas making an arch for the honored guest—it can be seen that the differences hold true for the interior as well. Walls richly patterned in mosaics and extravagantly carved and painted coffered ceilings make the grand throne room a complete world of Islamic design (FIG. 95). Geometric and curvilinear motifs, ogival Sassanian archways, gleaming marble floors and sumptuous silk draperies

FIG. 97
Istana **Kutei**, 1935: Tenggarong, East Kalimantan. Some rulers of this period embraced modernism and adopted European styles like the Art Deco of this palace.

complete the contrast with the open *pendopo*, where the interpenetration of internal and external space, the indefinable nature of the space soaring above into the receding roof structures and the ambiguity of light and shadow combine to give the impression of infinity.

The palace at Siak Sri Indrapura (FIG. 96), designed in 1889 with the help of an Italian architect, also expresses the Islamic themes so important in the Malay states of Sumatra. A glance at the map shows their closeness to the Malay Peninsula. Comparison with Malaysian buildings indicates the stylistic kinship between Sumatra and the Malay world, where monumental architecture also frequently adopted Mughal Indian models. In this case an eclectic freewheeling use of pointed domes, orientalist arcades and pointed arches more Gothic than Sassanian, with corner turrets defining the symmetrically arranged masses, creates an ensemble that says "palace" from every perspective. As at Medan, the interior is lavish in the public reception rooms. Upstairs the spaces are simpler, the matted wooden floors and plain walls suggesting that the private life of the Sultan was not as removed from Sumatran style as his ceremonial setting indicated.

THE INFLUENCE OF COLONIALISM

One notable aspect of the Siak palace introduces the final significant category of Indonesian royal architectural features: the buildings influenced by the colonial presence during the three hundred fifty years of Dutch tenure. Amid the splendor of carved arches and fretwork screens in Siak, it is somewhat startling to see an immense chandelier and an entire setting of dining-room furniture all made of twisted Venetian glass. By the nineteenth century, when Dutch hegemony in most regions had negated the military preoccupations of Indonesian rulers and left them free to cultivate the ceremonial and cultural aspects of their kingdoms, the images of power and prestige were increasingly associated with European style. Gilt chairs and tables, even thrones (indigenous ceremonial seats were not in chair form), velvet draperies, enormous gilded mirrors, crystal chandeliers and European-style silver and china all became normal accessories in palace life.

Ironically, the ruler who took this trend furthest was the last Sultan of Kutei, Aji Muhammad Parakesit, Sultan XIX, whose court in Tenggarong in East Kalimantan was near the site of the earliest recorded king in Indonesia, Mulavarman of the early fifth century. According to the records, the palace during the early twentieth century had been in Bugis style (not surprising in view of the strong Bugis strain in the Kutei genealogy), but was destroyed by fire. In an enthusiastic adoption of the progressive, in 1935 the Sultan constructed a palace in complete Art Deco style (FIG. 97). This commitment to full Western modernism epitomizes the conviction (held by many in Indonesia at the time and common in many developing countries) that only by eliminating all traces of difference between traditional regional culture and international modern civilization could developing countries participate fully in the world of the future. The costs in terms of the destruction of social integrity were not fully understood; they are still not appreciated today in many instances. The palace at Tenggarong, excellent building though it is in terms of international style, makes a convincing symbol of the anomaly of architecture without historical, cultural or climatic relevance as the setting for the oldest court in the archipelago.

Even in courts where there was no stimulus to replace damaged buildings, progressive rulers or princes seeking the cachet of *le dernier cri* employed Dutch or Dutch-trained architects to alter or add to their residential areas. In the old settings of the courts of Java certain European elements besides furnishings were introduced. Etched glass enclosed a dining area in the *kraton* in Yogyakarta; formal Victorian statuary decorated the buildings in Surakarta. Less visible but more basic alterations included plumbing improvements and electrification.

One of the happiest of such associations of traditional and modern, local and international, was that of Mangkunagoro VII and the Dutch architect Thomas Karsten, which began in 1917 and continued until 1942. The Mangkunagoro was an outstanding scholar and conservator of Indonesian culture. His interests were shared by Karsten, who throughout his life stressed the need to incorporate such culture into any social development. When the prince commissioned him to design an addition to the Mangkunagaran—a small *pendopo* for informal receptions, a bedroom, dressing room and bathroom for the prince's new wife, and the later addition of a dining room—Karsten believed that the new work should be homogeneous with the existing traditional architecture of the palace.[25]

Karsten's knowledge and understanding of indigenous architecture was deepened by concurrent restorations he was asked to make to the 1810 *Pendopo Agung* (FIG. 98), the *pringgitan* and the areas surrounding the *Dalem Agung*. He designed a *pendopo* (FIG. 99) and surrounding rooms where traditional roof structure and interplay of defined and open-ended spaces blended charmingly with some unobtrusive innovations. These included an octagonal plan, some experiments with terrazzo tile inlays on the floors, stained glass using Indonesian motifs in dining-room windows and bathroom skylight, and carved paneling and door details blending traditional techniques and subtle contemporary colors. The resulting suite has freshness and human scale without losing the spatial qualities of traditional Javanese architecture with its use of organic materials, its feeling of flow and its harmonious balance of vertical élan and horizontal calm.

Such sympathetic integration of the heritage of the past with the excitement and challenge of the new in the *Pracimusono*, as Karsten's pavilion was called, sums up the best of Indonesian palace architectural traditions. The ability to adopt and modify successive cultural elements, to absorb them into the autochthonous mainstream, in architecture as in other fields of art, was the reason that the courts continued to express the intrinsic nature of Indonesian culture.

IV. POMP AND CIRCUMSTANCE

The Court as Center of Ritual and Patronage

*[A]s gravel to cover the yard
[semiprecious] stones were used and
when they were raked by the feet of
the many passing serving-maidens they
shone and glittered like so many
shooting stars.[1]*

THE ROLE OF THE COURTS in the continuity of Indonesian culture is most visible in the arts, both plastic and performing. Sometimes this role was direct, when the ruler supported a dance troupe, for example, or musicians in the gamelan orchestra. Sometimes it was less obvious, as when ceremonies stimulated the making of regalia or cloth (FIG. 100/NO. 79) or when special performances required new instruments. In all these activities it was axiomatic that the production of material culture was secondary to the fulfillment of an ideal, the satisfying of a tradition.

The need for the ruler to impress his subjects with his might and magnificence, as outward signs of his royal capabilities and the prosperous state of his realm, led to what has been called the Cult of Glory.[2] Besides demonstrating the spiritual and moral aspects of the prince's power, the cultivation of his physical surroundings became an important part of the activities of the court. This was particularly so after the hegemony of the Netherlands government negated any true exercise of military power or political maneuvering by the courts. Although the Dutch made little effort to control any part of Bali except the north until the turn of the twentieth century, and despite prolonged and passionate resistance in Aceh until about the same time, most of the key points of the archipelago were under Dutch control by the early nineteenth century (even by the eighteenth century in Java). However, complete control of the government and the interior was restricted to Java, Minangkabau, Minahasa in North Sulawesi and Maluku. In these circumstances, stimulating the visible glory and the increasing refinement of the courts was vital to the maintenance of princely superiority. It has been suggested that the use of three different languages in Javanese to address superiors, equals or inferiors, came into existence only in the seventeenth century and was intensified as rulers sought to increase the social distance between their subjects

Ibu Sukeni, *wayang topeng* performance,
Kraton Kasepuhan, 1989. Cirebon, West Java.

Previous page:
FIG. 98
Pendopo Agung, Istana **Mangkunagaran**, 1810. Surakarta, Central Java. This *pendopo* with ceiling painted in cosmic symbols is among the largest and most majestic in Java.

and themselves.³ While this may account for a stricter codification of the practice, Tomé Pires observed in 1515 that there were two languages in Java according to rank and that class distinctions were firmly maintained.⁴

To understand the role of the courts in fostering and refining culture, it is logical to consider their ceremonies and the objects associated with them in five categories: activities connected with the ruler as host; music, dance and drama performance; literature and painting; ceremony deliberately emphasizing kingship; and rituals connected with the life cycle.

THE PRINCE AS HOST
Social receptions in the courts were based on the traditional offering and receiving of hospitality, where a relative balance of honor conferred and honor received has always been carefully maintained.⁵ By the nineteenth century, particularly in Java, these receptions demonstrated ever more subtle distinctions of rank through strictly regulated behavior and highly specific accoutrements. Dress was prominent among these indicators; batik patterns in Central Java, for example, became indicators of status. Some motifs, such as the intersecting circle *kawung*, which could also appear in other media such as jewelry (FIGS. 101, 102/NO. 55), were restricted to the sultan and his immediate family. Others in this category included the *jelamprang*, the mandala-like motif derived from Indian patola design that is related to the *kawung*; the *garuda* wings and tail *sawat* pattern; and some of the diagonal *parang rusak* (broken sword) designs. In Malay culture areas in Sumatra, Kalimantan and Sulawesi some colors, particularly yellow and white, were available only to princely families. Some styles of wrapping and wearing cloths like the *dodot* of Central Java were also exclusively royal (FIG. 103/NO. 74). Certain weav-

FIG. 99
Pendopo **Pracimusono**, *Istana* **Mangkunagaran**, 1917–20. Surakarta, Central Java. Thomas Karsten, architect. This *pendopo* for receiving private guests integrates traditional form with contemporary features.

ing techniques, like gold and silver *songkets* (supplementary weft brocaded silks), became identified with princes, as in Bali (FIG. 104/NO. 76), Deli (FIG. 105/NO. 83), Palembang (FIG. 106/NO. 85) and Sumbawa (FIG. 12/NO. 78), though probably more as a result of costliness than of proscriptive design. Some imported textiles like the double-*ikat* silk *patola* (FIG. 107/NO. 88) from Gujerat became necessary parts of royal costumes and of the hangings in the ceremonial *kobongan*, or ritual marriage bed. A prince of Maluku, rich from the clove trade, is said to have given another ruler a wedding present of five hundred of these *patola*, each equal in value to half a ton of cloves.[6]

In all these examples, with the exception of the *patola*, indigenous traditions of weaving and dyeing were the bases for these ceremonial cloths; they acquired their courtly status from a refinement of local craft techniques. Both cotton and silk were important items of export from Indonesia by the sixteenth century, cotton being produced in East Java, Bali, Sumbawa and Sulawesi and silk in Pasai in Sumatra. The seventeenth-century *Hikayat Raja-Raja Pasai* attributes to the first ruler the ability to convert worms to gold and silver, a possible reference to silkworms and the production of silk, which Albuquerque reported in 1511.[7]

Textiles rank among the greatest creations of Indonesia. Their variety of weaving techniques, resist dyeing methods[8] and motifs offer a profusion and beauty unsurpassed anywhere. The significance of weaving, an art representing the female portion in Indonesian clan symbols, is related to the crossing of the threads of the warp by the weft to make the fabric of the cosmos. The colors are also symbolic, the brown of earth and the blue of heaven being placed on the white of the air. These metaphysical principles were expanded by symbolic entities such as plants, animals, pavilions and mountains. The female act of weaving received its

FIG. 100/NO. 79
Kain songket, 19th century. Bima, East Sumbawa. Silk, gold thread, 112.8 × 103 cm.

FIGS. 101, 102/NO. 55a, b
Subang (**earplugs**), 14th–15th century. East
Java. Gold, emeralds, garnets(?), 4.34 × 1.04 cm.

FRONT

BACK

Opposite:
FIG. 103/NO. 74
Dodot pinarada mas (**royal ceremonial skirt
cloth**), 1910. Yogyakarta, Central Java. Cotton,
resist-dyed by batik wax process in natural
dyes, silk, gold leaf, fish protein glue,
210 × 379 cm.

143

Opposite:
FIG. 104/NO. 76
Kain songket, late 19th century. Klungkung(?),
Bali. Silk, cotton, gold thread, chemical dyes,
94 × 169 cm.

male complement in the process of dyeing, usually done by men in secret rituals where outsiders were forbidden.

The secret rites accompanying warp and weft tying and dyeing of the double-*ikat geringsing* (FIG. 108/NO. 75)[9] of Tenganan in Bali lend a special mystery to these sacred cloths, yet mystery is also an element in the subtle tones and iconic tribe and family motifs of weavings from Savu and Roti (NO. 87). The gold embroidery on a *geringsing* suggests that it was a princely piece, as do the rich and multitudinous motifs of a Timor queen's cloth (FIG. 109/NO. 86). The *kain tapis* skirt cloths from Lampung (FIG. 110/NO. 80; NO. 81), with their wealth of symbols and intricate *ikat* and embroidery, and the supplementary weft *ikat* cloth from Palembang (FIG. 111/NO. 84) are examples of the consistently high level of textile production even when not intended for royal use.[10]

By the nineteenth century an injection of Western elements, such as formal high-collared jackets of velvet with gold braiding, had modified the purely indigenous court dress, but accessories often retained their original form. The beaded bag, which is one of the royal appurtenances of the Raja of Baun, in Timor, draws on vernacular beading skills but adds the enrichment of gold beads (FIG. 112/NO. 50). A belt buckle for ceremonial dress in the Mangkunagaran court in Surakarta is studded with rubies and diamonds and inlaid with gold, but its basic material is iron (FIG. 113/NO. 52). A ceremonial belt (FIG. 114/NO. 53) from a princely Surakarta owner was made on a backstrap loom of human hair with no adornment beyond a restrained iron and gold buckle (*timang*) and sliding keeper (*lerep*). A fan for covering food or presenting a napkin in ceremonial serving of the sultan in Sumbawa Besar (NO. 49) is fashioned in gold though its form still resembles the palm-leaf, woven rattan or fragrant root-fiber examples made for the local market.

Jewelry in Indonesia is made of a broad range of materials and expresses many regional characteristics. It has been fashioned for almost all parts of the body—head, ears, neck, arms, torso, legs and feet—and evidence of this can be seen from as early as the ninth century, when elaborate jewelry was carved on the figures in the reliefs of the temples of Central Java (FIG. 31/NO. 6; FIG. 32). Some jewelry was involved in marriage exchange (FIG. 34/NO. 3), some in the adornment of performing artists, and some was important in ritual and ceremony.

Although the exquisite workmanship and precious materials of court jewelry put it in a class by itself, it often embodies the symbols that represent the myths of origin or links to religious power discussed in chapter 1. Thus it is not mere adornment, but emphasizes the links between ruler and race, ruler and supernatural forces. Some of the images used include the *naga* in bracelets from Gowa in Sulawesi (FIG. 43), a dragon in an ear pendant from East Java (FIG. 115/NO. 57), a crocodile-like snake in a chest ornament from Kalimantan (NO. 62), a *kala* (mythical monster) head from an East Javanese ear pendant (FIG. 116/NO. 56), a *gunungan* pendant from Bali (FIG. 117/NO. 63) and a double lotus on a ninth-century ring from Central Java (FIG. 118/NO. 60).

Probably no single object so embodies the mythological, spiritual, artistic and technical ideals of Indonesian society as does the *kris*, which, though important in other parts of Southeast Asia like Malaysia, is developed to a unique degree in the archipelago. A Javanese proverb lists five things essential to man's happiness: *wisma* (house), *wanita* (woman), *kukila* (singing bird), *turongga* (horse) and *curiga* (*kris*). No other object is more enshrined in mythology, stimulates more interest, or is held in such esteem and awe. The smithing perfection of the blades (FIG. 119; NO. 68) of this quintessential Indonesian weapon is enhanced in ceremonial *krises* (those worn for formal ceremonies as distinct from military occasions) by an elegance and richness in design of hilt (FIG. 120/NO. 72) and sheath (FIG. 52/NO. 67) that raise them to the levels of the world's greatest metalwork.

FIG. 105/NO. 83
Kain songket, 19th century. Batu Bara, North
Sumatra. Silk, gold thread, approx.
117 × 164 cm.

FIG. 106/NO. 85
Kain songket, late 19th or early 20th century.
Palembang, South Sumatra. Silk, gold thread,
silk thread, 212 × 79 cm.

Fig. 109/No. 86
Tais (**woman's ceremonial skirt**), 20th century.
Belu, West Timor. Cotton woven with
supplementary weft and complementary warp,
gold thread, natural dyes, 152 × 63 cm.

Opposite:
Fig. 107/No. 88
Patolu, 19th century. Gujerat, India. Silk woven
in double *ikat* technique, gold leaf, fish protein
glue, 378 × 109 cm.

Fig. 108/No. 75
Geringsing wayang kebo, 20th century(?).
Tenganan Pageringsingan, Bali. Handspun
cotton woven in double *ikat* technique, natural
dyes, gold thread embroidery, 213 × 55.4 cm.

The earliest definite date for the *kris* is the fourteenth century, as it is visible on the bas-reliefs of *candi* Panataran, but a depiction on such a state temple implies an established social role and suggests an older date for its evolution. Tomé Pires commented in 1515 that "every man in Java, rich or poor, must have a *kris* in his house, and a lance and a shield, and no man between the ages of twelve and eighty may go out of doors without a *kris* in his belt." Later he observed that the Bugis all wore *krises* also.[11] Although the symbolism of the *kris* is predominantly male, women wore them, too, as can be seen from an example of the nineteenth century that has an earlier blade (FIG. 121/NO. 73). One of the most prestigious gifts that a ruler could bestow was an important *kris*.

From the mystical power of the *empu* (smith), the rituals of the forging process,[12] the varieties of *pamor* (nickel-iron lamination) motif and the number and profile of the blade's curves, to the indefinable spirit of the weapon, the world of the *kris* is extremely complex. Smiths have always been seen as having magic power. *Kris*-making, where disparate elements are deconstructed and then fused into a new entity, has been seen as an allegory for the transformation of the human soul after death.[13] The iconography is further enriched by phallic symbolism, a reference made explicit in the huge linga sculpture with inset *kris* found at *candi* Sukuh.

On the technical side, sophistications of curve and *pamor* in the blade are only part of the lore, as is shown by encyclopedic manuscripts illustrating hundreds of blades and *pamor* designs. Several specialized studies indicate the depth of meaning, the social significance and the potency, both spiritual and sexual, implicit in this weapon.[14] Each *kris* is thought to have a spirit of its own that must be compatible with the owner's lest misfortune follow. This spirit may have a positive aspect: the form of certain weapons may invoke protection (FIG. 49). Possession of certain *kris* is equated with royal power, and there are many *kris* among the *pusaka* of all courts (FIGS. 120, 172/NOS. 72, 136), some of them having names and aristocratic titles (NO. 138). Ceremonial exchange of gifts among rulers often involved *kris*. Pakubuwono X (1893–1939) gave the ruler of Gianyar a Surakarta *kris* (FIG. 52/NO. 67), while the famous Nagasapto series of seven *krises* with seven *luk* (curves) made at the behest of Pakubuwono VII (1830–58) were given away by Pakubuwono X as grand gestures to other sovereigns, such as the King of Sweden, or commoners of note (FIG. 122).

One of the most pervasive social customs in the Indonesian archipelago, indeed in Southeast Asia as a whole, where it is considered to have originated, is the ceremony of *sirih* (betel) chewing. *Pinang*, the nut of the areca palm, is wrapped in the leaf of the betel vine along with crushed lime—originally from seashells—and sometimes tobacco and spices, and the whole quid is chewed for a prolonged period. A mildly narcotic effect is induced, much saliva flows, which necessitates frequent spitting, and over a long period the teeth become reddened. The habit is ancient; T'ang sources in China mentioned its place in marriage ceremonies, while Ma Huan commented in 1433 that guests were offered betel rather than tea.[15] In fact the ceremonial preparation and chewing of *sirih* quids accompanies all important rituals in Indonesia, its ingredients are offered to the spirits, and its symbolism is said to encompass sexuality, the heat of the *pinang* nut paired with the coolness of the *sirih* leaf, the long pod of the *sirih* vine contrasting with the round nut.[16]

For every ingredient and process connected with the betel ceremony a container or implement has evolved. There are pots with and without lids for the nuts, lime and spices, elongated holders for the leaves, tweezers and rods for picking up and mixing, nutcracker-like hinged tools for cutting, and a spittoon for the inevitable red saliva (FIG. 123/NO. 43). In every part of Indonesia sets of these objects have been made from every imaginable material and in a great range of

FIG. 110/NO. 81
Kain tapis (**woman's skirt cloth**), 19th century.
Lampung, South Sumatra. Cotton woven with
warp *ikat*, silk thread embroidery, natural dyes,
mica, 125 × 116 cm.

FIG. 111/NO. 84
Kain songket, late 19th or early 20th century.
Palembang, South Sumatra. Silk woven with
weft *ikat*, gold thread, 83 × 86 cm.

FIG. 112/NO. 50
Ceremonial bag, 19th century. Baun, West
Timor. Glass and coral trade beads, gold,
cotton, twine, 18 × 10 cm.

styles. Finely woven palm fiber, split rattan and grass are used in some areas, such as Kalimantan and Nusa Tenggara. Carved wood serves elsewhere, as does tortoiseshell. In Lampung there are exquisitely beaded boxes, in Palembang silver boxes linked with chains for carrying in the belt and also red lacquer sets. The forms sometimes mimic fruits like the mangosteen, are sometimes round and sometimes rectangular. Almost no traditional household lacks a set, commonly made of brass.

Honored guests in the courts, as elsewhere, were offered *sirih*, the preparation of it (as well as its presentation) being a courtesy of hospitality at rites-of-passage ceremonies. These included marriage and circumcision, both rituals influenced by Islam but incorporating older traditions. Another important ceremony where *sirih* was served was the tooth-filing rite. Sharp teeth are thought by the Balinese to be signs of the undesirable human traits of lust, anger, greed, stupidity, intoxication and jealousy, so the six upper front teeth are filed to render them even and to eliminate the bad characteristics. Even the ceremonies connected with death and burial are accompanied by the serving of *sirih*.

While the ingredients of the *sirih* quid presented in the courts were identical to those chewed elsewhere, the sets containing the different substances were more refined in craftsmanship and made of precious materials. Often they were gold (FIG. 124/NO. 38), sometimes studded with gems (FIG. 125/NO. 42), occasionally of repoussé (FIG. 126/NO. 41) or stained gold work (FIG. 123/NO. 43) and also of iron inlaid with gold (FIG. 127/NO. 45) utilizing a technique used in *kris*-making. Indeed, so central to the concept of ceremony is the betel custom that a set forms part of the essential regalia of a court. An example was included in a state gift presented in 1901 by Susuhunan Pakubuwono X to Queen Wilhelmina of the

FIG. 113/NO. 52
Timang (**buckle**), 19th century. Surakarta, Central Java. Iron, gold, rubies, diamonds, 12.2 × 11.2 × 1.5 cm.

Netherlands: a set of regalia, copies of the Surakarta *kraton* regalia, from one sovereign to another (FIG. 128/NO. 140).

THE RULER AS PATRON OF THE PERFORMING ARTS

The performing arts in Indonesia are extraordinarily varied and rich. A notable example is the dance, from the spear-brandishing, leaping and shouting war dances of the Dayak in Kalimantan to the stately and controlled *bedoyo*, a dance of the Javanese courts where nine female dancers glide almost imperceptibly over the *pendopo* (pavilion) floor, small movements from their classically turned-out feet scattering jasmine petals enfolded in their batik trains. Court dances in Kalimantan, in South Sulawesi and in Malay courts in Sumatra are similarly stately, showing some Javanese influence (or Balinese in the Lombok area) in turned-out posture and flexed arm and hand movements. Movements in the Sumatran case show more swaying body motion, perhaps an Arab influence in this region where Islamic cultural traditions have been more formative.

Lilting rhythms with overtones of Spanish and Portuguese music accompany the lively folk dances of Sumatra and Maluku, with twirling umbrellas and waving kerchiefs a cheerful contrast to the demonic trance-dances of Bali. The mesmerizing clapped rhythms of Aceh, the Arab-influenced syncopations of Riau music, the hypnotic chants of Bali's *kecak* dance (developed as recently as the 1930s when it was noted by Walter Spies and Beryl de Zoete) and the enigmatic subtlety of gamelan melody are only a few of the great diversity of musical and dance types found throughout the archipelago. Most of these themes and movements, while characteristic of vernacular dance, have also affected the style of court dance in many parts of Indonesia.

FIG. 114/NO. 53
Belt, ca. 1850. Surakarta, Central Java. Human hair, iron, gold, bronze, 99.7 × 16.5 × 1.9 cm.

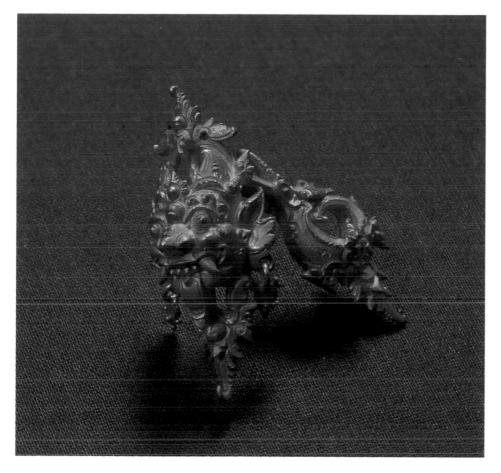

FIG. 115/NO. 57
Ear pendant in dragon form, 14th–15th
century. East Java. Gold, 3.6 × 4.6 cm.

157

FIG. 117/NO. 63
Hiasan dada (**chest ornament**), 19th century(?).
Klungkung, Bali. Gold, rubies, diamonds,
12.8 × 8.5 cm.

FIG. 118/NO. 60
Ring in double lotus form, 8th–9th century.
Central Java. Gold, 4.01 × 3.9 cm.

Opposite:
FIG. 119
Kris Nagakresna, 19th century. Surakarta, Central Java. Iron, nickel *pamor*, gold, diamonds, silver, ivory, sandalwood, *timaha* wood, 51.1 × 17.5 × 3.6 cm.

There is no doubt that the musical wonder of Indonesia is the gamelan,[17] an orchestra consisting largely of percussive bronze instruments keyed in two scales, the seven-toned *pelog* and the five-tone *slendro*. Although it is found elsewhere in Southeast Asia, its sounds and musicology in Indonesia have reached a sophistication and beauty—particularly in Java, but also in Bali—that place it in the company of the world's greatest musical traditions. The centerpiece of the gamelan orchestra is the large gong, its periodic sonorous note marking the basic sections of a composition's musical development. Gongs are surrounded with spiritual mystery and have always been associated with people of importance as a sign of status. Many are magically potent and are often given offerings and hung on elaborately carved stands (FIG. 129);[18] in recognition of their sacred nature, sometimes only especially designated people may touch them.

Other instruments that make up the gamelan ensemble include other percussive bronze instruments, domed like the *bonang*, *kenong* and *ketuk*, slatted in metallophone form (*saron*) (FIG. 130), with opposed plates in the cymbals (*kecer*) (FIG. 131) or with bronze strips suspended over bamboo resonators (*gender* and *slentem*) (FIG. 19).[19] There are also wooden xylophones (*gambang*) (FIG. 36/NO. 91) and hand-beaten drums (*kendang*) (sometimes stick-beaten in Bali). The continuous melody line is provided by the flute (*suling*) (FIG. 132/NO. 90) the *rebab* (two-stringed instrument played with a bow, FIG. 133/NO. 89) and the human voice. One of the finest musical groups based on gamelan instruments and melodic patterns is the small Sundanese *kecapi-suling*, a zither-like instrument and flute ensemble whose haunting rhythms have an unequalled subtlety and poignancy.

The gong is ancient, and the use of bronze for musical instruments goes back to Dongson times, the centuries immediately preceding and following the birth of Christ. It was used for ceremonial drums possibly connected with rain ceremonies.[20] A small gonglike instrument is depicted on Borobudur reliefs, as are drums, transverse flutes, cymbals, a two-stringed lute and a xylophone-like instrument. Larger gongs were established by the fourteenth century, since they are depicted on the friezes of *candi* Panataran. The word "gong" itself is Indonesian, and already by the sixteenth century, according to Portuguese accounts, gongs were an important export from Java and were symbols of royal rank in other parts of Indonesia. Other gamelan instruments developed later, the complete orchestra probably resembling its present form by the eighteenth century. Though gamelans have been owned by a wide range of wealthy people, the finest were made for palaces. A ruler often commissioned a new gamelan to mark his ascendancy, or some other special occasion, and most courts, such as the *Kraton* Ngayogyakarta Hadiningrat, the *Kraton* Surakarta Hadiningrat, the *Istana* Mangkunagaran and the *Istana* Pakualaman, have many gamelan ensembles.

Originally musical performance was probably connected with religious ceremonies, a link that survives today in the Sekaten (or Mulud) procession marking Mohammed's birthday, when a small gamelan is carried through the streets from palace to mosque and back. Gamelans were also carried into battle, perhaps summoning up supernatural powers to help the army.

One of the gamelan's most visible functions is to accompany dance and *wayang* performances, and those made for performances in the palaces of the rulers of Java are the apogée of the type. The gamelan is also pervasive in Bali, one of the most beautiful and melodious being that in the palace (*puri*) of Gianyar; the excellence of its tone is ascribed to the admixture of gold in the bronze of the *genders*.[21] Patronage such as that offered by a prince was important in the making of these orchestras because the instruments totaled more than thirty and the traditional bronze-casting methods made their creation a costly matter.

Costly also, and equally dependent on the patronage of the nobility, was the maintenance of a dance troupe. This entailed not only the support and training

FIG. 121/NO. 73
Patrem (**female dagger**), 17th and 19th century.
Surakarta, Central Java. Iron, nickel *pamor*,
gold, ivory, ebony, 34.2 × 4.8 × 3.6 cm.

Opposite:
FIG. 120/NO. 72
Kris, 19th century. Klungkung, Bali. Iron,
nickel *pamor*, gold, rubies, diamonds, wood,
76.2 × 11.7 × 5 cm.

FIG. 122
Kris Nagasapto, mid-17th century. Surakarta,
Central Java. Iron, nickel *pamor*, gold,
diamonds, wood, approx. 48 cm. One of the
seven Nagasapto *krises* with seven curves made
for Pakubuwono VII.

of the dancers, but also the provision of costumes, traditionally rich with gold-thread and gold-leaf ornamentation. Elaborate jewelry was required for performances of Javanese court dances like the *bedoyo* and *serimpi* and also for *wayang wong* performances—a more recent dance form—where unmasked men and women danced episodes from the Ramayana. Most spectacular are the dance headdresses, such as the gold and diamond crowns (FIG. 134/NO. 93) used for the *bedoyo* in the *Istana* Mangkunagaran and the ruby-studded example from Klungkung in Bali (NO. 92). Bracelets are also remarkable, as seen in a pair from Kalimantan in the form of a *garuda* (mythical bird) (FIG. 135/NO. 94) and a fourteenth-century example in *gunungan* form from Mojokerto, East Java (NO. 95). The jewelry for the classical dance strongly resembles that depicted on the god-king sculptures of the Majapahit era, almost certainly indicating a link between the court dancers and the demonstration of the ruler's divine connections (FIG. 31/NO. 6).

The masked dance (*wayang topeng*) is one of the oldest of the performing arts in Indonesia and was popular by the early sixteenth century, according to Tomé Pires. Masked dancers accompanying a royal circumcision in Banten were mentioned by a British traveler, Scott, in 1606.[22] Masks, effigies and fetishes are found in all parts of the country, often used in funeral processions or initiation and exorcism ceremonies in areas like Timor, Maluku and Batak lands, where autochthonous beliefs have persisted most strongly.[23] Death masks (FIG. 136/NO. 126) might have been the original mask form, or masks might have been developed to provide anonymity so that the performer became a more believable, less individual vessel for the personification of an ancestor, a god or a demon. The leader of the Sekaten procession on Mohammed's birthday wears a mask, one of the few examples of ritual use of masks in a post-Islamic setting and undoubtedly a relic of an earlier ceremony. Court masks, though made of wood and painted with gouache as were vernacular masks, were often gilded (FIGS. 137, 138/NOS.

FIG. 123/NO. 43
Paidon (**spittoon**), 19th century. Riau Lingga, East Sumatra. 18-carat gold, 11.7 × 19.3 cm.

FIG. 124/NO. 38
Sirih (betel) set, 19th century. Sumedang, West Java. Tray, spittoon, open container and five lidded
boxes: gold, 15.5 × 28.8 × 22.3 cm.

128, 130) and sometimes studded with gems, like the Kutei mask with its diamond teeth (FIG. 139/NO. 129).

As an entertainment—or perhaps more likely as a medium for instruction—the *topeng* dance is alleged by some Javanese to have been invented by *Sunan* Kalijaga, one of the nine *wali sanga* of Java's north coast cities in the Demak period of the sixteenth century. In the court setting where it was later refined the masked dance combines the enigmatic quality of the iconic *topeng* with the potent tensions implicit in the restrained energies and strict discipline of Javanese dance movements. The *topeng* reached its greatest subtlety and expressiveness in nineteenth-century creations like those collected by Raffles in the early part of the century (FIGS. 16, 140, 141)[24] and the Panji mask (FIG. 142/NO. 127) carved for Pakubuwono IX's son, a famous dancer, around 1875. In this period many princes were themselves skilled in mask-carving. Masked dance today is most seriously performed in Cirebon, perhaps reflecting a history of coastal origin and popularity that only later was absorbed into courtly practice. Its repertoire is the *gedog* cycle dealing with the hero Panji, equated with Arjuna in the Indic *purwa* cycle and considered by Rassers to be the mythological father of the Javanese people.[25]

The flowering of a traditional art under the patronage of the courts undoubtedly achieved its highest expression in the creation of *wayang kulit* (literally shadow of skin or leather), the shadow play, in which puppets of intricately carved, painted and gilded buffalo parchment are manipulated so that an overhead lamp throws their shadows on a white cotton screen. How old this drama is remains conjecture. It is mentioned in a ninth-century inscription in Bali, a tenth-century reference that may be to a shadow play in an inscription in Java, an eleventh-century chronicle, as well as by Tomé Pires in the early sixteenth century.

FIG. 125/NO. 42
Cupu (covered container) for lime, 19th century. Palembang, South Sumatra. Gold, diamonds, 5.7 × 5 cm.

Fig. 126/no. 41
Wadah (containers) for *pinang* and *gambir*, 19th century. Riau Lingga, East Sumatra. 22-carat gold, rubies, 5.9 × 8.1 and 6.2 × 8.2 cm.

Shadow puppets might have occurred earlier in China and been the inspiration for the Indonesian version,[26] or they might have come from India, where a first-century B.C. Buddhist text refers to what seems to be a shadow play and where, in Kerala, a form of it still exists. Carved leather puppets also exist in Turkey and Thailand; the latter were possibly derived from Indonesian examples.

Whatever its origins, the *wayang kulit* drama as it is known in Indonesia has developed to a unique level of refinement, with complex gamelan, song and poetry interludes set into the development of the plot as revealed by the puppet action; it has a completely Javanese or Balinese character.[27] The vocabulary of its equipment, such as the screen (*kelir*), the box containing the puppets (*kotak*) and the lamp (*blencong*) (FIG. 143/NO. 106) is totally indigenous despite the Indic origin of many of the stories in its repertoire. Most scholars of the *wayang* believe that performances were probably first connected with religious ceremonies, and all agree that the mythology draws on the deepest wells of symbolism. Still today certain plays (*lakons*) about Dewi Sri and Sadana are performed in connection with the rice harvest, and the *Murwakala* story is played in conjunction with the ritual purification ceremony (*ngruwat*).

The meaning of the shadow play has long been a subject for scholarly

FIG. 127/NO. 45
Kacip (betel nut cracker) in Twalen (Semar) **form,** 19th century. Lombok. Iron, gold, 18 × 7.7 × 1.1 cm.

speculation. Some judged the shadows to represent the souls of the ancestors in an intermediate state between invisibility and material presence. One theory sees them as the manifestation of the world of *kebatinen*, or hidden forces, a realization of imperceptible spiritual power,[28] an idea somewhat resembling the Sulawesi concept of *sumange'*, inner and invisible power, being manifest in shadows, footprints and whispers.[29]

The puppets are arranged to left and right of the *dalang*, the puppeteer, with the tree- or mountain-form puppet, the *kayon* or *gunungan*, in the center. Their long horn sticks are driven into one of a set of three banana palm trunks called *dhebog*. There may be as many as four hundred puppets to a *kotak* (box, set). Although the characters of the right side are commonly identified with the good and the left with its opponents,[30] there is no overt justification for such a categorical moral distinction; sympathetic characters exist on the left and characters on the right sometimes act reprehensibly.

A screen (*kelir*) hangs between the *dalang* and the audience, while an oil lamp (*blencong*), often in the form of a *garuda*, throws a flickering light on the puppets and projects their shadows onto the screen. The combination of the fluctuating quality of the flame and the animation of the puppets, constantly

FIG. 128/NO. 140
Upacara (regalia) replicas, 1901. Surakarta, Central Java. Gold.

whirled in and out of the scene, their arms manipulated by the *dalang* by the attached rods (*cempurit*), lends dynamic intensity to the scene. Behind the *dalang* sit the players of the gamelan, while to his left is the *kotak* where the *wayang* are usually stored. He knocks this box with one of two wooden mallets (*cempala*) to mark passages in the story; the larger is held in his hand, the smaller by his right toes. With his foot he also clangs a set of bronze plates (*kepyak*) for a different punctuation of the tale.[31]

This brief description of the action indicates the importance of the *dalang*. In addition to the demanding business of selecting, anchoring and manipulating the puppets in the constant cycle of scenes, he recites the Javanese poetry belonging to the *lakon*, foreshadows the plot in formal declamation and also speaks the dialogue, partly improvised, adapting his voice to the various characters; all the while he conducts the gamelan orchestra. The story develops in strictly prescribed fashion, but there is room for contemporary comment or moral interpretation in the conversation of the Panakawans, particularly Semar. This much-loved figure, a servant-clown also identified by some Indonesians with a pre-Indic deity, is sometimes used to make political comments or advocate new social ideas such as birth control.

The *dalang* has special status and power in society and is traditionally immune from retribution for any remarks critical of the government that he may place in the mouths of the Panakawan. As a master of words with their incalcu-

FIG. 129
Gamelan gong stand, before 1815. Java or Madura. Wood, painted and gilded, 187 × 195 cm. The double fish, a Majapahit royal motif, and crowned *nagas* and *garuda* show the courtly origin of this gong stand from the Raffles collection.

lable powers, he is in addition somewhat feared. His training is long and arduous, entailing the memorization of an enormous repertory, and is often learned from a relative.[32] Before a performance the *dalang* will meditate to seek spiritual inspiration for the seven-hour tour de force that lies ahead.

The dramatic material for the plays, which begin at about nine in the evening and continue until dawn, is in two main categories. One repertory, the *wayang purwa*, is largely derived from Indic sources, most commonly the Ramayana and Mahabharata epics (in Indonesian *Serat Rama* and *Serat Bratayudha*), as well as the Adiparwa and Arjuna Sasra Bau legends and old Indonesian myths.

Another cycle, indigenous legends concerned with characters such as Panji, Damar Wulan and Puyengan (FIG. 144/NO. 122), is called *wayang gedog*. Some of the best-known characters from the *wayang purwa* in the Bratayudha cycle are the heroes of the right phratry, notably the five Pandawa brothers (Yudistira [FIG. 56/NO. 115], Bima [FIG. 145/NO. 118], Arjuna [FIG. 57/NO. 109], Nakula and Sadewa). Others are their servant-clown attendants, the Panakawans (Gareng, Bagong, Petruk and Semar [FIG. 69/NO. 121]); the king-god Kresna (an incarnation of Visnu, FIG. 147; NO. 111) and the princess Srikandi (FIG. 148/NO. 119). Famous characters on the left, the side of the hundred Korawa brothers, include Baladewa (Kresna's brother), Kurupati, Karna, Durna and the princess Banuwati (FIG. 148/NO. 120). In the Ramayana cycle the heroes of the right include Rama (FIG.

FIG. 130
Saron barung (metallophone), before 1815. Java or Madura. Bronze, wood, pigment, gold leaf, tempera, fish glue medium, 48 × 100 cm.

Above:

FIG. 131

Kecer or *ricik* (**cymbals**), before 1815. Bali(?).
Bronze, wood, pigment, gold leaf, 30 × 44 cm.

Below:

FIG. 132/NO. 90

Suling (**flute**), 19th century. Klungkung, Bali.
Gold, rubies, diamonds, semiprecious stones,
glass, tortoiseshell, wood, 97.5 × 4.6 cm.

Opposite:

FIG. 133/NO. 89

Rebab (**stringed instrument**), 19th century.
Klungkung, Bali. Wood, coconut shell, gold,
silver, rubies, sapphires, semiprecious stones,
crystal, horsehair, gut, parchment, velvet,
92 × 18.4 × 8.5 cm.

Fig. 134/no. 93
Dance crown, 1920s. Surakarta, Central Java.
Gold, velvet and cotton ribbon, 18 × 24 × 24 cm.

146/NO. 110), his brother Laksmana and his wife Sita; they are aided by the monkey general Hanuman (FIG. 149/NO. 116). On the left the notable characters include the demon king Rahwana (FIG. 20/NO. 114; NO. 113) and the giant Kumbakarna.

Stylization of the *wayang*, with exaggeratedly long and slim arms and torsos, pointed noses, slanting eyes and elongated details of hair and clothing, seems to have been characteristic from the earliest days. There are suggestions that such distortions of naturalistic proportion were a response to Islamic proscriptions on the representation of the human form; advocates of this opinion cite the greater naturalism of *wayang kulit* in Bali, where Islam did not penetrate. Evidence to the contrary can be pointed out in the bas-reliefs of fourteenth-century pre-Islamic *candi* Panataran, where figures carved in typically *wayang* style are already present. The form is also apparent in a lamp of about the same time (NO. 105), its carved bronze figures themselves capable of throwing dramatic shadows when the lamp is lit.

The carving and painting of the oldest surviving *wayang kulit* are relatively simple. A seventeenth-century example from the National Museum in Denmark, already in the collection in 1669, is quite small and coarsely carved. While this Danish piece is probably a vernacular example (children in Javanese villages today still fashion simple *wayang* from twigs and grasses), one of the oldest court pieces in Indonesia, a *kuda* (horse) of the same century (from the time of Sultan Agung, according to *kraton* history) in the *pusaka* collection of the Yogyakarta sultanate, is also simply though vigorously carved and painted (FIG. 150).

A crocodile from the Raffles collection in the British Museum (therefore dated no later than 1816) is much more sophisticated, as is a slightly later Bima from the *Kraton* Kasepuhan in Cirebon (FIG. 145/NO. 118). The ultimate

FIG. 135/NO. 94
Kelat bahu (bracelets for the upper arm), 19th century. Kutei, Kalimantan. Gold, diamonds, 8.7 × 9.8 × 3.5 cm.

craftsmanship, however, was achieved in the *wayang* made later in the nineteenth century, when the protocol and artistic cultivation of the courts reached their apogée. The exquisite refinement of the Pakualaman Yudistira (FIG. 56/NO. 115) and the spirituality of the Surakarta Panji from the *Kyai* Dewa Kadung set are matchless, though less dazzling than the 1903 Kresna studded with diamonds from the Yogyakarta *kraton* (FIG. 147).

Several other forms of *wayang* plays exist. These include *wayang klitik* (or *kerucil*, small), *wayang beber* (unfolding), and *wayang golek*. One of the oldest is *wayang beber*, reported by Ma Huan in the 1433 voyage of Zheng He, where the *dalang* unrolls a painted paper scroll (FIG. 151/NO. 125) whose successive scenes depict the episodes in the same stories as those of the *wayang kulit* drama. Both scrolls and performances are exceedingly rare now, though the tradition is said to be maintained in Pacitan, East Java.

Wayang klitik are made of wood carved in low relief (FIG. 144/NO. 122; FIGS. 21, 152),[33] have leather arms and are manipulated without an intervening screen. The stories come from the *gedog* cycles and are also seldom performed these days. Their history is uncertain, but the Danish National Museum collection has an example from the seventeenth century.

Wayang golek, fully three-dimensional puppets with wooden arms and moveable head surmounting a central support rod hidden by cloth garments (FIG. 23/NO. 124), probably originated on the north coast of Java and are particularly popular in West Java. The repertoire in Central Java comprises stories from the Middle East about Amir Hamzah, uncle of the prophet Mohammed; in West Java the *gedog* and *purwa* cycles are also presented in *golek* plays, a much younger tradition than other *wayang* forms. However, a small *wayang golek*, the *gambyong* or *tayub* (FIG. 153/NO. 123), whose name derives from a word for dancers, appears at the end of the performance of the *wayang kulit lakon*.[34] The *golek* may be much older than its present performance format: the Batak people have an articulated puppet, the Si Galegale, that is manipulated in a complicated dance at the death rites of people without offspring and is clearly very ancient, as are the effigies of the dead, the *tau-tau*, of the Torajans in Sulawesi.

Another form of *wayang* exists about which very little is known. Apparently the only examples are in the Raffles collection in the British Museum, where the inventory lists them as *krucil gilig*, presumably a version of *kerucil golek*. Standing about sixteen inches tall, they are fully carved in solid wood with moveable wooden arms (FIGS. 22, 154)[35] and personify characters from the Damar Wulan tales. They once had long wooden rods attached to the feet (these rods were sawn off at some point between their acquisition in 1859 and the present), so they seem to have been designed for performance.

No account of any other such puppets exists, as far as can be determined; any notes Raffles might have made about them could have been lost when his ship, the *Fame*, burned at the time of his final voyage home to England in 1824. In his account of *wayang* in *The History of Java* of 1817 he mentions only *wayang kulit*, *wayang klitik* and *wayang beber*. They might have been part of the booty taken from the palace by the British when they defeated the forces of Hamengkubuwono II (1792–1810, 1811–12, 1826–28) in Yogyakarta in 1812. Or perhaps they were made on commission, which would account for their uniqueness, or possibly were a gift from Prince Natakusuma (the brother of Hamengkubuwono II), who had helped Raffles in subduing Yogyanese forces and was rewarded by the creation of the principality of the Pakualaman in 1813. In any case, the puppets' fine crafting and style of dress mark them as probable court pieces. They are remarkable as lively carvings, and they are particularly interesting as an early record of refined batik designs and of court dress and hair styles of the early nineteenth century. The intricacy of their batik motifs sets an earlier date than was previously assumed for the development of such sophisticated techniques.

Opposite:
FIG. 136/NO. 126
Death mask, 16th century(?). South Sulawesi. Gold, 21.25 × 18 cm.

Sculpture is probably one of the Indonesian arts best appreciated in the West, thanks to the exposure of the magnificent bas-reliefs of Central Java through publicity associated with the reconstruction of Borobudur. It reached splendid heights during the Hindu-Javanese period in both relief and freestanding stone pieces as well as in bronzes.[36] The reliefs of Borobudur tell the story of the Buddha's life and tales of others who tried to achieve enlightenment through his inspiration. Those of *candi* Loro Jonggrang at Prambanan relate the Ramayana story. The vitality and wealth of detail about courtly and vernacular life achieved by these sculptures is of a remarkably consistent standard, each panel skillfully carved and composed with careful attention to specific space, yet in harmony with the overall flow of the reliefs around the galleries of the monument. Like the narrative reliefs, the large standing sculptures of Hindu gods or Buddhist figures that were placed in central chambers of the temples are among the finest achievements of the art of Southeast Asia. In particular should be noted the figures in *candi* Mendut.

The East Javanese period from about the twelfth until the fifteenth centuries also produced distinguished bas-reliefs and portrait sculptures in stone (FIG. 31/NO. 6; FIG. 32). Both periods have an additional legacy of lost-wax bronze sculpture of great refinement, its character more in the mold of the calm and iconic sculpture of Sukhothai and Khmer pieces than that of dynamic Indian work.

After this classical period, carving skills besides those for architectural application were mostly exercised in woodworking. Examples include *wayang golek* and *wayang klitik* figures, cases and stands for gamelan instruments and images of iconic character and ritual significance like ancestor figures and *loro blonyo* sculptures, the so-called bridal pair of Dewi Sri and Dewa Sadono that stand in front of the ritual marriage bed in Javanese interiors.

The other important application of sculpture after the classical period was in architecture. Carving is pervasive in vernacular houses, whether in relatively simple fretwork in Bugis areas or intricate geometric motifs in low relief in Dayak, Batak, Torajan and Minangkabau lands. Exceptionally refined work was done for screens, external and internal, in the houses of Kudus and Japara on the north coast of Java, but fine architectural carving was also applied as decoration for palaces. In Sulawesi, Sumatra, Nusa Tenggara and Kalimantan carving sometimes showed considerable sophistication in relating motifs to architectural planes. In the second Mataram period in Java the sweep of the roof line and the simplicity of the columns of most *pendopos* eschewed decoration in favor of overall form in architectural usage, but in Cirebon some evidence survives, as in a carved panel (FIG. 87/NO. 37) and carved doors, that the old palace had distinguished relief sculpture.

Exquisite craftsmanship can be seen in small jewelry chests and cosmetic drawers from Central Java, but on the whole furniture was not important in traditional Indonesian craftsmanship, as it was not a central part of indigenous domestic equipment. This is perhaps why colonial influences are strong in the styles of chairs, tables and even thrones in chair form, objects that found a place in Indonesian life only after the colonial example. The making of litters and carriages, however, is an old skill, that will be examined later in this chapter.

In Bali, where the gap between the art of the *puri* (palace) and the art of the village has always been narrower than in other parts of Indonesia and where decoration is valued for its ability to express devotion to the gods, highly skilled sculpture was—and still is—visible in houses and temples throughout the island. Some work of exceptional refinement is visible in princely buildings, however, notably on the doors of *bales*, like those at Karangasem and on a pair from the *puri* in Singaraja (FIG. 155/NO. 36). Architectural features stimulating the most

FIG. 137/NO. 128
Topeng (mask), **Gunung Sari**, late 18th century.
Java. Wood, pigment, fish glue medium,
semiprecious stones, glass, 19 cm.

FIG. 138/NO. 130
Topeng (mask), **Srikandi**, late 19th or early 20th
century. Cirebon, West Java. Wood, pigment,
gold leaf, fish glue medium, leather teeth-thong,
17.5 × 14.5 × 10.2 cm.

FIG. 140
Topeng (mask), **Raden Antunan**, before 1815.
Central Java. Wood, pigment, gold leaf, fish
glue medium, 18 cm.

FIG. 141
Topeng (mask), **Raden Arya Gunung Sari**,
before 1815. Java. Wood, pigment, gold leaf, fish
glue medium, 18 cm.

FIG. 139/NO. 129
Topeng (mask), **Klono**(?), late 19th century.
Kutei, East Kalimantan. Wood, pigments, gold
leaf, fish glue medium, diamonds, hair,
19.3 × 17.6 × 12.5 cm.

FIG. 142/NO. 127
Topeng (mask), **Panji**, 19th century. Central
Java. *Kantil* wood, natural pigments, 24-carat
gold leaf, fish glue medium, leather teeth-thong,
18 × 15.4 × 9.5 cm.

spectacular Balinese sculpture are probably the *sendi*, the central figures on the cross-beams of *bale* roofs (FIG. 156/NO. 104). The creative fantasy that makes Balinese carving so lively and varied is also apparent in a *kris*-holder of the nineteenth century from Lombok (FIG. 157/NO. 66).

Painting in the Western fine arts sense has not been characteristic of Indonesian art until this century. Painterly skills were certainly employed in the decoration of *wayang kulit* and *wayang beber*, but the outstanding medium for graphic and coloristic skills traditionally has been the art of batik. The most important locus for fixed-plane painting has been architecture. Here painting, like sculpture, was an applied art in that it was dedicated to enhancing the meaning of life and the function of the building it embellished. In an architectural sense this meant illustrating the ideas that made the building significant, so the painting lining the roof of the Kerta Gosa judgment pavilion in Klungkung, for example (FIG. 61), demonstrates the workings of justice. Similarly, the fine gouache paintings on cloth in *wayang*-influenced Kamasan style that were made to decorate Balinese temples depict legends relevant to worship of the gods.

One further instance of painting in Indonesia has been almost entirely dependent on the courts: the art of manuscript writing and illustration. Copyists

FIG. 143/NO. 106
Blencong (*wayang* lamp), 1776. Central Java. Brass, 53.3 × 48.8 × 66.7 cm.

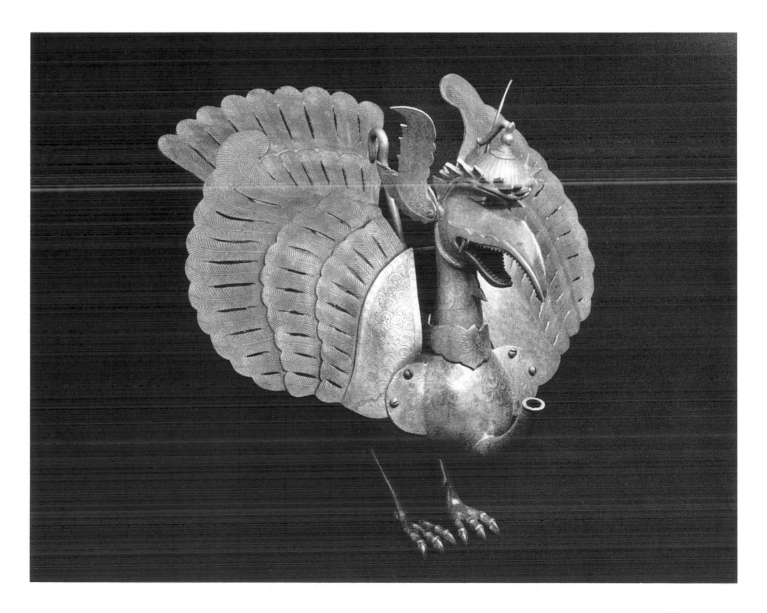

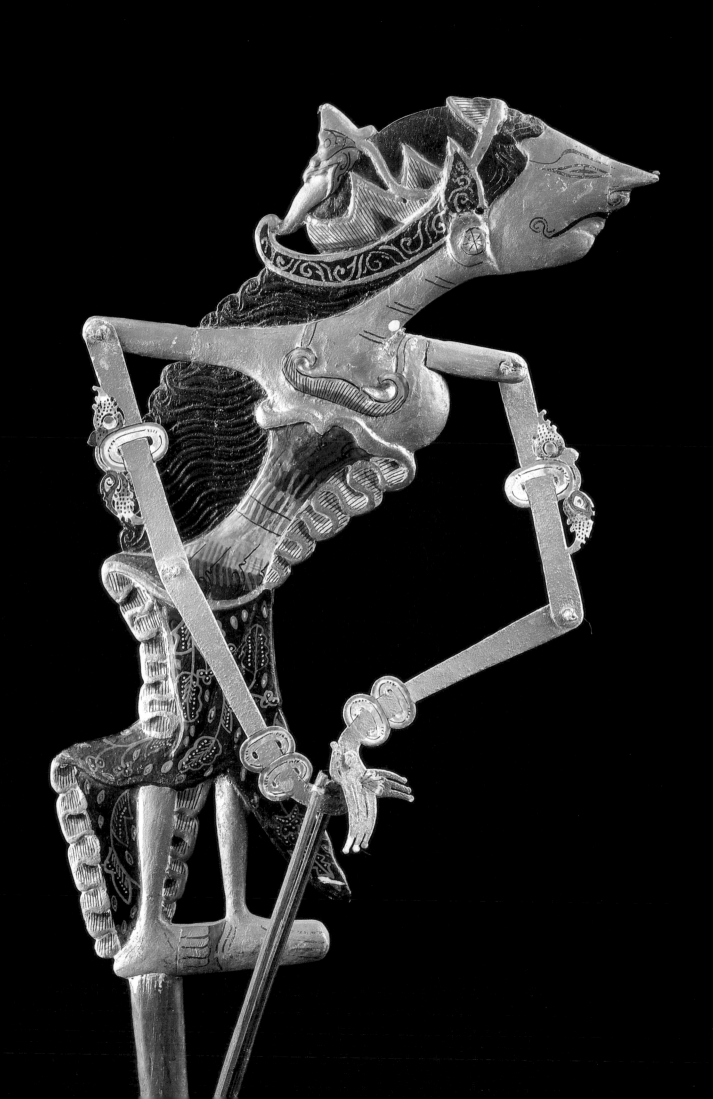

were commissioned by princes of the more important courts to ensure the continuity of old texts and to write out new works of prose and poetry. The laborious copying and illustrating of old texts, in a perpetual struggle to defeat the destructive forces of humidity, mold and insects, is a costly activity sustainable only by princely patronage (or today by other private or government support). The majority of Indonesian manuscripts, particularly the genealogies, chronicles and divination texts of Sulawesi and Sumatra, were not illustrated. In Java and Bali, however, some of the splendid books that were created from about the end of the eighteenth century were skillfully illuminated.

In Bali manuscripts were in *lontar* form (FIG. 158/NO. 96), palm leaf cut into lengths of about twenty inches held together by cords passing through perforations in the leaves. They were inscribed with a sharp stylus (NO. 97) and then rubbed with ink (NO. 98) to emphasize the incisions. They tell the stories of the Mahabharata and Ramayana epics as well as Balinese legends. One of the biggest collections is in the palace of the Raja of Singaraja. Many ancient Javanese manuscripts were preserved in Bali and Lombok when the disintegration of the Majapahit empire and the arrival of Islam in the new kingdoms of Demak and Mataram led to the destruction of literature of the Old Javanese type in Java itself.

Just as the courts were the chief patrons of manuscript writers and painters, palace libraries are the most important repositories of old manuscripts in Java, the majority of which are copies made in the nineteenth century of older works. Most of the painting in those that are illustrated is in *wayang* style, as in the *Serat Bratayudha* from the Yogyakarta *kraton* (FIG. 68) and the *Sela Rasa* manuscript in the Mackenzie collection of the British Library (FIG. 159/NO. 100). By the time later examples were produced, such as the *Dewa Ruci* manuscript (FIG. 160/NO. 101) of 1886, there was a mixture of stylized *wayang* mode with a more naturalistic style showing the influence of European perspective and realism. Along with this blending of techniques one finds unselfconscious anachronisms, as when the Bratayudha hero Bima in antique mythical form crosses the ocean in which a steamship is making way. Other palace productions include richly illustrated horoscope sequences and texts depicting hierarchies of signs of rank, such as umbrellas (FIG. 161/NO. 19).

Korans were copied in many areas, and manuscript versions survive in the palace collections of Tidore, Sumabawa Besar, Surakarta and Yogyakarta, as well as in museums that have inherited palace collections, as in Banjarbaru in Kalimantan and in Aceh. Some have decorative motifs and illuminated frontispieces, but most are extremely dilapidated. In general, although the manuscripts of Indonesia do not approach the level of Persian work, the vitality and freshness of the illustrations make them an important addition to the already extensive range of Indonesian art.

One question needs to be addressed in considering court patronage: to what extent did critical judgment and the deliberate search for style motivate the ruler? By and large, traditional skills and the continuity of theme underlay most of the products of palace craftsmen, but certain rulers were responsible for clearer choices in matters of taste. Pakubuwono II (1725–49) ordered a return to seventeenth-century script techniques. Mangkunagoro IV (1853–81) patronized *wayang* makers, as did Hamengkubuwono VIII (1921–39), whose passion for *wayang* stimulated much creativity before and during his reign. Mangkunagoro VII (1916–44), who made his palace an important center for innovation in performing and plastic arts, was another prince who exerted considerable personal influence on cultural trends. In Bali the artist has always had great freedom to interpret traditional form according to his own inspiration, which partly accounts for the vitality of craft in that island. Since the art created for the courts in Cirebon was produced by guildlike organizations in surrounding villages rather than in the

Opposite:
FIG. 144/NO. 122
Wayang klitik, Puyengan, 19th century. Central Java. Wood, leather, pigment, gold leaf, fish glue medium, rattan fastenings, 48.4 × 19.5 × 1 cm.

FIG. 145/NO. 118
Wayang kulit, **Bima**, 19th century. Cirebon,
West Java. Buffalo hide, pigment, gold leaf, fish
glue medium, buffalo horn, bone studs,
95 × 55 × 2.2 cm.

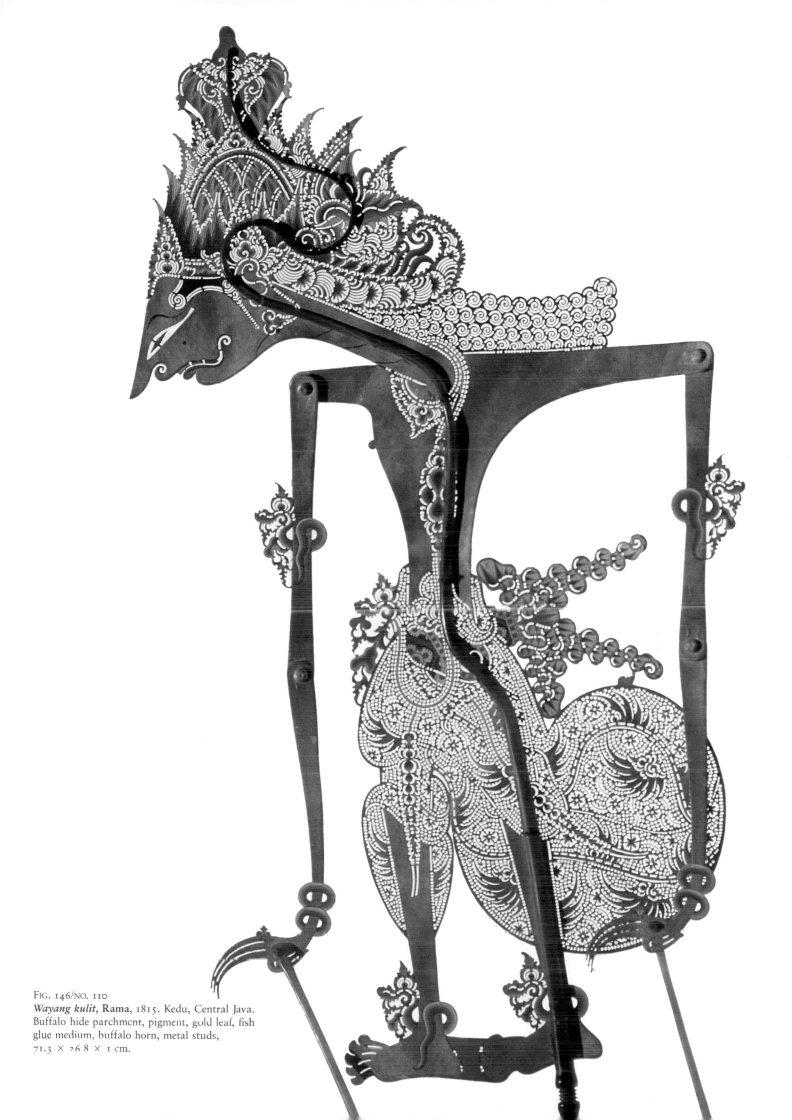

FIG. 146/NO. 110
Wayang kulit, **Rama**, 1815. Kedu, Central Java.
Buffalo hide parchment, pigment, gold leaf, fish
glue medium, buffalo horn, metal studs,
71.3 × 26.8 × 1 cm.

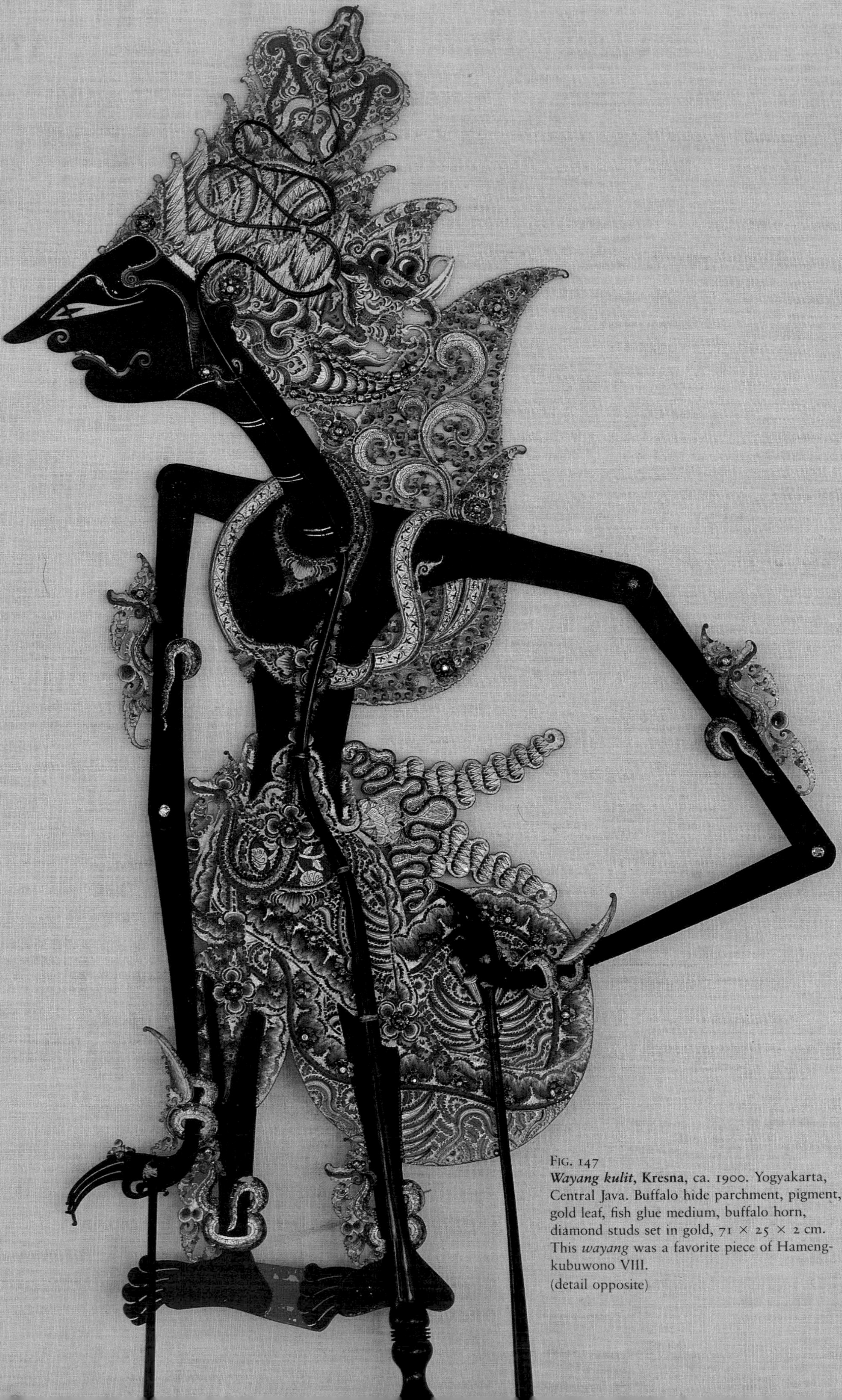

FIG. 147
Wayang kulit, **Kresna**, ca. 1900. Yogyakarta, Central Java. Buffalo hide parchment, pigment, gold leaf, fish glue medium, buffalo horn, diamond studs set in gold, 71 × 25 × 2 cm. This *wayang* was a favorite piece of Hamengkubuwono VIII.
(detail opposite)

FIG. 148/NOS. 119, 120
Wayang kulit, Banuwati (left), and *wayang
kulit*, Srikandi (right), 19th century. Cirebon,
West Java. Buffalo hide parchment, pigment,
gold leaf, fish glue medium, buffalo horn, bone
studs, 53 × 23 × 1.4 cm. (NO. 119),
55.5 × 21 × 1.4 cm. (NO. 120)

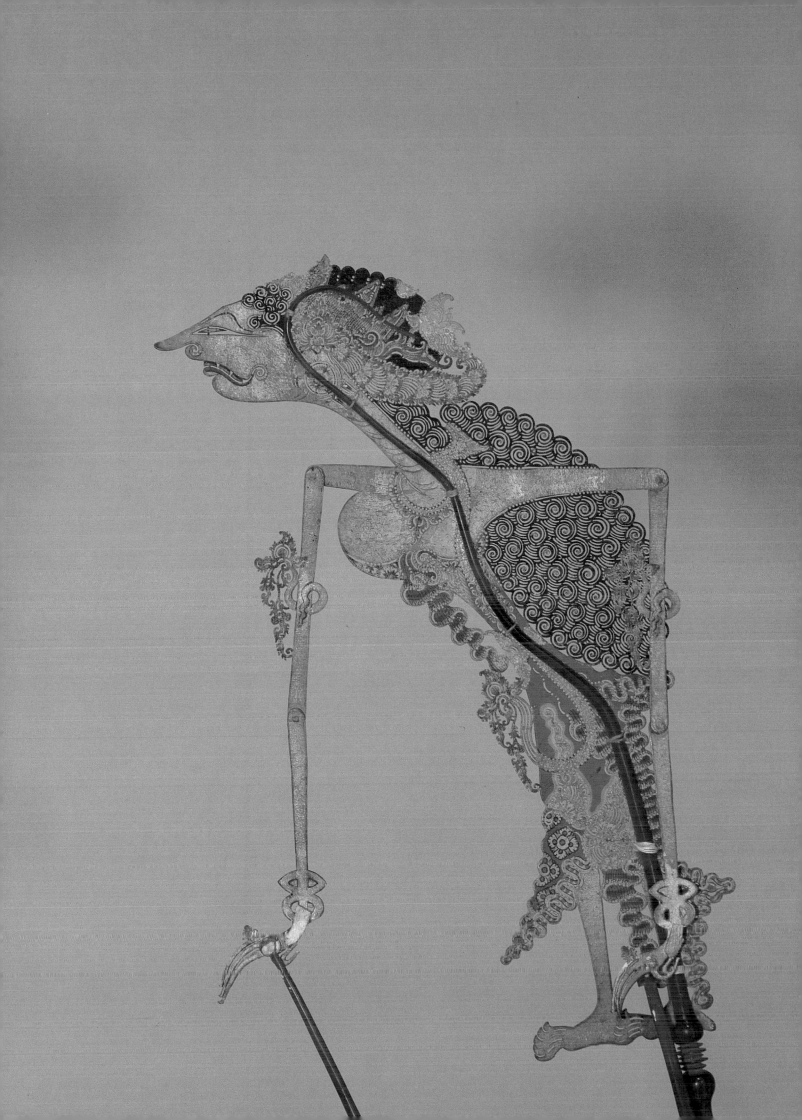

palaces themselves, the role of the courts in artistic production was more one of sustenance than stylistic innovation. This may explain the more robust character of Cirebon *wayang kulit* figures as compared to the greater refinements of those made in Central Java, though it does not account for the exceptional refinement of *wayang golek* from Cirebon (FIG. 23/NO. 124).

ROYAL REGALIA

Ceremonies that deliberately emphasized kingship are an important category of court ceremonies stimulating cultural production. These ceremonies were either public, as when the ruler went on formal procession before his subjects, or were enacted in the inner spaces of the palace before his courtiers. A royal progress must have been a dazzling occasion as long ago as the fourteenth century, according to the *Nagarakertagama*. Prapanca describes the royal retinue, with as many as four hundred carriages, their seats screened with *geringsing* cloths embroidered with gold, the woodwork "glittering with drawings of gold," preceding the king:

> Placed in the rear was the wagon of the Illustrious Prince, ornamented with gold and jewels, shining. Different was its aspect: with the body of a palanquin, entirely open, broad, radiant, its rays spreading. How great was the variety of the serving-men who accompanied him: of Janggala, Kadiri, Sedah, Panglarang, crowded, marching evenly, not to mention yet the [guardsmen], vested with authority, setting aside the retainers who had their places with the elephants and the horses.[37]

A painted scroll from the turn of the present century (FIG. 162/NO. 30) gives some idea of the pomp of a royal procession in Java, with the colorful uniforms of the

FIG. 150
Wayang kulit, kuda (horse), 17th century. Yogyakarta, Central Java. Buffalo hide parchment, pigment, gold leaf, fish glue medium, buffalo horn, metal studs, 75 × 78 × 2 cm. One of the oldest *wayang kulit* in the Yogyakarta *Kraton*, this horse is said to date from the time of Sultan Agung. The simple strength of its carving contrasts with the elaborate detail of 19th-century *wayang* like FIG. 56/NO. 115.

FIG. 151/NO. 125
Wayang beber, before 1852. Java. Watercolor
and ink on paper, wood batons, 71 × 289 cm.

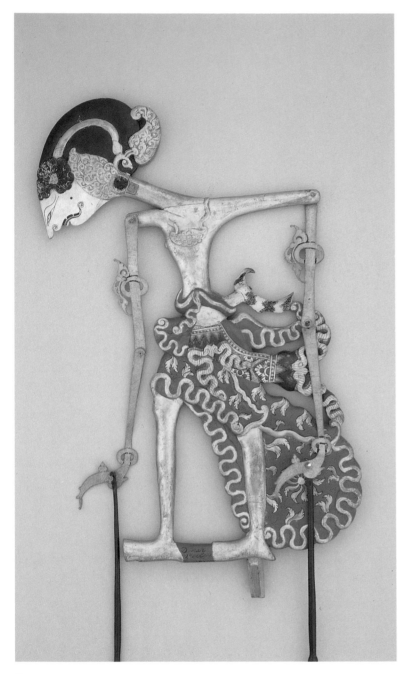

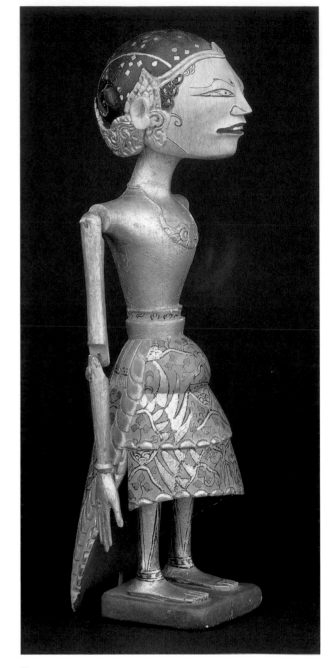

FIG. 152
Wayang klitik, **Raden Damar Wulan**, before 1815. Java. Wood, leather, pigment, gold leaf, fish glue medium, metal studs, 43 cm.

FIG. 154
Wayang gedog, **Raden Damar Wulan**, before 1815. Central Java. Wood, pigment, gold leaf, fish glue medium, rattan fastenings, 40 cm.

FIG. 153/NO. 123
Wayang golek, 19th century. Surakarta, Central Java. Wood, cotton cloth, diamonds, pigment, gold leaf, fish glue medium, fiber fastenings, 49 × 18 × 16 cm.

Opposite:
FIG. 155/NO. 36
Puri (palace) **doors**, late 18th or early 19th century. Singaraja, North Bali. *Nangka* (jackfruit) wood, painted and gilded, 211 × 210.9 × 31 cm.

FIG. 156/NO. 104
Sendi (pillar base) of Visnu mounted on Garuda, late 19th century. Singaraja(?), North Bali. *Nangka* (jackfruit) wood, pigment, fish glue medium, gold leaf, 71.5 × 70.2 × 41.5 cm.

FIG. 157/NO. 66
Kris-**holder and** *kris*, 19th century. Lombok.
Wood, pigment, gold leaf, iron, gold, rubies,
diamonds, ivory, 125.8 × 30.7 × 52 cm.

Fig. 158/no. 96
Lontar manuscript of **Smara Dahana**, second
half of 19th century. Singaraja, North Bali.
Palm leaf (incised and inked, polychromed and
gilded), string and coin, wood with polychrome
decoration; leaf: 5.3 × 49.5 cm; box:
7 × 8 × 53 cm.

202

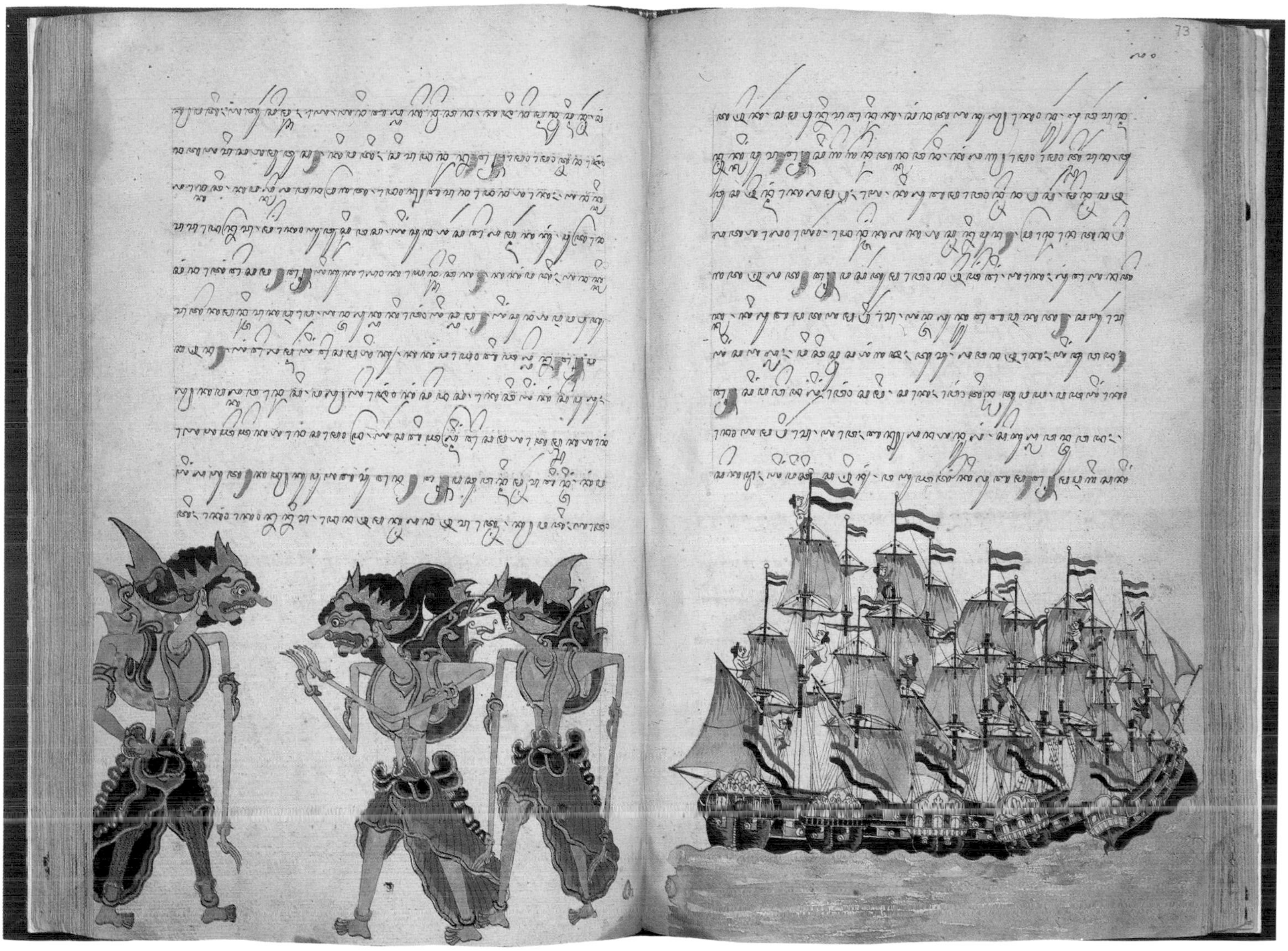

FIG. 159/NO. 100
Manuscript of Sela Rasa, 1804. Java. Ink on
European paper, polychrome watercolor, gold
leaf, cloth and leather binding, 40.3 × 20 cm.

Opposite:
FIG. 160/NO. 101
Manuscript of Dewa Ruci, 1886. Yogyakarta,
Central Java. Ink on European paper,
polychrome watercolor, gold leaf, leather
binding, 33.7 × 21 cm.

sovereign's regiments, the flash of weapons and jewels, the brilliant umbrellas of rank, the stately carriages all sweeping along to the accompaniment of gamelan music. Sometimes the ruler rode in a litter, exquisitely carved, gilded and painted, like a nineteenth-century example from Bali (FIG. 163/NO. 29); it was a tradition that the feet of the ruler should not publicly touch the ground. To this end the Sultan of Ternate wore silver shoes in Arabic style, a gift from the Dutch Governor-General Van der Capellen in the nineteenth century. Another version of the litter is the ceremonial cart, its figurehead carved in bird form like a ship's, in which the wives of nobles in Lampung were carried to feasts. Umbrellas of rank (FIG. 161/NO. 19) played a significant part in ceremony. The most important were gold, had elaborate finials (FIG. 164/NO. 33) and were reserved for the sovereign (FIG. 165). Other ranks were allowed to be sheltered by specific colors and forms, and golden umbrellas are still used to cover *pusaka* objects when they are moved from one place to another.

The most spectacular objects in Indonesian rulers' retinues, as the *Nagarakertagama* indicates, were probably the carriages. A closed carriage called Ratu Kencana (golden king), its form resembling the *kobongan* shrine, is represented in one of the *wayang kulit* from the Kyai Sebet set made for Mangkunagoro

FIG. 162/NO. 30
Scroll depicting a procession, ca. 1900. Java.
Watercolor and gold leaf on paper,
23 × 2045 cm.

FIG. 161/NO. 19
Manuscript on weapons and umbrellas of rank,
1815. Central Java. Paper, leather, ink,
watercolor, gold leaf, 26 × 20.5 × 1.5 cm.

Secretaris

2 *Redenas blanda*

Raden Toemenggoeng Kertonegoro
dan 8 Boepati

Boepoljoro dibawak panewoe mantri

Panen

IV and shows the fine craftsmanship of the traditional Javanese type (FIG. 9/NO. 31). The zenith of courtly carriage construction was undoubtedly reached in the still-existing Singhabarwang, Jempana Setia and Paksinagaliman carriages from Cirebon (FIGS. 166, 167). All three, it is claimed, belonged originally to the old Pakungwati *kraton*, but when the court was split into the Kasepuhan (elder) and Kanoman (younger) palaces in 1677,[38] the Kasepuhan received the Singhabarwang and the Kanoman the other two. The Singhabarwang,[39] said to date from 1549, was pulled by four white buffaloes and used by the sultan, its elephant head, eagle wings and lion body giving a powerful mythological impression reminiscent of the chariots of the gods in the friezes at Prambanan. The effect must have been greatly enhanced when the wings flapped as the carriage moved forward, the joints operated by an ingenious mechanism with a leather strap attached to a kind of piston.

The Jempana Setia, said to be from the same period, was possibly originally a litter and was used for the *permaisuri*, or senior wife; another theory suggests that it might once have carried royal princes during circumcision ceremonies. It is decorated with one of the finest existing examples of *megamendung-wadasan* carving. Its tightly furled curves and sinuous lines are very like the shapes of the grottoes depicted on the terra-cotta friezes found at Trawulan. The alleged early date of the carriage would place it within a century of the fifteenth- or

sixteenth-century demise of Majapahit, depending on which criterion of decline is invoked, the loss of power or the end of a dynasty. This date and its stylistic similarities with Majapahit sculpture demonstrate the link that the art of Cirebon provides between the last great East Java empire and the later Central Java kingdom of Mataram.[40] The Paksinagaliman in the Kanoman palace, also invoking the marvelous, completes the trio of carriages whose imagery is dominant (and more widely known) in the motifs of Cirebon batik.[41] Carriages from the courts of Surakarta and Yogyakarta are grand but of European style.

As might be expected, symbols of office were essential accompaniments to a ceremonial appearance by the ruler. One element of regalia either carried before or held by the prince is the *tongkat* (NO. 34), its resemblance to the Western staff making its function obvious. Paired lances (*tombak*) (FIG. 168/NO. 10) played a similar part, as did umbrellas and flags, and the ruler wore certain regalia items such as chains of office, a ceremonial hat of gold (*kuluk*) (FIG. 169/NO. 35) or perhaps of more vernacular materials (FIG. 170),[42] and ceremonial shoes. In Central Java he would be preceded by a set of *upacara*, which are ceremonial *pusaka* objects fashioned in gold, in some cases studded with diamonds, in the form of *sirih* (betel) ceremony objects, including a spittoon, a bowl and napkin for finger washing, a lamp, cosmetic containers and models of several creatures: a goose, a

Left:
FIG. 164/NO. 33
Umbrella finial, 8th–9th century. Cirebon, West Java. Gold, clay fill, 20.2 × 8.1 × 8.1 cm.

Right:
FIG. 165
Umbrella, 19th century. Surakarta, Central Java. Paper, wood, cotton string, gold leaf, pigment, 330 × 160 cm. The triple form and gilded surface of this ceremonial umbrella indicate the supreme rank of the Susuhunan, ruler of Surakarta.

deer, a peacock, a cock[43] and a snake.[44] The items in the collection vary somewhat in different Javanese palaces, and palaces elsewhere possessed regalia like the *upacara*; one example is a large container in snake form from the sultanate of Banjarmasin (FIG. 27/NO. 139), a court that was under considerable Javanese influence.

Within the palace, ceremonial appearances by the ruler that demonstrated his kingship also required the wearing or display of regalia. The *tongkats* would have been present (NO. 34), perhaps a ritual fan as in Riau Lingga (FIG. 171/NO. 48), *pusaka* state *kris* would have been worn (FIGS. 172, 173/NOS. 136, 138), and in some states, crowns. In Bima the state crown, encrusted with more than seven hundred diamonds (FIG. 174/NO. 133), has a shallow peaked brimless shape of Islamic origin, whereas the crowns of Banten (FIG. 175/NO. 134) and Gowa (FIG. 91) are domed, the latter also having a brim; their form may derive from a headdress based on the convention of the Buddha head covered with curls. The Gowa crown, named Salokoa and made of almost two kilograms of twenty-two carat gold (FIG. 91), was worn only at coronation rituals; Gowa Museum officials consider it to be from the fourteenth century. The crown of Sumedang (FIG. 176), a replica of one now lost that is said to have come from the ancient West Java kingdom of Pajajaran, resembles crowns on Hindu deity sculptures of Central

FIG. 166
Singhabarwang carriage, 16th century. Cirebon, West Java. The mythical powers of elephant, *garuda* and lion are invoked in this carriage used by the Sultan on ceremonial occasions.

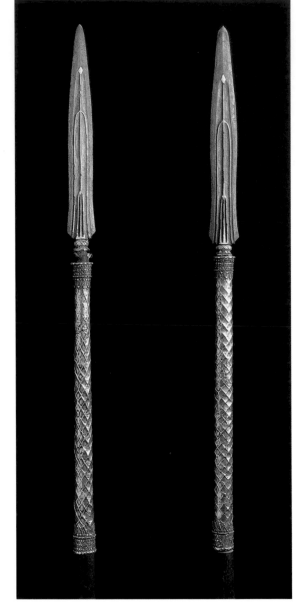

Fig. 167
Paksinagaliman carriage, 16th century. Cirebon, West Java. Bird, elephant and *naga* invoke respectively Islam and Arab culture, Hinduism and India, and Buddhism and China.

Fig. 168/no. 10
Pair of tombaks (lances), early 17th century. Bima, Sumbawa, possibly made in South Sulawesi. Head and sheath: gold, iron, nickel *pamor,* silver or zinc; shaft: *sawo* wood; 204 × 4.2 × 3 cm.

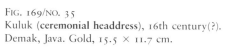

FIG. 169/NO. 35
Kuluk (**ceremonial headdress**), 16th century(?).
Demak, Java. Gold, 15.5 × 11.7 cm.

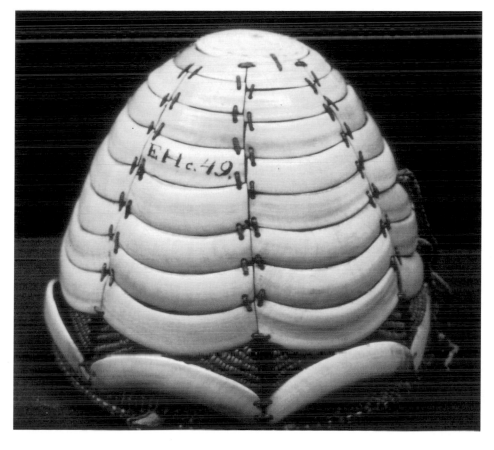

FIG. 170
Ceremonial headdress, late 17th–early 18th
century. Banten, West Java. Boar's tusks, shell,
coral, glass, rattan or palm twine, cotton,
rattan or bamboo frame, 17 cm.

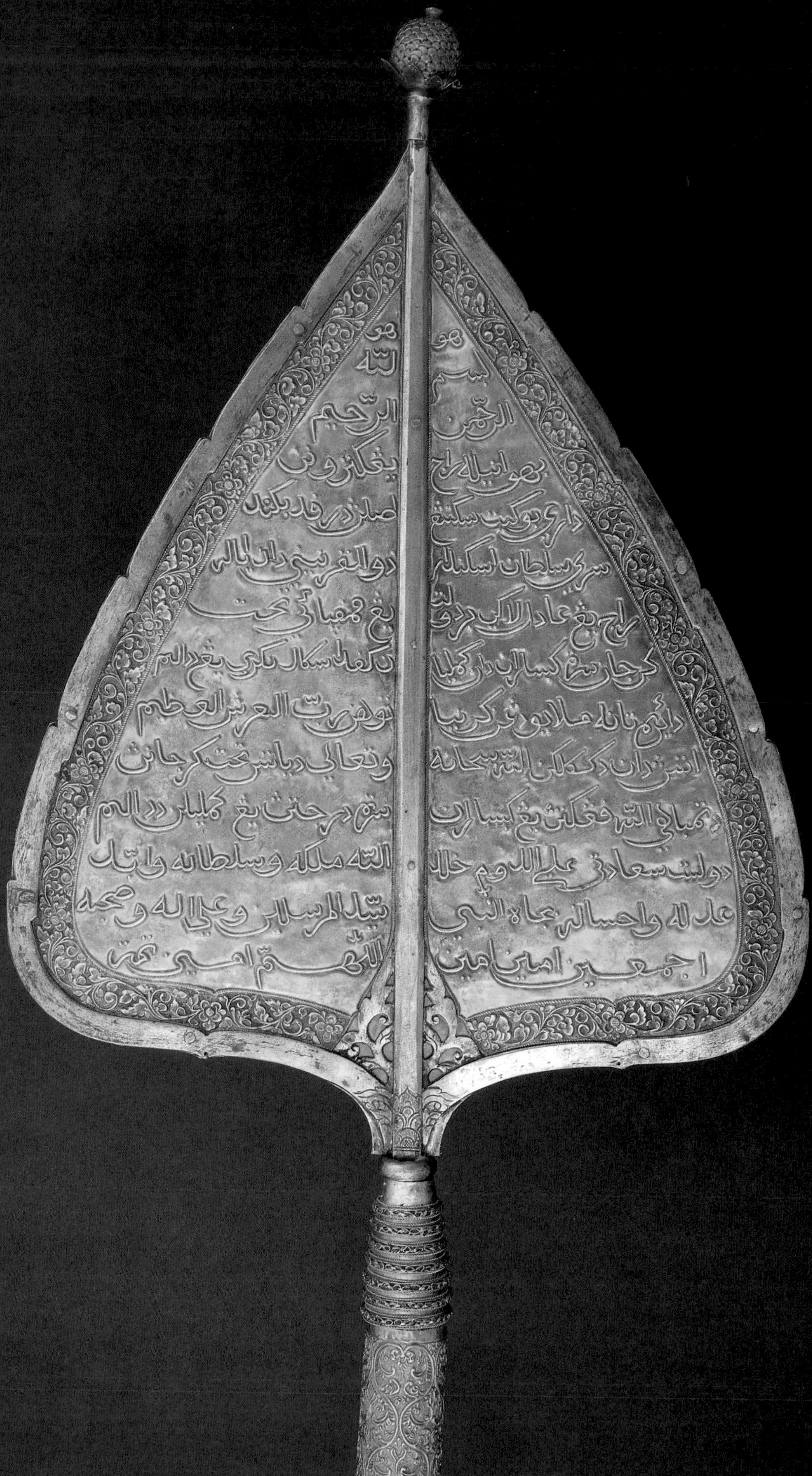
بسم الله
الرحمن الرحيم

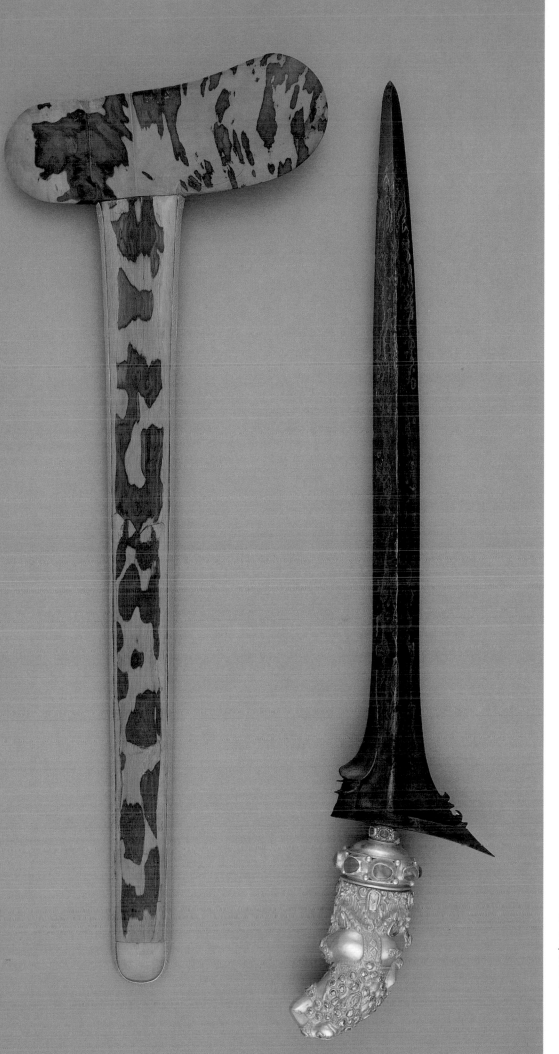

FIG. 172/NO. 136
State *kris*, early 19th
century. Gianyar Bali.
Iron, nickel *pamor*, gold,
rubies, diamonds, *pelet*
(*timaha*) wood,
63 × 19.5 × 5 cm.

Opposite:
FIG. 171/NO. 48
Jogan (**ritual fan**), 19th
century. Riau Lingga,
East Sumatra. Gold,
silver, 54.8 × 27.7 × 3 cm.

213

FIG. 174/NO. 133
Crown, 1790 or earlier. Bima, East Sumbawa. 22-carat gold stained red, diamonds, cloth lining, 17.2 × 10.5 cm.

FIG. 175/NO. 134
Crown, 18th century. Banten, West Java. Gold, rubies, diamonds, emeralds, pearls, enamel work, 16.5 × 19.3 cm.

Opposite:
FIG. 173/NO. 138
State kris, Tatarapa Sangajikai or Samparaja, 1634. Bima, East Sumbawa. Iron, nickel *pamor*, gold, diamonds, wood, silk ribbon, 50 × 14.4 × 6.1 cm.

FIG. 176
Crown, 19th century. Sumedang, West Java. Gold, approx. 25 × 25 cm. This crown is a replica of the original crown of Pajajaran, the early Sunda kingdom. Its form relates to crowns depicted on sculpture of the Hindu-Javanese period.

Opposite:
FIG. 177
Hamengkubuwono VII, Sultan of Yogyakarta, (1877–1921), ca. 1880. *Dodot* in royal *parang* design, *cindai* (trousers), *kuluk* (headdress) and *sumping* (head ornaments) all show royal rank.

FIG. 178/NO. 132
Pepadon (ceremonial seat), 19th century. Lampung, South Sumatra. Wood, 176 × 157 × 67 cm.

Java. In Java crowns are worn in the dance, but no longer by the ruler, who usually wears a slightly tapering flat-topped brimless hat like a fez, resembling the *kuluk* (FIG. 177): the gold crown of Majapahit disappeared during the 1678 attack of the rebel Madurese leader Trunajaya in Kediri. The most distinctive head adornment for the ruler in Java was the *sumping*, or earpiece (FIG. 35/NO. 65), which can be seen in Hindu-Javanese sculpture and also on *wayang* figures (such as Semar, FIG. 69/NO. 121) where it was an indicator of rank. The *sumping* also demonstrates the persistence of the mountain-form image, which it often resembles.

The throne as it is known in the West did not originally exist in Indonesia. The *pepadon* of Lampung (FIG. 178/NO. 132) was a ceremonial seat of honor for a member of the nobility, but not a throne for a ruler. In its backless version it resembles the stone ancestor seats of the Bataks and those in Nias. The usual seat of honor for a ruler in the Malay culture areas and in Sulawesi was a mat or silk cushion, or stack of cushions, often decorated at the ends with gold plaques. These were placed on a *bale*, or platform. In Bima the royal seat was a carpet elaborately embroidered with gold thread, also placed on a *bale*. In Java the king traditionally sat on a *dampar*, or low stool. The *Nagarakertagama* refers in canto 65 to a *singhasana* (lion throne) in Majapahit, but this was the seat created for a flower effigy representing the soul of the deceased queen in a *sraddha*, a posthumous ceremony held twelve years after her death.

Later, when colonial influences on the rulers, who were subsidized by the Dutch government, led to the introduction of many Western habits, thrones with

FIG. 179/NO. 143
Circumcision knife, 17th century. Java. Iron, gold, 19 × 4 cm.

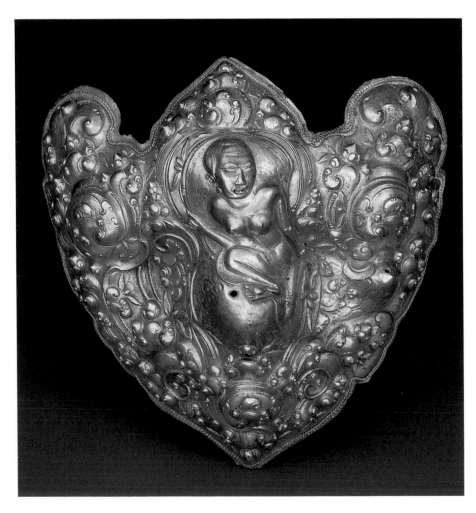

FIG. 180/NO. 142
Badong or *cupeng* (modesty plate), 14th or 15th century. Surakarta, Central Java. Gold, 15.8 × 15.6 × 5.2 cm.

backs and arms in European fashion were made. These are to be found most frequently in palaces in Sumatra and Kalimantan, though the *Kraton* Surakarta Hadiningrat had a throne that yielded a large quantity of melted gold when the disastrous fire of 1984 destroyed the ceremonial core of the palace. Although such thrones are usually sumptuously made, often of gold, they do not belong to the indigenous tradition so have no vernacular significance as symbols.

LIFE-CYCLE RITUALS

When the ruler participated in another category of ceremony, rituals connected with the life cycle, a dedicated set of objects accompanied his acts or the acts of those who performed in his name. Birth and first ground-touching ceremonies were less the province of princes than of men of religion, whether Islamic, Hindu or animist. The same thing can be said of those of marriage and death; procedures were followed in the courts, as they were among the population, in such matters as umbilicus severing and placenta preservation, ritual bathing of mother, hair-cutting of child and tooth-filing ceremonies. In Bali special crowns are worn during rites of passage ceremonies. Circumcision rites—an occasion for grand ceremonial processions in Malayan kingdoms—spawned delicately chased knives (FIG. 179/NO. 143) and clips (NO. 144) for the retention of the sarong to prevent its abrading the wound; sometimes these were gold-inlaid. In earlier centuries females wore modesty disks (*badong* or *cupeng*) to cover the pubic area. Perhaps these signified the onset of puberty or were connected with other rites of passage. For

Next page:
FIG. 183/NO. 145
Loro blonyo, 19th century. Surakarta, Central Java. Wood, pigment, fish glue medium, iron, gold, diamonds, semiprecious stones; male figure 56 × 28.5 × 27 cm, female figure 48.5 × 25.3 × 28 cm.

Left:
FIG. 181/NO. 64
Kalung (**necklace**), ca. 9th century. Gegerbitung village, Sukabumi, West Java. Gold, 30.5 × 28 × .7 cm.

Right:
FIG. 182/NO. 47
Tenong (**ceremonial stacked lacquer boxes**), 19th century. Palembang, South Sumatra. Wood, pigment, gold leaf, lacquer, 90 × 50 cm.

royal girls disks were richly modeled in gold (FIG. 180/NO. 142). An eighth- or ninth-century gold necklace (FIG. 181/NO. 64), with its mango-like yoni elements, its long spiral shells and its central phallus, may be an early fertility totem implying both male and female sexuality. In general, the court ceremonies differed not in essence but only in the elaborateness and richness of equipment from vernacular customs.

Marriage ceremonies are dominated by the bridal pair, who in most parts of Indonesia are granted the privilege of wearing princely clothing and jewelry for the occasion, whether or not they are of royal blood, and of being presented with special dowry gifts like the lacquer boxes that were present in the bridal chamber in Palembang (FIG. 182/NO. 47). The role of the ruler, therefore, is less distinct in this arena also, although his authority is implicit in the imagery. The ceremonial marriage bed (*petanen* or *kobongan*) (NO. 141) was once occupied by the bridal pair for the official consummation of the marriage, but the custom died out early in this century. During the ceremony the bridal couple sits in front of the shrine in attitudes resembling the poses of the bridal pair *loro blonyo* sculptures (FIG. 183/NO. 145), which are removed on these occasions. As another significant indication of the close relation between courtly and vernacular customs, these ceremonies do not greatly differ from court to village. Since the bridal couple is garbed like royalty, rank is not apparent; the only differences occur at the time of the exodus from the ceremony. If the bride is of higher rank than the groom, he must carry her. If they are of equal rank, they walk together with linked little fingers. The courts of Sumatra, Kalimantan and Sulawesi had marriage beds called *pel-*

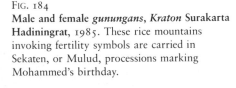

FIG. 184
Male and female *gunungans*, *Kraton* Surakarta Hadiningrat, 1985. These rice mountains invoking fertility symbols are carried in Sekaten, or Mulud, processions marking Mohammed's birthday.

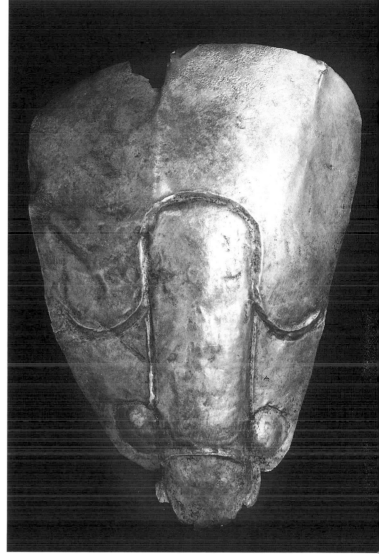

Fig. 185/no. 155a
Death mask, 11th–13th century. South Sulawesi.
Gold, 13.7 × 9.8 cm.

Fig. 186/no. 155b
Penis cover, 11th–13th century. South Sulawesi.
Gold, 10.5 × 7.3 cm.

Fig. 187/no. 147
Lelancang (**bowl for** *sajen*, **offerings**), early
19th century. Gianyar, Bali. Gold, rubies,
sapphires, ebony wood, 19.4 × 41.5 × 19 cm.

FIG. 188/NO. 148
Swamba (holy-water pot), *sasirat* (sprinkler)
and *tripada* (tripod stand), 17th century.
Gianyar, Bali. Gold, silver, rubies,
36 × 16.4 × 16 cm.

aminan (*lamming* in Sulawesi), which were hung sumptuously with gold-embroidered silks and before which ritual offerings were always placed for the spirits who inhabited the shrines.

One important annual ceremony in which the ruler participated was that of Sekaten (or Mulud), the celebration of Mohammed's birthday. In Java this ceremony still takes place. It is clearly the overlay of an indigenous rite by an Islamic one. A procession of the prince's troops, palace retainers and subjects from outlying villages accompanies a special gamelan (brought out some days earlier from the *kraton* mosque) from the *Mesjid Agung* (Great Mosque) back to the palace. Central to the procession are two large constructions, made of molded and decorated rice, called *gunungans*. One is male, one female (FIG. 184), and they are clearly fertility symbols dating from pre-Islamic times. After the reinstallation of the gamelan in the palace mosque, the *gunungans* are offered to the crowd, which eagerly seizes portions as tokens of fertility and good fortune.

Death rituals are not of great significance in Islamic cultures, so the most interesting regalia of this kind is to be found in Bali and in Tanah Toraja in Sulawesi, along with other areas where Islam has not dominated religious practice. That such rituals were once important in Java can be seen from the *Nagaraker-tagama*. Prapanca describes (in cantos 63–69) the posthumous *sraddha* ceremony for the king's grandmother, with its towerlike structures for the offering of food covered by gold and silver lids, its many-tiered viewing stands, ritual chanting of sacred texts, fire worship and the solemn progress of the lion throne accompanied by musicians playing trumpets and conches.

The elaborate cremation ceremonies of the Balinese princes are still famous today, with commoners scheduling their family members' death rites to share in the beneficence and organization of such costly events. The enormous funeral tower elaborately decorated and borne in solemn procession for great distances has formal connections with temple roofs, the importance of height and the invocation of the world mountain.

In Toraja, which is nominally Christian but where autochthonous beliefs have shaped many of the life-cycle rites, funeral ceremonies last five days and involve the participation of thousands of people in ritual presentation of buffaloes, pigs, palm wine and other gifts. Unlike the Balinese funeral, however, the Torajan funeral is not a custom whose ultimate expression depends on royal involvement. Other graves in South Sulawesi occasionally yield death masks (FIG. 185/NO. 155a) and penis covers (FIG. 186/NO. 155b), probably Sung period Chinese.

In Bali and in some areas in Sulawesi the mediation of the priest in life-cycle rituals was all-important, and the ruler's power was enhanced by the spiritual power personified in the man of religion. In Sulawesi this function was properly the province of the *bissu*, the transvestite mediums who were charged with conducting such ceremonies and guarding *pusaka*. In Bali purification ceremonies conducted by the *prohita*, the courtly temple priest, which follow cremations or precede rites to exorcise evil and gain spiritual insights, are always concerned with holy water and offerings. This has given rise to magnificent vessels (FIG. 187/NO. 147) whose richness is a tribute to the gods. The apparatus connected with priests' services is quite specialized, the ladles (NO. 151), spoons (NO. 152) and sprinklers (FIG. 188/NO. 148) made for palace temples often of exquisite workmanship. The forms of some of these attest to the antiquity of the practice, as a bronze example of the fourteenth century shows (NO. 150).

In Bali, effigies of the dead called *ukur* (measure) are made from Chinese copper or gold coins or plates strung together with wire or cord to establish the dimensions of the body. Usually these are burned with the body, but gold ones are retrieved before the cremation, as seen in an example from Lombok (FIG. 189/NO. 154). The imagery of death is most compellingly presented, however, in objects

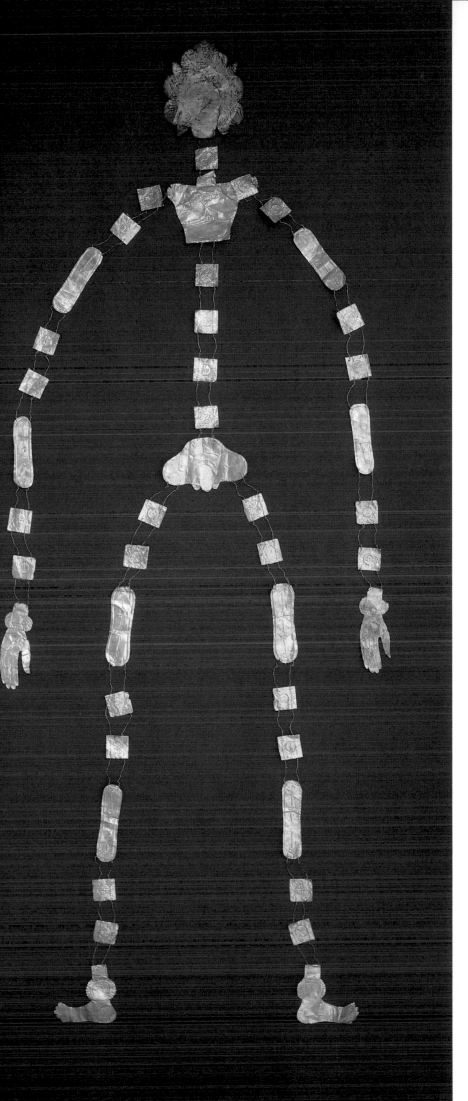

Fig. 189/no. 154
Ukur (measure of the corpse), 19th century(?).
Lombok. Gold, 136.7 × 30 × 1.5 cm.

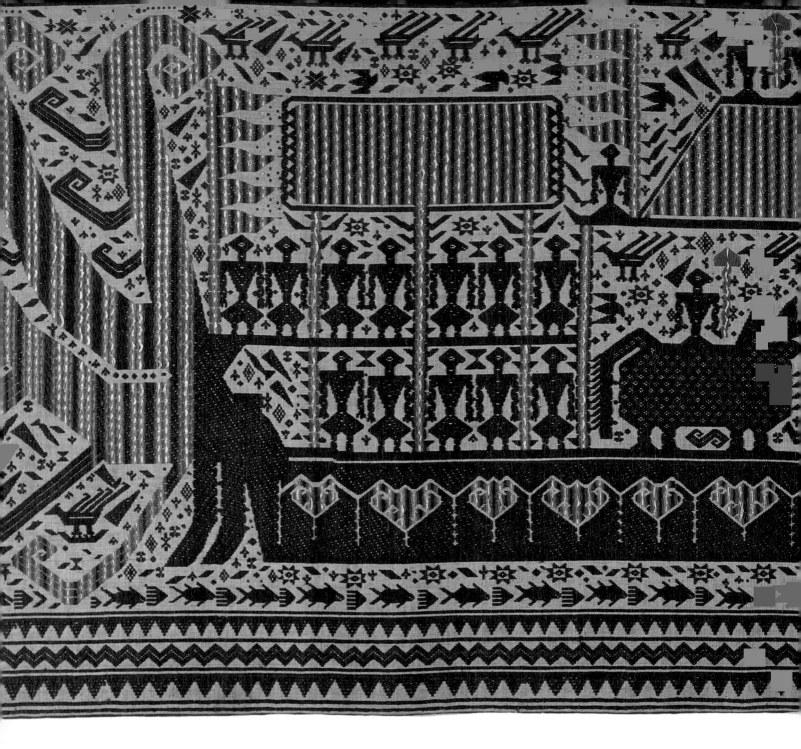

FIG. 190/NO. 157
Palepai (**ceremonial hanging**), 19th century.
Lampung, South Sumatra. Cotton,
supplementary weft, gold thread, 61 × 285 cm.

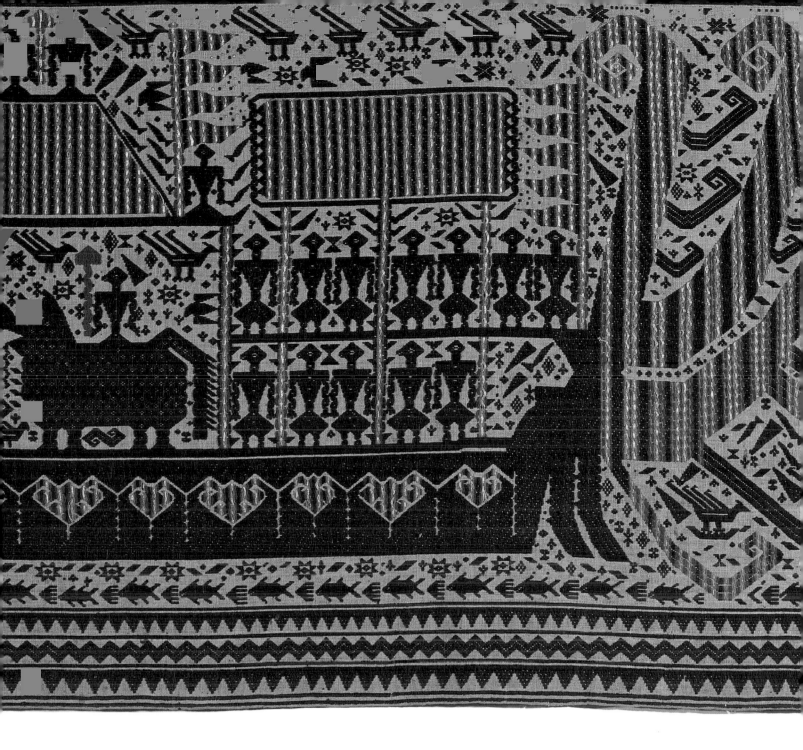

that touch on the autochthonous beliefs discussed in chapter 1. No objects later than the great funerary *candis* of Majapahit times so mysteriously hint at the life beyond than those that invoke those mythological images of the tree—the shrouds in Tanimbar have Trees of Life—and the ship. The great *palepai* of Lampung (FIGS. 45, 50, 190/NOS. 156a, 156b, 157), while portraying the life of the clan's leaders, offer potent messages of the continuity of the spirit, of the coexistence of the world of the present and the timeless world that precedes and follows it.

The autochthonous Indonesian belief in the continuum of the material and spiritual world and in the importance of its symbols is well expressed in a Karo Batak proverb:

> The *tondi* [soul] becomes *begu* [ghost],
> The hair becomes *ijuk* [palm fiber],
> The flesh becomes earth,
> The bones become stones,
> The blood becomes water
> The breath becomes wind.[45]

EPILOGUE

World Without End: The Significance of the Courts Today

Without a perspective on the future, the historical vision of the past is final and completed, and therefore false.[1]

THE INDEPENDENCE OF Indonesia was proclaimed on 17 August 1945. Since that time all previous political entities have been subsumed into the central authority of the Republic of Indonesia, with regional governors representing each province and a branching system of officials below the governors delegated to control districts and villages. The local administrative structure is not radically different from the system in effect during the later colonial period, with the all-important difference that supreme authority rests with the Indonesian government, the elected President being its highest official, that increasing numbers of other officials are also elected by popular choice, and that rank and office are no longer inherited.

At the time of the proclamation of independence, the Sultan of Yogyakarta sent a telegram ceding his territories and those of the Pakualam to the new Republic, so those courts continued to exercise considerable influence in the government. In the east of Indonesia, rulers of some of the smaller islands also continued to wield power for a few years. But by definition the power of the courts as it had survived under Dutch hegemony was no longer a central part of the political system of the independent Republic. The vitiation of many former rulers' authority inherent in the change was amplified by the nationalization of some of the territories that had belonged to them. Loss of land inevitably led to diminished revenues and reduced labor resources, and many princes lacked most of the material support for their former positions. Yet the traditional loyalties and fealties continued in many instances, particularly among older people, so that there was a tendency to downplay the possible role of the princes to avoid any political or social schism in the young nation.

In these circumstances one might have predicted the disappearance of the courts and all they stood for within a decade or so. In some cases this has proved accurate. Aceh's glory has vanished, and the royal family no longer plays even a social role. The same thing can be said for Banten and Pagarruyung. But there is a difference between these former courts, where all that remains of the original palaces are ruins, and places like Luwu and Bone, which are similarly without palace centers. Probably the underlying reason for the demise of the first group is their virtual elimination by the Dutch long before the days of Indonesian independence. Luwu, on the other hand, was devastated by resistance to both Dutch and Japanese considerably later than when the Acehnese Sultans faded from the scene; the court families were central to this resistance and therefore exerted a moral influence that remains today. Even without material glory, the former royal families have "white blood," and their traditional position is respected.

This holds true as well for areas where the palace still stands as a symbol of previous power and allegiance, even when it is no longer occupied by the princely family. Further examples are another Sulawesi court, Gowa, and the courts of Bima and Sumbawa Besar, of Kutei and Siak. In some of these cases the palace has been converted to a museum, where sometimes a member of the royal family acts as director. In this way the palace becomes part of municipal administration, and the descendants of the last ruler are the bridge between the past and present functions of the building. If the relationship can be worked out amicably, the interests of history and the conservation of culture are served with no disruption of political loyalties.

Other arrangements have followed in other areas. If the revenues and the organizing skills of the ruler continued to prove adequate for the upkeep of the palace, and if family members found satisfactory places in society, the cohesion of the family group and the continuity of the court as a center proved possible. This happened even in some small protocourts like Baun, but on the whole applied to larger centers like Pontianak and particularly to Bali and Java. As long as the former ruling family continued to live in the palace, there was a focus for some residue of old respect.

The most successful continuity has occurred where rulers were able to adapt to the changed circumstances by fitting the palace and the cultural legacy of the court into the new social structure of Indonesia. The most dramatic instance of this was the commitment of the late Sultan Hamengkubuwono IX of Yogyakarta to the cause of the revolution. In later days, inspired perhaps by the continuing example set by Yogyakarta, other rulers developed a role for their courts in a changed society. Traditional Indonesian skills of syncretism inspired some families to make their treasures available by creating museums within the palace. Letting the public at large see how the heritage of the courts related to the general cultural stream was achieved by scheduling tourist visits, training guides from the ranks of relatives and former retainers, and welcoming scholars to the libraries. Children in such progressive families were encouraged to acquire as fine an education as possible to enable them to become leaders in the new society on the basis of modern talents rather than on the old basis of inherited rights, to serve the Republic as they had once served the kingdom.

Such adaptability has ensured that the advice and protection a ruler once offered his subjects has in several courts been modified to fit the new democratic society. These days, for example, princes have become lawyers and diplomats, bankers and entrepreneurs, historians and teachers, or they have directly entered the civil service. Thus they have committed themselves to the new structures of government and made possible the continuation of their courts as social and cultural centers where their constituents can still turn for benign guidance and cultural focus. This kind of continuity can be a valuable transitional aid for people whose world is undergoing change more rapidly than a new welfare and education system or their own training can absorb. It can also be useful for a new regime: old loyalties can be attached to new ideals with as little disruption as possible.

In places where such enlightened response, or even a gradual pragmatic adjustment, has not been the norm, there is a danger that the court system may be seen as completely anachronistic and reactionary. The former subjects receive no moral or social sustenance, the former rulers do not see themselves as part of the new regime yet have neither authority nor resources to maintain the old ways, and the courts are in danger of becoming ultimately meaningless.

Apart from the obvious interest in survival on the part of the former rulers themselves, what arguments are there for the continuity of the courts' identity within the structure of the Republic of Indonesia? One of the important reasons for their relevance even in an age when they are not politically viable is the relationship of the courts to the larger society: the culture of the courts and vernacular culture are two aspects of the same mainstream. The refinements of the former have brought the latter to its highest expression and therefore are central to the cultural heritage of the nation.

The past is fused with the present identity of any person or polity. By deleting details, even those that seem to be redundant in a new frame, we reduce the round and complete three-dimensionality of history to a template. Two dimensions in the *wayang kulit* imply infinity because they are indefinable, because they hint at meanings beyond the seen limits, but the present robbed of the past is merely flat, the result of a reduction process, not an enlightenment.

Two days before his death on 21 December 1989, the inspiring humanist, intellectual and mystic Indonesian writer and teacher Soedjatmoko wrote a letter about the importance of keeping cultural traditions alive:

> In this period of major social transformation, here as well as in the world at large, there will be a need and a search for different modes of living and being [while still maintaining] a sense of cultural continuity, so essential to one's own sense of authenticity and creativity. Especially as the awareness is beginning to sink in that life on earth is non-sustainable at this high level of consumption of natural resources—irrespective of its inequity—and people begin to look for different lifestyles and values. Cultural diversity may turn out to be as important for mankind's future wellbeing as biological diversity.[2]

What role should the courts play in the Indonesia of tomorrow? Clearly, there are social obligations that some princes see as a continuing responsibility, but apart from that local commitment and any central national position to which they may be appointed, the princes of Indonesia can help their courts to continue as the guardians of cultural values. They can (and some already do) sponsor craftsmen of all kinds, carvers, musical instrument makers, puppet makers, painters, weavers and batikers, smiths and potters. They can also promote the performing arts, particularly music and the dance, by helping to maintain troupes, letting their gamelans and *pendopos* be used for rehearsals and performances, training new *dalangs* by letting their *wayang kulit* be used, offering their old textiles, puppets and jewelry as models for new creations.

All these activities are costly, as is the financial burden of maintaining historically important architecture, and while tourist visits can defray some of these expenses, much more revenue is needed. A fruitful relationship between the government and the princes, who offer incomparable resources for scholarship and tourism but who need financial support, has in many cases been reached, or will be in the future. Great care is needed to preserve the particularities and subtleties of the courts, but the effort is worthwhile. Setting the courts into the right social context is so clearly in the interests of everyone—government, princes, public and the outside world—that with time the courts could continue to make a vital contribution to the cultural heritage of Indonesia.

1a. *Tampan* (**ritual weaving**) (FIG. 46)
Lampung south coast, Sumatra, 19th century
Cotton, supplementary weft, 80 × 77.5 cm
Robert J. Holmgren and Anita E. Spertus,
no. I-132

1b. *Tampan* (**ritual weaving**) (FIG. 51)
Lampung south coast, Sumatra, 19th century
Cotton, supplementary weft, 85 × 70 cm
Robert J. Holmgren and Anita E. Spertus,
no. I-114

Tampan are ceremonial cloths used in
Lampung, South Sumatra, as seats during
rituals, covers for ritual gifts (especially
during marriages), places to lay the heads
of the dead and cappings for house-poles.
Some cloths have abstracted geometric,
vegetal, animal, ship or architectural motifs, but those from the coast, like NOS. 1a
and 1b, present specific scenes with elaborate ships carrying crew, passengers, animals and treasure cargo, the whole hung
with vegetal growths. They are set in a sea
full of marine creatures and smaller boats,
while birds fly freely in the sky. Since
weaving of this kind died out in Lampung
around 1900, the original purposes of the
cloths remain speculative. Scholars have
suggested that they depict ships of the
dead, and Holmgren and Spertus (1989)
have pointed out that imagery found on
tampans is associated with death rites in
Kalimantan. Another theory holds that the
ships are vessels bringing ancestor figures
from the Upperworld to earth. Holmgren
and Spertus believe that the ships symbolize organized communities where the
world of the ruler is depicted as a paradigm of prosperity. FIG. 46/NO. 1a shows a
couple, seemingly male and child or female, in a small pavilion, which resembles
the shrine in the center of the *gunungan*
(mountain form) of the *wayang kulit*, on
the left of the upper deck. The male and
the flanking figures outside (carrying
boxes, umbrellas and pennants) wear
krises (ceremonial daggers) and garments
resembling the aristocratic draped *dodot*
of Java (FIG. 103/NO. 74); Lampung was
under the hegemony of Banten for several
hundred years so Javanese influence is possible. The presence of a peacock and two
elephants, animals of prestige and rank,
on the lower level indicates that this is a
courtly scene.

Umbrellas of rank appear also in
NO. 1b, where a central pavilion shelters
five figures, one of whom again appears to
be a child. Below, two antlered creatures
face a Tree of Life. Crew members are
shown steering, keeping watch and manning the rigging. The treelike branching
growth attached to the masts—three in
both NOS. 1a and 1b—occurs to Holmgren
and Spertus as similar to the *sanggaran* of

Kalimantan, structures indicating places of
living sacrifice, which would be consistent
with the association of *tampan* with death
ships. They also consider that the imagery
of shipcloths combines Indic realism with
the stylized geometric and natural motifs
characteristic of Central Asian art; the latter might, they suggest, have been introduced by mainland Buddhist pilgrims
during the Dongson era (FIG. 44) or might
have arrived with the Austronesian
peoples.

Tampan are not only tours de force of
weaving but also remarkably dramatic
and iconic representations of lifelike
scenes. Their asymmetry lends spontaneity
without upsetting equilibrium, while the
crisp contrast of a small range of colors
invokes the symbolism of the shadows of
the *wayang kulit*. The feeling of allegory
is strong, the compression of the scene
having a genre character reinforcing the
mythological allusions to the world of the
ancestors and the journey of the soul from
one realm to the next.
Literature: Gittinger 1979:88–97; Holmgren
and Spertus 1989:72–85.

Wayang kulit
See FIG. 1/NO. 107, FIG. 9/NO. 31, FIG. 20/NO.
114, FIG. 33/NO.108, FIG. 37/NO. 2, FIG. 56/NO.
115, FIG. 57/NO. 109, FIG. 69/NO. 121, FIG.
145/NO. 118, FIG. 146/NO. 110, FIG. 147, FIG.
148/NOS. 119, 120, FIG. 149/NO. 116, FIG. 150,
NO. 111, NO. 112, NO. 113, NO. 117

The making of *wayang kulit*, or shadow
puppets, is a long and painstaking process. Skin of a female buffalo of about
four years of age, the ideal type for tex-
ture and strength, is dried, scraped and
cured for up to ten years to achieve stiff-
ness and eliminate warping and splitting.
On maturity, the skins are carved and
pierced to fashion the required character.
This technique involves extensive knowledge of iconography and physiognomy,
since all lines—angles of the head, slant of
eyes and mouth, profile of the body—are
specific to the character.

When carving is completed the figures
are painted, the traditional pigments including powdered burnt bone for white,
lampblack, indigo, yellow ochre and cin-
nabar for red in a gelatinous medium
mixed from dried egg-white. Gold leaf and
pigment are applied in a medium of protein glue derived from fish bones. The
cempurit, or manipulating rods, are made
of buffalo horn, while the studs attaching
the jointed arms to the torso are of metal
(sometimes gold), bone, bamboo or, in
rare courtly examples, gold studded with
diamonds (FIG. 147).

The history and role of *wayang kulit* in Javanese literature and society are described in chapter 4.

Literature: Kats (1923) 1984; Anderson 1965; Guritno et al. 1984; Keeler 1987.

2. *Wayang kulit*, shadow puppet, *gunungan* (FIG. 37)

Cirebon, West Java, 19th century
Buffalo hide, horn, pigment, fish-glue medium, gold leaf, 102.6 × 40.2 × 2.3 cm
Kraton Kasepuhan, Cirebon

The *gunungan* (mountain form), or *kayon* (Javanese; *kekayon*, tree form, in Bahasa Indonesia) is one of the most ambiguously symbolic pieces in the *wayang kulit* pantheon. It is placed in the center of the screen before the drama begins, separating the opposed groups of *wayang* characters that lie to right and left of the *dalang* (the puppeteer). Its mountain image implies the cosmic mountain; its tree manifestation refers to the Tree of Life (see chapter 1). Both authochthonous and Indic traditions see the tree as a link between Upper and Underworlds. For the Batak in Sumatra the tree represents the totality of the universe. For the Dayak in Kalimantan the Ngayu, their Tree of Life, has a serpent (*naga*) representing the Underworld in the lower of its two horizontal branches and a hornbill representing the Upperworld in the higher branches.

In Indic terms the tree on the *kayon* is usually considered to be the *nagasari* tree, which is also seen on the Hindu-Buddhist religious monuments of the eighth and ninth centuries in Central Java. The meditation undertaken by the *dalang* before a *wayang kulit* performance seeks a train of associations leading from the gods of the Hindu pantheon to the *kayon*. In the *gunungan*/*kayon* the tree is rooted centrally, its trunk a central vertical line, its branches inclining equally to left and right, thus showing the mutual sources of the opposed left and right groups in the drama's cast of characters.

In some *gunungans* there are pavilions with closed doors and apposed animals. In others there are pools (see FIG. 1/NO. 107). This Cirebon example, however, is almost exclusively a forest scene. A pair of high mountains lies behind small foothills outlined in *wadasan* (rock) form typical of the Chinese motifs that pervade *pasisir* (coastal) style. The hills are flanked by *lar*, or *garuda* (mythical bird) wings, a royal motif. The trunk of the tree curves sinuously up the *wayang*, two pairs of asymmetrical branches incline down, and the whole is seen through a delicate tracery of twigs and leaves. So graceful and luxu-

riant is the tree that it brings to mind a Paradise Tree dropping blessings on all who pass beneath it, an apt image to suggest the idyllic world of the kingdoms of the *wayang lakons* (plays) before the activities of men and supernatural beings upset the ideal balance.

3. *Mamuli*, ear pendant (FIG. 34)

East Sumba, possibly royal house of Kanatangu, 19th century
Gold, 12 × 10 cm
Australian National Gallery, Canberra, inv. no. 1984.255

Mamuli were part of the sacred heirlooms (*pusaka*) of noble families on Sumba and as metal objects played a masculine role in the exchanges effected at marriage rituals (textiles played the corresponding feminine role). *Mamuli* were kept in secret places, had links with ancestor spirits, and because of their potentially harmful supernatural powers were seldom brought into view. They were also sometimes buried with the corpse of the deceased and thus have connections with death rites.

Notwithstanding the male ritual significance of the *mamuli*, its yoni-like shape also suggests female sexuality as part of its ambiguous form. The mountain, sacred symbol of ancestor origin and the place of the spirit of the gods, is implicit in the form as well. Another meaning is suggested by the central line with its surrounding of delicate spiral meanders, the fissure resembling the trunk of the *wayang gunungan* connecting the Upperworld with the Underworld and suggesting the interpenetration of matter and void. The lower world or the sea can be inferred from the separation of the main body of the *mamuli* from its setting by a curving base that can be read as the form of a ship hull. The whole can thus perhaps be interpreted as a multiple image of earth, in the form of the mountain, air above the tree, and water and the Underworld below it. Mythologically the tree, with its implications of the Tree of Life, links all three regions. Such symbolism is appropriate for objects connected with rites of passage.

The two warriors standing on the base wear high frontal headdresses typical of the region, where vertical gold strips (or feathers) affixed to diadem bands serve as ritual regalia. They carry round bossed shields (FIG. 66/NO. 26) and lances (FIG. 7/NOS. 11, 12, FIG. 168/NO. 10) in their articulated arms. *Mamuli* were made in Sumba, but whether such exquisite workmanship as this one displays was commissioned from elsewhere or from specialist smiths, possibly Chinese, is not known.

Literature: Rodgers 1986:165–95; Holmgren and Spertus 1989:32–33.

Kris

See FIG. 2/NO. 69, FIG. 49/NO. 4, FIG. 52/NO. 67, FIG. 53/NO. 71, FIG. 64/NO. 22, FIG. 65/NO. 23, FIG. 119, FIG. 120/NO. 72, FIG. 121/NO. 73, FIG. 122, FIG. 157/NO. 66b, FIG. 172/NO. 136, FIG. 173/NO. 138, NO. 68, NO. 70, NO. 137

The history and philosophy of the *kris* deserve and have stimulated several dedicated studies. With its implications of potency the *kris* occupies a unique position in Indonesian philosophy and society (see chapter 4). Many *pusaka kris* are reputed to have the power to warn their owners of impending disaster. One such *kris* is said to have rattled violently the evening before a family crisis. The spiritual qualities of a *kris* account for its importance in royal *pusaka* collections and in the estimation of Indonesians, but the technical sophistication and artistic imagination that coalesce in its form can be appreciated at a different level.

The complex forging technique requires nickel or nickeliferous meteoritic iron to be beaten into iron in intricately controlled laminations; the material, the technique and the patterns produced are all referred to as *pamor*. After forging and tempering (a ceremony preceded by solemn offerings), the blade can be patinated with a mixture of lime juice and arsenicum to reveal the *pamor* pattern. Each part of the blade, each curve and projection, each indentation and line, has its proper name. This is also true of the sheath, the hilt and all their parts. The subtleties of meaning and style are almost infinite, but for general understanding the viewer should keep a few parts and characteristics in mind.

The blade (*wilah*) and its crosspiece (*ganja*) offer many profiles, from straight (FIG. 52/NO. 67) to multicurved (NO. 68) and *pamor* patterns, from simple striations (FIG. 52/NO. 67) to elaborately detailed emblems (FIG. 121/NO. 73). On the *ganja* solid gold is sometimes carved into delicate images of elephants, tigers, *kala* (monster) heads and floral patterns, or into snakes plated or inlaid with gold (NO. 68), while the blade may be covered with a continuous gold-scaled snake body (FIG. 2/NO. 69).

The grip (*ukiran*) may be fashioned from any of several materials: polished wood (NO. 68), ivory (NO. 70) or gold studded with jewels (FIG. 120/NO. 72). It can be abstracted (NO. 68) or figurative (FIG. 120/NO. 72). The junction of grip and crosspiece is protected by a metal collar (*selut*) encircling the lower part of the grip (NO. 67) or by a ring (*mendak*) covering the transition between crosspiece and

235

sheath, where the tang (*pesi*) projects from the blade through the crosspiece into the sheath (FIG. 53/NO. 71), or often by both (FIG. 2/NO. 69).

The sheath, which like the grip must be fashioned with the character of the blade in mind, can be of wood only (FIG. 172/NO. 136) or have an oversheath (*pendok*) of lacquer (FIG. 52/NO. 67) or metal, sometimes gilded brass or silver, sometimes gold (FIG. 53/NO. 71) or gold studded with gems (NO. 70). Its shape can be elaborately flanged in formal style (*ladrang*) (NO. 70), simpler and more compact (*gayaman*) (FIG. 52/NO. 67) or fashioned to cover the blade only with no projecting upper portion (*sandang walikat*) (FIG. 65/NO. 23).

The assembly of the parts is the responsibility of the sheathmaker, and the *kris*'s perfection is achieved in the eyes of the initiated only when every element in the ensemble is compatible with all the others. Sometimes a new owner (traditionally a *kris* should not be bought, but given or inherited) will make a new sheath or grip, so probably few blades, which are more durable, are today assembled with their original sheath and grip.

Literature: Rassers (1940) 1982; Hamzuri (1973) 1983; G. and B. Solyom 1978.

---

4. *Kris* (FIG. 49)

Surakarta, Central Java, late 19th century
Iron, nickel alloy, gold; grip: sandalwood; sheath: teak wood (*simbar jati*, branching teak), 44 × 15 × 3.7 cm
K.R.T. Hardjonagoro

This *kris* in the form of a Tree of Life was directly inspired by the *gunungan/kayon* figure in the *wayang kulit* drama (FIG. 37/NO. 2). In similar style to the *gunungan*, four pairs of birds sit on the downward-trailing branches, and the trunk is surmounted by a fan-shaped peacock with spread tail. *Krises* with Tree of Life motif were made to protect the world; the general invocation of the life force is reinforced here by the tree depicted, which is the *waringin*, the sheltering *kalpataru* or banyan tree of Buddhist philosophy. Other *krises* exist with a tree in relief on the blade, but the carved *karawang* (openwork) form of this one is unique. There are a few examples of old *krises* with a split in the center, once thought to be a flaw, but later considered deliberate, offering a view of the world beyond and linked with predicting the future. The blade's *pamor* is invisible. The *empu* (smith), from the reign of Pakubuwono X, is unknown. This *kris* is for ritual use; it is too wide and too short to be worn. (Information supplied by K.R.T. Hardjonagoro.)

5. Plaque (FIG. 30)

Desa Majasari, Purbolinggo, Banyumas, Central Java, 9th century
18-carat gold; frame: silver or zinc and copper alloy, 20 × 12.4 × 2 cm
Museum Nasional, Jakarta, inv. no. A29, found 1904 and noted by the Resident of Banyumas

This plaque depicting paired male and female standing figures is repoussé work. The large, long-stalked lotus held in the left hand of the male figure, the piled-curl headdresses and the tranquil simplicity of the piece identify it as Buddhistic; it is perhaps a votive plaque. Stylistically, the richly brocaded draped cloth of the male shows Indian influence (compare the Siva and Parvati sculptures, Museum Nasional inv. no. 519, illustrated in Fontein, Soekmono and Suleiman 1971). The richness of the jewelry suggests a royal pair: note the earrings, necklace and belt of the female and the caste-cord and lower- and upper-arm bracelets of both (compare NO. 95). Since their heads are encircled by an aureole and they stand under the protection of the lotus-umbrella, the connotation of Buddhist spiritual power, often unorthodoxically interpreted in kingly terms in Indonesia, is also present. The plaque may therefore be interpreted as possibly a god-king piece, though there is no indication that portraiture is involved. East Javanese examples of Hindu god-king sculptures are relatively well known (FIG. 31/NO. 6 and FIG. 32), but Buddhistic ones and specimens from the Central Javanese period are rare. The naturalism of the sculpting is typical of the early Central Java style and may be compared with the bas-reliefs on Borobudur.

Literature: *Notulen van de Algemeene en Bestuursvergaderingen van het Bataviaasch Genootschap van Kunstennen Wetenschappen* 1904; Fontein, Soekmono and Suleiman 1971:122.

6. God-king sculpture (FIG. 31)

East Java, ca. 1260
Andesite, 123 cm
Royal Tropical Institute, Tropenmuseum, Amsterdam, inv. no. A5950

This statue, identifiable as Siva from the fly whisk and rosary in the upper pair of arms, is probably from *candi* Kidal, the mortuary temple consecrated to Anusapati, second king of Singasari and stepson of the first, Ken Angrok, whom he murdered. Since Anusapati died in 1248 and since *sraddha* rites (the ceremony dedicating dead monarchs' temples) were held twelve years after death, the temple and this sculpture, whose iconic expression is consistent with a posthumous portrait, were presumably completed around 1260.

East Javanese monarchs were usually

portrayed as gods in such posthumous statues (see chapter 1). A similar example from about 1300 (FIG. 32) shows Kerterajasa, first king of Majapahit, as Vishnu; the beautiful thirteenth-century Prajnaparamita statue from *candi* Singasari (see Fontein et al. 1990, no. 24) is thought to be a portrait of Ken Dedes, mother of Anusapati and wife of Ken Angrok. Anusapati's front arms' *mudra* shows liberation from the cycle of rebirth (compare the eleventh-century mortuary statue of King Airlangga as Vishnu [Holt 1967:pl.51], and the subsidiary figures flanking Kerterajasa). Note the similarities between the king's crown and the crown of Sumedang (FIG. 176) and the sumptuousness of the textiles (compare FIG. 13/NO. 82) and jewelry, which also adorns the feet of the god-king.

Literature: Holt 1967: pl. 51; Van Brakel et al. 1987:100; Fontein et al. 1990: no. 24.

7. Letter in *lontar* form (FIG. 4)

Badung or Mengwi, Bali, 1768
Gold-copper alloy, 24 × 5.5 cm
The British Library, Oriental Collections, by permission of The British Library Board, London, inv. no. Egerton 765

This letter (written in Javanese-influenced Balinese) was sent by Kandjeng Kjai Angroerah Djambe of Badung and his fellow prince Kyai Angroerah Agoeng of Mengwi to Johannes Vos, the Governor and Director of the Vereenigde Oost-Indische Compagnie's (United East Indies Company, or VOC) northeast coast region of Java, in Semarang. It is inscribed on both sides, six lines of script on the front and five lines on the back. The size and shape of the letter conform to the proportions of the pages of Balinese manuscripts, called *lontar* (palm leaf) (see FIG. 158/NO. 96, NOS. 97, 98). This letter was acquired by the British Museum in 1839. The text states that the two senders, princes of Badung and Mengwi, acknowledge the letter of Governor Vos of Semarang and that they endorse his belief in the eternal friendship between the VOC and their states. They express anxiety over the possibility, inferred from Vos's letter, that any threat to this friendship might arise, and they declare that their territories have not been visited by the two East Javanese from Lamajang and Malang cited by Vos. They state that should these men appear, they will conform to the will of the VOC, passing on a rumor that one of the two has been seen in the territory of Karangasem. Finally, they acknowledge the receipt of two barrels of liqueur and some clothing from the Governor and announce that in return, in token of friendship, they are sending the Governor two slaves in the charge of two trusted associates.

The text was transcribed and translated into Dutch by J. Kats, who further investigated the matter by searching Dutch records. A 1765 letter to Vos from his departing predecessor warns of the interference of the Balinese in the often turbulent eastern areas of Java, where rebellious princes can always find "hiding nests" to carry out their "evil designs" (Kats [trans.] 1929:293). The Balinese, who have exerted ever-stronger influence in the Eastern Salient region, are suspected of aiding the escape to Bali of several instigators of uprisings against the VOC.

Presumably with this warning in mind, Vos wrote in October 1768 to the two Balinese princes named as the authors of the gold *lontar* letter. He praises their commitment to peace and friendship with the VOC and also their return of bounty seized by the princes from a shipwreck in the Mengwi district; such bounty capture was to remain a cause of friction between the Company and the Balinese. He goes on to demand their neutrality in matters concerning Java and their promise not to aid the Company's enemies or allow anyone from Java to enter their territories without an official pass from the Company. He concludes by announcing the dispatch of liqueur and clothing as gifts to the princes.

The gold *lontar* is clearly a reply to Vos's letter. An interesting footnote to the accuracy of political reporting can be read in a further exchange of letters between Vos and the Governor-General of the VOC, Van der Parra, in December 1768. The Balinese letter arrived on 21 December; on 24 December Vos wrote the Governor-General stating that the princes had promised "not to allow any traffic between Balemboangan and Bali." This distortion of what the princes had actually promised was consolidated by Van der Parra's letter to Vos on 31 December, in which he confirmed the princes' commitment to admitting nobody without permission from the Company. It is not hard to see why VOC relations with Indonesians were marred by accusations of broken promises and bad faith on both sides.

The princes' use of a precious metal rather than normal palm-leaf or European or Chinese paper for their letter shows both the cult of magnificence for the establishment of status, which Clifford Geertz (1980:13) has characterized as "power serving pomp," and the awareness that placating the VOC (though as the letter shows, not necessarily obeying it) was of great importance.

Literature: Kats (trans.) 1929, vol. 1:291–96; Geertz 1980.

8. Drawing of a river scene with *naga*-head boat (FIG. 42)

Java, 1811–13
Watercolor on paper, 50.8 × 30.5 cm
The British Library, India Office Library and Records, by permission of The British Library Board, London, WD 953, f.75(86)

The British commissioned many drawings during their governance of Java (1811–16), which was based on an agreement reached in the eighteenth century by the Dutch and the British about the balance of power in the Indonesian-Malay area and which was invoked, though not without fierce resistance from local Dutch forces, to protect Dutch overseas interests from the power of the French. Among the collectors were Thomas Stamford Raffles, who was the head of the British administration as lieutenant-governor, Colin Mackenzie, an officer in the British East India Company army, and Hermanus Christiaan Cornelius, formerly an engineer in the VOC marine and later employed by the British as surveyor of buildings in Central Java. Mackenzie and the others commissioned several draftsmen to draw and paint archaeological, social and topographic scenes. Some of these draftsmen were Indonesian, some Dutch, like Jacobus Flikkenschild, and some British, like John Newman, who was the artist of this river scene, part of a collection of 116 drawings made in Java under Mackenzie's supervision.

Both artistic quality and accuracy of observation of vegetation, dress and topographic detail in the work commissioned for Europeans varies from drawing to drawing. This skillfully painted example has a pleasing composition, avoids the sometimes banal rendition of tropical landscape and seems for the most part to offer reasonably authentic renditions of palm trees, mountains, conical hats, and canoes and their occupants. Its depiction of the boat with *naga*-head (snake) prow and sweeping *naga*-tail stern conforms with existing heads (FIG. 41/NO. 9). The drawing can therefore be taken as evidence that in the early nineteenth century such spectacular vessels were still in active use by princes, who were sheltered from the common gaze by screens hung around the boat's pavilion superstructure. The snake has mythological importance in Indonesia, being associated with many legends of origin and held to be ruler of water and thus connected to fertility (see chapter 1).

Literature: Archer 1969, vol. 2:446–65, 472–552; Archer and Bastin 1978.

9. Boat head in *naga* form (FIG. 41)

Surakarta, Central Java, 19th century(?)
Teak wood, painted and gilded, 78 × 30 × 71 cm
Kraton Surakarta Hadiningrat, inv. no. A781

This *naga* is linked to the same snake iconography mentioned for FIG. 42/NO. 8. The strongly detailed carving and the crown on the head mark it as a *kraton* (court) piece that, mounted on the prow of a royal boat, could well have inspired the wonder of the poet describing the boat of the King of Tallo in South Sulawesi (chapter 1). The crown resembles the dance crowns still worn in Bali and Java (FIG. 134/NO. 93). The rear-facing head carved from the back of the *naga*'s head is a *garuda mungkur*, the mythical bird *garuda* looking backward, placed at the rear of headdresses and crowns (NO. 92) as a protective talisman.

10a, b. Pair of *tombaks* (FIG. 168)

Bima, East Sumbawa, formerly state weapons of the Sultanate of Bima, possibly made in South Sulawesi, early 17th century
Head and sheath: gold, iron, nickel *pamor*, silver or zinc; shaft: *sawo* wood;
204 × 4.2 × 3 cm
Kabupaten Bima, East Sumbawa

Tombaks, spears or lances used for both fighting and ceremony, are prominent in collections of court *pusaka* weapons and are often shown in the *dalem* (inner sanctum) of the palace in specially constructed stands. This pair once flanked the ruler of Bima on formal occasions. The iron tip has nickel *pamor* and is inlaid with gold. This technique was known in Sulawesi as well as Java, and the diapering on the gold shaft cover is consistent with Sulawesi style and workmanship. The lower end is sheathed in a silver-white metal that may be zinc or a low silver alloy. Bima, which had always struggled for independence, was too favorably placed on the main eastern trade routes to escape the attention of larger powers. Early in the seventeenth century the Sulawesi kingdom of Makassar, newly converted to Islam, subjugated Bima and converted it to Islam as well; the dating of a Sulawesi-made *tombak* to that period is therefore appropriate historically as well as stylistically.

The residual red stain on the gold is characteristic of Bima treasures (FIG. 173/NO. 138, FIG. 174/NO. 133) and is also occasionally found on Riau objects (FIG. 123/NO. 43). It is obtained by heating sulphur, acid and salt together and dipping the gold object into the solution on strings made from palm leaf strips. If there is an admixture of silver in the gold, the color will not last well. To gain a more lasting color in this case, a brew of saltpeter, the sap of the purple tuber of a white-flowered wild orchid and salt is used. For pure gold, potash combined with "*air keras untuk emas*" (literally "strong liquid for gold," possibly mercury or a strong acid solution) will produce a rapid result. (Recipes provided by Bapak Massir Q. Abdullah, head of the museum service of Bima and a descendant of the noble *Raja Bicara* [prime minister] family.)

11. *Tombak* (FIG. 7)

Yogyakarta, Central Java, 17th century
Head: gold, iron, nickel *pamor*, silver or zinc; shaft: *timaha* wood; 277.6 × 5.7 (shaft 3.3) cm
Museum Nasional, Jakarta, inv. no. 1658

This lance came from *Raden Tumenggung* Merto Negoro, an aristocratic source that may account for its ascription as a *pusaka*. The exquisitely fashioned snake that supports the blade resembles the *naga* that is often found on royal *krises* (NOS. 68, 70). The gold inlay work is typical of Central Javanese smiths' skills. Such lances were clearly intended more for ceremonial display than for military use.

12. *Tombak* (FIG. 7)

Bone, South Sulawesi, 1872
Head: gold, silver, iron, nickel *pamor*; shaft: wood; 244.4 × 3.1 (shaft 2.4) cm
Museum Nasional, Jakarta, inv. no. 16966

This *tombak* was presented to "Goerinda Daeng Malala from Tanralili" by the Netherlands government for services rendered on 25 November 1872 during the attack on the reinforcements of the rebel "Karaeng Bontobonto in Barabatoewa." The text is inscribed around the gold casing of the lance shaft. Below it, on a silver casing, the text is written in Bugis script. The precedents for Dutch use of Indonesians in regional disputes are well documented. One of the most famous examples is their reliance on Arung Palakka of Bone to curb the power of the Sultan of Makassar in 1666, thus making their own use of a regional rivalry between the two powerful South Sulawesi states. It should be added that Arung Palakka gained great power and prestige from the victories won with VOC help. The episode commemorated on this lance seems to have a similar background, but no record is so far available to document what advantage, if any, accrued to Daeng Malala.

13. *Tombak* (FIG. 8)

Central Java, 17th century
Head: gold, silver, iron, nickel *pamor*; shaft: wood; 226 cm
Rijksmuseum voor Volkenkunde, Leiden, inv. no. 704-15

The *cakra* motif, usually associated with the sun and with Visnu, one of whose attributes it is, crowns the unusually thick and heavy shaft of this lance. This symbol invokes Hindu religious references but has been absorbed into Indonesian imagery of power and probably, given its likely Mataram date, does not have a specifically religious reference. The weapon was acquired with a group of others (see FIG. 8/NO. 14) in 1889 from an auction house.

14. *Tombak* (FIG. 8)

Central Java, 17th century
Head: gold, diamond, iron, nickel *pamor*; shaft: wood; 230 cm
Rijksmuseum voor Volkenkunde, Leiden, inv. no. 704-13

Acquired in a group with FIG. 8/NO. 13, this lance is decorated on the lower part of the blade with a cock with diamond eye intricately inlaid in gold. The cock, symbol of courage in the ritual *upacara* regalia of Central Javanese *kratons*, is an apt image to project in a ceremonial weapon.

15. *Tombak*

Siak Sri Indrapura, Riau Lingga, Sumatra, 18th century(?)
Head: silver, iron, nickel *pamor*, silk; shaft: wood; approx. 200 × 20 cm
Istana Siak Sri Indrapura

This ceremonial lance, one of the *pusaka* of the Siak palace, is most notable for its sheath. It bears twin snakes leaning against a Tree of Life, a symbol of fertility

and power for the dynasty, whose first ruler was Raja Kecil, Sultan Abdul Jalil Rakhmadsyah (1723–46). The sinuous decorations are in marked contrast to the more severe and restrained decorations on Javanese and Sulawesi *tombaks* and might have been the work of smiths from Palembang, a noted center for exuberant metal craft.

16. *Trisula* (three-pronged) lance head (FIG. 48)

Central Java, 17th century
Gold, iron, nickel *pamor*, 52.5 cm
Royal Tropical Institute, Tropenmuseum, Amsterdam, inv. no. 1698/464

This richly inlaid three-pointed lance-head comes from the Wurfbain collection. The thirteen *luk* (curves) of the central prong indicate the high prestige of this weapon, while the central vegetal meander on all three prongs suggests the Tree of Life, especially in conjunction with the central *tumpal* motif, which here also resembles the *gunungan* motif seen at the base of the Tree of Life on the *wayang kayon* (see FIG. 37/NO. 2).
Literature: Jasper and Mas Pirngadie 1912–27; Les Iles des Dieux 1956–57: no. 4/15.

17. *Tombak* head (FIG. 54)

Central Java, 17th century
Gold, silver, iron, nickel *pamor*, 64.5 cm
Royal Tropical Institute, Tropenmuseum, Amsterdam, inv. no. 1698/463

This lancehead has a similar provenance to FIG. 48/NO. 16. Clearly a piece of great iconographic importance, it invokes the image of Semar, one of the Panakawan servant-clown characters who attend the Pandawa princes in the Bratayudha *wayang* cycle. Semar is an ambiguous figure, since some legends see him as one of the pre-Indic gods and some as the brother of Batara Guru, a manifestation of Siva (see chapter 4), as well as the wise leader of the Panakawans. Semar's high status is shown by his draped dress, an aristocratic preserve as is his *sumping* (head ornament) (FIG. 35/NO. 65). To invoke Semar's presence is to draw on a mythical source of protection, so this lance must have had great ritual significance. Note the raised central rib of the blade, which resembles the central horn support of *wayang* puppets, and compare its silhouette with that of the *gunungan/kayon* figure (see FIG. 1/NO. 107, FIG. 37/NO. 2).
Literature: Jasper and Mas Pirngadie 1912–27; *Indonesian Art* 1948: no. 658; *Art Indonésien* 1952–53: no. 188.

18. *Dwisula* (two-pronged) lance head
(FIG. 63)

Central Java, 17th century
Silver, iron, nickel *pamor*, 42.5 × 11.5 × 3.5 cm
Samuel Eilenberg

The simplicity and lack of gold ornament of this blade suggest that it was used as a weapon rather than in ceremony. But the high quality of its intricately embossed and chased sheath with exuberant curvilinear floral motifs indicates that the weapon was held in esteem. For an Indonesian the quality of the forging of a weapon, the form of the blade and the character of the *pamor* design are more important than the value of the materials or the artistic elements of the sheath. The value of this *dwisula*, therefore, resides as much in the fine forging as in the silversmith's artistry.

19. Manuscript on weapons and umbrellas of rank (FIG. 161)

Central Java, 1815
Paper, leather, ink, watercolor, gold leaf,
26 × 20.5 × 1.5 cm
The House of Orange-Nassau Historic Collections Trust, The Hague, L. 1102

Manuscripts such as these are found in most of the palace libraries in Java and also in public and private collections. This example was a gift to King Willem III (1817–90) of the Netherlands. Such manuscripts are interesting as indications not only of style, but of hierarchy; specific forms and colors of umbrella, for example, are permitted only to certain ranks. Many older manuscripts kept in Indonesia have deteriorated greatly because of heat, humidity and tropical pests. The pristine condition of this one, kept in more temperate conditions in the Netherlands, gives the viewer a rare chance to appreciate the artist's skills.

20. *Parang* (sword) La Teya Riduni

Bone, South Sulawesi, once part of the regalia of the Sultan of Bone, 17th century
Gold, diamond, iron, nickel *pamor*, wood (sheath lining), 74 × 11 × 3 cm
Kabupaten Watampone, South Sulawesi

Pusaka weapons belonging to a *kraton*, such as cannons, *krises* and swords, frequently had their own names. The name of this sword means "will not die" in the Bugis language and has some ambiguity: it can refer to the protection offered to the bearer or to the sword itself. Traditionally it is said that the *parang* should be buried with the ruler, but on the third day it will rise again from the earth. The flat-bottomed sheath with its gold wire wrap-

ping is characteristic of Bugis weapons, as is the double loop of twisted gold, made to resemble cord and originally used for hanging the sword on the belt. The imagery probably derives from the binding of split rattan and the cords of palm fiber or grasses found on vernacular weapons.
Not in exhibition. Not illustrated.

21. *Parang* (sword)

Sumbawa Besar, West Sumbawa, reign of Sultan Amrullah (1836–82)
Gold, diamond, iron, nickel *pamor*; sheath and grip: wood, 75 cm
Family of the last Sultan of Semawa, Sultan Muhamad Kaharuddin III (1931–58)

The goldwork on this *parang* was made by the goldsmith Palima Sape during the long and prosperous reign of Sultan Amrullah, when many other regalia items were produced (NO. 49). Like Bima to the east, the dynasty of Semawa in western

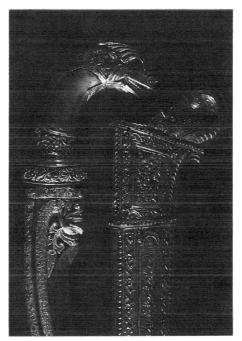

Sumbawa profited from the trading routes between the east and the main India-China shipping patterns. It, too, was influenced politically, socially and stylistically by the much larger power of the Bugis and Makassarese seafaring states to the north, but its goldwork remained distinctive. Although the VOC exercised control over the region from 1674, considerable autonomy continued. The form of the *naga* head on the grip resembles the insect larva forms found on Balinese grips. This shows another possible regional influence important for the West Nusa Tenggara province of

which Sumbawa and Lombok are the chief islands: Lombok, Sumbawa's western neighbor, was under Balinese control. The blade's snake is similar to those on Javanese *naga krises* and it might have been imported via South Sulawesi (FIG. 2/NO. 69, FIG. 65/NO. 23, FIG. 119, FIG. 122, NO. 68). Both densely embossed sheath and grip show traces of red staining similar to the color added to Bima goldwork and also found on Bugis pieces.

22. *Kris panjang* (FIG. 64)

Deli, Medan, North Sumatra, 19th century
Gold, iron, nickel *pamor*; sheath: wood, ivory; grip: wood; 72 × 13.2 × 3.8 cm
Museum Nasional, Jakarta, inv. no. E255

The strongly Sumatran style of this *kris panjang* (long *kris*) is apparent in the motifs of the *gayaman*-shaped *wrangka* (sheath), the *pendok* (oversheath), the *selut* (grip ring) and the *ukiran* (grip). The motifs on the ivory upper portion of the *wrangka* are densely carved and on the upper section of the *pendok* embossed and chased with a spiraling floral motif that is abstracted and formalized in a style very different from the loose and descriptive meanders of FIG. 49/NO. 4 and FIG. 48/NO. 16. The lower part of the *pendok* has a geometric motif applied in diagonal bands. These abstractions can be ascribed to the influence of Islam, which had a stronger effect on design in Sumatra than in Java. Islamic motifs are directly used on the *selut*, where a *mihrab*-shaped motif encircles the grip. They are suggested on the base of the *pendok*, with its finial composed of a series of knobs of varying diameter, and on the flat-topped cap of the *ukiran*. This is a form often found in Aceh, where Islamic influence was stronger than anywhere else in Indonesia.

The small *gunungan* or *tumpal* motif carved into the front of the sheath is perhaps a residual symbol from Sumatran myths of the mountain origin of their rulers. The shape of the grip, with its binding of fine gold wire and red staining, suggests Bugis influence. Since the mobile Bugis peoples had well-entrenched positions in many parts of the Straits of Melaka region and were prominent in trading patterns, their influence is not unusual in Sumatran style, especially in the eastern provinces.

23. *Kris pedang luwuk* (FIG. 65)

Surakarta, Central Java, 19th century or earlier
Gold, silver, diamonds, iron, nickel *pamor*, wood (sheath and grip), 67.5 × 7.2 × 3.5 cm
Museum Nasional, Jakarta, inv. no. E632

Since this straight-bladed *kris* was made in Surakarta and presented by the ruler of the Mangkunagaran palace to the Governor-General (no date mentioned), it is puzzling to find the word *luwuk* in the technical description. The word probably comes from the association of the South Sulawesi state of Luwu with a meteorite found there that according to legend was one of the sources of the nickeliferous iron necessary for *pamor*. The exquisite workmanship of the gold *naga* on the blade (which is possibly much older than the rest of the ensemble), the diamonds on the *mendak* (tang ring) and the repoussé goldwork on the *pendok* and *ukiran* mark it as a fine *kraton* piece.

24. *Siwai* (*rencong*) (FIG. 67)
Aceh, North Sumatra, 18th century
Gold, enamel, diamonds, iron, wood (sheath and grip), 37.4 × 11.2 cm
Museum Negeri Aceh, inv. no. 656

Ownership of the Acehnese dagger, the *rencong*, and the related *siwai* was restricted to the Sultan and other members of the royal family and the Hulubalang (in Acehnese, Ulee Balang), territorial leaders. Its form, clearly influenced by Islamic design, had several variations according to the shape of the grip and the angle of the blade. Many had enamel inlays and Arabic inscriptions on the grip, usually words from the Koran, signaling the importance of Islam to the warrior ethos of Aceh. The jewels on this example, a variant on the *rencong* shape called a *siwai*, signals its noble ownership; in fact, it was the property of the Sultan. The grip's geometric motifs and triple row of triangular forms show strong Arab influence. The *rencong* has symbolic importance in Aceh that can be compared, on a smaller scale, to the importance of the *kris* in Java, particularly since the warrior skills of the Acehnese, who were not finally conquered by the Dutch until the late nineteenth century, were a proud heritage long after combat was merely a memory in Java.

25. *Golok* La Nggunti Rante (FIG. 55)
Bali or Sri Lanka(?), once a state weapon of the Sultanate of Bima, East Sumbawa, 15th century(?)
Blade: iron, silver alloy, copper; handle: horn or wood; 28.5 × 5.4 × 2.3 cm
Kabupaten Bima, East Sumbawa

One of the most treasured *pusaka* of the royal family of Bima, this *golok* or knife probably came from Bali where its first user is claimed to have been the deity Batara Sang Bima, grandfather of Sang Bima, legendary founder of the Bimanese dynasty, in the thirteenth century (Bima is the warrior prince among the Pandawa princes in the Bratayudha cycle). It was the official weapon of the Sultan before

the existence of the state *kris*. It has been suggested that the blade might have had its origins in Sri Lanka.

The knife is said to have magic properties. It allegedly rattled during council meetings if traitors were present. More spectacularly, it was said to have flown from Bima to Manggarai in Flores in 1467 when Bima was attempting to take control of this neighboring island. By flying between the opposing forces it so awed the Florinese that they capitulated immediately, and the battle was won for Bima without bloodshed. The name means "cutter of chains" (*gunting rantai* in Bahasa Indonesia), and the weapon might once have been an execution knife. Iconographically the piece is unique. The motifs seem Javanese, though the curve of the handle has some Balinese larva-form echoes. The crouching beast facing forward near the front of the back edge of the blade seems to be a *kirin*, or mythical lion figure, whose nearest Indonesian equivalent is the Balinese *barong*, protector of good.
Literature: Coomaraswamy 1908: 337, pl. XVII, no. 2

26. *Perisai* (shield) (FIG. 66)
Banjarmasin, Kalimantan, 19th century
Gold, iron, 46.5 diameter × 9.3 cm
Museum Nasional, Jakarta, inv. no. E315

This shield was part of the royal regalia of the Sultan of Banjarmasin, where goldsmiths are thought to have operated already during the Majapahit empire period (thirteenth to fifteenth centuries). Kalimantan has been famous as a source of gold throughout known Indonesian history. The repoussé and chasing workmanship and the control of overall patterning, sympathetically keyed to the circular form, is sophisticated. A central lotus motif forms the heart of a sun with radiating undulating flames in *tumpal*- or *kris*-like form. Concentric rings of diapering underlying the flames resemble Kalimantan basketwork, while the outer ring of forms, suggesting leaves, fans or *gunungans*, is skillfully disposed in a continuous row of coiled lines. As in much Kalimantan work, though techniques may be syncretic, stylistic elements—in this case the reference to basketwork—continue to establish the locality of the piece.

27. *Tali banang* (swordbelt) (FIG. 6)
Bugis people, South Sulawesi, 19th century
Cotton, tablet woven, natural dye,
380 × 12 cm
Australian National Gallery, Canberra, inv. no. 1984. 1989

The Arabic inscription "There is no God but Allah and Muhammad is his prophet"

is woven into the band of this ceremonial piece in Kufic calligraphy. Tablet weaving using the tubular loop is rare, though bands using the tablet weaving technique are made for many purposes. Maxwell suggests that the three colors, white, indigo and red, might have invoked protection for the wearer, as such twining of these colors does in other parts of the region. To the element of animist belief this implies and to the Islamic culture expressed in the inscription can be added the Indic influence represented by the mandala motif that alternates along the swordbelt's length with an Austronesian geometric diamond motif.
Literature: Maxwell 1990.

28. Reins holder
Central Java, 18th century(?)
Iron, gold, ruby, 7.5 × 5.0 × 2.0 cm
Samuel Eilenberg

The reins holder was hooked over the belt of the horseman and the reins were then looped around the front section to free the hands for weapon use. The wealth and

power of a ruler could often be estimated by the magnificence of his army's cavalry trappings. While gold-inlaid iron work seems to have been typical for Javanese legions, in Bima the caparisons were of silver and gold with inlaid gems and bore the emblem of Bima, a double-headed eagle, which expressed spiritual and material power. The motifs on Javanese examples like this are usually talismanic figures like *nagas* or birds.

29. Litter (FIG. 163)

Bali, 19th century
Painted and gilded wood, 90 × 260 × 70 cm
Volkenkundig Museum Nusantara, Delft, inv.
no. S58-1

This litter probably belonged to someone of royal rank, since being carried in such a thronelike litter was the prerogative of high nobility. It was given to the museum soon after its founding in 1864. The donor was an instructor at the Royal Military Academy in Breda, training center for many of the army officers serving in Indonesia who, along with members of the Civil Service, were the chief conduit of Indonesian objects to the Netherlands.

The refined carving of the pair of crowned *nagas* that flank the footrest and of the pendant leaf motif that surrounds the footrest and seat (compare with the outer motif on the Banjarmasin shield, FIG. 66/NO. 26) is a further indication of the court origin of this piece. Paired *nagas* are a royal symbol and in addition have a deification implication (see the miniature litter-shrine for a divine image, FIG. 60/NO. 153). The paintings embellished with gold leaf are in Kamasan style, named for the village near Gelgel where Klungkung court painting was produced. The scenes depicted come from the Ramayana.
Literature: *Etnologische Verzameling* 1884; *Indonesische Kunst uit Eigen Bezit* 1964.

30. Scroll (FIG. 162)

Java, ca. 1900
Watercolor and gold leaf on paper,
23 × 2045 cm
Rijksmuseum voor Volkenkunde, Leiden, inv.
no. 1989-1

The artist of this comprehensive representation of the entourage of the Sultan (of Yogyakarta, presumably) proceeding with full ceremony to the residence of the senior Dutch official, the Resident, was Raden Bekel Djajeng Soedirdjo. Two dates are mentioned for the procession: 1 January and 31 August. The scroll gives a vivid impression of the spectacle of the public appearance of the Sultan. It also contains a wealth of detail, both visual and written in careful captions, about uniforms of the household troops, dress of courtiers and Dutch officials, *pusaka*, weapons, the gamelan orchestra, umbrellas of rank and carriages, thus providing a detailed account of the public image of the ruler at the beginning of this century. Note that the driver of the Sultan's carriage is a European, since no Javanese would presume to have his head elevated above the level of his monarch's.

31. *Wayang kulit*, carriage (FIG. 9)

Surakarta, Central Java, late 19th century
Buffalo hide parchment, buffalo horn, pigment, gold leaf, fish glue medium, 63.7 × 76.7 × 1.7 cm
Istana Mangkunagaran, Surakarta

This carriage (*kareta*) of Rata Kencana, golden sovereign, comes from a *pusaka kotak* (box or set) made at the instigation of Mangkunagoro IV (1853–81), a poet and a great patron of the arts. The pavilion-like enclosed seating area resembles the oldest pavilions in the *kratons* of Surakarta and Yogyakarta, one of the former having been carried from Kartasura when the court moved to Surakarta in 1746. It also has visual connections with the *kobongan* (ritual marriage bed) in the Surakarta *kraton* (FIG. 40), with its paired arched-backed *nagas* along the roof. In the *wayang* play it suggests the public movements of the prince, whose status would be indicated not only by the form of the carriage and the formal dress of the coachmen, but by the use of a pair of rare dappled horses.

32. Flag (or umbrella?) finial

Bone, South Sulawesi (or Minangkabau, Sumatra), once part of the regalia of the Sultan of Bone, 17th century(?)
Gold, 18 × 6 cm
Kabupaten Watampone, South Sulawesi

No documentation can be found for this piece, which in the opinion of some Watampone officials is an umbrella top and of others a flag finial. If it is the former, it is part of a ceremonial umbrella from Minangkabau. This huge gold umbrella was either captured by the Bone hero Arung Palakka when he aided the Dutch in subduing the people of that province in

August 1666 or presented to him by the people of Ulakan, who were so impressed by his valor that they declared him their king (see Leonard Andaya 1981). Though there are knobbed finials on some of the umbrellas on the bas-reliefs of Borobudur, the form does not resemble most existing finials, which are usually pointed (FIG. 164/NO. 33), so it is more likely to be the top of the raja's flag, Samparajae, the Great Defender. Flags were of great importance in Bugis and Makassarese regalia. This magnificent example of Indonesian goldsmithing probably predates the arrival of Islam in Sulawesi late in the sixteenth century, since the multitiered form and lotus flower as well as the Tree of Life or *gunungan* motifs are strongly Indic. *Not in exhibition*

33. Umbrella finial (FIG. 164)

Cirebon, West Java, 8th–9th century
Gold, clay fill, 20.2 × 8.1 × 8.1 cm
Museum Nasional, Jakarta, inv. no. A86

This exquisitely embossed and chased piece is decorated with motifs that cannot be precisely identified. Birds with clearly marked wings are found on the upper portion of the peak, whose nine-tiered tip is set into a lotus flower cupping, while small anthropomorphic figures are depicted on the lower section, which has a stupa-like form. The detailing resembles more the intricacy of crown finials than anything else, but its multitiered iconography clearly indicates a link with a high-ranking ruler, whose umbrella of state would have been one of the chief attributes of office. The motifs on the shaft sheath are mysterious and amorphous, with resemblances to the motifs on Dongson drums, the shape of Dongson axes and the equally mysterious amoebalike forms to be found on Lampung *tapis* cloths (NO. 81).

34a, b. Pair of *tongkats* (ceremonial staves)

Sabu (and?) Sulu, tributes to Ternate, 17th century or earlier
Silver, wood, 151 cm
Istana Ternate Museum, Maluku

Tongkats, or ceremonial staves, have been symbols of office in Indonesia since at least the eighth century, since they can be seen on the bas-reliefs of Borobudur. This pair, tribute to the Sultan from polities to the northeast of the Indonesian archipelago, once flanked the Sultan on official occasions. Sulu is in the Philippines island group, and Sabu (probably Sabah) is in the northwest of Borneo. Whether both areas contributed the *tongkats* or whether "Sulu" is a geographical locator for

"Sabu" is not clear. Whatever the case, both are a considerable distance from Ternate. That they were its tributaries indicates the power of this small and prosperous island within the Maluku area of the Spice Islands.

35. *Kuluk* (ceremonial headdress) (FIG. 169)

Demak, Java, 16th century(?)
Gold, 15.5 × 11.7 cm
Royal Tropical Institute, Tropenmuseum, Amsterdam, inv. no. 124/1

Demak, the first Islamic state in Java, was the strongest polity to emerge in the Central Java region after the decline of the East Java empire of Majapahit in the sixteenth century and remained dominant until the rise of Mataram in the seventeenth century. The form of this ceremonial headdress is a significant indication of some of the changes brought about by the Sultan's conversion to Islam. Hinduistic rulers, from the evidence of sculpture, wore tall tapering crowns. Buddhist princes and Bodhisattvas are shown with domed, helmetlike headdresses decorated with massed curls. The *kuluk*, by contrast, clearly derives its form from the fez. The shape has persisted, as can be seen from the photographs of Central Javanese rulers in more recent times (FIG. 177). The eight vertical bandings that climb the upper half of the *kuluk* continue over the top and taper into the central knob, a pleasing geometric disposition of the form that can also be seen in the state crown of Bima (FIG. 174/NO. 133). The foliate design that fills the upper panels and the lower wall has a formalized density that characterizes Islamic-period decoration.

Literature: Van Brakel et al. 1987:22, 263.

36. *Puri* (palace) doors (FIG. 155)

Singaraja, North Bali, late 18th or early 19th century
Nangka (jackfruit) wood, painted and gilded, 211 × 210.9 × 31 cm
Museum Bali, Denpasar

The Dutch conquered the forces of the Raja of Singaraja in 1843, which is presumably the acquisition date of these magnificent doors, which were reserved, on the evidence of the winged bird-lions, for the passage of the king and his consort. They may well be considerably older, since *nangka* wood, highly prized by the Balinese, is said to be highly resistant to insect pests and therefore lasts much longer than most dressed timber in tropical climates. The soft coloration of the wood is typical of older Balinese work, where only natural pigments (possibly coral in this case) mixed with gum Arabic were used.

Noteworthy in the carving is the influence of Chinese style in the winged lions and in the floral spirals of chrysanthemum flowers. Bali's arts show stronger influence from China than most other regions of Indonesia, a situation partly explained by the important role Chinese merchants played in the commerce and administration of Balinese states. Note the pierced carving of the *jenang*, the panels flanking the door jambs and the *gelung* surmounting the top of the doors. In characteristic Balinese fashion, the construction can be dismantled, the whole being ingeniously anchored by the *ambang*, the bar spanning the entire top edge.

37. Carved panel (FIG. 87)

Cirebon, West Java, 16th century
Wood, 43.7 × 109 × 5 cm
Kraton Kasepuhan, Cirebon

This panel, possibly a door lintel, is one of the few elements remaining from the original Pakungwati palace buildings of this senior princely *kraton* of Cirebon. The motifs of *wadasan* (rocks) and mountains are characteristic of Cirebon, which has been considerably influenced by Chinese style as a result of its coastal (*pasisir*) location. These motifs recur in Cirebon batiks and in the construction of the *kraton's* meditation grotto, Sunyaragi. The perspective rendering of the scene in the carving is also reminiscent of Chinese art, but offers a link with Majapahit, the direct ancestor of Cirebon style. Majapahit continued until about a century before the rise of Cirebon. Although Majapahit was a spent force politically, enough of it survived to ensure stylistic continuity. The connection can be seen clearly in the terra-cotta bas-relief panels from Maja-

pahit buildings found near Trawulan, which offer an obvious stylistic precedent for Cirebon carving like that in the Kasepuhan piece.

38a-h. *Sirih* (betel) set (FIG. 124)

Sumedang, West Java, 19th century (tray, spittoon, open container and five lidded boxes)
Gold, 15.5 × 28.8 × 22.3 cm overall
Museum Prabu Geusan Ulun, Sumedang

Complete sets of gold courtly *sirih* utensils like this one, part of the treasure devolving to the ruling prince of Sumedang, Pangeran Suria Kusumah Adinata, when he inherited the throne in 1836, are rare outside *pusaka* collections. The two small and three large covered boxes for *pinang* nut, tobacco, lime and spices are in *manggis* (mangosteen) form, while the flaring container for *sirih* leaves and the wide-rimmed spittoon (*paidon*) are the usual shape for these components. The preparation and serving of *sirih* was an important ceremony of hospitality throughout Indonesia and accompanied other important rituals and celebrations (see chapter 4). Sets were often made to local design, so *sirih* sets offer a fairly comprehensive vocabulary of regional styles and materials. The fruit form and embossed and chased floral decoration of these pieces are not strongly connected with any particular idiom, but they demonstrate the bounteousness of court hospitality and the meticulous craftsmanship stimulated by courtly patronage.

39a, b. *Sirih* boxes

Aceh, 20th century
Silver gilt, 12 × 21 × 14 cm and 5 × 11 × 6.4 cm
The House of Orange-Nassau Historic Collections Trust, The Hague, inv. nos. 3584, 3585

These containers for *pinang* nut or lime have a lobed form and abstracted, non-figurative motifs characteristic of Acehnese

design and attributable to the influence of Islam, which had first been officially established in Indonesia in Samudra and Pasai (in Aceh) in the late thirteenth century and which was (and still is) stronger in Aceh than in most other parts of the archipelago. These boxes were a ceremonial gift early in this century to Queen Wilhelmina of the Netherlands from the province of Aceh. It is not known whether they were made at that time or earlier, but they demonstrate the metalsmithing skills for which Aceh, affluent from the control and exploitation of Minangkabau gold mines in the seventeenth century, was famous.

40a, b. *Wadah* (containers) for tobacco and *sirih* leaves
(FIG. 10)

Bangkalen, Madura, 19th century
Gold, 11.4 × 9.7 × 4.8 and 11.3 × 10 × 5 cm
Museum Nasional, Jakarta, inv. nos. E670, E671

These containers are the usual shape for the presentation of the *sirih* leaf, in which the other ingredients in a *sirih* quid were wrapped, and of tobacco, which was sometimes added to the mixture. The heavy repoussé and chased gold sheet has perforations in the base for air circulation. The diagonally disposed flamelike *tumpal* motif, consisting of sinuous foliate strands, suggests the *parang rusak* design on batiks that were restricted to royal use in Central Java. Madura, lying just off the north coast of East Java, was strongly influenced by Java, where its ruling families had strong connections. The quality of these *wadahs* almost certainly indicates court provenance, in this case the court of Bangkalen in the west of the island, its closest point to Surabaya in East Java.

Literature: Van der Hoop 1949:303.

41a, b. *Wadah* for *pinang* and *gambir*
(FIG. 126)

Riau Lingga, East Sumatra, 19th century
22-carat gold, rubies, 5.9 × 8.1 and 6.2 × 8.2 cm
Museum Nasional, Jakarta, inv. nos. E10a, E10b

The exuberant repoussé and à-jour work of these containers is typical of the abstracted foliate and geometric designs of regions where Islamic beliefs influenced material culture. The richness of the pieces indicates the prosperity of the regions on the east coast of Sumatra that benefited from the thriving trade passing through the Straits of Melaka.

Literature: *Notulen* . . . 1904:121, no. 8 and Bijlage 7:cxiii.

42. *Cupu* (covered container) for lime
(FIG. 125)

Palembang, South Sumatra, 19th century
Gold, diamonds, 5.7 × 5 cm
Museum Nasional, Jakarta, inv. no. E251

This covered box is characteristic of the elaborate designs of Palembang culture. The area is famous for fine gilded woodcarving, gold work and textiles with rich supplementary wefts of gold thread (FIG. 111/NO. 84). The fine twisted gold wire filigree fashioned into tightly coiled spirals draws on a motif common in Austronesian cultures from as early as the Dongson era, ca. 300 B.C.–100 C.E. On the walls of the bowl they suggest Tree of Life forms within *gunungan* outlines. The harmonious relationship between the circular motifs and the globular form of the *cupu* shows a high level of sophistication; the compressed spiral band encircling the central diamond-studded section of the lid makes a pleasing transition from one medium to another. The surface of the underbody of the *cupu* shows traces of the red staining characteristic of Bugis–Riau Lingga and Bima goldwork.

43. *Paidon* (spittoon) (FIG. 123)

Riau Lingga, East Sumatra, 19th century
18-carat gold, 11.7 × 19.3 (foot 6.3) cm
Museum Nasional, Jakarta, inv. no. E7

The disposition of the paneled repoussé and chased motifs on the body and flaring lip of this spittoon, an important part of a *sirih* set because of the copious saliva stimulated by chewing the quid, is an outstanding example of metal design in Sumatra. Like the *kris* from Deli (FIG. 64/NO. 22) and the *cupu* from Palembang (FIG. 125/NO. 42), it has the red staining characteristic of regions exposed to Bugis influences. These influences were particularly strong in Riau Lingga, where the state was jointly ruled by a Malay-Riau dynasty and the Bugis Yang Di Pertuan Muda (see chapter 2).

Literature: *Notulen* . . . 1904.

44. Pipe (FIG. 11)

Lombok, 19th century
Gold, rubies, diamonds, 23 × 12.1 × 2.2 cm
Museum Nasional, Jakarta, inv. no. E1094

This exquisitely crafted pipe in *naga* form with jeweled head and four jeweled bands at the shaft joints might have been part of the Lombok treasure, captured when Netherlands forces sacked the Raja's palace at Cakranagara in 1894. The blend of fantasy and realism in the piece is typically Balinese—for Lombok was ruled by a dynasty descended from the Rajas of Karangasem—and is in marked contrast

to the formal abstraction of Islamic-influenced Sumatran design (FIG. 123/NO. 43, FIG. 125/NO. 42, FIG. 126/NO. 41).

45. *Kacip* (*pinang* nut cracker) in Twalen (Semar) form (FIG. 127)

Lombok, 19th century
Iron, gold, 18 × 7.7 × 1.1 cm
Museum Nasional, Jakarta, inv. no. E1025

The *kacip* was an essential accessory in the preparation of the *sirih* quid, since the *pinang* nut (betel from the areca palm) had to be cracked to be mixed into the other ingredients. The motif of Twalen, the Balinese equivalent of Semar, the popular Panakawan figure (FIG. 54/NO. 17), is ingeniously worked into the shape of the cracker. His *dodot* cloth, worn in Balinese fashion, is decorated with the common Chinese-derived Balinese motif of the *banji* (swastika), which represents the turning of the celestial bodies and symbolizes the sun, which is also depicted on his chest. Together with the benign image of Semar they suggest a good-fortune symbol.

Literature: Van der Hoop 1949:129.

46. *Kacip* (*pinang* nut cracker) in horse form

Badung, Bali, 19th century
Iron, gold, 26.6 × 8 × 1.4 cm
Museum Nasional, Jakarta, inv. no. E942

The fine detailing of the gold work on the horse's mane and tail, the amusing use of the curve of the blade for the horse's

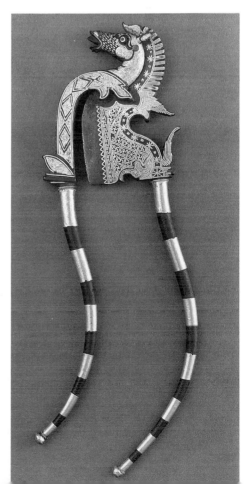

swelling chest and the vitality of the whole are typical of Balinese craft. Note the use of the *banji* motif here, as in FIG. 127/NO. 45.

Literature: *Koleksi Pilihan Museum Nasional* 1984:541, pl. 126.

47a-d. *Tenong* (ceremonial stacked lacquer boxes) (FIG. 182)

Palembang, South Sumatra, 19th century
Wood, pigment, gold leaf, lacquer, 90 × 50 cm
Royal Tropical Institute, Tropenmuseum, Amsterdam, inv. no. 3098-2a, b, c, d

Stacked lacquer boxes like this were a traditional female contribution to the contents of a bridal chamber. The lower portion was used for storing dowry textiles, the upper for food. The wood (sometimes bamboo or rattan) form was carved by Sumatran craftsmen, while the painting, gilding and lacquering was done by Chinese. This shared creation perhaps accounts for the two types of imagery present in the piece. The Indic nature of the tiered form, with its eight-sided base, lotus-shaped pedestal base and upper box, and stupalike top knob is in a different stylistic idiom from that of the decoration, which employs Chinese motifs like the chrysanthemum, the peony, the deer and the swastika, along with the *kawung* (interlocking circle) motif of indigenous origin.

Literature: Van Brakel et al. 1987:15, 262.

48. *Jogan* (ritual fan) (FIG. 171)

Riau Lingga, East Sumatra, 19th century
Gold, silver, 54.8 × 27.7 × 3 cm
Museum Nasional, Jakarta, inv. no. E13

Part of the *pusaka* regalia of the Sultan of Riau Lingga, this ritual fan in leaf or mountain shape evokes the symbolism of the *kayon* or *gunungan* of the *wayang* drama with all its implications of mountain and Tree of Life mythology. The Malay (proto-Bahasa Indonesia) text is written in Arabic characters and states that the kings of Melayu (the name for a kingdom that was situated where Riau Lingga later developed) are descended from Iskandar Zulkarnaen (Alexander the Great), who descended from *Bukit* Siguntang (Siguntang Mountain). The ritual expression of a myth of origin in the symbol-laden *gunungan* form is an indication of the importance of royal genealogies (see chapter 1).

Literature: *Notulen . . . 1904*; *Koleksi Pilihan Museum Nasional* 1980:288, pl.80.

49. *Jogan* (ritual fan)

Sumbawa Besar, West Sumbawa, 19th century
Gold, 50 × 30 cm
Family of last Sultan of Semawa, Sultan Muhamad Kaharuddin III (1931–58), Sumbawa Besar

While lacking the ritual significance of FIG. 171/NO. 48, this fan was used in the ceremonial presentation of a napkin, food and other offerings to the Sultan. It was made during the reign of Sultan Amrullah (1836–82), perhaps by the same goldsmith who crafted the gold on the *parang* (NO. 21). With its sun motif surrounded by foliate-*gunungan* forms and its snake-scaled handle, it clearly injected symbolic meaning into formal gestures.

Literature: Hitchcock 1988.

50. Ceremonial bag (FIG. 112)

Baun, West Timor, 19th century
Glass and coral trade beads, gold, cotton, twine, 18 × 10 cm
Raja of Baun, Timor

Beaded bags like this are common in Timor, an area that shares a beadwork tradition with other areas of Indonesia where Austronesian cultural traits have remained strong, such as Kalimantan, parts of Sumatra and Maluku. Another indication of the force of indigenous culture can be seen in the geometric motifs that are carefully delineated in contrasting bead colors. Used to carry personal possessions, including equipment for *sirih* preparation, beaded bags were not exclusively for princely use. The presence of many plain and openwork gold balls as part of the decoration indicates that this bag belonged to a person of rank. In fact it is one of the *pusaka* of the Raja of the small polity of Baun. Still carried on ceremonial occa-

sions, it illustrates how indigenous vernacular style forms the basis for the refined art associated with courts throughout Indonesia.

51. Belt

Savu, 19th century
Gold, 78 × 4.5 (clasp 10.8) cm
Royal Tropical Institute, Tropenmuseum, Amsterdam, inv. no. 3993-2

This belt with nine links and oval hooked clasp, which once belonged to the Raja of Savu, has a form similar to that of ceremonial dress belts from elsewhere in Indonesia. It was worn at the waist to anchor the long, over-folded woven skirt tubes typical of Nusa Tenggara (FIG. 109/NO. 86; NO. 87). The dense floral motifs have no specifically Savunese character, whereas the open lotus flower with seeds in the center of the clasp is an Indic motif, and the diagonal placement of the bands of floral meanders across the links suggests the *parang* designs of Javanese batiks. The date of the piece may explain its eclecticism, so different from the purely indigenous nature of the trident- and moon-

shaped frontal bands worn on the heads of Savunese nobility: outside influences had penetrated Savu by the time the polity had become centralized. These influences possibly affected the dress of courts which had not been defined earlier.

Literature: Wassing-Visser 1984:494; Van Brakel et al. 1987:189, 277.

52. *Timang* (buckle) (FIG. 113)

Surakarta, Central Java, 19th century
Iron, gold, rubies, diamonds,
12.2 × 11.2 × 1.5 cm
Wieneke de Groot

A gift to Wieneke de Groot's mother from a princess of the Mangkunagaran palace in Surakarta, this buckle would have been fixed to a belt of embroidered velvet or human hair (see FIG. 114/NO. 53) as part of ceremonial court dress. Such belts are still used to anchor a midriff sash of *cinde* (tie-dyed silk patterned to resemble Indian double-*ikat* silk *patola*, much used in court dress for trousers, sashes and scarves). It must originally have had a *lerep*, a narrower sliding piece (see FIG. 114/NO. 53) to retain the end of the belt. The *naga* motif is common in Surakarta buckles, which are often made in the gold-inlay technique found in weapons from the seventeenth century. They are seldom as big as this piece, in which the gems indicate the royal status of the original owner.

53. Belt with *timang* and *lerep*
(FIG. 114)

Surakarta, Central Java, ca. 1850
Human hair, iron, gold, bronze,
99.7 × 16.5 × 1.9 cm
K.R.T. Hardjonagoro

Human hair has a mystical importance in Indonesia. In Toraja, South Sulawesi, it is wrapped around swords as a talisman. In Batak ceremonies it is wrapped around magic staffs. Sometimes the hair of heroes is carefully preserved and is said to continue growing; this is believed of the hair of Arung Palakka, fixed to a diadem in the *pusaka* collection of the Raja of Bone, and of the hair connected to the state crowns of Ternate and Tidore. In some areas, such as Luwu in South Sulawesi, hair is considered to be an emanation of spiritual strength and cuttings of it are said to retain some of this power. In Java, too, it has spiritual power; the Sultan's hair (along with his nail clippings) is an important offering to Ratu Kidul, the goddess of the Southern Ocean. It is also thought to ward off black magic. Belts like this one were made from the hair of women but woven by men on backstrap looms (in contrast to the usual situation where women do the weaving). The motif on the densely woven fabric is *pola nitik* (small geometrical pattern). The elegant severity of the buckle (*timang*) and the sliding keeper (*lerep*) is appropriate for the accessories of this unusual example of Indonesia's textile tradition.

54a, b. *Glang* (bracelets) (FIG. 14)

Kutei, East Kalimantan, 19th century
Gold, 10.5 × 7 and 10.1 × 7.2 cm
Museum Nasional, Jakarta, inv. no. 1305a, b

The repoussé and chased motifs of these bracelets in part retain an indication of the origin of this tapering cylinder form. The horizontal bands probably represent what in earlier times had been a stack of separate bracelets; such stacks, and also bracelets like this pair, are still found in South Sulawesi. The other dominant motif is the foliate- and floral-infilled *gunungan*, with its pan-archipelagic symbolism of ancestor worship. The pair possibly came from the Kutei court collection.

55a, b. *Subang* (earplugs) (FIGS. 101, 102)

East Java, 14th–15th century
Gold, emeralds, garnets(?), 4.34 × 1.04 cm
Samuel Eilenberg-Jonathan Rosen Collection

Earplugs like this, which were set into the earlobe, can be seen on stone reliefs of the ninth century in Central Java and of contemporary East Java temples. The back of this pair is decorated with the *kawung* motif (an exclusively royal pattern in Javanese batik) in a circle resembling a *cakra*, Visnu's symbolic weapon, surrounded by diamond-shaped forms suggesting sun rays. The front (which fits concentrically over the back) presents two intricately crafted scenes enclosed in a four-lobed rosette that is echoed in the central motif. Gemstones once studded the inner points of the lobes and are still present at the central points.

Set in each of the eight lobes is a human figure, none like any other. A seated figure is placed in the lower lobe of each earplug. On the left the figure is a meditating male; on the right it seems to be an infant. A seated figure is also placed at upper center of both earplugs, but on the left the figure is a female with side-placed legs and sinuously swayed torso and on the right a cross-legged male. On the left earplug the figures in the left and right lobes are males standing with outer hands on hips, inner arms crooked and holding what looks like a weapon. On the right piece the left figure is a standing female, inclining slightly forward, with an elaborate wimplelike headdress suggesting rank, while the right is a standing male with outer hand on hip like the pair on the left earplug but with inner hand held down. He wears a headdress that may be a crown. Each earplug presents a genre scene in its own right; together they may tell a story. The placement of limbs, the direction of weight thrust and the inclination of heads are all unmistakably designed so that each scene balances and relates to the other; the vitality and muscular tension expressed in these minuscule figures is clearly pertinent to a specific relationship.

One possible interpretation of the iconography suggests a king's attempt to gain enlightenment through meditation. The left scene may show a king in meditation, protected by guards and watched over by a heavenly nymph. The right may show his achievement: having been elevated to a higher state of consciousness, he leaves behind the three material connections of

rank (himself in kingly dress), family (the baby) and women (the female figure on the left). Whatever the intended meaning of the scene, these earplugs are masterpieces of Indonesian goldsmithing.

56. Ear pendant in *kala* (monster)-head form (FIG. 116)

East Java, 14th–15th century
Gold, 3.59 × 3.06 cm
Samuel Eilenberg-Jonathan Rosen Collection

Kala heads with exaggerated noses, bulbous eyes, and flame-surrounded heads, sometimes half-head, sometimes also having fanged mouths and protruding tongues like this one, are found in many places in Indonesia. The most prominent *kala* images surmount gateways and stairs in temples, particularly those of the Majapahit era contemporary with this ear pendant. Sheaths of *krises* from Madura commonly have them, as do the grips of some Balinese *krises*. The *kala* is a talisman against evil, and its image is invoked for spiritual protection. The remarkably fine workmanship of this piece, incorporating such minute detail as an earring hooped through the *kala*'s own ear, is typical of East Javanese jewelry of this period.

57. Ear pendant in dragon form
(FIG. 115)

East Java, 14th–15th century
Gold, 3.6 × 4.6 cm
Royal Tropical Institute, Tropenmuseum, Amsterdam, inv. no. 1771/8

This beast is unquestionably a dragon and not a *naga* (snake) of the usual form, since it has two feet. The filigree work decorating the chest and head and the vitality of the creature, with its arched back and curved tail, are products of exceptional craftsmanship.

Literature: *Art Indonésien* 1952–53:no. 141; *Les Iles des Dieux* 1956–57:19, no. 4/16.

58a, b. Ear pendants in quasi-bird form (FIG. 15)

East Java, 14th–15th century
Gold, 7.5 × 3.4 cm
Royal Tropical Institute, Tropenmuseum, Amsterdam, inv. no. 1771/3 & 4

Delicate filigree and chasing characterize these ear pendants as they do NO. 59. The ambiguity of the forms adds interest to the balance of mass and void; some are zoomorphic, some foliate or flamelike, and all are subsumed into an assured handling of design.

Literature: *Art Indonésien* 1952–53:nos. 145, 146; *Les Iles des Dieux* 1956–57:19, no.4/16.

59a, b. Ear pendants in quasi-elephant form

East Java, 14th–15th century
Gold, amethyst, 4.7 × 2.6 cm
Royal Tropical Institute, Tropenmuseum,
Amsterdam, inv. no. 1771/1 & 2

The sinuous curves of the flame- or featherlike motifs and the masterly balance of the curved main stems, including the piece

that suggests an elephant's trunk, swirling in opposed directions in the abstracted design of these ear pendants offer another example of the consummate art of East Javanese goldsmiths.

60. Ring in double lotus form (FIG. 118)

Central Java, 8th–9th century
Gold, 4.01 × 3.9 cm
Samuel Eilenberg-Jonathan Rosen Collection

The iconography of this massive ring with its double row of flamelike lotus petals is not clear. It was probably a thumb ring. The engraved motifs include *lar* (wing) and foliate forms placed in relation to a central stem with some suggestion of a Tree of Life. The central motif is the most puzzling. It could be intended as a Visnu-connected conch, or it could be a larvalike shape deriving from the same source as the anthropomorphic forms on the stem of the roughly contemporary umbrella finial, FIG. 164/NO. 33.

61. Ring in phoenix form (FIG. 47)

Java, 14th–15th century(?)
Gold, 2.28 cm
Samuel Eilenberg-Jonathan Rosen Collection

The phoenix motif so artfully disposed to fill the circular space of this signet ring suggests that the piece might have come from Cirebon or some other coastal state. Such states, continuously exposed to maritime trade, were deeply influenced by Chinese designs such as the phoenix, which was popular in ceramics and embroidered silks.

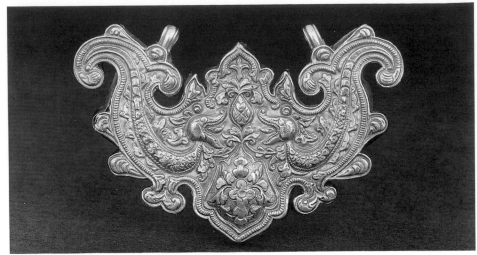

62. *Hiasan dada* (chest ornament)

Kutei, Kalimantan, 19th century(?)
Gold, copper, 8.1 × 11.3 × 1 cm
Museum Nasional, Jakarta, inv. no. E1211

In characteristic Kalimantan fashion the *naga* forms that dominate this pendant have local references; their long open jaws suggest crocodiles rather than snakes, though the pointed tongues and heads are snakelike. The *gunungan* shape of the piece, of repoussé work and chasing, draws on autochthonous themes, while the foliate motifs and the multilobed niche framing the central symmetrical motif show the influence of Islamic design.

63. *Hiasan dada* (chest ornament) (FIG. 117)

Klungkung, Bali, 19th century(?)
Gold, rubies, diamonds, 12.8 × 8.5 cm (chain 9.7 cm)
Museum Nasional, Jakarta, inv. no. E821

This pendant resembles those worn by Balinese dancers, its leaf or inverted mountain (*gunungan*) shape also comparable to the *cupeng* or *badong* (modesty disks for the pubic area, FIG. 180/NO. 142) once worn by women. The high standard of craftsmanship and the richness of the gems make it likely that the piece came from the Klungkung *puri* (palace) collection.

64. *Kalung* (necklace) (FIG. 181)

Gegerbitung village, Sukabumi, West Java, ca. 9th century
Gold, 30.5 × 28 × .7 cm
Museum Nasional, Jakarta, inv. no. 1483

The twenty pieces making up this necklace have three forms. All the motifs have strong Indic iconography, from the nine cast shell forms with their Visnu overtones and the ten repoussé and chased pieces in mango shape, a common Indian motif, to the central phallus. The fertility symbolism is clear: the mango motifs, with their indication of a central cleft, have yoni connotations and the phallus represents the linga. A practice that might have originated in India, since it is mentioned in the *Kama Sutra* of the sixth century, but was widespread in Southeast Asia, is revealed by the presence of penis inserts in the form of small balls on the phallus. The oldest dated example so far of a penis insert found in Southeast Asia occurs in a bronze dog of the fourth century. The practice of inserting bells, balls and cuboid objects under the skin of the penis, or of driving pins through it, or of attaching rings, rosettes or *cakra*-shaped disks around it, seems to have been carried out among many peoples (see NO. 155b). Who might have worn such devices and for what reason is not known, though many explanations, including female gratification in an Austronesian region where female autonomy was considerable, have been suggested, as has the idea that it was an indication of high rank.

Literature: Brown, Edwards and Moore 1988.

65. *Sumping* (head ornament) (FIG. 35)

Java, 14th–15th century(?)
Gold, 7.4 × 5.3 cm
Royal Tropical Institute, Tropenmuseum,
Amsterdam, inv. no. 1771/21

The *sumping* was placed on the head behind the ear and was the prerogative of high rank. It can be seen in many *wayang kulit* figures (see Semar, FIG. 69/NO. 121) and can be seen today as royal head adornment or wedding decoration. The exquisite goldsmithing of this piece, with its *gunungan* form and central elephant motif (the elephant always has connotations of power and rank, and sometimes implies the auspicious elephant-god Ganesha), marks it as a Majapahit creation.

Literature: *Indonesian Art* 1948:no. 8.

66a, b. *Kris*-holder and *kris* (FIG. 157)
Lombok, 19th century
Wood, pigment, gold leaf, iron, gold, rubies,
diamonds, ivory, 125.8 × 30.7 × 52 cm
(holder), 53 × 17.5 cm (*kris*)
Museum Nasional, Jakarta, inv. nos. E1018,
E1015

Though spectacular as sculptures and used
to flank the seat of honor of the ruler in
Bali and Lombok, *kris*-holders were not
designed to hold the most sacred *krises*,
which would have been kept in *pusaka*
boxes and brought out only on ceremonial
occasions. The character depicted here is
the popular Hanuman, the white monkey
general of the monkey army that supported Rama in the Ramayana epic (FIG.
149/NO. 116). His gold-edged loincloth,
gold necklace, *sumping*, shoulder ornaments, bracelets and anklets indicate his
high rank. The *kris*, also from Lombok,
has a *wrangka* (sheath) in *gayaman* (plain,
in mango form) shape with *tunggal kukus*
(ribbon of steam) and *kembang pala* (nutmeg flower) *pamor* motifs on the blade.

67. *Kris* (FIG. 52)
Surakarta, Central Java, 19th century
Gold, iron, nickel *pamor*, diamonds, rubies,
wood, pigment, gold leaf, lacquer, copper,
52 × 17 × 4 cm
Dr. Mr. Ide Anak Agung Gde Agung, Puri
Agung, Gianyar

A gift from the Susuhunan Pakubuwono
X of Surakarta (1893–1939) to the ruler
of Gianyar, Ide Anak Agung Ngurah
Agung (ruling 1912–60 though never consecrated into the family dynastic title of
Manggis) on an official visit to Gianyar in
1928, this *kris* is of the kind given in
brotherhood. It was made by the Susuhunan's favorite *empu* (smith), Joyo-
sukago, who worked in the last quarter of
the nineteenth century and early in the
twentieth century. It is a *pengapit kris*,
that is, a guardian of *pusaka*, and is kept
with the most sacred heirlooms.

The blade's *pamor* is in the *beras wutah*
(scattered rice) motif, its shape *jalak* (the
name of a black bird). The *ganja* (crosspiece) is gold-inlaid, the *mendak* (tang
ring) studded with rubies and the *selut*
(grip ring) with diamonds. The *ukiran*
(grip), in *nungga semi* (old tree resprout-
ing) form, is of *kemuning bang* wood, the
wrangka (sheath) in *gayaman* shape, its
interior of *mentaos* wood and its *pendok*
(oversheath) of lacquered copper. The
most striking feature of the sheath is the
alas-alasan (mountain and forest motifs,
sometimes with animal figures) decoration
in paint and gold leaf on the upper portion of the *wrangka* and on its lower
portion under the *pendok* on a white

background (restricted to princely ownership). The charming animal and plant figures are set in repeated *gunungan* shapes
interspersed with insets of fish- or reptile-
scale motif. In the center of the *gambar* is
the coat-of-arms of the Pakubuwono line
comprising an oval medallion containing
the sun, a star, the crescent moon and the
earth (the last pierced by a nail, the earth-
anchoring *paku* of the dynastic title), with
rice and cotton plants flanking the oval.
Literature: Hamzuri (1973) 1983:figs. 9, 10.

68. *Kris*, Nagasasra
Cirebon, West Java, 17th century
Gold, iron, nickel *pamor*, wood,
46.9 × 10.8 × 2.8 cm
Museum Nasional, Jakarta, inv. no. E450

This *naga*-decorated *kris* with eleven *luk*
(waves or curves) from the era of Sultan
Agung offers a perfect fusion of the iron-

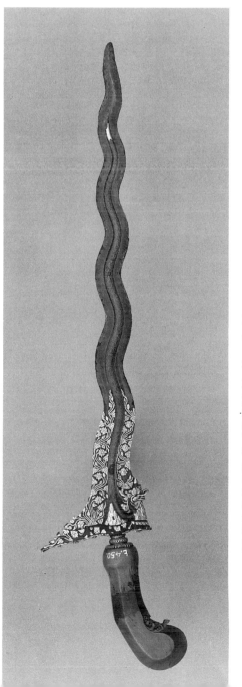

smith's and goldsmith's arts. The crowned
naga's body follows the sinuous shape of
the blade, while its elaborate gold-inlaid
headdress echoes the forms of the floral
meander encrusting the first three *luk*. The
finely chiseled figure of a small seated deer
is tucked into the space between the *ganja*
(crosspiece) and the first curve of the
naga's body in a further illustration of this
kris's complete integration of form and
decoration. The *pamor* motif is *sekar pala*
(nutmeg flower). Although the provenance
of the *kris* is Cirebon, the workmanship is
typical of Central Java.

69. *Kris*, Nagasasra (FIG. 2)
Surakarta, Central Java, early 19th century
Iron, nickel *pamor*, gold, silver, diamonds,
wood, 48 cm
Royal Tropical Institute, Tropenmuseum,
Amsterdam, inv. no. H2

This nine-*luk kris* with its dominant *naga*
imagery shows the height of sophistication
of the *empu* (smiths) of the early nineteenth century. It is interesting to compare
it with NO. 68, where the *naga* form is
also central. The older *kris* is still predominantly a weapon, the decorative elements merged with but not dominating
the iron smithing. This example is clearly
a ceremonial piece of *kraton* quality where
refinement of form and lavishness of material, including heavy gold on the *naga*
body and the diamonds studding the *selut*,
replace the robustness of the earlier piece.
The *gambar* (the *wrangka* top) is of the
formal flaring *ladrang* shape, the *pendok*
(oversheath) is of silver in the open-
fronted *blewah* style.
Literature: Van Brakel et al. 1987:213, 280.

70. *Kris*
Yogyakarta, Central Java, 19th century(?)
Iron, nickel *pamor*, gold, diamonds, wood,
ivory, 48 cm
The Orange-Nassau Historic Collections Trust,
The Hague, inv. no. 3567

A present from Sultan Hamengkubuwono
VIII to Queen Wilhelmina of the Netherlands on the occasion of her twenty-five
year jubilee in 1923, this eleven-*luk kris*
offers another variant of the *naga* form to
compare with FIG. 2/NO. 69 and NO. 68.
The snake's body is more delicate and
sinuous and relates more closely to the
pamor pattern (probably *laring gangsir*
[cricket wings]). The *wrangka* has a
diamond-studded gold *pendok* (sheath
cover) decorated with bird and foliate motifs and ivory top in *ladrang* shape. The
ivory in the grip, which is in anthropomorphic form, and the ivory in the

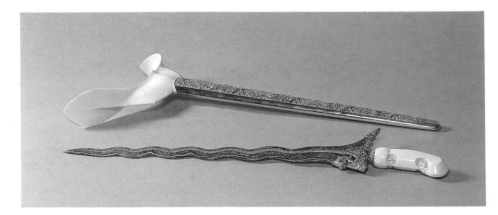

wrangka top mark the *kris* as a piece from Yogyakarta as distinct from Surakarta, where ivory was not traditionally used.

71. *Kris* (FIG. 53)

Riau Lingga, East Sumatra, 19th century
Iron, nickel *pamor*, gold, rubies, diamonds, wood, 37 × 11 cm
Museum Nasional, Jakarta, inv. no. E28

This magnificent *kris* demonstrates the close link between the Riau Lingga Sultanate and Bugis princes. The style of the *wrangka* is characteristic of Sulawesi weapons, having a flat base, twine-wrapped pattern on the lower end and more rectangular upper portion than Javanese examples of the *ladrang* shape (compare with NO. 70). The double loop of gold cord is also typical of Bugis models, whereas the dense foliate motif covering the central stem and the upper part of the sheath as well as the grip are Sumatran in character, as is the rosette of diamonds and rubies on the sheath cord. The *selut* is chased gold, the *mendak* a ring of diamonds; the blade has seven *luk*.

Literature: Hamzuri (1973) 1983:123, no. 26.

72. *Kris* (FIG. 120)

Klungkung, Bali, 19th century
Iron, nickel *pamor*, gold, rubies, diamonds, wood, 76.2 × 11.7 × 5 cm
Museum Nasional, Jakarta, inv. no. E793

This state *kris* for ceremonial use invokes talismanic protection through the *raksasa* (demon) figure (commonly found on Balinese *krises*) on the *ukiran* (grip) and the *kala* (monster) head on the sheath, which is in *sandang walikat* form. The blade's *pamor* design is *lemmet* (not clear). Both the finely worked gold of the grip and sheath and the lavish use of large gems mark it as a court piece.

73. *Patrem* (female dagger) (FIG. 121)

Surakarta, Central Java, 17th and 19th century
Iron, nickel *pamor*, gold, ivory, ebony, 34.2 × 4.8 × 3.6 cm
Haryono Guritno

The blade of this *kris* has *kulit semangka* (watermelon rind) *pamor* and like NO. 68, dates from the seventeenth century. The *kris* was put together around 1880 and belonged to one of the daughters of Pakubuwono IX (1861–93). *Krises* for women (note that this one is barely half the size of the male *krises* preceding it) were usually weapons for the defense of life and virtue; the smallest were sometimes worn concealed in the coiffure; the larger, like this example, were tucked into the sash. The elaborately carved ivory *ukiran* (grip), in the form *kembang temu* (ginger flower), is from Madura, and the ebony sheath of the simple *sandang walikat* type has two gold repoussé oversheath parts with foliate motif.

74. *Dodot pinarada mas* (royal ceremonial skirt cloth) (FIG. 103)

Yogyakarta, Central Java, 1910
Cotton, resist-dyed by batik wax process in natural dyes, silk, gold leaf, fish protein glue, 210 × 379 cm
Australian National Gallery, Canberra, inv. no. 1984.3165

Wearing the large *dodot* cloth is a prerogative of members of the royal courts of Java; it is worn bulkily draped around the hips and thighs (see the *wayang* figures FIG. 57/NO. 109, FIG. 146/NO. 110, NO. 111) on ceremonial occasions. This one is unusually densely decorated, with *prada* (gold leaf) enriching the complex batik design. The design comprises *semen* (forest elements with *gunungan* [mountain] forms, a motif with fertility implications) combined with *lar* (wing) and *sawat* (the wings and tail of the *garuda*, the giant mythical bird of Indonesian legend) that covers most of the cloth. Traditionally the *sawat* motif was reserved for royalty. Out-

lining the lozenge-shaped central panel of appliqué silk is a border of *lidah api* (tongue of flame) motif; in the curved and hooked form seen here the motif is also known as *cemukiran*.

Literature: Van der Hoop 1949; Gittinger 1979; Maxwell 1990.

75. *Geringsing wayang kebo* (cloth for sacred use or apparel) (FIG. 108)

Tenganan Pageringsingan, Bali, 20th century(?)
Handspun cotton woven in double *ikat* technique, natural dyes, gold thread embroidery, 213 × 55.4 cm
Australian National Gallery, Canberra, inv. no. 1982.2308

Geringsing cloths, made only in the village of Tenganan, have a sacred significance throughout Bali. They are used or worn in varying sizes and shapes at weddings, cremations, tooth-filing and healing ceremonies. The wearing of *geringsing* is a sign of status, and a cloth like this, with its rich gold embroidery, is of exceptional importance.

The dyeing process, performed by men, is accompanied by rituals and is shrouded in mystery to maintain the sacred nature of the creation. The weaving is done by women on a back-strap loom. There is a continuous warp, which is cut if the cloth is used to wrap the breast or waist or to hang from the shoulder, but left intact if the piece is to be an offering to the gods. Making a cloth can take up to eight years.

After the handspun threads have been soaked for more than a month in oil and ash and slowly dried, the double *ikat* technique requires intricate measuring and binding of both warp and weft threads to provide a resist pattern during dyeing. The dyeing of the traditional indigo color is forbidden in Tenganan itself, so this step in the process is carried out in the nearby village of Bugbug. Red dyeing is done in Tenganan, either in addition to the indigo to produce a purplish black or to make predominantly red *geringsing*. Repeated dye baths are required to obtain the deep coloration. The red, purplish black and the cream ground color may represent respectively the Hindu gods Brahma, Visnu and Isvara (compare FIG. 6/NO. 27) and thus partly account for the sacred nature of *geringsing* and its suitability, if the warp threads are uncut, as a ritual offering in temple ceremonies (Gittinger; Maxwell).

Maxwell surmises that the small missing portion at one end of this cloth might have been used in a healing ritual for someone of high rank. Such practices are well known in Bali and also occur with Indian silk *patola* cloths, whose motifs of eight-lobed rosettes, mandala-like shapes and *nitik* forms (small geometrical figures inspired by woven motifs) were the inspiration for *geringsing* designs (see FIG. 107/NO. 88). Maxwell suggests that the central four-pointed motif (with stepped profile enclosing a similar shape containing a square form) resembles a stupa that in turn symbolizes the cosmic mountain.

This *geringsing* has twenty-four symmetrically grouped figures, three in each quadrant of both halves of the cloth, that are depicted in stylized *wayang* form (hence its ascription as a *geringsing wayang kebo*). Gittinger interprets the three figures on similar cloths as a priest (the central figure with swathed headdress), a suppliant (the figure with bent head and hands in devotional position facing the priest) and the priest's wife (with hand on knee and elbow bent back in a pose reminiscent of dancers and figures on the bas-reliefs of East Javanese temples of the Majapahit period). The devotional implications of the iconography of these types of *geringsing* compare with the earplugs, FIGS. 101, 102/NO. 55 and make them especially suitable for temple offerings.
Literature: Gittinger 1979; Maxwell 1990.

76. *Kain songket* (cloth with supplementary weft) (FIG. 104)
Klungkung(?), Bali, late 19th century
Silk, cotton, gold thread, chemical dyes, 94 × 169 cm
Museum Bali, Denpasar, inv. no. E 1b. 3287

Silk cloths with supplementary weft in imported gold-wrapped thread and sometimes also brightly colored cotton thread, as here, traditionally were woven by women of high caste and are still made in villages near the former princely courts. They were worn for social and religious ceremonies by both men and women, either as skirt cloths or chest and hip cloths. This example is a *saput*, a man's chest and hip cloth, worn above the skirt cloth. The motifs include *karang* (Balinese equivalent of *kala*, monster) figures, whose presence probably invokes protection; crowned *nagas* with implications of royal rank, power and fertility; birds; butterflies; fish; stars; flames; *nitik* (small geometric elements); and in the triangular *tumpal* shapes at each end, Trees of Life. The overall design is both vertically and horizontally symmetrical (compare the *geringsing* cloth, FIG. 108/NO. 75). The placement of the motifs, seemingly spontaneous, even whimsical, yet with a careful control of scale and space, exemplifies the Balinese mastery of design and space. The brightness of the colored threads indicates chemical dyes and establishes that the piece cannot be more than a hundred years old.

77. *Kain songket* (cloth with supplementary weft) (FIG. 18)
Klungkung(?), Bali, late 19th century
Silk, gold and silver thread, chemical dyes, 110 × 150 cm
Museum Bali, Denpasar, inv. no. E 1b. 3297

This cloth, like FIG. 104/NO. 76, is a *saput* to be worn by a high-ranking man on ceremonial occasions. Its motifs, alternately gold and silver, are more formalized than those of FIG. 104/NO. 76. The design is symmetrical in only the horizontal plane, which is divided into layers by nineteen narrow bands separating rows of the chief design element, a geometrical abstraction of a halved *ketupat* (single serving of rice cooked in a container of coconut leaves folded into a triangular shape). These forms have diagonals alternating in direction in both planes, which gives the design a three-dimensional effect. The invocation of rice, like the double row of *tumpal* shapes containing Trees of Life at each end of the cloth, implies fertility and ancestor links. Other motifs include stars, interlocked keys and the zig-zag pattern known as teeth of the *barong* (the mythical lionlike figure traditionally said to represent the forces of good in a Balinese dance named for him, where he is pitted against the destructive Rangda, ruler of witches). Like the images depicted in FIG. 108/NO. 75 and FIG. 104/NO. 76, these motifs symbolize ideas of the universe and the life force appropriate to Balinese rituals.

78. *Kain songket* (cloth with supplementary weft) (FIG. 12)
Semawa, West Sumbawa (Sumbawa Besar), early 20th century(?)
Silk, cotton, silver thread, 117 × 164 cm
Collection of the Australian Museum, Sydney, inv. no. E 66721

The complex technique of working the highly detailed motifs of the supplementary weft of the *songket* cloths of Sumbawa was once reserved for women of the court. Unlike the gold and silver threads used in Bali, which were imported, those of Sumbawa were locally made of pulled wire wrapped around cotton fibers. The costliness of the workmanship and materials of these textiles restricted their use to the high nobility, and the lavishness and sophistication of this cloth distinguishes it as a court cloth. This is an exceptionally rare piece.

The iconography of the motifs on this cloth, which is a man's wedding sarong, can be compared in its complexity to that of the ship cloths of Lampung (FIG. 45/NO.

156a, FIG. 46/NO. 1a, FIG. 50/NO. 156b, FIG. 51/NO. 1b, FIG. 190/NO. 157). The surface is divided into panels of indigo and purple background color bordered with rows of *tumpal* motifs. In rectangular areas within the indigo panels, a scene is repeated showing a male figure standing above a pavilion that may itself be on a ship, gesturing with one hand at a triple-masted ship on which stand three female figures. These figures may represent the male and female partners of the marriage ceremony, perhaps the arrival of the female half of the ancestors, perhaps both. Small ships bearing a single figure and a Tree of Life are repeated down the panels with purple background. Other motifs include Trees of Life within the *tumpals*, birds, crabs, *lidah api* (tongues of flame), and geometric and floral elements.
Literature: Hitchcock 1988:14–21.

79. *Kain songket* (cloth with supplementary weft) (FIG. 100)
Bima, East Sumbawa, 19th century
Silk, gold thread, 112.8 × 103 cm
Ibu Siti Maryam Rachmat, S. H.

This cloth, an heirloom of the Bima royal family, was used as the wedding sarong for the *Permaisuri* (queen or senior wife). It was worn by Ibu Suri Kaharuddin, a daughter of the Sultan of Bima and the sister of the present owner, when she married the last Sultan of Semawa, West Sumbawa, Sultan Muhamad Kaharuddin III (1931–58), the thirteenth sultan since the arrival of the Netherlands East Indies Company in the princedom in 1674. A pattern of diagonally crossing end-to-end spirals with eight-lobed rosettes in the resulting lozenge-shaped spaces covers the main body of the cloth. The *kepala* (head, or central, panel) has bands of floral motifs edging two rows of slender *tumpals* with Tree of Life infill facing complementary *tumpals* with abstracted floral design. A broad ribbon of brocaded gold is applied to the lower edge of this rich court textile.

80. *Kain tapis* (woman's skirt cloth)
Lampung, South Sumatra, 19th century
Cotton woven with warp *ikat*, silk thread embroidery, natural dyes, 124 × 67 cm
Royal Tropical Institute, Tropenmuseum, Amsterdam, inv. no. 1772-1332

The *tapis* cloths of Lampung, like the *palepai* (FIG. 45/NO. 156a, FIG. 50/NO. 156b, FIG. 190/NO. 157) and *tampan* (FIG. 46/NO. 1a, FIG. 51/NO. 1b) ship cloths, are among the most notable achievements of Indonesian textile artists, though their production largely ceased at the beginning

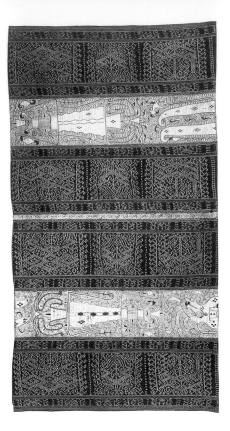

of this century. They can be classified in three main types. One, lavishly embroidered with gold thread, was made in the south and southeast of Lampung province. Another, from the southwest coast, is covered with small pieces of mirror or mica. The third, which FIG. 110/NO. 81 and NO. 80 exemplify, comes from the inland mountains and is characterized by alternating bands of subtle warp *ikat* and silk embroidery. All were made to be worn on ceremonial occasions.

Like all sarongs made from the relatively narrow panels resulting from backstrap loom weaving, this cloth is seamed across the horizontal center. It has been left in tubular form, with vertical seam intact, unlike NO. 81, which has been opened. Three principal images are represented in the *ikat* motifs on this example, each set repeated in both halves of the skirt: a ship related to the soul or ancestor ships of the *palepai*, a Tree of Life and a *gunungan* figure. All three are strongly stylized in angular shapes that spring from the Austronesian tradition, whose early forms can be seen in bronze decoration from the Dongson period (the centuries straddling the beginning of the Christian era). Other *tapis* have more abstracted *ikat* patterns, like NO. 81, or formal motifs derived from Indian *patola* cloths.

The iconography of the embroidered panels, in which the imagery reads at right angles to the *ikat* panels, is less clear. Though the outlines of the figures have anthropomorphic proportions, the tangled curves and waving lines of their bases suggest marine creatures, perhaps squid or octopus, while the inner shapes and the tendrils flowing from the arms are foliate.

All the elements and their inhabitants seem to be in a composite form. Other *tapis* embroideries depict ameboid creatures, some with young; most of the motifs support Holmgren and Spertus's interpretation of them as fertility signs.

Literature: Jasper and Mas Pirngadie 1912–27; Gittinger 1979:79–84; Holmgren and Spertus 1989:94–101.

81. *Kain tapis* (woman's skirt cloth) (FIG. 110)

Lampung, South Sumatra, 19th century
Cotton woven with warp *ikat*, silk thread embroidery, natural dyes, mica, 125 × 116 cm
Royal Tropical Institute, Tropenmuseum, Amsterdam, inv. no. 1772-1514

The reddish-brown ground of this *tapis* reveals a motif of sharply angled lozenge-shaped forms with hooked ends, perhaps highly stylized mountain forms. The Austronesian-derived geometric pattern, more abstracted than the motifs in NO. 80, relates to the patterning found on outer island textiles and carving. The embroidered motifs, cryptically anthropomorphic in NO. 80 but here more legible and clearly related to the imagery of ship cloths, have ship forms carrying and flanked by human figures. The larger figures wear elaborate headdresses; one in particular wears a spiraling, perhaps feather, creation. Others, who seem to be female, have snakelike heads and lower limbs like calipers enclosing a nucleus or a single sinuous snake form running down the center. The ships bear Trees of Life, closed pavilions and large boxes, perhaps heirlooms, perhaps dowry. As with many of these mysterious textiles, the profusion of detail presents more questions than answers.

Literature: Jasper and Mas Pirngadie 1912–27; Gittinger 1979:79–84; Holmgren and Spertus 1989:94–101.

82. *Kain songket* (cloth with supplementary weft) (FIG. 13)

Pandai Sikek, Minangkabau, West Sumatra, late 19th or early 20th century
Silk, gold thread, 46 × 175 cm
Rijksmuseum voor Volkenkunde, Leiden, inv. no. 2299-150

The consistent shape of the motifs surrounding the dominant lozenge patterning of this cloth establishes its turn of the century date. The use of five threads to the pattern stick is also characteristic of the date: earlier cloths had fewer and were coarser. The lozenges symbolize a piece of the special cake (*wajik*) that was mandatory at Minangkabau ceremonies. The vertical motifs represent *pinang* palm trunks; the alternating light and dark rectangles may indicate woven rattan strips or seeds of the *sirih* vine. Both *pinang* nut and

sirih seed are central to hospitality rites, and, like the *wajik* cake, are associated with the ceremonies where this shoulder cloth would have been worn. (Information on motifs provided by A. and J. Summerfield.)

83. *Kain songket* (cloth with supplementary weft) (FIG. 105)

Batu Bara, North Sumatra, 19th century
Silk, gold thread, approx. 117 × 164 cm
Tengku Luckman Sinar, Deli Sultanate, Medan

This sarong, woven in a village about thirty-five miles from Medan that is noted for its weaving, is an heirloom piece from the Deli Sultanate, one of the Malay princedoms (*kerajaans*) of Sumatra. Its design is a blend of Islamic-inspired stylized motifs such as trefoils, as well as eight-lobed flowers and other *ceplok* shapes (small abstracted figures based on rosettes and centered figures that derive from Indian *patola*) with realistic depictions of fish and crocodiles in facing pairs.

84. *Kain songket* (cloth with supplementary weft) (FIG. 111)

Palembang, South Sumatra, late 19th or early 20th century
Silk woven with weft *ikat*, gold thread, 83 × 86 cm
Rijksmuseum voor Volkenkunde, Leiden, inv. no. 370-2869

The rich red-and-gold *ikat* silks of Palembang have a cosmopolitan blend of indigenous techniques like *ikat* and supplementary weft with foreign elements like *patola* motifs, gold thread and chemical dyes. The exuberance of the colors and the carefully modulated placement of the gold border panels and small decorative elements in this piece are typical of Palembang ceremonial pieces.

85. *Kain songket* (cloth with supplementary weft) (FIG. 106)

Palembang, South Sumatra, late 19th or early 20th century
Silk, gold thread, silk thread, 212 × 79 cm
Royal Tropical Institute, Tropenmuseum, Amsterdam, inv. no. 2781-2

This textile is a *slendang*, or shoulder cloth. Its overall pattern of rosettes, stars and mandalas in gold highlighted with colored silks is bounded on the sides by thick gold supplementary weft borders with running geometric and floral motifs and on the ends by *tumpals* interspersed with sprouting plant forms and by dense wafer sections. The subjugation of natural imagery to formalized and stylized motifs is typical of Indonesian textile art in strongly Islamic regions.

Literature: Jasper and Mas Pirngadie 1912.

86. *Tais* (woman's ceremonial skirt)
(FIG. 109)

Tetum people, Belu, West Timor, 20th century
Cotton woven with supplementary weft and complementary warp, gold thread, natural dyes,
152 × 63 cm
Australian National Gallery, Canberra, inv. no. 1984.1104

This richly ornamented skirt is covered with geometric designs typical of the east of Indonesia, where the indigenous Austronesian culture has been less affected by Indic and Islamic influences than has the west. The stylized anthropomorphic figures are also typical of the region. The piece is notable for the exuberance of its asymmetrical patterning, for the brilliance of its supplementary weft (known as *raroti* in the Tetum area) and for its elements of gold thread, which indicate that it was made for a high-ranking woman such as a ruler's wife or daughter.
Literature: Maxwell 1990.

87. Royal cloth
Termanu, Roti
Cotton, 163 × 83 cm
James J. Fox

This nobleman's cloth from the central domain of Termanu on the island of Roti (Rote) displays the strongest possible assertion of royalty. In its design format,

patterning and principal motifs, this cloth shows the influence of specific silk *patola* textiles that were given by the Dutch East Indies Company to the rulers of the island as formal recognition of their raja status.

When the supply of these textiles ceased, the rulers of the island adapted the motifs and transferred them to their *ikat* cloths. The wearing of cloths with these motifs was reserved as the exclusive prerogative of the high nobility of the island.

The center field of this cloth contains an alternating arrangement of Roti's two main noble motifs: the eight-pointed *jelamprang* pattern known in Roti as *dula nggeo* and the linked half-rhomboid pattern known as *dula penis*. The *dula penis* motif is especially associated with the domain of Termanu, which was for most of the Dutch East Indies Company period the most powerful of the domains of Roti.

The *dula penis* motif is a Rotinese interpretation of a *patola* design: it takes as its center point what is, in effect, the intersection of two adjoining *patola* motifs. (Written by James J. Fox.)

88. *Patolu* (FIG. 107)
Gujerat, India, 19th century
Silk woven in double *ikat* technique, gold leaf, fish protein glue, 378 × 109 cm
Iwan Tirta

Patola cloths have long been prized in Indonesia, their use on ceremonial occasions and at rites of passage being common throughout the archipelago. It is not certain when *patola* first appeared in Indonesia, but records of textile trade with India go back to the fifth century of the Christian era, when Chinese dynastic records recount an Indonesian diplomatic mission bringing Indian cloth as part of its tribute. *Patola* might already have been made in India by that date. A temple built by silk weavers in Rajasthan in the fifth century has an inscription describing a weaving technique resembling the *patola* method, while an eleventh-century poem from Gujerat refers to such cloths. God-king statues of the Majapahit era, like that of Kerterajasa in FIG. 32, wear textiles patterned in *patola* motifs. Later records equate the value of one *patolu* with half a ton of cloves (see chapter 4). As important as their intrinsic value is the influence *patola* had on Indonesian design. The eight-lobed rosettes, the stars, the mandala and the *jelamprang* (an eight-pointed *cakra*-derived figure set in a circle, related to the overlapping circle *kawung* motif), all having directionally aware elements in what are known as *ceplok* designs, are derived from *patola*, and they appear throughout

Indonesia on both woven and batiked textiles. Sometimes cloths decorated with these adapted designs are known as *cinde* or *cindai*.

The high value and rarity of *patola* made them a status symbol, and they have always been associated with royalty. Used in the courts of Central Java as skirt cloths, *slendangs* and formal trousers, and drapings for the ceremonial marriage bed, they have taken on strongly Indonesian values despite their foreign origin. This *patolu* is a particularly interesting example, having been a *pusaka* of the court of Yogyakarta and then decorated with *prada* (gold leaf) especially for the marriage of one of the princesses of the *Kraton* Ngayogyakarta Hadiningrat to the ruler of the Mangkunagaran court (who later assumed the title Mangkunagoro VII) in Surakarta in 1920.
Literature: Wastraprema 1988; Sarabhai 1988.

89a, b. *Rebab* (stringed instrument)
(FIG. 133)
Klungkung, Bali, 19th century
Wood, coconut shell, gold, silver, rubies, sapphires, semiprecious stones, crystal, horsehair, gut, parchment, velvet,
92 × 18.4 × 8.5 cm
Museum Nasional, Jakarta, inv. no. E829

The two-stringed *rebab* is one of the few instruments in the gamelan orchestra, along with the flute and the human voice, that plays a continuous melody line as distinct from a percussive one. Unlike most of the percussion instruments, which are indigenous, it is of Arabic origin. The loose stringing of both gut strings and horsehair bow produce a plaintive quavering tone; there is no fingerboard. This example is unusually richly decorated and was possibly made for the *puri* (court) in Klungkung.
Literature: McPhee 1966; Kunst (1949) 1973; Lindsay (1979) 1985; Kartomi 1985.

90. *Suling* (flute) (FIG. 132)
Klungkung, Bali, 19th century
Wood, gold, rubies, diamonds, semiprecious stones, glass, tortoiseshell, 97.5 × 4.6 cm
Museum Nasional, Jakarta, inv. no. E833

This elaborately decorated six-holed flute possibly comes, on the evidence of the gem work, from the same source as FIG. 133/NO. 89. The *suling*, end blown in Bali and Java, is the principal melody carrier in the gamelan and its only wind instrument.

91. *Gambang* (xylophone) (FIG. 36)

Cirebon, West Java, 18th century
Wood, bronze, rope, pigment, 29 × 65 × 23.3 cm
Kraton Kasepuhan, Cirebon

Although this piece from the Siketuyung gamelan of 1748 is described as a *gambang* in the palace museum, its size and the number and material of its keys classify it as a *saron penerus* in the nomenclature of Javanese gamelans. Possibly the ascriptions of Sundanese (West Javanese) gamelans differ in this respect. The curvilinear carving that makes it an unmistakably Cirebon piece depicts clouds (*megamendung*) and rocks (*wadasan*) in a style that has been strongly influenced by Chinese design. It is one of thirteen instruments in this *slendro*-scale gamelan.

92. Dance crown

Klungkung, Bali, 19th century
Gold, rubies, rattan, 41.5 × 24.5 × 30 cm
Museum Nasional, Jakarta, inv. no. E827

Dance in Bali originated as performance for the gods in temple grounds. Although some Balinese dance today is secular, the act of dancing, like all Balinese artistic expression, retains characteristics of an offering to divine powers. Something of the Hindu association of kings with gods has influenced the costume for dance, particularly those dances performed in *puri* (palace) temples under the patronage of princes. This crown has the upswept *kekayon* (tree) form used for the headdress of the *baris* and *legong* dances. The *baris* dance is a warrior dance performed by men; the *legong*, derived from the temple dance *gambuh* that has Majapahit origins, is performed by prepubescent girls. During the performance the dancer's head is decked with fresh flowers that tremble like the gold flowers of the crown, refracting

the light and dispersing their fragrance with the movements of the dancer. The richness of this ruby-studded version—with its *lar sumping* (wing headpieces) and rear-facing peacock tail fanned against the *gunungan* form and its talismanic *garuda mungkur* guarding the dancer's back—suggests that it was used by the palace dancers of Klungkung.

Literature: De Zoete and Spies (1938) 1973; Bandem and deBoer 1981.

93. Dance crown (FIG. 134)

Surakarta, Central Java, 1920s
Gold, diamonds, velvet and cotton ribbon, 18 × 24 × 24 cm
Istana Mangkunagaran, Surakarta

This crown is one of nine made for dancers in the *bedoyo* dance at the instigation of Mangkunagoro VII, a noted patron of the arts. The *bedoyo* is one of the oldest court dances of Java, traditionally performed by royal princesses and seen only by the members of the court. The *sumping* and diadem of the crown resemble those on temple bas-reliefs and sculpture of the Majapahit era (see FIG. 31/NO. 6). The style of the gold work is a replica of the original crown of Cirebon; the Chinese influence on coastal culture can be seen in the crown's curving and undulating profile and embossing, which resemble the cloud and rock (*megamendung* and *wadasan*) motifs typical of Cirebon art.

94a, b. *Kelat bahu* (bracelets for the upper arm) (FIG. 135)

Kutei, Kalimantan, 19th century
Gold, diamonds, 8.7 × 9.8 × 3.5 cm
Museum Nasional, Jakarta, inv. nos. E1316, E1336

Bracelets like these adorn the arms of dancers in all parts of Indonesia where Indic culture has influenced the dance, particularly in Java and Bali. Kalimantan was one of the earliest areas in Indonesia to have lasting signs of Indian contact—epigraphic material exists from the fifth century—but in later centuries Indic influences were more likely to have come by way of Java. The form of the mythical *garuda* always suggests an invocation of divine protection, and the dancer wearing these bracelets would be performing a dance from the Indian-influenced tradition rather than indigenous Kalimantan sources.

95. *Kelat bahu* (bracelet for the upper arm)

Kuteran *desa* (village), Mojokerto, East Java, 14th–15th century
Gold, 15.5 × 21.5 cm
Museum Nasional, Jakarta, inv. no. A965

This form of bracelet can be seen on the statues and figures in the friezes of eighth- and ninth-century temples in Central Java

and also on those from the Majapahit era (thirteenth to fifteenth centuries). The repoussé work of curling leaves and bosses resembling gemstones and the delicate beadwork limning the piece testify to the high standards of the Majapahit goldsmiths' art.

96. *Lontar* manuscript of *Smara Dahana* (FIG. 158)

Singaraja, North Bali, second half of 19th century
34 folios on palm leaf (*lontar*), 33 incised and inked, 2 also polychromed and gilded, wood with polychrome decoration, string and coin, 5.3 × 49.5 cm (leaf), 7 × 8 × 53 cm (box)
Peter Worsley

The oldest known manuscript on palm leaf (*lontar*: ron means leaf, *tal* means tree) is an Indian fragment dating from the second century. The first evidence for the existence of such manuscripts in Indonesia occurs in about 800 on the Buddhist monument of Borobudur, where two bas-reliefs show a Boddhisattva and companions of the future Buddha holding them. No extant texts are as old as that, but the tradition of copying manuscripts was revered in the first Mataram period in Java (coinciding with the great eighth- to ninth-century Hindu-Buddhist temples of Central Java) and continued until the end of the civilization associated with the Majapahit empire in the sixteenth century. When the forces and moral imperatives of Islam gradually assumed control of Java by the seventeenth century, the Javanese traditions of literature and art were preserved in Bali, where scholars continued to copy Old Javanese poetry and history, texts of which are known from the tenth century. Sometimes these manuscripts were written in the Javanese language and, from the early ninth century, also in Javanese script. Later in Bali they were sometimes written in Javanese language and Balinese script. The most important conservation of Java's manuscripts, however, was carried out in Balinese script and language; the preservation of Old Javanese literature lay in the hands of the Balinese for centuries. The onslaught of tropical heat, humidity and pests sets the maximum life of a *lontar* at about a century. Existing manuscripts like this one are therefore distant but direct descendants of the originals, lovingly copied in a venerated tradition.

This *Smara Dahana* is the descendant of a *kakawin* (Old Javanese poem in Indian meter) and was written by the poet Dharmaja, probably toward the end of the twelfth century. Dharmaja worked in the court of King Kameswara of Kediri, for whom the poem might have been written. (According to some scholars, King Kameswara might have been the model for Panji, the hero of the epic containing the *gedog* stories so popular in the *wayang kulit* repertory of Java and Bali.) The poem, called "The Burning of the God of Love," relates the story of the creation of Ganesha, the elephant god, by Siva and Uma, and the anger of Siva, who was attempting ascetic meditation on Mount Meru and was distracted by Kama Jaya, god of sensual love. His anger, expressed in a glare from his third eye, consumed Kama Jaya, whose wife, Ratih, also entered the fire. As spirits the two attempted reunion in the persons of Siva and Uma.

The illustrations of this manuscript are of rare refinement and unusual profusion. *Lontar* leaves are made of palm leaves cut and dried and then incised with an iron stylus (NO. 97); ink made of burnt *kemiri* nuts (an oily nut similar to the macadamia) is rubbed into the grooves (NO. 98). Pigments are added in the same way. The exquisite detail and extraordinary vitality and fantasy of the drawing, which is the precursor of the style of later Kamasan painting (FIG. 26/NO. 103), combines mythical figures depicted in *wayang* stylization with realistically rendered animals, vegetation and architecture. The imagery of this manuscript suggests a world with a unique and compelling aesthetic.

Literature: Pigeaud 1967; Zoetmulder 1974; Guy 1982; *Donald Friend's Bali* 1990.

97. Knife for *lontar* incision
Toyang *desa*, East Lombok, 20th century
Iron, 17.5 × 5.8 × .2 cm
Museum Negeri Nusa Tenggara Barat, Mataram, Lombok, inv. no. 1531

Since many of the *lontar* manuscripts in Lombok relate the same stories as the *wayang lakon* (plays), local scholars suggest that the people of the Sasak region of the island where this knife was made might have fashioned the knife in *wayang* form to invoke the spirit of the character (who here resembles the hero Amir Hamzah of the Menak cycle) to help in the depiction of the tales.

98. Pen holder and inkwell
Lombok, late 19th or early 20th century
Brass, 19 × 3.2 × 1.5 cm (well 4 cm)
Museum Negeri Nusa Tenggara Barat, Mataram, Lombok, inv. no. 1254

The pen (*kalam*) used to copy manuscript texts, particularly the Koran, was kept in containers like this slender model with its attached inkwell decorated with a scallop shell. The barrel is inscribed with Arabic letters and small abstracted motifs.

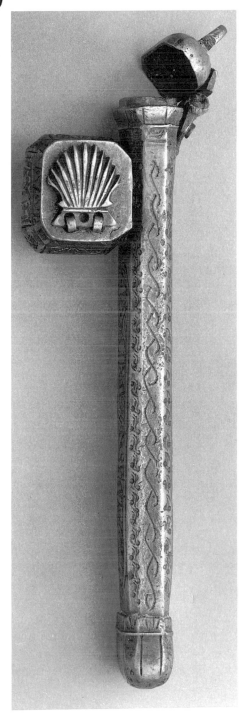

99. Manuscript of *Serat Ambiya*
(FIG. 24)

Yogyakarta, Central Java, 1844
1,267 pages of text, ink on European paper, with 122 blank pages and 102 illustrated in polychrome watercolor and gold leaf, leather binding (one cover missing), 38 × 28 × 15 cm
Museum Sonobudoyo, Yogyakarta, inv. no. SK132

This manuscript in *macapat* (meter derived from popular Javanese poetry) verse with its richly illustrated pages contains a collection of stories about the hundred *nabis*, or Islamic prophets, beginning with the creation of the world and ending with Nabi Penutup and his friends. Transcribed by Raden Arya Suryamisena, it was not produced by scholars within the *pesantren* (center for Islamic study and education), but almost certainly, on the evidence of the style of its decoration and the form of the writing, by the *kraton* of Yogyakarta in the time of Hamengkubuwono V (1822–55). (Information supplied by Banis Isma'un of the museum staff and T. E. Behrend, research scholar.)

100. Manuscript of *Sela Rasa*
(FIG. 159)

Java, 1804
294 pages (5 blank), ink on European paper, polychrome illustrations in watercolor and gold leaf, cloth and leather binding (new), 40.3 × 20 cm
The British Library, India Office Library and Records, by permission of The British Library Board, London, inv. no. Java 28, Mackenzie Collection B 32, 1823

Manuscript production was largely the province of the courts; the support of the scholars responsible for the painstaking work of writing, copying and illustrating was dependent on the kind of patronage found nowhere else. Some rulers were not only scholars but themselves authors of prose and poetry, notably Pakubuwono III (1749–88), Pakubuwono IV (1788–1820) and Mangkunagoro IV (1853–81), all of Surakarta, and Hamengkubuwono II (1792–1810) of Yogyakarta. Sometimes members of the royal families worked on the actual inscribing of the manuscripts. Ricklefs (1974:195) quotes the eighteenth-century *Serat Surja Radja*, in which the author says that the Crown Prince of Yogyakarta executed some of the inscriptions and that his wives were among those who painted and gilded it.

Colin Mackenzie (1753?–1821) was a lieutenant-colonel (later colonel) in the British Indian Army who served from 1811 until 1813 as the commanding engineer in Java during the British interregnum of 1811–16. When the British attacked the court of Yogyakarta in 1812 he acquired many manuscripts from the *kraton* library. He later sold them to the East India Company, whence they came to the India Office Library. (See FIG. 42/NO. 8 for a drawing in the Mackenzie collection.) The manuscript of *Sela Rasa*, however, was acquired in Surabaya from a "Mr. Rothenbühler" in February 1812. The original owner, noted on the first page in Javanese, seems to have been one "Nyonya Sakeber" (Ricklefs and Voorhoeve 1977:61 interpret this as either "Madame Schaber" or "*gezaghebber*," director, manager). The flyleaf is annotated in English "The History of Seloe Rodjo, an Ancient Prince of Tjampa." Though the provenance indicates Dutch owners and the tale itself is not one commonly found in *kraton* collections, the quality of the execution suggests court artisans.

This manuscript is in excellent condition. The European climate is much less destructive than that of Indonesia, so old texts stored in Britain, the Netherlands and Germany have been well conserved. What distinguishes it particularly is its clear and brilliantly colored illustrations. The figures are depicted in *wayang* style, with elongated slender limbs and facial features, but the formalism of the technique is transcended by the liveliness of the scenes, with their great variety of detailing in such items as textiles and in the rigging and manning of the European ships portrayed. We are presented with a whole visual world, not merely a formalized adjunct to the tale.
Literature: Ricklefs 1974; Ricklefs and Voorhoeve 1977; Lindsay, Soetanto and Feinstein 1987.

101. Manuscript of *Dewa Ruci*
(FIG. 160)

Yogyakarta, Central Java, 1886.
70 pages (64 illustrated), ink on European paper, polychrome watercolor and gold leaf, leather binding, 33.7 × 21 cm.
National Gallery of Victoria, Melbourne, presented by the Friends of the Gallery Library in memory of Tina Wentcher, 1982, inv. no. AS29/1982

The popular tale of Dewa Ruci concerns the search for the water of life by the Pandawa warrior hero Bima. Although Bima, whose importance in Java is indicated by the role he plays in the sculpture of *Candi* Sukuh in Central Java, is a Mahabharata character, the Dewa Ruci story is unique to the *Bratayudha*, the Indonesian version of the *Bharatayudha*.

In the opinion of M. C. Ricklefs (personal communication; Guy) this manuscript was painted by the same court painter, Jayadipura, who illustrated the *Bratayudha* (FIG. 68) for Sultan Hamengkubuwono VII (1877–1921). Certainly the painter employs the same lively mix of formalized *wayang* style with European realism and exhibits a similar skill in massing groups of figures so that the intricate details of the profiles are subsumed into a balanced rhythm of line and color. Like the *Bratayudha*, the *Dewa Ruci* combines naturalistic landscape with fantastic creatures and to an even greater extent juxtaposes mythical elements with contemporary details.
Literature: Guy 1982: 71, no. 112.

102. Manuscript of *Rama Kawi*
(FIG. 25)

Yogyakarta, Central Java, late 18th century
342 pages, ink on Dutch paper, title pages illuminated with polychrome watercolor and gold leaf, leather binding, 31 × 19.5 cm
Royal Asiatic Society, London, Raffles Java 4, Raffles Collection, 1830

Ricklefs and Voorhoeve point out that the style of illumination of the title pages of this manuscript is similar to that in the Yogyakarta court manuscript of the *babad* (chronicle) in Raffles Java 6 (in the Royal Asiatic Society), which is dated 1726 in the Javanese calendar (equivalent to 1799 in the Christian era). The author of the *babad* is identified as Raden Adipati Danureja II, chief minister of Yogyakarta, 1799–1811. It also resembles another late eighteenth-century Yogyakarta *kraton* manuscript, *Kanjeng Kyai Surya Raja*. On this basis it is reasonable to assume that the exceptionally handsome *Rama Kawi*, a variation on the Ramayana repertory of tales, is also a court piece and that it was among the manuscripts Raffles acquired after the capture of the *kraton* in 1812.
Literature: Ricklefs and Voorhoeve 1977:78, no. 117.

103. Ramayana scene (FIG. 26)

Klungkung area, Bali, 20th century
Pigment and gold leaf on cotton, 150 × 139 cm
Museum Bali, Denpasar, inv. no. 835

This painting of an episode in the Balinese version of the Hindu epic of the Ramayana is in the style practiced for many generations in Kamasan, one of the villages making up the town of Gelgel. Gelgel was the site of the *Puri Gde* (chief palace) of the Dewa Agung, Bali's senior prince, until he transferred his court a few miles to Klungkung nearly two centuries ago. Within the village a section called Banjar Sangging (ward of painters) and another called Banjar Pande Mas (ward of goldsmiths) are occupied by families concerned with painting and gold work.

Painting in Bali, like all Balinese art and craft, is strongly motivated by and dedicated to religion. It was traditionally done at the behest of the princes and was used to decorate their palaces and temples. One type consisted of long cloth strips (*ider-ider*) telling complete stories that were hung along pavilion eaves. Another form, *langse*, was in rectangular format and was used as a screening curtain before a ceremonial bed. A third kind was *tabing*, of which FIG. 26/NO. 103 is an example, which was placed behind the ceremonial bed or behind altars in temples.

Although the patrons of painting were aristocratic (members of the three upper castes [*triwangsa*] of Hinduistic Bali, the Brahmana, the Ksatria and the Wesia), the painters themselves were commoners (Sudra) who injected elements of Balinese life beyond the *puri* into their work. This typically Balinese phenomenon of vigorous popular participation has made art central in the social life of the island and has ensured its vitality and continuity.

The painters traditionally used hand-ground local ochres, imported Chinese vermilion (*kincu*), lamp-black and some vegetable dyes in a medium of Chinese protein glue (*lim Cina* or *ancur*, extracted from fish scales). They prepared the cloth by immersion in a rice paste followed by polishing with a cowrie shell to ensure a smooth surface for the inked outline of the figures in the drawing. Color, in graduated washes, was applied next; then the drawing was retouched for finer detailing. If the patron was rich and the painting important, gold leaf (*prada*) would be applied to highlight important areas.

The behavior of kings and warriors in the Ramayana was important as a moral example for the princes of Bali. This painting tells the story of the battle between the monkey army fighting on behalf of Rama and led by its general, Hanuman, and the forces of the demon king Rahwana, as Rama attempts to recover his wife Sita, whom Rahwana has abducted. Hanuman wears the magic black- and-white checked cloth (*kain poleng*) often used in Balinese rituals and found on statues in temple grounds. He has been endowed by the gods with invulnerability and special spiritual qualities. In this picture he appears three times, as the story of the battle progresses from left to right. The demon (*raksasa*) army is defeated, and Indrajit, the magically potent son of Rahwana, is killed. The flames signify the burning of Rahwana's palace, set alight by Hanuman's tail when Rahwana attempts to burn the monkey general. The scattered petals at the top of the picture may be petals rained down from heaven or dry

leaves blown into the air by the fierceness of the battle.

The usual placement of the good and evil characters at the right and left of the scene, respectively, is reversed here, perhaps because the demons are to be driven from the territory they occupy to signify the yielding of what they unjustly hold, that is, Sita. The painting also has a vertical reading that indicates rank. The lower characters are for the most part without clothing and coarser in physical type; many of them fight with their bare hands. As the eye travels up the picture the characters are more elaborately dressed, until, at the top level, refined beings with elaborate crowns and *sumping* (head ornaments) indicating high rank wield gilded weapons. This view of the world expresses the hierarchical order of the universe that is traditional in Kamasan painting. Hanuman's divinely endowed qualities of physical and spiritual strength enable him to transcend the normal barriers between refined gods and humanity on the one hand and coarse demons and beasts on the other. He appears at a mediating central level, reconciling the disparate elements. This bond between opposite groups is ideologically similar to the way the different strata of Balinese society, where caste divisions do not operate as divisively as they do in India, are connected through art.

Literature: Forge 1978; Worsley 1984.

104. *Sendi* (pillar base) of Visnu mounted on Garuda (FIG. 156)

Singaraja(?), North Bali, late 19th century
Nangka (jackfruit) wood, pigments, fish glue medium, gold leaf, 71.5 × 70.2 × 41.5 cm
Museum Bali, Denpasar, inv. no. DM 4337

Sendi are bases for the pillars springing from the cross-beams and supporting the roof beams of Balinese ceremonial pavilions. Often they were decorated with sculptures like this example that invoked protection for the building. Visnu is identifiable from the holy-water container in his hand and from his mount, the mythical bird Garuda, who achieved this distinction by refraining from drinking the holy water of life after stealing it from the gods to heal his sick mother. Garuda is in turn supported by an elephant, a *naga* and a *karang* (monster), all symbols of protection. The exuberance of the sculpture is typical of an aspect of Balinese art that pervades the architecture of temples, house pavilions and gates.

105. Oil lamp

East Java, 14th–15th century
Bronze, 16.7 × 19 × 10 cm (chain 32.6 cm)
Collection University of Amsterdam, on loan to the Royal Tropical Institute, Tropenmuseum, Amsterdam, inv. no. 2960-119

This hanging oil lamp provides evidence for the pre-Islamic emergence of the stylization of sculpture in *wayang* form and hence for the early development of *wayang* itself. The three figures decorating the lamp are almost two-dimensional, and it is imaginable that when the lamp was lit they would cast a shadow in somewhat the way *wayang kulit* puppets' forms are projected onto the screen. The largest figure, a high-ranking personage from the evidence of his headdress, may be Bima holding in his hand the water of life, the quest for which is related in the Dewa Ruci story.

106. *Blencong* (*wayang* lamp) (FIG. 143)

Central Java, 1776
Brass, 53.3 × 48.8 × 66.7 cm
Museum Wayang, Jakarta, inv. no. MW/J/71

The *blencong* provides the traditional lighting for a *wayang kulit* performance, being hung above the *dalang*'s head behind the *kelir* (screen) so that its coconut oil-fueled flame projects a flickering light on the puppets. The mobile nature of the light animates the projected shadows, an illusion that modern lights fail to impart. The *garuda* is a common form for old *blencongs*, perhaps because of its talismanic qualities; another frequently used and probably older form for the lamp is the *gunungan*. By holding the *wayang* at varying distances from the lamp, the *dalang* affects the size of the shadow: a piece held close to the flame projects an expanded image, so that a character may assume superhuman dimensions; puppets brandished at a distance from the screen can suggest sweeping movements through space and imply long journeys. Once fixed into the *dhebog* (the banana trunk base) close to the screen, the *wayang* casts a sharply etched shadow where individual movements of the arms can underscore the dialogue. This *blencong* was presented to the museum in 1976 by Colonel C. A. Heshuisius, whose family had acquired it in the nineteenth century.

107. *Wayang kulit* (shadow puppet), *gunungan* (*kayon*) (FIG. 1)

Yogyakarta, Central Java, Ngabean set, 1917–42
Buffalo hide parchment, pigment, gold leaf, fish glue medium, buffalo horn, 109.8 × 48.3 × 2.7 cm
Museum Wayang, Jakarta, inv. no. 180/MW/A/97

The *gunungan* with its ambiguous mountain-tree form is the central piece in the arrangement of *wayang* in the *dhebog* on both sides of the screen (see FIG. 37/NO. 2). In the center of some *gunungans* there is a pavilion, a male symbol alluding to the fertility implications of the *kobongan* shrine. This example has a *blumbang* (pool), a female symbol and several guardian figures: *raksasa* (demons) at the bottom, *makara* (mythical dolphin-*naga* creatures) flanking the pool, a *kala* head above it, then apposed buffalo (representing the forces of good) and tiger (evil). A *naga* curls sinuously around the trunk of the Tree of Life while the whole *alas-alasan* (forest life) scene is animated by monkeys and several varieties of bird.

A complete *kotak* (set) of *wayang kulit*, which may comprise 400 or more puppets, typically takes twenty-five years to make. This piece and FIG. 57/NO. 109, and NOS. 111 and 112 were commissioned by Prince Ngabean, the older brother of Hamengkubuwono VIII, and demonstrate the high standards of carving and painting inspired by aristocratic patronage. (Information about this and the other *wayang kulit* examples was supplied by Bapak Haryono Guritno.)

Literature: Kats (1923) 1984; Anderson 1965; Guritno et al. 1984; Keeler 1987.

108. *Wayang kulit*, Batara Guru (FIG. 33)

Magelang, Central Java, 1870
Buffalo hide parchment, pigment, gold leaf, fish glue medium, buffalo horn, semiprecious stones, 74.7 × 27 × 1.7 cm
Museum Wayang, Jakarta, Po Liem Collection, Gift of Bapak Harjono, inv. no. 54/WK/IN

This richly decorated set was ordered by Po Liem, a wealthy Chinese merchant from Muntilan, Central Java. It was made by Ki Guno Kerti of Magelang who, like most renowned *wayang* makers, possibly worked for a *kraton*, in this case that of

Yogyakarta, and executed private commissions in his own time. The date of this piece is 1870, expressed in the *sangkala* (date cryptogram) of the Java year 1792 revealed in the entwined snakes that almost conceal the bull Nandi, the mount of Siva. In the *wayang purwa* repertory drawn from the Bratayudha epic Siva is represented by Batara Guru, here shown with Indic-derived *mahkota*, or crown (compare the crowns of Gowa, FIG. 91, and of Banten, FIG. 175/NO. 134) and *praba*, the wing-shaped backpiece, a kingly symbol. His head piece (*sumping*) is in the form *sureng pati* (from the Javanese *suro ing pati*, daring death), which is also an indicator of princely rank. The batik motif is the *parang*, traditionally restricted to the nobility, and he wears a thread-form necklace (*kalung ulur-ulur*) and anklets (*gelang kroncong*).

109. *Wayang kulit*, Arjuna (FIG. 57)

Yogyakarta, Central Java, Ngabean set, 1917–42
Buffalo hide parchment, pigment, gold leaf, fish glue medium, buffalo horn, bone studs, 69.5 × 28 × 1.5 cm
Museum Wayang, Jakarta, inv. no. 192/MW/A/97

Made for Prince Ngabean (like FIG. 1/NO. 107), this Arjuna figure exemplifies many of the characteristics of the Yogyakarta *wayang* style. The eye is more slitted than in Surakarta examples (see NO. 117) and the surface decoration and carving are rich and intricate, more explicit but less spiritual. Yogyakarta *wayang* have slightly longer arms than Surakarta puppets and are consequently harder for the *dalang* to manipulate. In a complete *wayang kotak* there are several versions of Arjuna, one of the most important characters in the Bratayudha cycle of the *wayang purwa* repertory, to represent different moods or phases (*wondo*). These include *wondo mangu* (in doubt), *wondo kanjut* (carried away by the charms of a princess), *wondo malatsih* (attractive to others), *wondo kinanti* (mature), as well as *wondo janggleng* (calm and sure of himself), the *wondo* of this figure. Arjuna appears under nine different names in addition to his own: Parta, Canaka, Margana, Pandusivi, Kombangaliali, Indratanaya, Prabukaliti, Dananjaya and Palguno.

Arjuna is one of the princely Pandawa brothers and the prototypical hero who is fearless in battle but refined, attractive to women but capable of great asceticism. Here he wears the princely draped *dodot* cloth with *limar sisik* (scales) and *garuda* wings and tail *sawat* motifs, and a *manggaran*, a *kris* stylized as garlands of flowers in the *wayang* convention for the

satriya (princely warrior) caste. His *sumping* is in *waderan* (fish) form and his hairstyle (*gelung*) in *supit urang*, or shrimp style. In keeping with the maturity and enlightenment gained through meditation that are expressed in this *wondo*, he wears no jewelry, a sign of purity.

110. *Wayang kulit*, Rama (FIG. 146)

Kedu, Central Java, 1815
Buffalo hide parchment, pigment, gold leaf, fish glue medium, buffalo horn, metal studs, 71.3 × 26.8 × 1 cm
Museum Wayang, Jakarta, gift of Air Marshall (ret.) Boediardjo, inv. no. 89/MW/A/65

Rama, the banished heir to the throne of Ngayodhya and the hero of the Ramayana cycle of the *wayang purwa* repertory, wears a *mahkota* (crown; compare FIG. 176, the crown of Sumedang) but no *praba*, so is not personified as a king in this puppet. Rama's *dodot* is patterned with the *semen* (foliate) motif; his *sumping* is the kingly *sureng pati* (compare FIG. 33/NO. 108). This piece, as old as the Raffles collection of *wayang kulit* from the British Museum, demonstrates that refinement of *wayang* carving was already highly developed early in the nineteenth century. Though not of courtly provenance, this piece's Kedu origin places it in the mainstream of the stylistic evolution of Yogyakarta *wayang* from the Demak origins they share with the Surakarta tradition. The latter evolved from Demak through Pajang and Kartasura, the former through Kedu.

111. *Wayang kulit*, Kresna

Yogyakarta, Central Java, Ngabean set, 1917–42
Buffalo hide parchment, pigment, gold leaf, fish glue medium, buffalo horn, metal studs, 70.3 × 21.4 × 1.8 cm
Museum Wayang, Jakarta, inv. no. 184/MW/A/97

Kresna, always black (compare the diamond-studded example, FIG. 147), is

first cousin to the Pandawa brothers on the side of their mother, Kunti, but also an incarnation of Visnu in the Bratayudha cycle of the *wayang purwa* repertory and a character whose judgment and resourcefulness is central to the eventual victory of the Pandawa faction in their war against the Korawa. He is depicted here in full kingly dress with *praba* and crown and in *wondo gendreh* (relaxed mood). With rich jewelry—snake form *kelat bahu* and *gelang kroncong* (upper arm bracelets and anklets) and also necklace (*kalung*) in *naga karangrang* form—and his arrogant head position (contrast FIG. 57/NO. 109, FIG. 146/NO. 110), he clearly projects an image of power.

112. *Wayang kulit*, Werkudara (Bima)

Yogyakarta, Central Java, Ngabean set, 1917–42
Buffalo hide parchment, pigment, gold leaf, fish glue medium, buffalo horn, bone studs, 95.3 × 44.4 × 2.2 cm
Museum Wayang, Jakarta, inv. no. 104/MW/A/97

Bima, one of the Pandawa brothers in the Bratayudha cycle of the *wayang purwa* repertory, here in his manifestation of Werkudara, is a fearless warrior of legendary strength who can stride effortlessly over vast distances. His courage and honesty make him one of the most popular *wayang* characters, even though his great size, coarse nose and bulging eyes are uncharacteristic for a heroic figure. His physical prowess has a divine origin: he is the son of the god of the winds, Sang Hyang Bayu, and the grandson of the supreme deity, Batara Guru, a provenance he shares with the monkey general Hanuman (see FIG. 149/NO. 116). Father and sons are the only *wayang* characters with the sharp poisoned fingernails (*pancanaka*) that make them invincible; all three wear the sacred *kain poleng* checked in red (for Brahma), black (for Visnu and Kresna), white (for Siva, or Batara Guru) and yel-

low (for Surya, the sun god, the father of the Pandawas' half-brother Karna, one of the most charismatic characters on the Korawa, or left, side). Bima has a *sumping* in *pudhak sinumpet* form (like a flower behind the ear) and a *gelung* (hair coil) in a style known as *minang koro* (compare FIG. 149/NO. 116).

113. *Wayang kulit*, Rahwana

Yogyakarta, Central Java, ca. 1900
Buffalo hide parchment, pigment, gold leaf, fish glue medium, buffalo horn, metal studs, 94 × 36 × 2 cm
Kraton Ngayogyakarta Hadiningrat

This puppet belongs to a set made for Hamengkubuwono VIII (1921–39), who was exceptionally interested in *wayang*,

before he became Sultan. Its ten arms make it technically unique. Rahwana (Dasamuka), the evil king of Ngalenka, abducts Sita (Sinta) from her husband Rama in the Ramayana cycle of the *wayang purwa* repertory. His coarse features and bulging eyes mark him for the unsympathetic character he is, despite the kingly adornments of his elaborate crown, sumptuous jewelry, *parang rusak* motif batik and *patola* trousers.

114. *Wayang kulit*, Rahwana (FIG. 20)

Surakarta, Central Java, mid–19th century
Buffalo hide parchment, pigment, gold leaf, fish glue medium, buffalo horn, metal studs, 90 × 38 × 1.8 cm
Istana Mangkunagaran, Surakarta, *Kyai* Sebet set

This Rahwana expresses some of the characteristics that differentiate Surakarta *wayang kulit* from Yogyakarta examples. Note the restrained palette and surface

patterning compared with NO. 113. Although individual details of costume and face are finer and more elaborate in the Yogyakarta example, the characterization of the more restrained Surakarta *wayang* is stronger. Compare also the longer arms of the Yogyakarta puppet. The *Kyai* Sebet set to which this Rahwana belongs was made for Mangkunagoro IV (1853–81), a noted poet and patron of the arts.

115. *Wayang kulit*, Yudistira (FIG. 56)

Yogyakarta, Central Java, mid–19th century
Buffalo hide parchment, pigment, gold leaf, fish glue medium, buffalo horn, metal studs, approx. 70 × 28 × 1.5 cm
Istana Pakualaman, Yogyakarta, *Kyai* Djimat set

Yudistira is the oldest of the Pandawa brothers, heroes of the right faction in the Bratayudha cycle of the *wayang purwa* repertory. He is a model of moral behavior, never lying or showing anger. In this manifestation, made for the noted patron of the arts Pakualam II (1829–58), he is of pure and mature character, as shown by his lack of jewelry. His hair style (*gelung*) is *keling* (black), and he wears an unusual double *sumping waderan*. The Pakualaman Kyai Djimat *wayang* are among the finest ever made. The carving is exceptionally fine and even extends to the *cempurit* (manipulating rods attached to the arms). Note that the *kris* is explicitly depicted and not represented in the usual way by a *manggaran*, the stylized flower garland.

116. *Wayang kulit*, Hanuman (FIG. 149)

Yogyakarta, Central Java, mid–19th century
Buffalo hide parchment, pigment, gold leaf, fish glue medium, buffalo horn, metal studs, 76.2 × 43 × 1.7 cm
Istana Pakualaman, Yogyakarta, *Kyai* Djimat set

The monkey general Hanuman, the rescuer of Sita from her abductor, Rahwana, is one of the most popular characters in the Ramayana cycle of the *wayang purwa* repertory. Characterized by his white color (other members of the monkey army are grey), he shares with his half-brother Bima (see NO. 112) not only the fearsome sharp fingernails and talismanic checked *kain poleng* but also phenomenal strength and speed of motion. Like Bima he has *gelung* (hairstyle) *minang koro* and a *sumping* in *pudhak sinumpet* (flower behind the ear) form. He is sumptuously bejeweled, with bands on his tail, upper and lower legs and arms as well as around his neck. He comes from the same set as FIG. 56/NO. 115.

117. *Wayang kulit*, Panji

Surakarta, Central Java, late 19th century
Buffalo hide parchment, pigment, gold leaf, fish
glue medium, buffalo horn, metal studs,
60.5 × 24.7 × 1.7 cm
Museum Radya Pustaka, Surakarta, inv. no.
R 15

Unlike the *wayang* characters so far discussed, Panji comes from the *wayang gedog* repertory, which enjoyed its greatest popularity in East Java. He is the quintes-

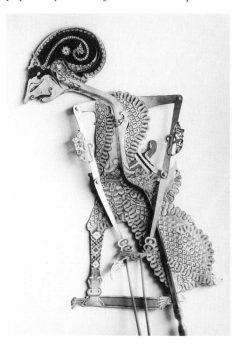

sential Javanese hero, an indigenous equivalent of Arjuna. Fine examples of *gedog* puppets are relatively rare in Central Javanese collections. This Panji comes from the collection of the *Kepatihan* (the establishment of the prince who was the Prime Minister of the Susuhunan of Surakarta) and was made in about 1890. Characteristic of Panji is the *tekas* hairstyle (*gelung*), the *grabahan* (unhusked grain of rice) eye shape, the backswept long *rapekan* sweep of the *dodot* cloth in *sisik* (scale) motif and the *kris* with formal *ladrang* sheath (*wrangka*). Like Arjuna, Panji has several *wondos* (moods); here he is shown as Panji *sepuh* (mature).

118. *Wayang kulit*, Bima (FIG. 145)

Cirebon, West Java, 19th century
Buffalo hide parchment, pigment, gold leaf, fish
glue medium, buffalo horn, bone studs,
95 × 55 × 2.2 cm
Kraton Kasepuhan, Cirebon

The *wayang kulit* of Cirebon are an interesting group. Stylistically they seem to serve as a link between an older form, perhaps already developed in Majapahit

times and probably the direct ancestor of the more naturalistic Balinese *wayang kulit*, and the more refined style of Central Javanese examples that derived from Demak either via Kedu or Pajang. The vitality of this Bima example springs not from intricate carving but from the vigor of its profile. The expression of character is more direct than in NO. 112. Noteworthy on this *wayang* are the gold *kala* heads in low relief decorating the thighs.

119. *Wayang kulit*, Srikandi (FIG. 148)

Cirebon, West Java, 19th century
Buffalo hide parchment, pigment, gold leaf, fish
glue medium, buffalo horn, bone studs,
53 × 23 × 1.4 cm
Kraton Kasepuhan, Cirebon

Srikandi is one of Arjuna's wives in the Bratayudha cycle of the *wayang purwa*. Quite unlike the conventional ideal of a wife, she is outspoken, argumentative, generous, a keen huntress and capable warrior who has become a symbol of the liberated woman in modern Indonesia. Her luxuriant hair is crowned by a coronet and she wears *patolu* cloth and upper arm bracelets (*kelat bahu*) in talismanic *garuda mungkur* form.

120. *Wayang kulit*, Banuwati (FIG. 148)

Cirebon, West Java, 19th century
Buffalo hide parchment, pigment, gold leaf, fish
glue medium, buffalo horn, bone studs,
55.5 × 21 × 1.4 cm
Kraton Kasepuhan, Cirebon

Although married to King Suyudana of Ngastina, Banuwati behaves equivocally in betraying secrets of the kingdom to the Pandawas. She had a secret love affair with Arjuna, who married her after her husband's death. The somewhat arrogant tilt of her head and her disdainful smile represent her imperious character. Her jewelry is elaborate and includes a bracelet with *garuda mungkur*, befitting a queen, and unlike the Banuwati puppets from Central Java, she wears a *slendang* (scarf) over her shoulders. Both this figure and FIG. 148/NO. 119 typify the expressiveness of Cirebon *wayang*.

121. *Wayang kulit*, Semar (FIG. 69)

Cirebon, West Java, 19th century
Buffalo hide parchment, pigment, gold leaf, fish
glue medium, buffalo horn, metal studs,
66 × 39 × 3.5 cm
Kraton Kasepuhan, Cirebon

An ambiguous figure who is both powerful god and gentle comic, the grossly fat and somewhat hermaphroditic Semar is the best-loved character in the *wayang*

kulit drama. Semar is the leader of the Panakawans, the servant clowns who attend the Pandawas and who spring from the autochthonous cultural stream rather than from the Indic tradition. This Cirebon example has a movable jaw, which adds to his animation while in use, and wears heavy bracelets at the wrists and a *gunungan*-form *sumping* (see FIG. 35/NO. 65). So popular is Semar, with a reputation for protection, that he is incorporated into objects outside the *wayang* world (see FIG. 127/NO. 45 and FIG. 54/NO. 17).

122. *Wayang klitik*, Puyengan (FIG. 144)

Central Java, 19th century
Wood, leather, pigment, gold leaf, fish glue
medium, rattan fastenings, 48.4 × 19.5 × 1 cm
Istana Mangkunagaran, Surakarta

Wayang klitik (small), also called *wayang krucil*, are wooden puppets carved in low relief with jointed leather arms. This form of the *wayang* drama existed as early as the seventeenth century, since an example exists in the National Museum of Denmark, but it is seldom performed today. The stories are drawn from the *wayang gedog* repertory concerning the adventures of Panji and Damar Wulan. Panji is the Javanese hero comparable to Arjuna in the *wayang purwa* repertory, and Damar Wulan is the young hero who thwarted the enmity of his Prime Minister uncle, Patih Logender, and the Patih's sons, conquered the opponents of the Queen of Majapahit and later married her, becoming king. This latter cycle, originating in East Java, was usually presented by *wayang klitik*, though it did appear in the other *wayang* media. The Damar Wulan cycle character Dewi Puyengan, whose rank is visible in this puppet's crown with its backward-looking talisman of the *garuda mungkur*, is one of two princesses held captive by Menak Jingga, the king of a vassal state of Majapahit, Balambangan, in the eastern salient of East Java. Humiliated by the Majapahit queen's rejection of his marriage proposal, Menak Jingga declares war on her empire. In a vision the queen, Prabu Kenya Kencana Wungu (purple-gold virgin queen), is told that the only warrior capable of defeating Menak Jingga is Damar Wulan, now imprisoned by Patih Logender in punishment for an alleged crime and for having married his daughter. Released from captivity, Damar Wulan succeeds in killing Menak Jingga with the help of the two princesses, whose lover he becomes.

Presentation of the Damar Wulan cycle was particularly popular at the Mangkunagaran palace; a musical and choreographed version of the play called

Langendriya was written in the time of Mangkunagoro IV (1853–81). The *wayang klitik* set to which Dewi Puyengan belongs probably dates from his reign.

123. *Wayang golek* (FIG. 153)

Surakarta, Central Java, 19th century
Wood, cotton cloth, diamonds, pigment, gold leaf, fish glue medium, fiber fastenings,
49 × 18 × 16 cm
K.R.T. Hardjonagoro

Though the *wayang golek* repertory in Central Java usually comprises the Islamic Amir Hamzah stories belonging to the Menak cycle (as distinct from West Java, where *golek* performance is very popular and includes *purwa* and *gedog* cycles as well), this example does not belong to that group. It is the small figure sometimes called *tayub* (union) or *gambyong* (after a famous dancer) that emerges at the end of the *wayang kulit* performance, as the dawn is breaking, to perform a dance. The tradition may spring from an old custom whereby a dancer communicates with the crowd (hence *tayub* from *tayupan*, to seek union) after the dance (compare Balinese *gambuh*, NO. 92). The *golek* sends a message to the viewers to make them consider the philosophy of the *lakon*. The refinement of carving, the *parang rusak* motif on the hand-drawn (*tulis*) batik and the diamond ear studs of this example mark it as a probable court piece.

124. *Wayang golek,* Kencana Wungu (FIG. 23)

Cirebon, West Java, before 1881
Wood, cotton and silk cloth, pigment, gold leaf, fish glue medium, metal fastenings, 47.1 cm
Rijksmuseum voor Volkenkunde, Leiden, inv. no. 264-248

This exceptionally fine *wayang golek*, acquired in 1881, might have belonged to one of the Cirebon courts or have come from one of the wealthy Chinese families in the coastal region. The character Kencana Wungu is also known as Prabu Kenya Kencana Wungu, the Queen of Majapahit in the Damar Wulan cycle (see FIG. 144/NO. 122). Her crown, with extended curved piece framing the cheekbones, is characteristic of Cirebon style (compare the dance crown, FIG. 134/NO. 93), while her dress, with its exclusively monarchial motif of *parang rusak barong* executed in *prada* (gold leaf) on the *dodot*, indicates her ruler status. The *plangi* (tie-dyed, literally rainbow) scarf (*slendang*) is exceptionally long, indicating its use as a ceremonial or dance scarf. The *golek* play in this region, known as *wayang cepak*, was characterized by the dancing movements the puppets made as they entered

the scene, so the long *slendang* used continuously by Javanese dancers is possibly an indication of this feature.

Literature: Van Dongen, Forrer and van Gulik, 1987.

125. *Wayang beber* (FIG. 151)

Java, before 1852
Paper, watercolor, ink, wood batons,
71 × 289 cm
Rijksmuseum voor Volkenkunde, Leiden, inv. no. 360-5256

Already in existence in 1433, when described by Ma Huan during a voyage with Admiral Zheng He, *wayang beber* (folding) has disappeared except from the region near Pacitan, on the south coast of East Java. The story in this form of *wayang* drama is told while the *dalang* unrolls the scroll from left to right, a graphic narrative technique comparable to that of the visual storytelling in the *ider-ider* hanging in Balinese temples and palaces. This example relates an episode from the Panji cycle. The illustrations are in classic *wayang* style (compare with the manuscripts FIG. 68, FIG. 159/NO. 100, FIG. 160/NO. 101) with exaggeratedly slender limbs and facial features and with landscape presented in the same manner (unlike the method in the manuscripts, where landscape is presented naturalistically). The scenes are divided from one another by formally stylized floral motifs and are furthermore composed so that the action of each scene is centered in its own visual field and is not confused with those on either side. At the same time its composition is in harmony with the whole, so the overall impression is homogeneous. Within the scenes there is a skilled balance of mass with the line of action, so each has a dynamism that contributes to the vitality of the entire scroll.

Literature: Thomsen 1980:218, 237.

126. Death mask (FIG. 136)

South Sulawesi, 16th century(?)
Gold, 21.25 × 18 cm
Suaka Peninggalan Sejarah dan Purbakala, Ujung Pandang, South Sulawesi

It is not known when the custom of placing death masks over the faces of the dead began in Indonesia, nor which peoples practiced the custom. In the last century, before a *wayang kulit* performance, the *dalang* would dance with *topeng* for spiritual contact with the cosmos. This example, weighing 68 grams, was unearthed accidentally by a farmer in 1966 in the village of Ujung Loe in the district of Pangkalene in South Sulawesi. There are precedents for the custom in China (see

FIG. 185/NO. 155a), and it is possible that gold death masks found in Indonesia were either from Chinese graves or from indigenous ones, maintaining a custom that arrived with the Austronesian peoples in their original migration from southwest China. The Torajans of South Sulawesi make effigies of the dead (*tau-tau*), but these are placed apart from the body. In Bali when the corpse is burned it is accompanied by an *ukur* (see FIG. 189/NO. 154), a skeleton of coins strung to the measure of the deceased, but the closest parallel to placing a mask on the face is probably the Balinese practice of placing a gold ring with a ruby (*mon-mon*) in the mouth of the deceased.

Whether death masks were the prototypes for *topeng* (dance masks) is conjectural though likely. Dance probably originated as a part of religious rites, particularly those concerned with death, when the spirit of the deceased could enter the body of the dancer. Certainly the mask lends an anonymity and indefinability enabling the performer to transcend material ties and embody universal themes.

127. *Topeng* (mask), Panji (FIG. 142)

Central Java, 19th century
Kantil wood, natural pigments, 24-carat gold leaf, fish glue medium (*ancur lempeng*, from fish scales), leather teeth-thong,
18 × 15.4 × 9.5 cm
K.R.T. Hardjonagoro

Topeng have always commanded respect within *kraton* circles. Both Pakubuwono III (1749–88) and Pakubuwono IV (1788–1820) carved them, and princes both carved and wore them, among them Prince Kusumadilaga of the early nineteenth century. This mask, for example, was owned by a famous royal dancer, Prince Prabuwinoto, a son of Pakubuwono IX (1861–93). The Panji dance, expressing the ideal embodiment of spiritual grace, is one of the most ritually important of the masked dances of Java. It is usually presented in a group of four dances (each with its specific mask) showing four stages of the worldliness and spirituality of man.

The masked dance possibly evolved from the legend of Visnu who, on looking at the world and finding it evil, descended and danced to promote the spiritual energy to change it, wearing a mask to preserve his anonymity. Other theorists believe it comes from rites of initiation, showing the ideal state of man contrasted with different levels of worldly behavior.

The Panji mask is usually gold (white in Cirebon), signifying purity and refinement, since his character is an East Javanese role model. The unusual green of this mask may imply the invocation of Visnu or a connection with Sadono, a manifestation of Visnu. Thus it may seek to invoke fertility and agriculture associations. Pigments in old masks like this one, as in Balinese painting and carving (FIG. 26/NO. 103, FIG. 156/NO. 104), are made from local ochres, indigo and lamp-black, with only the red *kincu* and the gold *prada* imported from China. The iconic simplicity of this finely carved mask with its delicately drawn details of eyes, brows and nose makes it a masterpiece of the genre. (Information supplied by K.R.T. Hardjonagoro.)

128. *Topeng*, Gunung Sari (FIG. 137)
Java, late 18th century
Wood (probably *mentaos*), pigment, fish glue medium, semiprecious stones, glass, 19 cm
Society of the Friends of Asiatic Art on loan to the Rijksmuseum, Amsterdam, inv. no. MAK 262

Gunung Sari is a prince of Kediri, the brother of Panji's wife Candra Kirana (sometimes also referred to as the princess of Daha) in the Panji cycle of stories. The carving of this mask is of unusual subtlety, the modulations of the facial planes and the enigmatic curl of the lips the work of a consummate artist. The richness of the crown indicates possible courtly patronage.
Literature: Van Lelyveld 1929:299–305; Visser 1948:pl. 369; *Oosterse schatten* 1954:no. 720.

129. *Topeng*, Klono(?) (FIG. 139)
Kutei, East Kalimantan, late 19th century
Wood, pigments, gold leaf, fish glue medium, diamonds, hair, 19.3 × 17.6 × 12.5 cm
Museum Nasional, Jakarta, inv. no. E1303

From the evidence of its unusually lavish decoration, with diamonds studding the teeth and repoussé gold plaques set into a gold diadem, this mask probably came from the court collection in Kutei. The form of the jeweled shapes on the crown have affinities with those on FIG. 137/NO. 128, but the character is of a much less refined nature, so the persona is likely to be Klono, a foreign king who threatens Kediri because he wants to capture Candra Kirana (see NO. 128) for himself. Although the mask has a crown and is white, both features that could indicate nobility, the protruding eyes are signs of coarseness and imply an ignoble character.

130. *Topeng*, Srikandi (FIG. 138)
Cirebon, West Java, late 19th or early 20th century
Wood, pigment, gold leaf, fish glue medium, leather teeth-thong, 17.5 × 14.5 × 10.2 cm
Istana Mangkunagaran, Surakarta

Srikandi is a character from the Bratayudha cycle, one of the wives of Arjuna and a strong personality who is a noted Amazon and has recently become a symbol of women's liberation in Indonesia. This mask comes from the famous collection amassed by Mangkunagoro VII (1916–44) in the 1920s and 1930s. The Cirebon examples were acquired from the Captain of the Chinese community in Semarang in the coastal region thought to have been the source of the masked dance. Characteristic of Cirebon masks are the sharper carving and the two small lines drawn below the eyelid, as well as the more direct expression of personality compared with the more inscrutable nature of Central Javanese masks. This accessibility is a quality the masks have in common with *wayang kulit* from Cirebon (see FIG. 69/NO. 121, FIG. 145/NO. 118, FIG. 148/NO. 119, FIG. 148/NO. 120).

131. *Telek* (mask) (FIG. 17)
Bali, 20th century(?)
Pole wood, fish glue patination, 15.6 × 12.5 × 6 cm
Museum Bali, Denpasar, inv. no. DM 437

Court and vernacular art in Bali are closely allied, so that the refinement of this piece, which in Java would indicate a court provenance, is not an identifying characteristic. The mask represents one of the five female retainers of the Barong, the gigantic mythical lion figure who represents good in the popular dance depicting the struggle against evil as personified by the female witch, Rangda. Though not of noble rank, the character exhibits the *halus* (refined) qualities inherent in the simplicity that suggests the power of good that her master embodies.

132. *Pepadon* (ceremonial seat) (FIG. 178)
Abung people, Lampung, South Sumatra, 19th century
Wood, 176 × 157 × 67 cm
Australian National Gallery, Canberra, inv. no. 1985.1982

The role of *pepadons* in ceremonies of rank in Lampung is still somewhat uncertain. In some cases the seats were a status perquisite available after the giving of a feast of merit, a custom that seems to have coincided with the Javanization of Lampung during the late colonial period, when

Lampung and its prosperous pepper trade were dominated by Banten. The origins seem to predate this period, however. According to Schnitger, *pepadons* were allowed to belong only to a man who had cut off four heads. In the village of Ogan Lima and neighboring villages *pepadons* àre considered *pusaka* and kept either in the roof, the Upperworld area of the house, or under precious cloths in the living area. Women and strangers are forbidden to see some *pepadons*; some have a guardian function that may manifest itself as a snake that appears when unauthorized people intrude in the owner's house (see chapter 1).

Pepadons are occasionally only slab seats on short legs, but sometimes, as in this case, they have backs (*sasako*) with elaborate carving. These often depict the Tree of Life and have paired *nagas* flanking the central panel. Hooykaas quotes Galestin's opinion that Balinese kings leaned against such ceremonial backrests, while the Bataks' ritual stone ancestor seats had back slabs that were similar to the megaliths found in Minangkabau and could have been a precedent for *pepadon* backs. Certainly the iconography of the *pepadon* with its Tree of Life (paired in this example), rampant snakes, luxuriant foliage and animal imagery is consistent with a tradition of the ruler's association with these symbols of fertility and protection. It is not, however, a symbol of the ruler in the sense of a western throne, since there are several in each clan, but rather an indication of the social status of the individual owner.
Literature: F. M. Schnitger (1938) 1964; J. Hooykaas 1957.

133. Crown (FIG. 174)
Bima, East Sumbawa, 1790 or earlier
22-carat gold stained red, diamonds, cloth lining, 17.2 × 10.5 cm
Kabupaten Bima, East Sumbawa, for the Sultan of Bima

The name of this crown, the state crown of Bima, is Songko Masa Sangajikai (king's golden crown). Symbolizing the precept of *dou la-o dana na* (the raja upholds society and the state), it is one of the three *pusaka* (heirlooms) legitimizing the installation of the ruler as Sangaji, or Sultan. The others are the state *kris* (FIG. 173/NO. 138) and the ceremonial umbrella of *lontar* (palm leaf) decked with gold fittings symbolizing the ruler's protection of the realm. The form of the crown shows Bugis influence, but it was made in Bima, either copying an earlier one dating from the sixteenth century (made by the twelfth

Raja of the pre-Islamic dynasty known as Dewa Maja Paruwa) or restoring it. The first ruler to be consecrated with it was Syafiuddin (1791–95), Sultan IX of the Dewa Dalam Bawa dynasty of the colonial era.

The red stain (see FIG. 168/NO. 10) is characteristic of the work of Bimanese goldsmiths, who were influenced by Balinese craftsmen in the use of the Chinese-derived foliate motifs like those of the crown's à-jour and embossed body. The former wealth of Bima—a kingdom ideally situated to profit from the maritime trading patterns between the spice islands of Maluku and the large polities of Java and Sumatra and which dominated Flores and Sumba for four centuries until the mid-nineteenth century—can be deduced from the impressive total of more than seven hundred fine diamonds that contribute to its weight of nearly three and a half pounds (one and a half kilograms).

134. Crown (FIG. 175)
Banten, West Java, 18th century
Gold, rubies, diamonds, emeralds, pearls, enamel work, 16.5 × 19.3 cm
Museum Nasional, Jakarta, inv. no. E587

Both the crown's stylized foliate motifs in the à-jour work, where a Tree of Life motif is formalized into niche shapes in repeated panels, and the enameling on the upper segment demonstrate the strong influence of Islamic design on the art of this strongly Muslim sultanate. Though the crown is probably only about two hundred years old, clearly it has been exposed to prototypes similar to Salokoa, the fourteenth- or fifteenth-century crown of Gowa (FIG. 91). A possible source for the stupa shape of both is the helmetlike headdress, with decorations in the form of Buddha hair-curls, that was worn by the *wajrayana* (priest) during rituals of a sect of Buddhism that was patronized by the rulers of Majapahit. The top of this stupa-shaped headdress (a remarkable example of which belongs to the Rijksmuseum voor Volkenkunde in Leiden, illustrated in Van Dongen, Forrer and Van Gulik 1987:111) also offers a source for the later secular crowns. It is in the form of a *vajra*, a Buddhist priest's scepter that symbolizes enlightenment, its curved prongs enclosing a crystal. The Leiden example lacks this gem, but a similar piece (destroyed in the fire at the Colonial Exhibition in Paris in 1931) still had a crystal. With this precedent in mind it is interesting to note the curved prongs clasping the gem on top of the Banten crown and vertical pieces on the Gowa crown that could be an abstraction from prongs supporting a finial gem. If this theory is correct, the crown of Banten, in this case fusing Indic and Islamic imagery, could be an important example of the syncretism that pervades Indonesian art and society. (Information on *vajra* and *Vajrayana* ritual headdresses and similar objects in Tibet and Nepal was supplied by Dra. Pauline Lunsingh Scheurleer of the Rijksmusem, Amsterdam.)
Literature: Van Dongen, Forrer and Van Gulik 1987:110–11; Scheurleer and Klokke 1988.

135. Clip for sarong
Central Java, 18th century or earlier.
Iron, gold, 8.5 × 6.6 × 1.5 cm
Collection of Samuel Eilenberg

The gold and iron work of this clip resembles that of the *krises* and lances (nos. 13, 14, 68) forged during the great period of Javanese smithing from the seventeenth to the nineteenth century. Its *naga* (snake) image indicates that it might have been used by an aristocratic boy after his circumcision. Such clips were hooked over the sarong at the waist and supported a stick that projected forward to keep the cloth from rubbing the wound. The elaborate craftsmanship of pieces like this clip and no. 14 testifies to the significance of circumcision as one of the most important rites of passage in post-Islamic Java.

136. State *kris* (FIG. 172)
Gianyar, Bali, early 19th century
Iron, nickel *pamor*, gold, rubies, diamonds, *pelet* (*timaha*) wood, 63 × 19.5 × 5 cm
Dr. Mr. Ide Anak Agung Gde Agung, Puri Agung, Gianyar

The *pamor* of this *kris* is from meteoritic nickeliferous iron, not typical for Balinese *krises*, and is in the *paku pipit* (fern frond) motif. The *ukiran* (grip) is in the form of a *buta nawosari* (ogre carrying a *nagasari* flower, the *nagapuspa* flower of the Buddha) in *peperutan* (bellied) shape, an anthropomorphic figure empowered to guard the spirit of the *kris* and the well-being of the owner. The gold sheet of the grip (reserved for the nobility) is molded over a mixture of resin and crushed brick called *gegalasari*. The large rubies and diamonds of the grip, the *mendak* (tang ring) and the *wewer* (Balinese for *selut*, grip ring) indicate the courtly status of the owner. The wood of the sheath, which is in *gayaman* form, is covered with a gold *pendok* on one side only, since *pelet* wood (the same as *timaha* in Java) is considered a gift from the gods and should not be hidden.

digenous fertility symbol with later Hindu overtones of the goddess Sri Devi. Sri is a relic of Indic religious knowledge in daily life that was once pervasive but has now been lost.

Known often as a bridal pair, *loro blonyo* sit in front of the *kobongan*, the ritual marriage bed that is also known as a shrine for Dewi Sri and may originally have been devised as a place for her to rest. In a palace this bed is in the *dalem*, or inner sanctum. In the area where the figures sit there are often accoutrements of daily life, such as toilet and cosmetic sets and *sirih* objects; offerings will also sometimes be placed there. Although associated with the marriage bed and described as a bridal pair, the *loro blonyo* are not present during the marriage ceremony. They are replaced by the bridal couple sitting in front of the *kobongan* in the same pose as the sculptures, thus emphasizing the importance of fertility symbols during the marriage rites without the actual presence of a Hinduistic or animist symbol. In Surakarta the presence of *loro blonyo* was restricted to noble families, but in Yogyakarta any family was permitted to own a pair. Non-noble pairs (see FIG. 3/NO. 146) were sometimes carved in standing position and often made of painted terra cotta, but court pieces were always carved of wood and depicted the figures in *halus* (refined) kneeling position.

One very fine pair (FIG. 38) was made in about 1875 by K.R.T. Wreksodiningrat, the grandfather of Mangkunagoro VIII's wife and the brother of the *Patih* (chief minister) of Pakubuwono X. The rare combination of refinement and humanism, of spirituality without remoteness, makes them masterpieces of the type. In the Surakarta and Yogyakarta *kratons*, *loro blonyo* are not placed in the *dalem* but instead set in the *Patihan*, the chief minister's residence, where the most sacred *loro blonyo* were kept. That is the provenance of this example, shown in court dress (note in particular Dewi Sri's *plangi* breast-cloth and Sadono's *timang* and *lerep* belt buckles; see FIG. 113/NO. 52, FIG. 114/NO. 53); they belonged to the *Patih* Sosolodiningrat of Surakarta in the last quarter of the nineteenth century. Made by an unknown artist, they are of incomparable quality. The carving of the faces has a serenity and simplicity reminiscent of the finest Buddhist sculpture and the most iconic masks (such as FIGS. 16, 140, 141), that of the bodies suggests meditative calm coupled with an unforgettable spirit of inner intensity.
Literature: B. and M. Ashabranner 1980:112–19.

146a, b. *Loro Blonyo* (FIG. 3)
Yogyakarta, Central Java, early 19th century
Wood, pigment, gold leaf, fish glue medium, copper gilt, silk, cotton; male figure 58 cm, female figure 54.5 cm
Rijksmuseum voor Volkenkunde, Leiden, inv. no. 360-7463, 360-7464

These standing *loro blonyo* figures, acquired by the museum in 1883 from the Royal Cabinet of Rarities, pose a question. Since standing *loro blonyo* are usually of vernacular origin and court pairs are always kneeling with legs tucked beneath the body, how can one account for the courtly refinement of these examples? The carving and painting of the ritually white faces is extremely delicate; they are dressed as a royal bridal pair and wear *patola* with *prada* (gold) for sarong and trousers. Sadono wears a *dodot* and Dewi Sri a *prada*-decorated breast cloth. Their jewelry is of the ceremonial style and they wear diadems, all of which suggest that they have a court provenance. The style of the carving is reminiscent of the *gambyong wayang golek* (FIG. 153/NO. 123).
Literature: Van Dongen, Forrer and Van Gulik 1987:82, 83.

147. *Lelancang* (bowl for *sajen*, offerings) (FIG. 187)
Gianyar, Bali, early 19th century
Gold, rubies, sapphires, ebony wood, 19.4 × 41.5 × 19 cm
Dr. Mr. Ide Anak Agung Gde Agung, Puri Agung, Gianyar

Boat-shaped bowls (see chapter 1) were used in temple ceremonies to present the gods with offerings and fragrant flowers. This example, made by a *puri* craftsman, is a fine example of Balinese goldsmithing. It is of twenty-two-carat gold and Burmese jewels and has an unusual repoussé design that depicts a Bratayudha story on the upper portion. The base, which was made later, has a more normal floral (*kekayunan*) motif.

148a–c. *Swamba* (holy-water pot), *sasirat* (sprinkler) and *tripada* (tripod stand) (FIG. 188)
Gianyar, Bali, 17th century
Gold, silver, rubies, sapphires, 36 × 16.4 × 16 cm overall (pot 14.6, sprinkler 30, tripod 10.9 cm)
Dr. Mr. Ide Anak Agung Gde Agung, Puri Agung, Gianyar

Containers of water made holy by rituals conducted by the Brahman *pedanda* or *prohita* priests are used in several Balinese ceremonies, including temple festivals, tooth-filings and marriage rituals. The motif of this *tripada*—three lions (*singa asti*) supporting three pillars—symbolizes beauty and spirituality, a typical Balinese blending of aesthetic and religious meanings. The priest, uttering ritual prayers, sprinkles the water, pours and swallows some of it in motions repeated three times, after which the water inside the *swamba* is deemed to have become *air tirta* (holy water) with great religious validity and vitality.

The triple structure of the ensemble represents three levels of the wisdom of life that comes from Siva, the uppermost level to be achieved in trance by the repeated chanting of sacred formulas (*mantra*). Though the chasing of the tripod and the elegant restraint of the pot are of considerable artistry, the most remarkable element in this holy-water set is undoubtedly the exquisite filigree sprinkler. A linga symbol (appropriate to Siva), it consists of eight delicate prongs, cupped by a lotus flower and set in wire so that they tremble when moved. Each prong has a meaning. The *gada* (hooked pieces) signify strength; the *trisula* (trident) stands for power and righteousness, the *tombak* (lance) for astuteness, the *naga* for human authority, while the *cakra*, a sun symbol, represents the emblem of Krishna. The central twined rope symbolizes the power of the cosmos that binds passion with restraint and sobriety. The gems also have meaning, the sapphires standing for purity and the rubies for force. (Information about the iconography of this item, as for many of the other Balinese objects, was provided by Dr. Mr. Ide Anak Agung Gde Agung.)

149a, b. *Sangku* (holy-water beaker) with lid (FIG. 59)
South Bali, 19th century or earlier
Silver gilt, rubies, 11.2 × 6 cm
Rijksmuseum voor Volkenkunde, Leiden, inv. no. 3077-1

The function of this *sangku* is similar to that of NO. 148 and, like it, is certainly of *puri* provenance. The repoussé and chased motifs include foliate meanders and a birdlike form.

150a, b. *Sangku suddhamala* (zodiac beaker) with lid
East Java, 1356
Bronze, 14 cm
Collection Mr. and Mrs. Oorthuys, on loan to the Rijksmuseum, Amsterdam, loan no. 24

Beakers of this type, with figures representing signs of the zodiac in relief around the lower sides and unidentified *wayang*-like beings (one resembles Semar) in the upper row, have been preserved in Bali as *pusaka* and are still used as holy-water containers in East Java on the slopes of

Mount Bromo. Many of them are dated, as is this one; the figures 1277 are placed above the bird motif (Saka dating system, equivalent to 1356 of the Christian era). Literature: Scheurleer and Klokke 1988:45–46, 143.

151. *Siwur* (or *gayung*, ladle)

Klungkung, Bali, 19th century(?)
Gold, wood, 45.4 × 8.2 × 7.2 cm
Museum Nasional, Jakarta, inv. no. E776

Although attached to a handle, the bowl of this ladle with its small pouring-spout closely resembles the form of the *swamba* in FIG. 188/NO. 148. Like that vessel, it was used for pouring—as distinct from sprinkling—holy water during purification ceremonies in Balinese temples.

152. *Sendok* (spoon)

Badung, Bali, 19th century(?)
Gold, tortoiseshell, rubies, wood,
39.8 × 6 × 2.9 cm
Museum Nasional, Jakarta, inv. no. E931

The elegance of the curve of the bowl and the gold-banded handle of this ceremonial spoon with its ruby-studded collar is typical of the importance attached to the design of even simple objects in Bali, where ideally all human endeavor is pleasing to the gods.

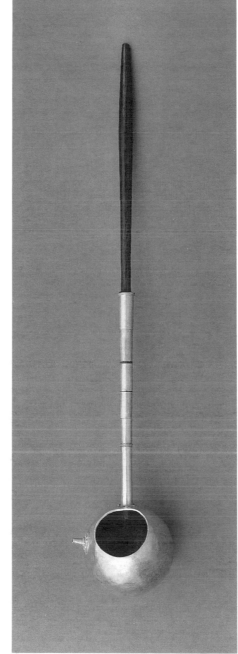

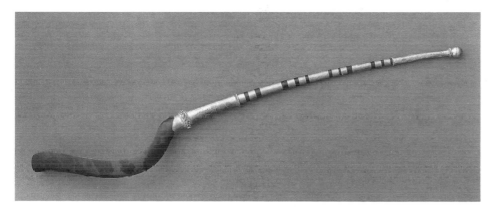

153. *Wahana* (miniature vehicle for a votive figure) (FIG. 60)

Bali, 20th century
Wood, pigments, gold leaf, fish glue medium, lacquer, 48.5 × 49 × 22 cm
Collection of the Australian Museum, Sydney, inv. no. E66858

This type of box, like miniature litters and other boxes in the form of birds and animals, is designed to contain the symbol of a deity and is used to carry that figure to the temple in procession. The consecrated effigy, known as an *arca lingga*, is then ready to become the temporary receptacle for the spirit of the god when he or she chooses to arrive. The two crowned *nagas* carried on the back of a turtle bring to mind the legend that the island of Bali rests on the back of Bedawan Nala, the Underworld turtle held between the coils of two serpents in the form of Anantabhoga and Basuki. The tigerlike beast crouching on the *nagas'* backs probably represents the forces of evil.

154. *Ukur* (measure of the corpse) (FIG. 189)

Lombok, 19th century(?)
Gold, 136.7 × 30 × 1.5 cm
Museum Nasional, Jakarta, inv. no. E1019

Ukurs (*sukat* in High Balinese) are skeletons of the dead, usually made of *kepengs* (Chinese coins) strung together with cotton to the exact measure of the body to ensure that the body can be properly reconstituted in the next incarnation. They are burned with the body during the cremation ceremony, a process that would seem to negate their stated purpose, which is in any case contrary to the principle of cremation, an act that liberates the soul from its earthly form to enable it to rise to a higher level of being.

In noble families the *ukur* was made of gold plaques with chased designs strung together with wire as in this example. According to Wirz, they were fixed to a matrix of bamboo rods; such a frame no longer exists for FIG. 189/NO. 154. In the account of Covarrubias, the gold versions were not burned with the corpse but saved as heirlooms, a *kepeng* substitute replacing them before the funeral tower was ignited. This would account for the survival of this example, whose provenance is Lombok, an island dominated by Balinese culture.

Literature: Wirz 1928:28; Covarrubias 1937:366–67. (I am grateful to John Stowell for translating the German.)

155a, b. Death mask and penis cover
(FIGS. 185, 186)
South Sulawesi, 11th–13th century
Gold; mask: 13.7 × 9.8 cm; cover: 10.5 × 7.3 cm
Samuel Eilenberg

The date for this mask and penis cover is posited on the evidence of its discovery site: both pieces were found in a grave containing Sung-period (960–1279) porcelain. Since the practice of burying porcelain with the corpse was common in this region, much excavation in search of interred Chinese, Sawankalok and Vietnamese wares has recently been carried out and has unearthed a few death masks like this (compare FIG. 136/NO. 126, discovered accidentally by a farmer). The custom of placing bronze or silver death masks on the face was known in China during the Liao dynasty (907–1125), which may indicate any of several possibilities: a Chinese corpse in the grave, a tighter time frame for the making of these pieces, the geographical origin of the deceased or his forebears, the date when his forebears left China, or a combination of all these data. The use of gold reflects available local materials and possibly the status of the deceased.

One aberrant item in this reasoning based on Chinese historical factors is the penis cover, which is rare: the form and concept relate to Austronesian traditions rather than Chinese. This distinction is strengthened by the depiction of penis inserts (see FIG. 181/NO. 64) on the cover; these also indicate an indigenous rather than a foreign tradition. The conjunction of two traditions represented by these two objects placed on the same corpse may be another example of the syncretizing tendencies of Indonesian culture.

156a. *Palepai* (ceremonial hanging)
(FIG. 45)
Kalianda, Southeast Lampung, Sumatra, 19th century
Cotton, supplementary weft, 63.5 × 266.7 cm
Robert J. Holmgren and Anita E. Spertus, inv. no. I-387

Palepai, like *tampan*, were used on ceremonial occasions, but their use was restricted to the nobility. They were hung as a backdrop to the owner during marriage ceremonies, formal public gatherings (sometimes with the *pepadon* seat of rank placed in front) and for death rites. The imagery presents large ships that convey in microcosm all the accoutrements of an aristocratic life and its rites of passage and all the necessities for journeys of the soul and the ancestors. This example's paired images suggest that it was used in a marriage ceremony, the treasure-boxes, shrines, pennants and elephants of one set of characters balanced by those of the other. The different nature of the Trees of Life that flank the ship—one with Dongson-derived hooked branches, the other with slender upward-reaching branches decked with hangings—may indicate the different aspects of the two parties concerned. The scene is teeming with figures, groups of people, birds and subsidiary vessels, all skillfully integrated into the shapes defined by the steeply curving prow and stern and the ranks of oars.
Literature: Holmgren and Spertus 1989:86–93; Gittinger 1979:88–91.

156b. *Palepai* (ceremonial hanging)
(FIG. 50)
Semangka Bay, South Lampung, Sumatra, 19th century
Cotton, supplementary weft, 67.7 × 245.1 cm
Robert J. Holmgren and Anita E. Spertus, inv. no. I-276

This blue ship, like the red-prowed ship (FIG. 45/NO. 156a), has matched pavilions, banners, and small suspended structures that seem to contain offering tables. Unlike the other ship it contains only two people; the small figures filling in the surrounding spaces are much more abstracted and geometrical. Moreover, it contains a central Tree of Life but is accompanied by an external tree on one side only. It is a less vital but more iconic scene.
Literature: Holmgren and Spertus 1989:86–93; Gittinger 1979:88–91.

157. *Palepai* (ceremonial hanging)
(FIG. 190)
South Lampung, Sumatra, 19th century
Cotton, supplementary weft, gold thread, 61 × 285 cm
Royal Tropical Institute, Tropenmuseum, Amsterdam, inv. no. 1969-4

This gold embellished *palepai* is outstanding in the perfection of its symmetry and its mastery of spatial organization. The main elements of two *gunungan*-shaped Trees of Life flanking the ship are delicately balanced by the dispersal of subsidiary echoing shapes. No fewer than six small Trees of Life, alternating blue and red, surround each main tree, while a second series of hooked oars, also alternating blue and red, branches out from each of the three steeply angled prow and stern elements. Gittinger suggests that red color in *palepai* ships signifies the sacred realm and blue the earthly one. On that basis this cloth presents a microcosm where the two are in perfect balance and harmony. All the people depicted beneath the trees, in the main ship and on the small ships to the left and right are standing strictly at attention, all attired in formal *dodot* cloths. Birds, fish and small geometric elements are distributed over the entire surface, giving vitality to the space without detracting from the dominant architectonics of the design. One has the impression of a powerful dynasty confronting and dominating both this world and the next in this masterpiece of weaving.
Literature: Gittinger 1979.

CHRONOLOGY

early 3rd century C.E.:
Indirect Chinese evidence of Sumatran trading centers.

early 4th century:
Barbarian invasion of North China closes trade route across Central Asia; development of maritime route for trade in luxury goods from West Asia to China.

ca. 400:
Reign of King Mulavarman in Kutei, East Kalimantan, referred to in Indic inscriptions.

413–14:
Chinese Buddhist pilgrim Fa Hsien, sailing from India to China, reports "pagans" in Java.

424:
Kashmiri Prince Gunavarman sails from India to China by way of Indonesia.

ca. 450:
Inscriptions near Bogor record earliest Indonesian irrigation works and reveal Brahman connections of King Purnavarman of Tarumanagara, West Java.

ca. 500:
Sumatran camphor and benzoin supplied to China in lieu of Persian frankincense and myrrh by state in region of Palembang.

7th century:
Emergence of Srivijayan kingdom centered in Palembang.

671–95:
Visit to Srivijaya and Melayu (now Jambi) by Chinese Buddhist pilgrim I Tsing indicates an important center of Buddhist learning.

late 7th century:
Earliest known inscriptions in Old Malay recorded in Srivijaya.

732:
Saivite sanctuary inscription records erection of linga by King Sanjaya of Mataram, Central Java.

778:
Inscription in *Candi* Kalasan near Yogyakarta, Central Java, celebrates Sailendra Buddhist King Rakryan Panangkaran.

ca. 800:
Construction of Borobudur by the Sailendra dynasty.

856:
Ratu Boko inscription celebrates victories of a Saivite monarch.

907:
Kedu stone records predecessors of Maharaja Belitung dating back to Sanjaya.

929–47:
Reign of Sindok; center of power now in East Java.

second half of 10th century:
Many embassies from Srivijaya to China.

1006:
Srivijayan attack on King Dharmawamsa, East Java.

1019–49:
Reign of Airlangga in East Java; writing of *Arjunawiwaha*.

1025:
Chola raid on Srivijaya.

late 13th century:
Sukhothai kingdom in Thailand; emergence of Singosari kingdom in East Java under Kertanagara (1268–92).

1289:
Kertanagara insults Chinese delegation in a gesture signaling refusal to pay tribute to Chinese emperor.

1292:
Visit of Marco Polo to Sumatra.

1297:
Gravestone commemorates first Muslim ruler of Samudra, North Sumatra.

early 14th century:
Samudra and other North Sumatra ports becoming trade centers; Kublai Khan demanding submission of Southeast Asian states.

14th century:
Emergence of Majapahit, centered in Trawulan, East Java, under its first king, Kertarajasa Jayavardhana (1293–1309). Empire lasts until ca. 1520; dynasty continues several decades longer.

1356–75:
Reign of Adityavarman in Minangkabau.

1365:
Writing of *Nagarakertagama* in reign of Hayam Wuruk (1350–1389).

1368:
Ming victory in China; restrictions on trade with China.

early 15th century:
Founding of Melaka.

1416:
Ma Huan, Chinese Muslim, visits Java.

1511:
Portuguese conquest of Melaka under Alfonso de Albuquerque.

1512–15:
Tomé Pires in Melaka; reports in *Suma Oriental* that most of Sumatra is Muslim.

early 16th century:
Kingdom of Pajajaran in West Java. Founding of Acehnese kingdom in North Sumatra; first Sultan Ali Mughayat Syah dies 1530. Rise of Demak in Central Java as coastal areas embrace Islam. Rulers of Ternate, Tidore and Bacan in North Maluku converted to Islam. Decline of Majapahit.

1527:
Sunan Gunung Jati, one of the *wali sanga* Islamic holy men, claims Banten, West Java, from the Pajajaran kingdom.

1546–47:
Spanish missionary Francis Xavier begins attempt to convert states of Maluku to Catholicism.

1552:
Sunan Gunung Jati establishes royal line in Cirebon, West Java.

1552–70:
Reign of Hasanuddin II in Banten, which gains ascendancy over Lampung, South Sumatra, and its pepper trade.

1579:
Molana Yusup (1570–80), third Sultan of Banten, conquers Pajajaran, the last major Hindu-Buddhist state in Java.

1582–1601:
Reign of Panembahan Senapati Ingalaga, founder of second Mataram empire.

1595–97:
First Netherlands expedition to Java.

early 17th century:
Javanese rulers adopt Islam.

1600:
Elizabeth I of England grants charter to East India Company.

1602:
Vereenigde Oost-Indische Compagnie (United East Indies Company), or the VOC, established in the Netherlands.

1605:
King of Gowa, South Sulawesi, adopts Islam.

1607–36:
Reign of Sultan Iskandar Muda in Aceh.

1613–45:
Reign of Sultan Agung of Mataram; adopts title of Susuhunan in 1624.

1641:
VOC conquers Melaka.

mid-17th century:
Spread of Dutch control of Maluku.

1666:
Defeat of Gowa by VOC aided by La Tenritatta to Unru', or Arung Palakka, of Bone, South Sulawesi (1634–96).

1667:
Treaty of Bungaya establishes Gowa submission to VOC.

1675–79:
Rebellion of Prince Trunajaya of Madura suppressed with help of Arung Palakka.

1681:
Establishment of VOC in Roti, East Nusa Tenggara.

1684:
Anti-VOC uprising in Java led by the Balinese slave Surapati.

1704–08:
First Javanese War of Succession; Amangkurat III (1703–05) of Mataram challenged by his uncle, Pangeran Puger, who becomes Pakubuwono I (1705–19).

1705–34:
Pusaka of Kartasura, capital of Mataram, lost during exile of Amangkurat III in Sri Lanka.

1719–23:
Second Javanese War of Succession; Amangkurat IV (1719–26) challenged by his brothers and uncle.

1740:
Massacre of 10,000 Chinese in Batavia by VOC forces and their slaves.

1741:
Forces of Pakubuwono II (1726–49) attack VOC garrison at Kartasura. Cakraningrat IV of West Madura (1718–46) assists the VOC in exchange for an end to his vassalage to Mataram.

1742:
Cakraningrat's forces conquer Kartasura.

1743:
In return for being re-established on his throne, Pakubuwono II yields huge concessions to the VOC for control of the north coast and rivers of Java.

1746:
After further rebellions, Cakraningrat IV exiled to Sri Lanka.

1746:
Pakubuwono II moves the court of Mataram from Kartasura to Surakarta.

1746–57:
Third Javanese War of Succession; Pakubuwono II and Pakubuwono III (1749–88) challenged by Pangeran Mangkubumi (later Hamengkubuwono I of Yogyakarta [1749–92]) and Raden Mas Said (later Mangkunagoro I [1757–95]).

1750:
Rebellion against VOC control by Banten; Sultan exiled.

1753:
Exiled son of Banten Sultan brought back, made Sultan Zainal Askyikin (1753–77) under control of VOC.

1755:
Mangkubumi takes the title of Sultan.

1755:
Treaty of Giyanti between VOC and the Javanese divides Central Java into two kingdoms, Surakarta and Yogyakarta.

1757:
Raden Mas Said, after split with Hamengkubuwono I and oath of allegiance to Surakarta, receives part of Surakarta land and the title of Mangkunagoro I.

1771–74:
Legal codes and land settlements between Surakarta and Yogyakarta. Armed conflict is gradually replaced by marriage diplomacy in Java.

1780s:
Beginning of Islamic reform movement in Minangkabau.

1796–1800:
Collapse and dissolution of the VOC. Formal government of the Indies by the Netherlands government (at this time under French control).

1808:
Forces of Mangkunagoro II (1796–1835) named the Mangkunagaran Legion on the order of Governor-General Herman Willem Daendels (1808–11).

1811–16:
British interregnum in Java under Lieutenant-Governor Thomas Stamford Raffles.

1811–18:
Rebellion of Palembang against foreign rule.

1813:
Pangeran Natakusuma granted part of Yogyakarta territory and made Pakualam I (1813–29).

1815:
Minangkabau royal family murdered by Islamic Padri reformers.

1821–38:
Padri War between Islamic forces in Minangkabau, mostly under the leadership of Tuanku Imam Bonjol, and Netherlands colonial forces. The Dutch control the region after 1838.

1825–30:
Java War, a rebellion splitting Javanese loyalties and involving the Dutch, led by Pangeran Diponagoro (Diponagara), son of Hamengkubuwono III. After the war much of the lands of the courts annexed by the Dutch.

1825:
Netherlands forces defeat Bone with the help of the Makassarese.

ca. 1830:
Netherlands treaties with Pontianak, Mempawah, Sambas and other West Kalimantan states.

1830:
Beginning of *Cultuurstelsel*, the forced cultivation by Indonesian farmers of cash crops for Dutch trade.

1838, 1846:
Netherlands expeditions against Flores, East Nusa Tenggara.

1840:
Treaty between the Dutch and the state of Siak, Sumatra.

1845–49:
Netherlands attacks on Buleleng, North Bali.

1854:
Acehnese control of Langkat, Deli and Serdang states of North Sumatra.

1858:
Siak under full control of the Dutch.

1859–63:
Banjarmasin War between Netherlands and Banjarmasin forces under Pangeran Antasari.

1872:
Batak War between the Bataks and the Dutch; resistance against the Dutch until 1895.

1873:
Aceh War; protracted and fierce resistance under Sultan Ibrahim Muhammad Syah (1895–1907) until 1903 and under the Islamic *ulamas* until 1912.

1882:
North Bali directly under Dutch rule.

1906:
Puputans (ritual mass suicide of rulers and court in battles against the Dutch) in Den Pasar, Pamecutan and Tabanan, Bali.

1942–45:
Japanese occupation of Indonesia during World War II.

1945:
Proclamation of Indonesian independence on 17 August.

1950:
Formation of the Republic of Indonesia.

GLOSSARY

adat: traditional

alun-alun: square to north (sometimes also south) of *kraton*

atap: roof thatch made of palm leaf

badong, cupeng: disk to cover female pubic area

bale: pavilion; platform

blencong: oil lamp used in *wayang kulit* performance

bupati: chief of an Administrative Region

candi: temple

cempurit: rod for manipulating arms of *wayang kulit*

cupeng: see *badong*

dalang: master of the *wayang* performance

dalem: lit. inside; the inner sanctuary of a palace

desa: village

devaraja: god-king cult

dhebog: banana tree trunk into which puppets are fixed during *wayang* performance

dodot: large ceremonial cloth used for Javanese court dress

empu: smith

garuda: giant mythical bird resembling eagle

gedek: paneling made of woven split rattan

gelung: hair knot or loop

geringsing (gringsing): double *ikat* cloth from Tengganan, Bali

glang (gelang): bracelet

gunungan (kayon, kekayon): mountain form; *wayang* figure placed centrally at beginning and end of *wayang kulit lakon*

ikat: textile with tie-dyed warp or weft, or occasionally both (double ikat)

istana: palace

kabupaten: district under the control of a *bupati*

kahiangan: sacred natural terrace or mountain temple

kain songket: brocaded cloth with supplementary weft

kain tapis: embroidered cloth from Lampung, Sumatra

kala: monster

kalung: necklace

kawala-gusti: subject-lord relationship

kayon, kekayon: see *gunungan*

kebatinen: hidden spiritual force

kelir: stretched cloth screen for *wayang kulit* play

kesakten: imbued with mysterious spiritual power

kobongan (krobongan): ritual marriage bed (see *lamming, pelaminan*)

kotak: box for *wayang* storage; set of *wayang kulit*

kraton: court, palace

kris: short stabbing weapon with great spiritual and artistic significance

kuluk: ceremonial hat resembling a tall fez

lakon: *wayang* play

lamming: ritual marriage bed (see *kobongan, pelaminan*)

lancang kuning: lit. yellow boat; ceremonial boat

lontar: palm leaf page or manuscript

loro blonyo: paired sculptures of Dewi Sri, goddess of rice, and her brother and spouse, Sadono

makara: mythical dolphin-snake creature

mamuli: ear pendant

medan: square in front of palace; cf. *alun-alun*

megamendung: cloud motif of Chinese origin, especially in Cirebon design

naga: snake, mythical creature with ritual dragon associations

negara: state, principality

palepai: long ship cloth from Lampung, Sumatra

pamor: nickel lamination of *kris* blade

panembahan: commander

patola: silk double-*ikat* cloths from Gujerat, India

pelaminan: ritual marriage bed (see *lamming, kobongan*)

pendopo: open pillared pavilion

pepadon: ceremonial seat of honor in Lampung

permaisuri: senior wife of ruler; consort

petanen: frame of a *kobongan* or *lamming*

pinang: betel nut

pringgitan: area in a palace between *pendopo* and *dalem* where *wayang kulit* plays are often performed

pura: temple (Balinese)

puri: palace (Balinese)

pusaka: heirloom, often sacred

rencong: Acehnese dagger (see *siwai*)

sajen: ceremonial offerings

sangkala: date cryptogram

sendi: pillar base surmounting cross-beam of Balinese roof structure

silsilah: genealogical tree

sirap: wood shingles

sirih: leaf of *sirih* vine used to wrap ingredients of betel quid; ceremony of preparing and serving betel nut

siti inggil: lit. high place; area of *kraton* where ruler ceremonially receives subjects in audience

siwai: dagger used by Acehnese nobility (see *rencong*)

subak: Balinese social organization controlling irrigation water for rice growing

sumping: decoration covering ear in noble ceremonial dress

surambi: *pendopo*-form verandah or porch in front of Javanese mosque

taman: garden

taman sari: pleasure garden, meditation garden

tampan: square ceremonial ship cloth from Lampung, Sumatra

tombak: spear or lance

tongkat: ceremonial staff

topeng: mask

tumpal: triangular border motif

ukur: a measure

upacara: ceremony; ceremonial regalia carried in Javanese royal processions

wadah: container

wadasan: rock motif of Chinese origin, especially in Cirebon

wahyu: supernatural spiritual power

wali, wali sanga: Islamic saints of the early days of Islam in Java

waringin: variety of *ficus*, banyan tree, often found on the *alun-alun* in front of Central Javanese *kratons*

wayang beber: painted scroll depicting a *wayang lakon* which is related by the *dalang* as he unrolls it

wayang gedog: *wayang* play repertory of indigenous origin

wayang golek: three-dimensional wooden puppets with jointed wooden arms and cloth dress; popular in West Java

wayang klitik, kerucil: wooden puppets carved in bas-relief with manipulable parchment arms

wayang kulit: lit. leather shadow; buffalo hide parchment shadow puppet

wayang purwa: lit. ancient *wayang*; *wayang* play repertory of Indic origin

wayang topeng: play enacted by human actors wearing a mask

wayong wong, wayang orang: drama enacted by human actors

NOTES

INTRODUCTION

1. François Valentijn 1724–26, vol. 5:310; see Soedjatmoko et al. 1965 (1968):160.

2. *Bahasa Indonesia*, the national language of Indonesia, is based on *Bahasa Melayu*, or Malay. This was the original language of much of East Sumatra and the Malay Peninsula and became the lingua franca of the seafarers and merchants who traveled around this region and beyond in trading patterns that reached as far as India and China. Recent studies (see Keith Taylor, in Hall and Whitmore 1976) confirm long-held theories that Indonesian-Malay seamen ventured as far afield as Madagascar.

3. Raffles (1817) 1978, vol. 1:4.

4. These include Fontein, Soekmono and Suleiman 1971; G. and B. Solyom 1978; Gittinger 1979; Thomsen 1980; Wassing-Visser 1984; Elliott 1984; Rodgers 1986; Van Brakel et al. 1987; Scheurleer and Klokke 1988; Holmgren and Spertus 1989.

5. There are many overlapping calendar systems for the centuries and regions discussed in this book: Buddhist, Christian, Islamic, with Saka and Java chronologies in Indonesia itself. For the sake of consistency and ease of comparison, all dates in the text are of the Christian era unless otherwise stated.

6. For information on the complex deciphering of the identities and names of early Indonesian states based on transliteration from Chinese records, see Wolters (1967) 1974.

7. This brief outline of kingdoms spanning fourteen centuries is not complete even for Java, omitting the West Java kingdoms of Pajajaran, Banten and Cirebon, as well as other coastal states and the polities of East Java. Kalimantan, Sulawesi, Sumatra, Bali, Maluku and West and East Nusa Tenggara also have long and complex histories and waxing and waning comparative regional dominance.

8. This offering bowl (FIG. 28) belongs to a temple near the goldsmiths' ward in Gelgel. This temple was the site of the most renowned metal work before the kingdom moved its seat to Klungkung. The sculpture of the scenes depicted on the lid is in the manner of the carvings of Majapahit times (thirteenth to fifteenth centuries) representing human or divine figures in niches in the manner of statues in temple chambers. Since the heritage of craftsmanship in Bali is uninterrupted from that era until the present, it is difficult to judge the age of a gold or silver artifact on stylistic or iconographic grounds. The family guarding the bowl estimates its age at around two hundred years, but it could be older. During the *odalan* (the birthday festival of the temple that occurs once every 210 days) the bowl is filled with cut leaves of young coconut and flowers as offerings to the gods and placed in the temple for three days.

CHAPTER 1

1. *Nagarakertagama*, canto 1, stanza 4, quoted in Pigeaud 1960–63, vol. 3:4. The *Nagarakertagama*, originally entitled *Desa Warnana* (Description of the Country), describes events in the court of the Majapaphit king Rajasanagara, or Hayam Wuruk (r. 1350–89) in the years 1353 to 1364. It also lists the names and dates of previous rulers of the kingdoms of East Java and describes their funerary temples. Prapanca (a *parab*, or penname) was a Buddhist court poet who accompanied the king on the official royal journeys through his domains. His descriptions of palaces, people, ceremonies and countryside give an invaluable account of a great empire at its apogée.

2. See Heine-Geldern 1956, Mabbett 1969 and Aeusrivongse 1976.

3. See, for example, Van Leur 1955; Schrieke 1957; Coedès 1964 (1968); Wolters 1967; Zoetmulder 1974.

4. Hall 1985:105–107.

5. Dates ascribed to rulers refer to their reigns, not their life spans, unless otherwise noted.

6. O'Connor 1972:59.

7. Hinzler 1985:138.

8. Forman 1977:105.

9. From a conversation with Taufik Abdullah of LIPI in 1988 it appears that for some the connotation is also with mountain.

10. Schnitger 1938 (1964):185.

11. Forman 1977:105.

12. This duality is expressed in the alternative name for the *gunungan*, *kayon*, Javanese for "tree" (*kekayon* in Indonesian). One of the *dalangs*, or puppet masters, performing in the Kraton Kasepuhan (the palace of the senior sultan of Cirebon, West Java) claimed that *kayon* is the word most used by *dalangs*.

13. Errington 1989; personal observation, 1972 to present.

14. Hitchcock 1990 and personal observation in Bima and Sumbawa Besar in 1988 and in Sulawesi from 1972 to 1988.

15. This idea was put forward in conversation with Dr. Soewito Santoso in 1988.

16. Reid 1988:20–23.

17. Loeb (1935) 1985:123.

18. In a rather strained analogy, Rassers (1925) 1982 suggests that the incestuous relationship of Sadana and Sri, consummated only after isolation and meditation undergone by both after trial, is the origin of the right and left phratries of the Javanese people, which are represented by the right and left groupings of the shadow puppets during the *wayang kulit* drama.

19. Keeler 1987:44.

20. Personal observation, 1985, *desa* Tambak, near Kartasura.

21. Further examples will be described in chapter 4.

22. Hall 1985:81–90.

23. Hall 1985:284.

24. Hall 1985:83.

25. In this context it is interesting to note parallels with Yggdrasil, the Nordic Tree and Snake of the World.

26. Oral information from the residents of Ogan Lima and nearby villages in Lampung in 1988.

27. Bapak Haryono Guritno, conversation with the author, Jakarta, 1988.

28. *Sja'ir Perang Mengkasar*, lines 161–65, in Koster 1985:60. This historical poem, written in Malay shortly after the event by Enci' Amin, secretary to the Sultan of the Makassar kingdom of Gowa, describes the 1668–69 war between Gowa and the united forces of another Sulawesi prince, the Bone leader Arung Palakka, and the United East Indies Company (the Vereenigde Oost-Indische Compagnie, or VOC).

29. Rassers (1940) 1982; Hamzuri (1973) 1983; G. and B. Solyom 1978.

30. Mentioned in discussions between the author and the director of the Provincial Museum, Pontianak, West Kalimantan, and the scholar of Malay architecture and literature, Tenas Effendy, Pekanbaru, Riau, East Sumatra, 1987.

31. Quoted in Manguin 1986:190.

32. B. Andaya 1975:28.

33. Manguin 1986:190.

34. Errington 1989:75.

35. Taylor 1976:27.

36. Ras 1968:93.

37. This is another instance of the universality of myths, with the Greek parallel of the birth of Aphrodite from the foam of the sea.

38. Hall 1976:66.

39. Tabrani Rab, physician and Malay scholar, conversation with the author, Pekanbaru, Riau, 1987.

40. The best account is an unpublished paper, "Local Perceptions of Ancient Maritime Trade in Insular Southeast Asia," delivered in 1987 at the Museum Nasional, Jakarta, by Pierre-Yves Manguin. See also Adams 1977.

41. La Ode Manarfa, Sultan of Buton, conversation with the author, 1986.

42. Wolters has pointed out the similarities between the ships depicted on Dongson bronze drums and ships of the dead found in Dayak cave paintings in Sarawak; see Wolters (1967) 1974:177.

43. Most notably, Gittinger 1972, 1979; Holmgren and Spertus 1980, 1989; Holmgren 1991.

44. The present Raja of Baun, conversation with the author, Timor, 1988.

CHAPTER 2

1. *Hikayat Raja Raja Pasai*, late fourteenth century. Quoted in Supomo 1979:177, from Hill 1960:161.

2. Letter from the Dutch Governor of the northeast coast of Java to the Susuhunan of Surakarta, late eighteenth century. In Kumar 1979:200, quoting from the *babad*, or chronicle (by Purwasastra, about the kingdom of Balambangan in the Eastern Salient of Java), LOr 2185 in the catalogue of Javanese manuscripts in the Netherlands by Pigeaud, *Literature of Java*, vol. II, 1987. Purwasastra incorporates into his account the full text of both internal and external VOC, or Vereenigde Oost-Indische Compagnie (United East Indies Company), letters. It is thus possible to see how correspondence between VOC officials belied the subservient attitude expressed in letters to the Susuhunan.

3. Moedjanto 1986:4; the phrase in Javanese is *ratu agung-binathara, bau dhendha nyakrawati* (celestially grand king who defends the law and rules the world).

4. See note 2.

5. The Surakarta court comprised only half of the Mataram kingdom as defined by Sultan Agung's conquests. The Treaty of Giyanti of 1755 had formalized its division between the Susuhunan of Surakarta and the Sultan of Yogyakarta, while 1757 and 1813 saw further fragmentation when the courts of the Mangkunagoro (formed from part of Surakarta's domains) and the Pakualam (carved from Yogyakarta territory) were established, respectively.

6. The country had been devastated by Sultan Agung's campaigns, the most disastrous of which was a failed attack on VOC forces at Batavia (now Jakarta). A policy of suppressing opposition by exterminating rivals did not succeed in damping criticism, and the expense of futile battles further undermined prosperity. The eventual insurrection of the Crown Prince, aided by Trunajaya, a prince of Madura, led to the king's dependence on the intervention of VOC forces, at his own expense, to bolster his authority. Mounting debts and lack of popular support bound the king and his son, Amangkurat II (1677–1703), into ever more vitiating concessions to the VOC.

7. After the collapse of the VOC in 1798, there were several confused years in Indonesia (while the Netherlands was dominated by the French during the Napoleonic period) under first the Batavian Republic and then the Batavian Kingdom, followed by five years of a radically different administration during the British interregnum of 1811–16.

8. There is no place in a book of this scope to trace in detail the complicated dynastic histories of Javanese courts, let alone the hundreds of Indonesian courts throughout the archipelago. Excellent coverage in English of the history of Indonesia is provided by Hall (1955) 1968 and Ricklefs 1981, among others; see bibliography.

9. In particular, see Wolters (1967) 1974.

10. Wolters (1967) 1974:209.

11. Exciting research into formations discovered through aerial survey may produce further evidence soon.

12. Geertz 1980.

13. Moertono (1968) 1981 and Anderson 1972.

14. Wolters 1982.

15. Kulke 1986.

16. Christie 1986 and Lansing 1979.

17. De Casparis 1956, 1986a, 1986b; Boechari (1965) 1968; Wisseman 1977; Christie 1986; Atmodjo and Sukarto 1986.

18. Hall 1976, 1985.

19. Kathirithamby-Wells 1985; Abdullah 1985; personal communication with Abdullah 1988.

20. Marsden (1811) 1966:168.

21. Committed to writing in 1822 from the recitation of the *mantri*, or religious leader, Singa Maharaja of Munjota; see Kathirithamby-Wells 1985:131–39.

22. Castles 1975.

23. See in particular the catalogue of the exhibition *Beyond the Java Sea*, Taylor 1991.

24. Geertz 1960; Anderson 1972; Keeler 1987; Errington 1989.

25. The contrast between eminence and incomprehensibility is expressed by two Javanese words of Persian derivation, *lair* (apparent, perceptible) and *batin* (invisible, imperceptible), that can both be qualifiers of *kesakten* (nonmaterial potency or supernatural power, *kesaktian* in Bahasa Indonesia). These can be contrasted to *kakuwatan*, a broader and more straightforward meaning of strength.

26. Anderson 1972:7.

27. Errington 1989:35. *Sumange'* is qualified according to whether it is visible (*talle'*) or invisible (*malinrung*).

28. Note the titles of Javanese rulers: Pakubuwono and Pakualam mean "nail of the world"; Hamengkubuwono means "the lap of the world," as does Mangkunagoro.

29. Koster 1985:46.

30. Moertono (1968) 1981:62.

31. The *wali sanga* were the nine holy men, known as Islamic saints, who were among the early leaders in the establishment of Islam in Java in the fifteenth century.

32. The Cirebon chronicles *Purwaka Caruban Nagari* and *Babad Cerbon* distinguish clearly between Fatahillah and Sunan Gunung Jati. It is claimed that the latter died in 1568, Fatahillah in 1570, and a grave is identified for each in the royal mausoleum of Cirebon on Mount Sembung. See Abdurachman 1982.

33. Moertono (1968) 1981:53.

34. Fox 1979c:19.

35. Supomo 1979:178.

36. A by no means exhaustive check of genealogies throughout Indonesia beyond Java shows family links between Lampung and Banten; Siak (in Sumatra) and Johor in the Malay peninsula; Riau Lingga (also in Sumatra) and Bone (in Sulawesi); the Kadriah palace in Pontianak and Luwu, Brunei, Sambas and Mempawa (all but Luwu in Kalimantan); Mampawa and Ambon (in Maluku); Sambas and Melaka, Sarawak (in Borneo) and Sukadana (in Kalimantan); Tenggarong and Dayak families (in Kalimantan also); Banjarmasin and Melayu-Jambi (in Sumatra); Savu (in East Nusa Tenggara) and Baun (in Timor); Sumbawa, Bima (both in West Nusa Tenggara) and Gowa (in Sulawesi); Ternate and Jailolo (in Maluku); and Lombok (in West Nusa Tenggara) and Bali.

37. The Bugis were also involved in the government of Johor from about the same time.

38. See Errington 1989 for an enlightening study of white blood in Luwu.

39. Errington 1989:23–25; L. Andaya 1977:9, 1979:368.

40. Matheson 1975:13.

41. Moertono (1968) 1981:64. The author points out that the Dutch scholar Hooykaas identifies the jacket with the skin of the snake-king, ruler of the Underworld, and with the

rainbow, a bridge to the Upperworld, which provides an explanation for its role as connector of man with other realms.

42. Their names are Ra Mas, Ra Putir, Sambir, Pajang, Ratu Kilat, Pangeran Rajajani and Panglima Guntur.

43. L. Andaya 1975; it is significant that there has been considerable discussion in both Gowa and Bone about whether the regional government offices or the former palace is the more appropriate place to guard the *pusaka*.

44. Gerritsen 1985.

45. Although Islam dominated policy more overtly and formatively in Aceh than in most other Indonesian states, it is noteworthy that there were four queens on its throne. A practice so contravening Islamic dictums about the role of women reflects the tolerant nature of Islam in Indonesia. There has been much discussion about the origins of the Muslim faith in the archipelago, where the earliest ruler to be converted seems to have been Sultan Malik as-Salih of Samudra, an early state on the north coast of Sumatra in what is now the province of Aceh; his tombstone is dated the equivalent of 1297. It is not the earliest Muslim tombstone, however; that dates from 1082, the grave of a woman in East Java, but it is unclear whether it indicates an Indonesian Muslim or a foreigner. Both Gujerat and South India, as well as China, Bengal, Arabia, Egypt and Persia (see Ricklefs 1981:chap. 1) have at times been proposed as the source, but Johns (1975) and Ricklefs (1981:12) have presented an interesting argument for the involvement of Sufi mystics.

46. Geertz 1980:68–86.

47. Wisseman 1977; Christie 1986.

48. Wolters (1967) 1974; Hall 1985; Reid 1988.

49. *Nagarakertagama*, canto 66, stanza 3, translated in Pigeaud 1960–63, vol. 3:77.

50. Reid 1988:23–24.

51. Detailed analysis of the trading patterns and economic development of the myriad states of Indonesia before independence in 1945 is far beyond the scope of this book. Post–World War II scholarship has begun to fill in the lacunae in this field. In particular the work of Van Leur 1955, Schrieke 1966, Wolters (1967) 1974, Hall 1985 and Reid 1988, as well as papers presented in valuable conferences and edited by Hall and Whitmore 1976, Hutterer 1977, Kartodirdjo 1986 and Marr and Milner 1986 are essential reading.

52. Moertono (1968) 1981.

53. Kumar 1980.

54. *Serat Kala Tida*, stanza 2; this "Poem of a Time of Darkness," ca. 1873, is translated by and quoted in Anderson 1979:219.

55. Information provided by Idwar Saleh, scholar at the Teachers' Training Institute in Banjarmasin.

56. Moertono (1968) 1981:75.

57. Keeler 1987.

58. The manuscript of *Serat* (book) *Bratayudha*, based on the section of the Mahabharata epic that deals with the war between the Pandawa and Korawa families, is one of the finest illustrated manuscripts in *kraton* collections. The story is based on a twelfth-century Old Javanese *kakawin* (poetry written in Old Javanese language with Indian meter) by the poets *mpu* Sedah and *mpu* Panuluh. The brilliant illustrations are the work of the court painter of Sultan Hamengkubuwono VII (1877–1921), K.R.T. Jayadipura, who was possibly also the artist responsible for the painting in FIG. 160/NO. 101. Like that manuscript, it employs a combination of naturalistic figures and landscapes in European-influenced perspective rendering with heroes and fantastic demons presented in traditional stylized *wayang* form. See Lindsay, Soetanto and Feinstein 1987.

CHAPTER 3

1. *Nagarakertagama*, canto 12, stanza 5, quoted in Pigeaud 1960–63, vol. 3:15. Tikta Shriphala is another name for Majapahit.

2. The *mandapa* was common in South India and Sri Lanka and fulfilled both sacred and royal-secular functions, as at Vijayanagara. Sometimes the *mandapa* was a freestanding open structure, sometimes closed with interior columns, and sometimes a pillared veranda-like structure open on three sides and attached on the fourth to an interior chamber. At Anuradhapura in eighth- and ninth-century Sri Lanka such buildings seem to have been monastic and quasi-residential (information provided by Dr. George Michell, historian of the archaeology and architecture of the Indian subcontinent).

3. De Casparis 1956.

4. Around 832, on the death of his father Samaratunga, the heir to the Sailendra dynasty, Prince Balaputra (who might have had Srivijaya family connections through his mother), seems to have moved to Srivijaya (probably as a result of Sailendra defeat), married a Srivijaya princess and eventually become ruler of the Sumatra kingdom.

5. De Casparis 1950.

6. I am grateful to the noted epigrapher Dr. Buchari for making me aware of these interpretations.

7. I am indebted to Dr. Bambang Prasetyo, archaeologist in charge of the Ratu Boko site in the regional office of the Department of Archaeology at Bogem, for a detailed tour and explanation of recent conjectures about the identity and functions of the buildings at Ratu Boko.

8. A comprehensive account of this still-existing Surakarta *kraton*, the replacement of an earlier one at Kartasura, can be found in Behrend 1983.

9. The symbolism of the Kasepuhan *siti inggil* was provided through the expertise of Bapak M. Sjafei Soeryagoenawan of Sukabumi.

10. The gates are described as "split" in reference to Siva's escape from imprisonment by splitting apart the cell in which he was confined.

11. The name derives from *ringgit*, High Javanese for puppet.

12. "Ceremonial axis" is a term adopted by Behrend 1983.

13. Maclaine Pont 1924, 1926, 1927.

14. Maclaine Pont, whose research from 1924 to 1942 did much to establish the layout of Majapahit, pointed out that the main axis turned left, not right, at Majapahit. He explained it in terms of the relationships between the palace and the Buddhist and Saivite temples.

15. Dr. Sunarjo of the Department of Archaeology, in charge of research at Trawulan, kindly explained the recent work at the site.

16. Michrob 1987; Ambary, Michrob and Miksic 1988. The history of the founding of Banten's Islamic dynasty, like that of Cirebon, is complicated by conflicting accounts of the identity of Falatehan. I am grateful for the advice of Dr. Hasan Ambary and Drs. Halwany Michrob about current opinions on Banten's origins. See also Koster 1985:46.

17. Lombard 1968.

18. Lombard 1968; Abdurachman 1982.

19. The most recent conclusions about the structure and symbolism of Sunyaragi were kindly provided by Bapak R. J. Djayakelana, an archaeologist working on the site.

20. Lansing 1979.

21. Ricklefs 1981:31.

22. A fascinating and comprehensive analysis of the Hinduistic ideas underlying the Moslem structure of the Aceh court as revealed in the *Bustan as-Salatin* was presented by L. F. Brakel at a 1973 colloquium; see Brakel 1975.

23. Brakel points out that the Indonesian word for cave, *goa*, comes from the Sanskrit *guha*, which means hidden, secret, available only to the ascetic. Brakel 1975:61.

24. Brakel 1975.

25. Jessup 1988.

CHAPTER 4

1. Moertono (1968) 1981:72, quoting Ch. te Mechelen, ed., "Drie Teksten van Toneelstukken uit de Wajang Poerwa" (three texts of *wayang purwa* plays), Verhandelingen van het *Koninklijk Bataviaasch Genootschap van Kunsten en Wetenschappen* (Proceedings of the Royal Batavian Society of Arts and Sciences) 43 (1882):2.

2. Moertono (1968) 1981:60–73; Geertz 1980.

3. Moedjanto 1986. Moedjanto bases his theory on the absence of distinctions of language level in Old Javanese literature. Current Javanese has three major levels: *krama* is High Javanese, *madya* middle level and *ngoko* low level. There are two further subdivisions for specialized application, for example, *krama inggil* for exclusive court usage. Speech levels also exist in Sundanese and Balinese. So complicated is the usage and so subtle the distinctions of status and relative power inherent in it, that in delicate situations many Javanese today prefer to use Bahasa Indonesia, the national language derived from Malay roots, which has no levels.

4. Pires (1515) 1944:199.

5. See Errington 1989:110–15.

6. Reid 1988:90–96.

7. Reid 1988.

8. The most frequently used resist dyeing methods are batik, in which the pattern is drawn or stamped on cloth in hot wax (or occasionally rice paste); *ikat* (tie), in which warp or weft threads and, in the case of double *ikat*, both, are bound tightly in the desired pattern; and *plangi*, *nitik* and *tritik*, in which cloth is gathered by needle and thread or pinched and tied into the motif. In all cases the cloth or thread is then dyed, the protected areas being immune to the dye bath. The process is repeated several times if, as is usual, more than one color is involved, and is laborious and demanding.

9. Its motifs are derived from the Indian *patola* cloth, an indication of aristocratic usage.

10. To do justice to the textiles of any area of Indonesia, let alone the entire tradition, only specialized studies can suffice. Recommended, among others cited in the bibliography, are Van der Hoop 1949; Gittinger 1979; Wastraprema 1988; Holmgren and Spertus 1989; Maxwell 1990 and Tirta 1990.

11. Pires (1515) 1944:179, 227.

12. See the bas-relief from *candi* Sukuh in Fontein et al. 1990.

13. O'Connor 1985.

14. Rassers (1940) 1982; Hill (1956) 1970; G. and B. Solyom 1978. Notable among unpublished experts in the field is the polymath scholar of Javanese culture, K.R.T. Hardjonagoro of Surakarta, who is a generous mentor in this as in so many other fields.

15. Reid 1988:42–44.

16. Reid 1988:42–44.

17. From the Low Javanese (*ngoko*) word *gamel*, the verb to make, to do, to work and, by association, a metal-working hammer; the name indicates the predominantly percussive nature of the orchestra. See Kunst (1949) 1973; Lindsay (1979) 1985; Becker 1979; Kartomi 1985.

18. One potent gong, thought to date from Majapahit times, is kept by a Pasuruan (East Java) Chinese family that has ancestors from that royal dynasty. It is said to be a *gong setan* (devil) because all who strike it are alleged to die within one year.

19. The *saron* is a percussion instrument with metal keys spanning one octave; the keys are suspended over a resonator. It comes in three lengths that determine its pitch from highest (*penerus*) through middle (*barung*) to lowest (*demung*). Although the original 1859 register entry for this piece notes it as a *saron demung*, its size confirms it as a *saron barung*. The player strikes the key with a mallet in the right hand while damping the preceding note with the left.

The *saron* (FIG. 130) belongs to one of two gamelans brought back to England by Raffles. One was presented to the British Museum and the other, known as the Claydon gamelan, was given to the forebears of the Verney family of Claydon House, Buckinghamshire. It is not clear where the gamelans were made. Some writers suggest Madura, famous for exuberant and fantastical carving, and others East Java as

likelier sources than Central Java with its more restrained style. Scott-Kemball (1985) believes that the British Museum gamelan was a *pusaka* given to Raffles by Sultan Cakraningrat II (1815–47) of Bangkalan, West Madura, in gratitude for the British guarantee of the continuance of his sultanate title. The court provenance is reinforced by the presence on the top piece of the gong stand (FIG. 129) of a double fish with crowned *naga* heads supporting a crowned *garuda*; this symbol was the insignia of the second king of Majapahit, whose son was sent to rule Madura.

The British Museum *slentem* (metallophone) (FIG. 19) comes from the same gamelan as the *saron*. A *slentem* usually has seven metal keys suspended over a resonating chamber, not a shallow box like the chamber of a *saron*, but a series of bamboo tubes suspended below the keys. The classification of this piece is problematical: it is registered as a *slentem* in the 1859 inventory, and its length (longer than the *saron*'s, which is an octave higher than the *slentem*) is consistent with this ascription, but it lacks the *slentem*'s usual tubular resonators and has instead a shallow trough resonator like the *saron*. Scott-Kemball's answer to the puzzle is to suggest that the piece was originally intended to be a *gambang gangsa* (a xylophone with fourteen to sixteen wooden keys and a comparable length to the *slentem*). The presence in the resonating chamber of broken-off stumps of restraining pegs, which are found in *gambang* but not in *saron*, is evidence for her theory.

The cymbals (*kecer* or *ricik*) (FIG. 131) are usually included in the Raffles gamelan list (Fagg 1970) but according to Scott-Kemball do not belong to it. Most of the gamelan pieces were presented to the British Museum in 1859 by the Reverend Charles Raffles Flint, Raffles's nephew and heir, after the death of Raffles's widow. A synopsis was included but no complete documentation accompanied the collection. Some pieces were retained by the family until 1939, when they were given to the museum by Flint's granddaughter, Mrs. J. H. Drake. Scott-Kemball carefully compared the items and inventory dates of both donations and concluded that the cymbals (*kecer*) belonging to the gamelan were in the later gift. Her argument is convincing on stylistic grounds: the realism of the carving is quite unlike the fantasy of the mythical creatures of the Raffles gamelan. She suggests that the cymbals are in fact *ricik* from Bali, where goose carvings are still popular today.

20. See Taylor 1991.

21. The *gender*, one of the instruments in which bronze slabs are suspended over bamboo resonators, is played with two mallets simultaneously. The sequential playing and damping of the keys with both hands—to prevent jarring continuation of the previous note into the tone of the next—require great skill.

22. Reid 1988:206.

23. Taylor 1991.

24. The masks in the Raffles collection are among the finest Indonesian masks in existence. The three enigmatic and noble pieces portray characters from the Panji cycle of the *wayang gedog* repertory. The subtlety of the line of the

eye, the delicacy of the drawing of brows and nostrils and the ascetic planes of cheeks and brow impart an iconic refinement to these pieces. Decorative touches are so strongly subsumed into the pervasive style that the lifelike detail in the painting of the hairs of the eyebrows is not at odds with the stylization of the tendril-like inner line of the brows. There is no documentation to establish the provenance of the masks Raffles collected, but the unique quality suggests that they could have come from the Yogyakarta *kraton* collection.

25. Rassers (1959) 1982:1,925, 1,931.

26. It seems that the earliest reference in China dates from the early eleventh century.

27. For explanation of *wayang* identity and meaning I am grateful to the noted scholars of the subject, Bapak Haryono Guritno and Air-Marshal (ret.) Boediardjo.

28. Keeler 1987.

29. See chapter 2. In a somewhat far-fetched theory, another scholar sees in the *wayang* drama the history of the Javanese people, the two opposed groups of puppets arranged to the left and right of the *dalang* representing the two phratries, older and younger, of exogamous societies. Rassers (1959) 1982.

30. Right and left are located in reference to where the *dalang* sits, not to the screen as seen from the audience side.

31. Guritno et al. 1984.

32. See Keeler 1987.

33. The Damar Wulan cycle is part of the *wayang gedog* repertory. FIG. 152 shows the prince Damar Wulan himself, the hero who married the Queen of Majapahit after defeating her enemies and thwarting the evil designs of his uncle, the Prime Minister *Patih* Logender. He can be compared to Arjuna and Panji as a prototypical hero, fearless in battle and irresistible to women. The name of FIG. 21 is probably a corruption of Sondong Sanjata, a bearer of arms, and the figure is likely to be a member of Damar Wulan's forces. The Raffles *wayang klitik* collection, acquired between 1811 and 1815, is finely carved with detailed depiction of textile motifs and courtly dress and possibly came from the Yogyakarta *kraton*.

34. Pushing his theory of *wayang* as symbols of evolution very far, Rassers suggests that this figure may be an image of the mythical mother of the tribe, the relic of a much older set of beings. Rassers (1959) 1982.

35. These figures are from a seemingly unique set of forty-seven puppets (called *wayang keruchil gilig* in the museum inventory) that is part of the Raffles collection. The puppets combine the largely wood composition of *wayang klitik* with the three-dimensional characteristics of *wayang golek*; the movable arms are made of wood, not of leather as with *wayang klitik*. The remains of placement spikes on the bases, sawn off at some point after the museum acquired the figures, suggest that they were intended for performance. They are expressive as carvings and in addition offer evidence that highly refined batik designs were developed earlier than was thought likely. The provenance of the set, which comprises the characters from the Damar

Wulan cycle in the *wayang gedog* repertory (see note 33), is unknown. They might have been acquired by Raffles at the time of the conquest of the Yogyakarta *kraton* in 1812, they might have been a gift from the Sultan, or perhaps they were commissioned (see Forge 1989).

The two characters portrayed in FIG. 22 and FIG. 154 are Ng Setro, probably a corruption of Layang Seta, and Damar Wulan (light of the moon) himself. The arrogance of Layang Seta, cousin to Damar Wulan and son to the scheming Prime Minister Patih Logender, is well expressed in the angle of the head and the boldness of the face, which can be contrasted with the nobility—the esteemed *halus*, or refined, quality—suggested by Damar Wulan's modest carriage of head and restrained expression suggesting spiritual superiority. (See *The Graphic* 1928; Scott-Kemball 1985; Forge 1989.)

36. See Fontein et al. 1990.

37. *Nagarakertagama*, canto 18, stanza 5, in Pigeaud 1960–63, vol. 3:24.

38. A later subdivision created the junior houses of Kaprabonan and Kacirebonan in 1683 and 1811, respectively.

39. Its full title is Singhabarwang *Penambahan* Pakungwati, meaning the lion commander of Pakungwati; both *singha* and *barwang* (*barong*) mean lion.

40. The art of Bali provides a similar continuity from Majapahit style to the present, an influence attributed to the overlordship of Java during Hayam Wuruk's empire.

41. The Kanoman museum curator explained that this carriage also invoked three creatures, the bird (*peksi*, phoenix), the snake (*naga*) and the elephant (*liman*, *gajah*). It also represented three cultures, since the peacock represents the Arab world and Islam, the snake means China and Buddhism, while the elephant stands for India and Hinduism.

42. The Danes were important traders in the West Java arena when the Dutch and British were vying with the earlier established Portuguese for control of Indies trade. Danish collections of Indonesian artifacts are among the oldest in the world, having been started in the mid-seventeenth century by Ole Worm. His 1710 Art Chamber inventory names Banten as the source of this headdress, but although Danish traders had considerable contact with the Sultan of Banten between 1620 and 1682 (when a treaty between the Sultan and the VOC closed the region to other nations), it is unlikely that it originated there: the Sultan was Muslim and the use of boar's tusks would have been unthinkable. The materials suggest Kalimantan as the likeliest provenance, since pigs are not proscribed among the Dyaks and since coral beadwork is common there. Such beadwork was also common in Lampung, South Sumatra, but by the seventeenth century Lampung was also Muslim. The formal connotations of the nine-tiered stack of meticulously cut and fitted teeth and the shape resembling Buddhistic curled headdresses suggest an Indic stylistic legacy, an intriguing conjunction of Hindu-Buddhist imagery with pre-Islamic materials. (See Wulff 1980.)

43. The cock is of great importance in Indonesia, as can be seen from the continuing widespread interest in cock-fighting. Although this ritual sport, an occasion for gambling, is now restricted, the practice was once connected with religious rites. Its importance as an exercise in status struggles, as a symbol of play in deadly earnest, is discussed in Geertz 1973, and it is also linked with sacrificial offerings of atonement to the gods; see Reid 1988:189–94.

44. I am indebted to H.H. Prince Joyokusumo of the Yogyakarta *kraton* for an explanation of the *upacara*, which are given the honorific title *Kanjeng Kyai* in that palace. The animals and objects have symbolic meanings: the goose (*banyak*) stands for purity, the deer (*dalang*) for intelligence, the cock (*sawung*) for courage, the peacock (*galing*) for beauty, the snake (*harda walika*) for power, the cosmetic containers for perfection, the finger bowl and napkin for cleanliness, the lamp for knowledge and the spittoon for faithfulness and commitment (presumably on the principle that what has been spat out is unretractable).

45. Loeb (1935) 1985:80.

EPILOGUE

1. Karl Jaspers, *Vom Ursprung und Ziel der Geschichte* (Zurich, 1949):181, quoted in Soedjatmoko (1965) 1968:408.

2. Soedjatmoko to the author, Jakarta, 19 December 1989.

BIBLIOGRAPHY

Abdullah, Taufik, ed. 1985. *Literature and History*. Papers of the Fourth Indonesian-Dutch History Conference, Yogyakarta, July 1983, vol. 2. Yogyakarta: Gadjah Mada University Press.

————. 1985. Islam, History, and Social Change in Minangkabau. In Thomas and von Benda-Beckmann, 141–56.

Abdurachman, Paramita R. 1972. Traditional Batik Textiles and Ikat Weaves. London: Perwanira, The Association of Indonesian Women.

————, ed. 1982. *Cerbon*. Jakarta: PT Djaya Pirusa.

Adams, Marie Jeanne. 1969. *System and Meaning in East Sumba Textile Design: A Study in Traditional Indonesian Art*. Southeast Asia Studies, Cultural Report 16. New Haven: Yale University.

————. 1977. A "Forgotten" Bronze Ship and a Recently Discovered Bronze Weaver from Eastern Indonesia: A Problem Paper. *Asian Perspectives* 20(1):87–109.

Aeusrivongse, Nidhi. 1976. Devaraja Cult and Khmer Kingship at Angkor. In Hall and Whitmore, 107–48.

Al-Attas, Syed Muhammad Naguib. 1966. *Raniri and the Wujudiyyah of 17th-Century Acheh*. Monograph 3. Singapore: Malaysian Branch of the Royal Asiatic Society.

Aman, S. D. B. (1976) 1986. *Folk Tales from Indonesia*. Jakarta: Djambatan.

Ambary, Hasan Muarif, and Halwany Michrob. 1988. *Geger Cilegon 1888: Peranan Pejuang Banten Melawan Penjajah Belanda*, Serang, Panitia Hari Jadi ke 462, Pemerintah Daerah Tingkat II, Kabupaten Serang.

————, Halwany Michrob and John N. Miksic, eds. 1988. *Katalogus Koleksi Data Arkeologi Banten*. Jakarta: Direktorat Perlingungan dan Pembinaan Peninggalan Sejarah dan Purbakala.

Andaya, Barbara Watson. 1975. The Nature of the State in 18th-Century Perak. In Reid and Castles, 22–35.

————, and Virginia Matheson. 1979. Islamic Thought and Malay Tradition: The Writings of Raja Ali Haji of Riau (ca. 1809–ca. 1870). In Reid and Marr, 108–28.

Andaya, Leonard Y. 1975. The Nature of Kingship in Bone. In Reid and Castles, 115–25.

————. 1975. The Structure of Power in Seventeenth-Century Johor. In Reid and Castles, 1–11.

————. 1977. Arung Palakka and Kahar Muzakkar: A Study of the Hero Figure in Bugis-Makassar Society. In *People and Society in Indonesia; A Biographical Approach*, 1–11. Clayton, Victoria, Australia: Monash University.

————. 1979. A Village Perception of Arung Palakka and the Makassar War of 1666–69. In Reid and Marr, 360–78.

————. 1981. *The Heritage of Arung Palakka, A History of South Sulawesi (Celebes) in the Seventeenth Century*. Verhandelingen van het Koninklijk Instituut voor Taal-, Land- en Volkenkunde 91. The Hague: Martinus Nijhoff.

————. 1984. Kingship-adat rivalry and the Role of Islam in South Sulawesi. *Journal of Southeast Asian History* 15(1): 22–42.

Anderson, Benedict R. O'G. 1965. *Mythology and the Tolerance of the Javanese*. Ithaca, N.Y.: Cornell University Modern Indonesia Project.

————. 1972. The Idea of Power in Javanese Culture. In *Culture and Politics in Indonesia*, ed. Claire Holt, Benedict Anderson and James Siegel, 1–69. Ithaca, N. Y.: Cornell University Press.

————. 1979. A Time of Darkness and a Time of Light: Transposition in Early Indonesian Nationalist Thought. In Reid and Marr, 219–48.

Archer, Mildred. 1969. *British Drawings in the India Office Library*. 2 vols. London: Her Majesty's Stationery Office.

————, and John Bastin. 1978. *The Raffles Drawings in the India Office Library, London*. Kuala Lumpur: Oxford University Press.

Art Indonésien (exhibition catalogue). 1952–53. Brussels: Palais des Beaux Arts.

Ashabranner, Brent and Martha. 1980. Loro Blonyo: Traditional Sculpture of Central Java. *Arts of Asia* (May–June 1980): 112–19.

Asmar, Teguh, and Bennet Bronson. 1973. *Laporan Ekskavasi Ratu Baka*. Philadelphia and Jakarta: The University of Pennsylvania Museum, Lembaga Purbakala dan Peninggalan Nasional.

Atmadi, Parmono. 1988. *Some Architectural Design Principles of Temples in Java*. Yogyakarta: Gadjah Mada University Press.

Atmodjo, M. M. and K. Sukarto. 1986. Some short notes on agricultural data from ancient Balinese inscriptions. In Kartodirdjo, 25–64.

Bandem, I Made, and Fredrik Eugene deBoer. 1981. *Kaja and Kelod, Balinese Dance in Transition*. Selangor: Oxford University Press.

Barrett Jones, Antoinette M. 1984. *Early Tenth Century Java from the Inscriptions, A Study of Economic, Social and Administrative Conditions in the First Quarter of the Century*. Verhandelingen van het Koninklijk Instituut voor Taal-, Land- en Volkenkunde 107, Dordrecht/Cinnaminson: Foris.

Becker, Judith. 1979. Time and Tune in Java. In *The Imagination of Reality: Essays in Southeast Asian Coherence Systems*, ed. A. L. Becker and A. A. Yengoyan, 197–210. Norwood, N.J.: Ablex Publishing Corp.

Behrend, Timothy Earle. 1983. *Kraton and Cosmos in Traditional Java*. Master's thesis, University of Wisconsin—Madison.

Belo, Jane, ed. 1970. *Traditional Balinese Culture*. New York and London: Columbia University Press.

Bernet Kempers, A. J. 1959. *Ancient Indonesian Art*. Amsterdam: Van der Peet.

Boechari. (1965) 1968. Epigraphy and Indonesian Historiography. In Soedjatmoko et al., 47–73.

Bondan, Molly. 1982. *Candi in Central Java, Indonesia.* Semarang: Provincial Government of Central Java.

Boon, James. 1977. *The Anthropological Romance of Bali, 1597–1972: Dynamic Perspectives in Marriage and Caste, Politics and Religion.* Cambridge: Cambridge University Press.

Boow, Justine. 1986. *Mbatik Manah: Symbols and Status in Central Javanese Batik Making.* Ph.D thesis, University of Western Australia.

Bosch, F. D. K. (1948) 1960. *The Golden Germ: An Introduction to Indian Symbolism.* 's-Gravenhage: Mouton & Co.

———, ed. 1961. *Selected Studies in Indonesian Archaeology.* Koninklijk Instituut voor Taal-, Land- en Volkenkunde Translation Series 5. 's-Gravenhage: Martinus Nijhoff.

Brakel, J. H. van, D. A. P. van Duuren, H. J. Gortzak, Wilhelmina H. Kal and B. C. Meulenbeld, eds. 1987. *Budaya Indonesia* (exhibition catalogue). Amsterdam:Koninklijk Instituut voor de Tropen.

Brakel, L. F. 1975. State and statecraft in 17th-century Aceh. In Reid and Castles, 56–66.

Brown, Donald E., James W. Edwards and Ruth P. Moore. 1988. *The Penis Inserts of Southeast Asia, an Annotated Bibliography with an Overview and Comparative Perspectives.* Occasional Paper 15. Berkeley: University of California Center for South and Southeast Asia Studies.

Bruner, Edward M., and Judith O. Becker, eds. 1979. *Art, Ritual and Society in Indonesia.* Southeast Asia Series, no. 53. Athens, Ohio: Ohio University Center for International Studies.

Buurman, Peter. 1980. *Wayang Golek, De fascinerende wereld van het klassieke West-Javaanse poppenspel.* Amsterdam: A. W. Sijthoff.

Carey, Peter. 1974. *The Cultural Ecology of Early Nineteenth- Century Java: Pangeran Dipanagara, a Case Study.* Occasional Paper 24. Singapore: Institute of Southeast Asian Studies.

———. 1981. *Babad Dipanagara, An Account of the Outbreak of the Java War (1825–30).* Monograph 9. Kuala Lumpur: Malaysian Branch of the Royal Asiatic Society.

Casparis, J. G. de. 1950. *Inscripties uit de Cailendra-Tijd. Prasasti Indonesia* I. Bandung: Djawatan Purbakala Republik Indonesia.

———. 1956. *Selected Inscriptions from the Seventh to the Ninth Century A.D.. Prasasti Indonesia* II. Bandung: Djawatan Purbakala Republik Indonesia.

———. 1981. Pour une histoire sociale de l'ancienne Java, principalement au Xe. s. *Archipel* 21: 125–52.

———. 1986a. Some Notes on Relations between Central and Local Government in Ancient Java. In Marr and Milner, 49–64.

———. 1986b. The evolution of the socioeconomic status of the East-Javanese village and its inhabitants. In Kartodirdjo, 3–24.

Castles, Lance. 1975. Statelessness and State-forming Tendencies among the Bataks before Colonial Rule. In Reid and Castles, 67–76.

Chambert-Loir, Henri. 1980. Les sources malaises de l'histoire de Bima. *Archipel* 20: 269–80.

———, ed. 1982. *Syair Kerajaan Bima.* Jakarta and Bandung: Lembaga Penelitian Perancis untuk Timor Jauh, Ecole Française d'Extrême-Orient.

Christie, Jan Wisseman. 1986. Negara, Mandala, and Despotic State: Images of Early Java. In Marr and Milner, 65–94.

Coèdes, G. (1964) 1968. Ed. Walter F. Vella, trans. Susan Brown Cowing. *The Indianized States of Southeast Asia.* Honolulu: East-West Center Press.

Coomaraswamy, K. 1908. *Mediaeval Sinhalese Art.* Gloucester: Essex House Press.

Covarrubias, Miguel. 1937. *Island of Bali.* New York: Alfred A. Knopf.

Crawfurd, John. 1820. *History of the Indian Archipelago.* 3 vols. Edinburgh: A. Constable.

Djelantik, A. A. M. 1986. *Balinese Paintings.* Singapore: Oxford University Press.

Dobbin, Christine. 1975. The Exercise of Authority in Minangkabau in the late 18th century. In Reid and Castles, 77–89.

Donald Friend's Bali. 1990 (exhibition catalogue). Sydney: Art Gallery of New South Wales.

Dongen, Paul L. F. van, Matthi Forrer and Willem R. van Gulik. 1987. *Topstukken uit het Rijksmuseum voor Volkenkunde (Masterpieces from the National Museum of Ethnology).* Leiden: Rijksmuseum voor Volkenkunde.

Duff-Cooper, Andrew. 1984. An Essay in Balinese Aesthetics. Occasional Paper 7. Hull, England: University of Hull Centre for South-East Asian Studies.

Elliott, Inger McCabe. 1984. *Batik, fabled cloth of Java.* New York: Clarkson N. Potter; Canada: General Publishing Co.

Errington, Shelly. 1989. *Meaning and Power in a Southeast Asian Realm.* Princeton: Princeton University Press.

Ethnographic Objects in The Royal Danish Kunstkammer 1650–1800, 1980. Copenhagen: National Museum of Denmark.

Etnologische Verzameling (museum catalogue). 1884. Delft: Volkenkundig Museum Nusantara.

Fagg, William. 1970. *The Raffles Gamelan: A Historical Note.* London: The Trustees of the British Museum.

Feldman, Jerome, ed. 1985. *The Eloquent Dead, Ancestral Sculpture of Indonesia and Southeast Asia* (exhibition catalogue). Los Angeles: Museum of Cultural History, University of California.

Fischer, Joseph. 1979. *Threads of Tradition, Textiles of Indonesia and Sarawak* (exhibition catalogue). Berkeley: Lowie Museum of Anthropology and University Art Museum, University of California.

Fontein, Jan, R. Soekmono and Satyawati Suleiman. 1971. *Ancient Indonesian Art of the Central and Eastern Javanese Periods.* New York: The Asia Society.

———, R. Soekmono and Edi Sedyawati. 1990. *The Sculpture of Indonesia.* Washington, D.C.: National Gallery of Art; New York: Harry N. Abrams, Inc.

Forge, Anthony. 1978. *Balinese Traditional Paintings.* Sydney: The Australian Museum.

———. 1989. Batik Patterns of the Early Nineteenth Century. In Gittinger, 91–106.

Forman, Shepard. 1977. East Timor: Exchange and Political Hierarchy at the Time of the European Discoveries. In Hutterer, 97–112.

Fox, James J. 1971. A Rotinese Dynastic Genealogy, Structure and Event. In *The Translation of Culture,* ed. T. O. Beidelman, 37–77. London: Tavistock.

———. 1979a. A Tale of Two States: Ecology and the Political Economy of Inequality on the Island of Roti. In *Social and Ecological Systems,* ed. P. C. Burnham and R. F. Ellen, 19–42. London: Academic Press.

———. 1979b. Figure Shark and Pattern Crocodile: The Foundation of the Textile Traditions of Roti and Ndao/1. In Gittinger 1980, 39–55.

———. 1979c. "Standing" in Time and Place: The Structure of Rotinese Historical Narratives. In Reid and Marr, 10–25.

———, ed. 1980. *The Flow of Life: Essays on Eastern Indonesia.* Cambridge, Mass.: Harvard University Press.

Fraassen, Christiaan Frans van. 1987. *Ternate, de Molukken en de Indonesische Archipel.* Ph.D. diss., University of Leiden.

Geertz, Clifford. 1960. *The Religion of Java.* Chicago: University of Chicago Press.

———. 1973. Deep Play: Notes on the Balinese Cockfight. In Geertz, *The Interpretation of Cultures, Selected Essays by Clifford Geertz.* 412–53. New York: Basic Books.

———. 1980. *Negara: The Theater State in Nineteenth-Century Bali.* Princeton: Princeton University Press.

Gerritsen, W. P. 1985. *Hikayat Iskandar Dzu'l Karnain, as seen by a western medievalist.* In Abdullah, 3–28.

Gessick, L., ed. 1983. *Centers, Symbols and Hierarchies: Essay on the Classical States of Southeast Asia.* Monograph 26. New Haven: Yale University Southeast Asia Studies.

Gittinger, Mattiebelle. 1972. *A Study of the Ship Cloths of South Sumatra: Their Design and Usage*. Ph.D. diss., Columbia University.

———. 1979. *Splendid Symbols, Textiles and Tradition in Indonesia* (exhibition catalogue). Washington, D.C.: The Textile Museum.

———, ed. 1980. *Indonesian Textiles*. Irene Emery Roundtable on Museum Textiles, 1979 Proceedings. Washington, D.C.: The Textile Museum.

———, ed. 1989. *To Speak with Cloth: Studies in Indonesian Textiles*. Los Angeles: Museum of Cultural History, University of California.

Groenendael, Victoria M. Clara. 1985. *The Dalang Behind the Wayang, the Role of the Surakarta and the Yogyakarta Dalang in Indonesian-Javanese Society*. Verhandelingen van het Koninklijk Instituut voor Taal-, Land-en Volkenkunde 114. Dordrecht-Cinnaminson: Foris.

Guritno, Pandam, Haryono Guritno, Teguh S. Djamal and Molly Bondan. 1984. *Lordly Shades: Wayang Purwa Indonesia*. Jakarta: Citra Indonesia, PT Jayakarta Agung Offset.

Guy, John. 1982. *Palm Leaf and Paper: Illustrated Manuscripts of India and Southeast Asia* (exhibition catalogue). Melbourne: National Gallery of Victoria.

Hall, D. G. E. (1955) 1968. *A History of South-East Asia*. 3rd ed. Basingstoke and London: Macmillan.

Hall, Kenneth R. 1976. State and Statecraft in Early Srivijaya. In Hall and Whitmore, 61–105.

———. 1985. *Maritime Trade and State Development in Early Southeast Asia*. Honolulu: University of Hawaii Press.

———, and John K. Whitmore. 1976. *Explorations in Early Southeast Asian Statecraft*. Papers on South and Southeast Asia, no. 11. Ann Arbor: University of Michigan.

Hamzuri. (1973) 1983. *Petunjuk Singkat Tentang Keris*. Jakarta: Museum Nasional.

Harmonic, Gilbert. 1987. *Le Langage Des Dieux: Cultes et Pouvoirs Pré-Islamiques en Pays Bugis, Célèbes Sud, Indonésie*. Paris: Edition du Centre National de la Recherche Scientifique.

Heine-Geldern, Robert. 1956. *Conceptions of State and Kingship in Southeast Asia*. Data Paper No. 18. Ithaca, N.Y.: Cornell University Southeast Asia Program.

Hidding, K. A. H. 1931. De Beteekenis van de Kakajon. *Tijdschrift voor Indische Taal-, Land-en Volkenkunde* 71. Batavia: Koninklijk Bataviaasch Genootschap van Kunsten en Wetenschappen.

Hill, A. H. (1956) 1970. *The Keris and other Malay Weapons*. Journal of the Malaysian Branch of the Royal Asiatic Society 29 (4).

———. 1960. *Hikayat Raja-Raja Pasai*. Journal of the Malaysian Branch of the Royal Asiatic Society 33 (2).

Himpunan Wastraprema. 1988. *Cindai: Pengembaraan Kain Patola India*. Jakarta: PT Jayakara Agung Offset.

Hinzler, H.I.R. 1985. The Usana Bali as a source of history. In Abdullah, 124–64.

Hitchcock, Michael. 1988. Fabrics for a Sultan. *Hali* 35:14–21.

———. 1990. *Court Arts and Trade in Indonesia, Bima and Komodo*. London: Ethnographica.

Hobart, Angela. 1985. *Balinese Shadow Play Figures, Their social and ritual significance*. British Museum Occasional Paper 49. London: Trustees of the British Museum.

Hobart, Mark, and Robert H. Taylor, eds. 1986. *Context, Meaning, and Power in Southeast Asia*. Ithaca, N.Y.: Cornell University Southeast Asia Program.

Holmgren, Robert J. (Forthcoming.) *Art of an Old Indonesian Culture*.

———, and Anita E. Spertus. 1980. Iampan Pasisir: Pictorial Documents of an Ancient Indonesian Coastal Culture. In Gittinger, 157–98.

———, and Anita E. Spertus. 1989. *Early Indonesian Textiles from Three Island Cultures: Sumba, Toraja, Lampung* (exhibition catalogue). New York: Metropolitan Museum of Art and Harry N. Abrams, Inc.

Holt, Claire. 1967. *Art in Indonesia, Continuities and Change*. Ithaca, N.Y.: Cornell University Press.

Hood, Mantle, 1969. The Effect of Medieval Technology on Musical Style in the Orient, *Selected Reports* 1(3): 147–170. Los Angeles: Institute of Ethnomusicology, University of California, Los Angeles.

Hooykaas, C. 1973. *Religion in Bali*. Leiden: E. J. Brill.

Hooykaas, Jacoba. 1957. Upon a white stone under a Nagasari-Tree, *Bijdragen tot de Taal-, Land-en Volkenkunde* 113(4):324–340.

Hoop, A. J. N. Th. à Th. van der. 1949. *Indonesische Siermotieven*. Bandung: Koninklijk Bataviaasch Genootschap van Kunsten en Wetenschappen.

Hospital, Clifford. 1984. *The Righteous Demon, A Study of Bali*. Vancouver: University of British Columbia Press.

Hutterer, Karl L., ed. 1977. *Economic Exchange and Social Interaction in Southeast Asia: Perspectives from Prehistory, History and Ethnography*. Papers on South and Southeast Asia, 13. Ann Arbor: University of Michigan.

Les Iles des Dieux (exhibition catalogue). 1956–57. Neuchâtel, Switzerland: Musée d'Ethnographie.

Indonesian Art (exhibition catalogue). 1948. New York: The Asia Institute.

Indonesische Kunst uit Eigen Bezit (museum catalogue). 1964. Delft: Volkenkundig Museum Nusantara.

L'Islam en Indonésie. 1985. Archipel, 29–30: entire issues.

Jasper, J. E., and Mas Pirngadie. 1912–27. *De inlandsche kunstnijverheid in Nederlandsch Indië*. 5 vols. The Hague: Mouton and Company.

Jessup, Helen Ibbitson. 1985. Dutch Architectural Visions of the Indonesian Tradition. In *Muqarnas* 3, The Aga Khan Program for Islamic Architecture, ed. Oleg Grabar, 138–61. Leiden: E. J. Brill.

———. 1988. *Netherlands Architecture in Indonesia, 1900–1942*. Ph.D. thesis, Courtauld Institute of Art, London University; forthcoming, New York: The Architectural History Foundation.

Johns, A. H. 1965. *The Gift Addressed to the Spirit of the Prophet*. Canberra: Australian National University.

———. 1975. Islam in Southeast Asia: Reflections and new directions. *Indonesia* 19:33–55.

———. 1979. The Turning Image: Myth and Reality in Malay Perceptions of the Past. In Reid and Marr, 43–67.

Jonge, H. M. Ch. de. 1984. *Juragans en Bandols: Tussenhandelaren op het Eiland Madura*. Ph.D. diss., University of Nijmegen.

———. 1986. Heyday and demise of the apanage system in Sumenep (Madura). In Kartodirdjo, 241–69.

Kahlenberg, Mary Hunt, ed. 1977. *Textile Traditions of Indonesia* (exhibition catalogue). Los Angeles: Los Angeles County Museum of Art.

Karow, Otto. 1987. *Terrakottakunst des Reiches Majapahpit in Ostjava* (exhibition catalogue). Frankfurt am Main: Museum für Volkerkunde.

Karsten, Herman Thomas. 1917–21, 1937–43. Unpublished letters to Mangkunagoro VII and the Mangkunagaran administration concerning palace extensions and renovations, in the Mangkunagaran library, Surakarta.

Kartini, Raden Adjeng. (1964) 1976. *Letters of a Javanese Princess*. Hongkong: W. W. Norton and Heinemann Educational Books (Asia) Ltd.

Kartiwa, Suwati. 1987. Trans. Judi Achjadi and Toto Tazir. *Kain Songket Indonesia (Songket Weaving in Indonesia)*. Jakarta: Djambatan.

———. 1987. Trans. Judi Achjadi. *Tenun Ikat (Indonesian Ikats)*. Jakarta: Djambatan.

Kartomi, Margaret J. 1985. *Musical Instruments of Indonesia: An Introductory Handbook*. Melbourne: Indonesian Arts Society and Monash University.

Kartodirdjo, Sartono, ed. 1986. *Agrarian History*. Papers of the Fourth Indonesian-Dutch History Conference, July 1983, vol. 1. Yogyakarta: Gadjah Mada University Press.

Kathirithamby-Wells, J. 1985. Myth and Reality: Minangkabau institutional traditions in the rantau. In Thomas, 121–40.

————, and Muhammad Yusoff Hashim. 1985. *The Syair Mukomuko: Some Historical Aspects of a Nineteenth Century Sumatran Court Chronicle*. Monograph 13. Kuala Lumpur: Malaysian Branch of the Royal Asiatic Society.

————, ed. 1986. *Thomas Barnes' Expedition to Kerinci in 1818*. Occasional Paper 7. Canterbury, England: University of Kent Centre of South-East Asian Studies.

Kats, J. (1923) 1984. *De Wajang Poerwa, een Vorm van Javaans Toneel*. Dordrecht: Koninklijk Instituut voor Taal-, Land- en Volkenkunde, Foris.

————, trans. 1929. Een Balische brief van 1768 aan den Gouverneur van Java's Noordkust. In *Feestbundel uitgegeven door het Koninklijk Bataviaasch Genootschap van Kunsten en Wetenschappen bij gelegenheid van zijn 150 jarig bestaan, 1778–1928*. Weltevreden 1:291–96.

Keeler, Ward. 1983. *Symbolic Dimensions of the Javanese House*. Working Paper 29. Clayton, Victoria, Australia: Monash University Centre of Southeast Asian Studies.

————. 1987. *Javanese Shadow Plays, Javanese Selves*. Princeton: Princeton University Press.

Kipp, Rita Smith, and Susan Rodgers, eds. 1987. *Indonesian Religions in Transition*. Tucson: University of Arizona Press.

Koentjaraningrat. 1985. *Javanese Culture*. Singapore: Institute of Southeast Asian Studies and Oxford University Press.

Koleksi Pilihan Museum Nasional (museum catalogues). 1 (1980); 2 (1984); 3 (1985–86). Jakarta.

Koster, G. L. 1985. The *kerajaan* at war: On the genre heroic-historical *syair*. In Abdullah, 29–72.

Koutsoukis, Albert, trans. 1970. *Indonesian Folk Tales*. Adelaide: Rigby Limited.

Kulke, Hermann. 1978. *The Devaraja Cult*. Data Paper 108. Ithaca, N.Y.: Cornell University Southeast Asia Program.

————. 1986. The Early and the Imperial Kingdom in Southeast Asian History. In Marr and Milner, 1–22.

Kumar, Ann. 1979. Javanese Historiography in and of the "Colonial Period": A Case Study. In Reid and Marr, 187–206.

————. 1980. Javanese Court Society and Politics in the Late Eighteenth Century: The Record of a Lady Soldier. *Indonesia* 29 (May) and 30 (October).

Kunst, Jaap. (1949) 1973. *Music in Java, Its Theory and Its Technique*. The Hague: Martinus Nijhoff.

Laksono, P. M. 1986. *Tradition in Javanese Social Structure, Kingdom and Countryside*. Trans. E. G. Koentjoro. Yogyakarta: Gadjah Mada University Press.

Langewis, Laurens, and Frits A. Wagner. 1964. *Decorative Art in Indonesian Textiles*. Amsterdam: Van der Peet.

Lansing, J. Stephen. 1979. The Formation of the Court-Village Axis in the Balinese Arts. In Bruner and Becker, 10–29.

Lelyveld, Th. B. van. 1929. Iets over het Masker en over het Javaansche Masker. *Maandblad voor Beëldende Kunsten* 6(10): 299–305. Amsterdam: J. H. de Bussy.

Leur, J. C. van. 1955. *Indonesian Trade and Society, Essays in Asian Social and Economic History*. The Hague and Bandung: W. van Hoeve.

Lindsay, Jennifer. (1979) 1985. *Javanese Gamelan*. Singapore: Oxford University Press.

————, R. M. Soetanto and Alan Feinstein. 1987. *A Preliminary Descriptive Catalogue of the Manuscripts of the Kraton Yogyakarta*. Sydney: University of Sydney and the Ford Foundation.

Loeb, Edwin M. (1935) 1985. *Sumatra, Its History and People*. Singapore: Oxford University Press.

Lohuizen-de Leeuw, J. E. van. 1984. *Indo-Javanese Metalwork* (exhibition catalogue). Stuttgart: Linden-Museum.

Lombard, Denys. 1968. Jardins à Java. *Arts Asiatiques* 20:135–83.

Mabbett, I. W. 1969. Dewaraja. *Journal of Southeast Asian History* 10:202–23.

————. 1977. The "Indianization" of Southeast Asia: Reflections on the Prehistoric Sources. *Journal of Southeast Asian Studies* 8(1):1–14; 8(2):143–61.

Maclaine Pont, Henri. 1924. *Overzicht van de Overwegingen welke geleid hebben tot de oprichting van de Oudheidkundige Vereeniging "Majapahit."* Weltevreden, (Java).

————. 1925. *Madjapahit, Poging tot Reconstructie van het Stadsplan nagezocht op het Terrein aan de Hand van den Middeleeuwschen Dichter Prapanca*. Weltevreden, (Java).

————. 1926. De Historische Rol van Madjapahit, een Hypothese door Ir. H. Maclaine Pont. *Djawa* 6:294–317.

————. 1927. Inleiding tot het Bezoek aan het Emplacement en aan de Bouwvallen van Madjapahit. *Djawa* 7:171–74.

McKay, E., ed. 1976. *Studies in Indonesian History*. Carlton, Australia: Melbourne University Press.

Macknight, C. C. 1974. The I La Galigo Epic Cycle of South Celebes and Its Diffusion. *Indonesia* 17:161–69.

————. 1979. The Emergence of Civilisation in South Celebes and elsewhere. In Reid and Castles, 126–35.

McPhee, Colin. (1947) 1985. *A House in Bali*. Kuala Lumpur: Oxford University Press.

————. 1966. *Music in Bali, A Study in Form and Instrumental Organization in Balinese Orchestral Music*. New Haven: Yale University Press.

Mangkunagoro VII. 1957. Trans. Claire Holt. *On the Wayang Kulit (Purwa) and Its Symbolic and Mystical Elements*. Data Paper 27. Ithaca, N.Y.: Cornell University Southeast Asia Program.

Manguin, Pierre-Yves. 1986. Shipshape Societies: Boat Symbolism and Political Systems in Insular Southeast Asia. In Marr and Milner, 187–214.

————. 1987a. Local Perceptions of Ancient Maritime Trade in Insular Southeast Asia. Paper presented at the Seminar Kebaharian ASEAN, Museum Nasional, Jakarta.

————. 1987b. "Etudes Sumatranaises, I. Palembang et Sriwijaya: Anciennes Hypothèses, Recherches Nouvelles (Palembang Ouest). Bulletin de l'Ecole Française d'Extrême-Orient 76:337–402.

Marr, David G., and A. C. Milner. 1986. *Southeast Asia in the 9th to 14th centuries*. Singapore: Institute of Southeast Asian Studies and Research School of Pacific Studies, Australian National University.

Marsden, William. (1811) 1966. *The History of Sumatra*. London. Repr. Kuala Lumpur: Oxford University Press.

Martindo. 1982. *Laporan Pemugaran Tamansari Sunyaragi, Cirebon, 1981–1982*. Jawa Barat: Departemen Pendidikan dan Kebudayaan, Kantor Wilayah Propinsi Jawa Barat.

Marzuki, Yasir, and Fred D. Awuy. N.d. *Namo Buddhaya*. Amsterdam: Indonesische Overzeese Bank.

Matheson, Virginia. 1975. Concepts of State in the *Tuhfat al Nafis* ("The Precious Gift"). In Reid and Castles, 12–21.

————. 1982. Conflict Without Resolution, the Banjarmasin War 1859–1905. Paper for the Asian Studies Association of Australia, Monash University. Clayton, Victoria, Australia.

Maxwell, Robyn. 1990. *Tradition, Trade, and Transformation: Textiles of Southeast Asia*. Canberra: Australian National Gallery and Oxford University Press.

Mededeelingen van de Kirtya Liefrinck van der Tuuk (communications of the van der Tuuk association) 16. 1941. Lombok-Nummer, Singaraja, Yogyakarta.

Michrob, Halwany. 1987. *A Hypothetical Reconstruction of the Islamic City of Banten, Indonesia*. Master's thesis, University of Pennsylvania.

Milner, A. C. 1982. *Kerajaan: Malay Political Culture on the Eve of Colonial Rule*. Tucson: Association for Asian Studies and University of Arizona Press.

Moedjanto, G. 1986. *The Concept of Power in Javanese Culture*. Yogyakarta: Gadjah Mada University Press.

Moebirman. 1967. *Wayang Purwa, the shadow play of Indonesia*. Jakarta: Yayasan Pelita Wisata.

———. 1970. *Keris and Other Weapons of Indonesia*. Jakarta: Yayasan Pelita Wisata.

———. 1980: *Keris, Senjata Pusaka*. Jakarta: Yayasan Sapta Karya.

Moertono, Soemarsaid. (1968) 1981. *State and Statecraft in Old Java: A Study of the Later Mataram Period, 16th to 19th Century*. Ithaca, N.Y.: Cornell Modern Indonesia Project.

Moor, Maggie de, and Wilhelmina H. Kal. 1983. *Indonesische Sieraden* (exhibition catalogue). Amsterdam: Tropenmuseum and Terra, Zutphen.

Nederlandsch Indië Oud en Nieuw. 1931. No. 15. Weltevreden (Java).

Nihom, Max. 1986. Ruler and Realm: The Division of Airlangga's Kingdom in the Fourteenth Century. *Indonesia* 42:78–100.

Noorduyn, J. 1978. Majapahit in the Fifteenth Century. *Bijdragen tot Taal-, Land- en Volkenkunde* 134:207–74.

———, with Brian E. Colless. 1975. The Eastern Kings in Majapahit. *Bijdragen tot Taal-, Land- en Volkenkunde* 131:479–89.

Notulen van de Algemeene en Bestuursvergaderingen van het Bataviaasch Genootschap van Kunsten en Wetenschappen (Minutes of the Public and Board Meetings of the Batavia Society for Arts and Sciences). 1904. Batavia.

O'Connor, Stanley J. 1966. Ritual Deposit Boxes in Southeast Asian Sanctuaries. *Artibus Asiae* 28:53–60.

———. 1972. *Hindu Gods of Peninsular Siam*. Switzerland: Ascona.

———. 1985. Metallurgy and Immortality at Candi Sukuh, Central Java. *Indonesia* 39: 52–69.

Oosterse Schatten (exhibition catalogue). 1954. Amsterdam: Rijksmuseum.

Partini, as told to Roswitha Pamoentjak Singgih. 1986. *Partini, Tulisan Kehidupan Seorang Putri Mangkunagaran, Recollections of a Mangkunagaran Princess*. Jakarta: Djambatan.

Pelras, Christian. 1971. Hiérarchie et Pouvoir Traditionnels en pays Wadjo' (Célèbes). *Archipel* 1:169–91; 2:197–223.

———. 1981. Célèbes-Sud avant l'Islam, selon les premiers témoignages étrangers. *Archipel* 21: 153–86.

Pigeaud, Theodore G. Th. 1960–63. *Java in the 14th Century; A Study in Cultural History; the Nagara-Kertagama by Rakawi Prapanca of Majapahit, 1365 A.D.* 5 vols. Koninklijk Instituut voor Taal-, Land- en Volkenkunde Translation Series 4. The Hague: Martinus Nijhoff.

———. 1967. *Literature of Java, Vol. I, Synopsis of Javanese Literature 900–1900 A.D.* Koninklijk Instituut voor Taal-, Land- en Volkenkunde Translation Series 3. The Hague: Martinus Nijhoff.

———, and H. J. de Graaf. 1976. *Islamic States in Java 1500–1700. Verhandelingen van het Koninklijk Instituut voor Taal-, Land- en Volkenkunde* 70. The Hague: Martinus Nijhoff.

Pires, Tomé. (1515) 1944. *The Suma Oriental of Tomé Pires*. Trans. A. Cortesao. London: Hakluyt Society.

Polo, Marco. (1298) 1958. *The Travels of Marco Polo*. Trans. Ronald Latham. Harmondsworth: Penguin Books.

Raffles, Thomas Stamford. (1817) 1978. *The History of Java*. 2 vols. London. Repr. Kuala Lumpur, Oxford University Press.

Ramseyer, Urs. 1977. *The Art and Culture of Bali*. Oxford: Oxford University Press.

Ras, J. J. 1968. *Hikajat Bandjar: A Study in Malay Historiography*. Koninklijk Instituut voor Taal-, Land- en Volkenkunde. The Hague: Martinus Nijhoff.

Rassers, W. H. (1925) 1982. On the Origin of the Javanese Theatre. In Rassers (1959) 1982.

———. (1940) 1982. On the Javanese Kris. In Rassers (1959) 1982.

———. (1959) 1982. *Panji, The Culture Hero, a Structural Study of Religion in Java*. The Hague: Martinus Nijhoff.

Reid, Anthony. 1975. Trade and the Problem of Royal Power in Aceh. c. 1550–1700. In Reid and Castles, 45–55.

———. 1988. *Southeast Asia in the Age of Commerce 1450–1680. Volume I, The Lands Below the Winds*. New Haven: Yale University Press.

———, and David Marr, eds. 1979. *Perceptions of the Past in Southeast Asia*. Singapore: Heinemann Educational Books (Asia) Ltd.

———, and Lance Castles, eds. 1975. *Pre-Colonial State Systems in Southeast Asia*. Monographs of the Malaysian Branch of the Royal Asiatic Society 6. Kuala Lumpur.

Resink, G. J., Claude Guillot, Cécile Bigeon and Jan Hostetler. 1982. Hommage à Kanjeng Gusti Ratu Kidul. *Archipel* 24:97–142.

Rhodius, Hans, and John Darling. 1980. *Walter Spies and Balinese Art*. Ed. John Stowell. Amsterdam: Terra, Zutphen.

Ricklefs, M. C. 1974. *Jogjakarta under Sultan Mangkubumi 1749–1792: A History of the Division of Java*. London: Oxford University Press.

———. 1981. *A History of Modern Indonesia c. 1300 to the present*. Basingstoke and London: Macmillan.

———. N.d. The Missing Pusakas of Kartasura, 1705–37. In *Bahasa, Sastra, Budaya*, 601–30. Yogyakarta: Gadjah Mada University Press.

———, and P. Voorhoeve. 1977. *Indonesian Manuscripts in Great Britain*. Oxford: Oxford University Press.

Rodgers, Susan. 1986. *L'Or des Iles: Bijoux et Ornements d'Indonésie, de Malaisie et des Philippines dans les Collections du Musée Barbier-Mueller* (exhibition catalogue). Trans. Monique Barbier-Mueller. Geneva: Musée Barbier-Mueller.

Santosa, Soewito. 1970. *Babad Tanah Jawi (Galuh Mataram)*. Jakarta: CV Citra Jaya.

Sarabhai, Mrinolini. 1988. *Patolas and Resist-Dyed Fabrics of India* (exhibition catalogue). Middletown, N.J.: Grantha Corp.

Satari, Sri Soejatmi. 1978. New Finds in Northern Central Java. *Bulletin of the Research Centre of Archaeology of Indonesia* 13. Jakarta.

———. 1981. Mountains and Caves in Art: New Finds of Terracotta Miniatures in Kudus, Central Java. *Bulletin of the Research Centre of Archaeology of Indonesia* 15. Jakarta.

Satiadinata, Ii Suchriah, Putri Minerva Mutiara, Sutrisno. 1988. *The Diversity of ASEAN Jewelry* (exhibition catalogue). Jakarta: Museum Nasional, Department of Education and Culture.

Scheurleer, Pauline Lunsingh-, and Marijke J. Klokke. 1988. *Divine Bronze, Ancient Indonesian Bronzes from A.D. 600–1600* (exhibition catalogue). Amsterdam: Rijksmuseum; Leiden: E. J. Brill.

Schnitger, F. M. (1938) 1964. *Forgotten Kingdoms in Sumatra*. Photomechanical reprint. Leiden: E. J. Brill.

———. 1942. Les Terrasses Mégalithiques de Java. *Revue des Arts Asiatiques* 13(3–4): 101–114.

Schrieke, B. (1955) 1966, 1957. *Indonesian Sociological Studies. Selected Writings of B. Schieke*, part 1; *Ruler and Realm in Early Java*, part 2. The Hague: W. van Hoeve.

Scott-Kemball, Jeune. 1970. *Javanese Shadow Puppets, The Raffles Collection in the British Museum*. London: Trustees of the British Museum.

———. Unpublished manuscript about the Raffles gamelan, British Museum Department of Ethnography.

———. 1985. Unpublished notes about the Raffles *wayang* figures, National Gallery of Victoria, Melbourne.

Setten van der Meer, N. C. van. 1979. *Sawah cultivation in ancient Java: Aspects of development during the Indo-Javanese period, 5th to 15th century*. Faculty of Asian Studies Monograph 22. Canberra: Australian National University Press.

Siegel, James T. 1969. *The Rope of God*. Berkeley: University of California Press.

Soedarsono. 1984. *Wayang Wong, The State Ritual Dance Drama in The Court of Yogyakarta*. Yogyakarta: Gadjah Mada University Press.

———, ed. 1986. *Kesenian, Bahasa dan Folklor Jawa*. Yogyakarta: Departemen Pendidikan dan Kebudayaan.

Soedjatmoko. (1965) 1968. *The Indonesian Historian and His Time*. In Soedjatmoko et al. 404–16.

Soedjatmoko, Mohammad Ali, G. J. Resink, and G. McT. Kahin, eds. (1965) 1968. *An Introduction to Indonesian Historiography*. Ithaca, N.Y.: Cornell University Press.

Soekmono, R. 1969. Gurah: The Link Between the Central and the East-Javanese Arts. *Bulletin of the Archaeological Institute of the Republic of Indonesia* 6. Jakarta.

Solomonik, I. N. 1980. Wayang Purwa Puppets: The Language of the Silhouette. *Bijdragen tot Taal-, Land- en Volkenkunde* 136:482–497.

Solyom, Garrett and Bronwen. 1978. *The World of the Javanese Keris* (exhibition catalogue). Honolulu: East-West Center.

Southeast Asian Ministers of Education Organisation—Project in Archaeology and Fine Arts (SEAMEO-SPAFA). 1983. *Final Report*. Bangkok, Consultative Workshop on Archaeological and Environmental Studies on Srivijaya (T-W3); 1985: (I-W2b).

Stohr, W., W. Marschall, J.-P. Barbier, C. H. M. Nooy-Palm, J. B. Ave, and J. de Hoog. 1982. *Art of the archaic Indonesians* (exhibition catalogue). Dallas: Dallas Museum of Fine Arts.

Stowell, John. Forthcoming. Biography of Walter Spies.

Stutterheim, W. F. 1931. The Meaning of the Hindu-Javanese Candi. *Journal of the American Oriental Society* 51:1–15.

———. 1937. *De Oudheden-Collectie van Z. H. Mangkoenagoro VII te Soerakarta*. *Djawa* (extra nummer). Yogyakarta: Djawa Instituut.

———. 1956. *Studies in Indonesian Archaeology*. Koninklijk Instituut voor Taal-, Land- en Volkenkunde Translation Series. The Hague: Martinus Nijhoff.

Sudjiman, Panuti H. M. 1983. *Adat Raja-Raja Melayu*. Jakarta: Penerbit Universitas Indonesia.

Suleiman, Satyawati. N.d. *The Ancient History of Indonesia*. Jakarta: Yayasan Purbakala.

Supomo, S. 1972. "Lord of the Mountains" in the Fourteenth-Century Kakawin. *Bijdragen tot de Taal-, Land- en Volkenkunde* (Leiden) 128: 281–97.

———. 1979. The Image of Majapahit in Later Javanese and Indonesian Writing. In Reid and Marr, 171–85.

Surjodiningrat, Wasisto. 1971. *Gamelan, Dance and Wayang in Jogjakarta*. Yogyakarta: Gadjah Mada University Press.

Sutherland, Heather. 1973–74. Notes on Java's Regent Families, Parts 1–2. *Indonesia* 16:113–48; 17:1–42.

———. 1979. *The Making of a Bureaucratic Elite, The Colonial Transformation of the Javanese Priyayi*. Singapore: Asian Studies Association of Australia.

Sweeney, Amin. 1980. *Authors and Audiences in Traditional Malay Literature*. Monograph 20. Center for South and Southeast Asia Studies. Berkeley: University of California.

Tardjan, Hadidjaja and Kamajaya, trans. 1978–79. *Serat Centhini Dituturkan dalam Bahasa Indonesia*. Vols. 1a–1b. Yogyakarta: U.P. Indonesia.

Taylor, Keith. 1976. Madagascar in the Ancient Malayo-Polynesian Myths. In Hall and Whitmore, 25–60.

Taylor, Paul Michael, and Lorraine V. Aragon. 1991. *Beyond the Java Sea: Art of Indonesia's Outer Islands*. New York: Harry N. Abrams, Inc.

The Graphic, 11 August 1928. Illustration of *wayang gedog* figure from the British Museum Raffles Collection.

Thomas, Lynn L., and Franz von Benda-Beckmann, eds. 1985. *Change and Continuity in Minangkabau: Local, Regional, and Historical Perspectives on West Sumatra*. Southeast Asia Series Monograph 71. Athens, Ohio: Ohio University Center for Southeast Asia.

Thomsen, M., ed. 1980. *Java und Bali, Buddhas, Götter, Heden, Dämonen* (exhibition catalogue). Stuttgart: Linden Museum and Philipp von Zabern.

Tirta, Iwan. (Forthcoming.) *A Tale of Indonesian Batik*. Jakarta: Gaya Favorit.

Tirtaamidjaja, Nusjirwan, Jazir Marzuki and B. R. O'G. Anderson. 1966. *Batik: Pola and Tjorak—Pattern and Motif*. Jakarta: Djambatan.

Tjan Tjoe Siem. 1969. Masques Javanais. *Arts Asiatiques* (Paris) 20:185–208.

Valentijn, François. 1724–26. *Oud en Nieuw Oost-Indiën*. 8 vols. Dordrecht and Amsterdam.

Velde, Pieter van de, ed. 1984. *Prehistoric Indonesia, a Reader*. Leiden, Foris and Koninklijk Instituut voor Taal-, Land- en Volkenkunde.

Veldhuisen-Djajasoebrata, Alit. 1984. *Bloemen van het heelal: De kleurrijke wereld van de textiel op Java*. Amsterdam and Rotterdam: Museum voor Land- en Volkenkunde, Rotterdam, A.W. Sijthoff.

Vickers, Adrian. 1989. *Bali: A Paradise Created*. Penguin Books, Australia.

Visser, H. F. E. 1948. *Asiatic Art in Private Collections of Holland and Belgium*. Amsterdam.

Wagner, Frits A., trans. Inès Vromen. 1961. *Indonésie, L'Art d'un Archipel*. Paris: Editions Albin Michel.

Wang Gungwu. 1958. *The Nanhai Trade, A Study of the Early History of Chinese Trade in the South China Sea*. Journal of the Malayan Branch of the Royal Asiatic Society 31. Kuala Lumpur.

Wassing, René S. 1983. *De Wereld van de Wayang, de schim van het verleden werpt zijn schaduw vooruit*. Delft: Volkenkundig Museum Nusantara.

Wassing-Visser, Rita. 1984. *Sieraden en Lichaamsversiering uit Indonesië* (exhibition catalogue). Delft: Volkenkundig Museum Nusantara.

———. N.d. *Weefsels en Adatkostuums uit Indonesië* (exhibition catalogue). Delft: Volkenkundig Museum Nusantara.

Wastraprema. 1988. *Cindai, Pengembaraan Kain Patola India* (exhibition catalogue). Ed. Soedarmadji Damais. Jakarta: PT Jakarta Agung Offset.

Wessing, Robert. 1988. The Gunongan in Banda Aceh, Indonesia: Agni's Fire in Allah's Paradise? *Archipel* 35:157–194.

Wirz, P. 1928. *Der Totenkult auf Bali*. Stuttgart: Strecker und Schroeder.

Wisseman, J. 1977. Markets and Trade in Pre-Majapahit Java. In Hutterer, 197–212.

Wolff Schoemaker, C. P. 1924. *Aesthetik en Oorsprong der Hindoe-Kunst op Java*. Semarang: Van Dorp.

Wolters, O. W. (1967) 1974. *Early Indonesian Commerce: A study of the origins of Srivijaya*. Ithaca and London: Cornell University Press.

———. 1982: *History, Culture, and Region in Southeast Asian Perspectives*. Singapore: Institute of Southeast Asian Studies.

———. 1986. Restudying Some Chinese Writings on Sriwijaya. *Indonesia* 42:1–41.

Worsley, P. J. 1972. *Babad Buleleng: A Balinese Dynastic Genealogy*. Bibliotheca Indonesica 8. The Hague.

———. 1975. Preliminary Remarks on the concept of Kingship in the *Babad Buleleng*. In Reid and Castles, 108–13.

———. 1984. E 74168. *Review of Indonesian and Malaysian Affairs* 18 (winter): 64–109.

———. 1988. Three Balinese Paintings of the Narrative Arjunawiwaha. *Archipel* 35:129–156.

Wulff, Inger. 1979. Krydderiernes verden. In *Det Indianske Kammer*, 26–41. Copenhagen: National Museum of Denmark.

Yudoyono, Bambang. 1984. *Gamelan Jawa, Awal Mula, Makna dan Masa Depannya*. Jakarta: PT Karya Unipress.

Zoete, Beryl de, and Walter Spies. (1938) 1973. *Dance and Drama in Bali*. London: Faber and Faber; repr. Singapore: Oxford University Press.

Zoetmulder, P. J. 1935. *Pantheisme en Monisme in de Javaansche Soeloek-Litteratuur*. Nijmegen: J. J. Berkhout.

———. 1974. *Kalangwan: A Survey of Old Javanese Literature*. Koninklijk Instituut voor Taal-, Land- en Volkenkunde Translation Series 16. The Hague: Martinus Nijhoff.

Zurbuchen, Mary Sabina. 1987. *The Language of Balinese Shadow Theater*. Princeton: Princeton University Press.

282

COLLECTION CREDITS

Introduction

FIGS. 16, 19, 21–22, The Trustees of the British Museum, London; FIG. 28, Pura Balebatur, Gelgel, Bali

Chapter I

FIG. 32, Museum Nasional, Jakarta; FIG. 38, K.R.T. Hardjonagoro; FIG. 39, Wieneke de Groot; FIG. 43, Balla Lampoa Museum, Sungguminasa, South Sulawesi; FIG. 44, Sikka, East Flores

Chapter II

FIG. 68, *Kraton* Ngayogyakarta Hadiningrat, Yogyakarta

Chapter III

FIG. 91, Balla Lampoa Museum, Sungguminasa, South Sulawesi

Chapter IV

FIG. 119, Haryono Guritno; FIG. 122, K.R.T. Hardjonagoro; FIGS. 129, 130–31, 140–41, 152, 154, The Trustees of the British Museum, London; FIGS. 147, 150, *Kraton* Ngayogyakarta Hadiningrat, Yogyakarta; FIG. 165, *Kraton* Surakarta Hadiningrat; FIG. 166, *Kraton* Kasepuhan, Cirebon; FIG. 167, *Kraton* Kanoman, Cirebon; FIG. 170, The National Museum of Denmark, Copenhagen; FIG. 176, Museum Prabu Geusan Ulun, Sumedang

PHOTOGRAPH CREDITS

FIGS. 1, 6–7, 9–11, 14, 16–22, 24–28, 30, 32–34, 36–41, 43, 47, 49, 52–53, 55–57, 60–61, 64–69, 75–77, 79, 84–88, 91, 98, 100, 101–4, 107–9, 113–14, 117–27, 130–36, 138–50, 152–58, 164–68, 171–72, 174–76, 178, 180–81, 183, 187–89, NOS. 32, 46, 62, 68, 92, 95, 97, 98, 113, 151–52, John Gollings; FIGS. 2, 15, 31, 35, 48, 54, 106, 110, 115, 169, 179, 182, 190, NOS. 51, 59, 80, 105, Dirk Bakker, by permission of the Royal Tropical Institute, Tropenmuseum, Amsterdam; FIGS. 3, 8, 13, 23, 59, 111, 151, 162–63, NO. 141, Dirk Bakker; FIG. 4, The British Library, Oriental Collections, by permission of The British Library Board, London; FIGS. 5, 12, 105, 111–12, 116, 173, NO. 135, Dana Levy; FIGS. 42, 159, The British Library, India Office Library and Records, by permission of The British Library Board, London; FIG. 44, Hugh O'Neill; FIGS. 45, 50, John Bigelow Taylor; FIGS. 46, 51, Robert J. Holmgren; FIG. 63, NOS. 28, 144, Paul Hickman; FIGS. 58, 62, 70–74, 78, 83, 89–90, 93, 95–97, 99, 112, 170, 184, NOS. 15, 21, 34, 49, 117, Helen Jessup; FIG. 92, Charles Warner; FIG. 94, Kleingrothe, by permission of VIDOC, department of the Royal Tropical Institute, Amsterdam; FIGS. 128, 161, NOS. 39, 70, The House of Orange–Nassau Historic Collections Trust, The Hague; FIG. 129, reproduced by courtesy of the Trustees of The British Museum, London; FIG. 137, NO. 150, Rijksmuseum–Stichting, Amsterdam; FIG. 160, John Gollings, reproduced by permission of the National Gallery of Victoria, Melbourne; FIG. 177, by permission of VIDOC, department of the Royal Tropical Institute, Amsterdam; FIGS. 185–86, courtesy of Dr. Samuel Eilenberg; NO. 87, James J. Fox.

FIG. 29, by permission of the Royal Institute of Linguistics and Anthropology, Leiden; FIG. 80, after a plan by Zimmerman, from *Tijdschrift van het Bataviaasch Genootschap*, NO. 58, 1919; FIG. 81, courtesy of Suaka Peninggalan Sejarah dan Purbakala DIY, Bogem, Kalasan; FIG. 82, after a plan from Maclaine Pont, 1925.

Photographs on pages 1, 4–5, 22, 48, 72, 104, 136, 230, by John Gollings.